SPACE PLANNING FOR COMMERCIAL AND RESIDENTIAL INTERIORS

SPACE PLANNING FOR COMMERCIAL AND RESIDENTIAL INTERIORS

SAM KUBBA, Ph.D.

McGRAW-HILL
New York   Chicago   San Francisco   Lisbon   London
Madrid   Mexico City   Milan   New Delhi   San Juan
Seoul   Singapore   Sydney   Toronto

The McGraw·Hill Companies

234567890 BKM BKM 09876

ISBN 0-07-138191-0

The sponsoring editor for this book was Cary Sullivan and the production supervisor was Sherri Souffrance. It was set in Avant Garde by Lone Wolf Enterprises, Ltd.

 This book is printed on recycled, acid-free paper containing a minimum of 50% recycled, de-inked fiber.

McGraw-Hill books are available at special quantity discounts to use as premiums and sales promotions, or for use in corporate training programs. For more information, please write to the Director of Special Sales, McGraw-Hill Professional, Two Penn Plaza, New York, NY 10121-2298. Or contact your local bookstore.

To my mother and father,
Who bestowed on me the gift of life.
And to my wife and four children,
Whose love and affection inspired me on.

CONTENTS

Chapter Three: Space Planning and Design Fundamentals   105

Chapter Four: Communication and Drafting Methods   143

Chapter Five: Human, Social, and Psychological Factors   187

Chapter Six: Project Cost Analysis   223

Chapter 7: Furniture and Furnishings: Assessment and Procurement   247

Chapter Eight: Building Codes and Standards   295

Chapter Nine: Barrier Free Design—ADA Requirements   337

Chapter 10: Computer Drafting and Software Systems   379

Chapter Eleven: Technical Issues   **415**

Chapter Twelve: Security Issues   **447**

Chapter Thirteen: Specification Writing   **463**

Chapter Fourteen: Epilogue and Future Trends   499

Glossary   505

Bibliography   517

Index   521

ACKNOWLEDGMENTS

A book of this scope would not have been possible without the active and passive support of many friends, colleagues, and scholars who have contributed greatly to my thinking and insights during the writing of this book, and who were instrumental in the crystallization and formulation of my thoughts on many of the subjects and issues discussed within. To them I am heavily indebted, as I am to the innumerable people and organizations that have contributed ideas, comments, photographs, illustrations, and other items that have helped make this book a reality instead of a pipe-dream.

I must also confess that without the enthusiasm and encouragement of Lone Wolf Enterprises, Ltd., this book might never have seen the light of day. Thus, my special thanks to Roger Woodson, President of Lone Wolf Enterprises, for his continuous support, advice, and assistance in the fostering of this book. I would also especially like to salute and express my deepest appreciation to Rick Sutherland and Barb Karg, who edited and produced the book, provided me with invaluable expertise, talent, and counsel, and managed (with their wonderful sense of humor) to carry me through the final stretch. It is refreshing to know that editors of their kind and caliber still exist. I thought they had become extinct. I also wish to acknowledge Ellen Weider, another highly valued and dedicated member of the Lone Wolf team, who did the copyedit for the manuscript.

The author especially wishes to express a deep appreciation to the distinguished architecture and planning firm of Hellmuth, Obata + Kassabaum, P.C. (HOK), and the pioneering furniture manufacturer, Herman Miller, Inc., who went out of their way to be helpful and to whom I am deeply indebted. At HOK, I would particularly like to express my gratitude to Bill Stinger, senior principal in the Washington office, and Susan Grossinger, Senior Vice President HOK Interiors, in the Los Angeles office for their continuous support. Also at HOK, I wish to acknowledge the assistance of Juliette Lam, Susan Mitchell-Katzes, Audrey Hoge, and Sandy Mendler for providing me with the cover photograph and other essential information and illustrations.

At Herman Miller, Inc., I wish to thank Corporate Communications Director Mark Schurman and Corporate Archivist Robert Viol for their continuous support and advice, and Robert Viol for putting up with my constant requests and providing me with many of the wonderful illustrations depicting the Action Office, Ethospace, the new Resolve System, and other excellent products that enhance this book. Also at

Herman Miller, my heart-felt thanks to Gail Toliver, Strategic Design Consultant, and Karen Witzel, 3D Marketing Renderer, for providing typical questionnaires and illustrations at such short notice.

Thanks are also extended to Jan Lakin, Director of Media Relations at Gensler, Architects and Interior Designers, to Steve Millnick of Gerard Engineering and Kazim Abbud, Consulting Engineer, for reviewing the Technical Issues section in Chapter 11, and for their expert comments and suggestions. I also wish to acknowledge architect Jasna Bijelic of Davies, Carter, Scott, Architects and Interior Designers, Jeanine Hill of Steelcase PR for putting at my disposal many excellent images, Georgy Olivieri, Director of Architecture and Design Markets at Teknion for the many fine illustrations and advice she provided, Angie Flory of ARCOM Master Systems for information and catalogues on specification software, my friends and colleagues at Inspection & Valuation International, Inc. (IVI), perhaps the largest and most reputable Due Diligence firm in the country, and to architects Wil McBeath and Robert Cox.

Chapter 11 would not have been complete without the illustrations provided by Jim Keener and Daphne Correa of Platts (a Division of The McGraw-Hill Companies). Molly Murray, manager with the CAP Division of The McGraw-Hill Companies, provided me with a wealth of information on this incredible software package. To these wonderful professionals, I can only say, "Thank you."

Finally, I would like to thank my wife, Ibtesam, for her continuous love and support, and for drawing several of the CAD and line illustrations. I also wish to thank the many people who mean so much to me and who kept me going with their enthusiasm and knowledge. I relied upon them in so many ways: for advice, support, and motivation. Without them, I could not have completed this book.

Some images © 2002--www.arttoday.com

ABOUT THE AUTHOR

Sam Kubba is the principal partner of Kubba Design, a firm noted for its work in architecture, interior design, and project management. Dr. Kubba has extensive experience in all types and all aspects of architectural and interior design and construction, including residential, hospitality, corporate facilities, retail, renovations, restaurants, and high-rise commercial structures. A member of the American Institute of Architects, the American Society of Interior Designers, and the Royal Institute of British Architects, he has lectured widely on architecture, archeology, interior design, furniture, and art. Kubba Design has headquarters in Herndon, Virginia.

FOREWORD

AN INNOVATIVE APPROACH TO
SPACE PLANNING AND DESIGN

An understanding of the use and allocation of space is a cornerstone in the many design disciplines that shape our built environment today. Knowledge of space planning and programming are essential tools in conceiving a successful project. Programming and space planning, once considered "pre-design" services by architects, have now taken their roles as an integral part of the entire design process; from conception of the project right through to the analysis of how the occupants use the new facility.

Our built environment is no longer shaped by the master architect as much as it is by collaborative teams of specialists working together and contributing their own expertise and experience. The increasing specialization of design disciplines has been a response to the increasing sophistication of our buildings, and the activities and people that inhabit them.

Design firms and individual design practitioners often build reputations based upon individual building types; museums, sports arenas, and hospitals among them. Large design services firms increasingly organize groups of experts into practice groups for retail, hotels, and office buildings. So it is with the practice of space planning and programming. Space planning, programming and interior design professionals not only are recognized as having unique skills and experience, but have developed specialized practice areas for university and educational facilities, laboratories, and hotels as well as the office and residential areas of practice.

Space planning and programming have certainly become a recognized area of expertise essential to the design process. When a client seeks to build a new college, for example, the team most likely includes a professional space planner with educational experience and expertise. The evidence of this specialization is apparent. Today, there are entire design practices built upon the specialized skills required to undertake the programming and space planning for colleges and higher education facilities.

The specialization of separate expertise for space planning is enabled by the quantum leap in our ability to electronically transmit, store, and analyze data, drawings, and design documents. Any individual facility can be "benchmarked" against several others of the same use. In the competitive commercial real estate markets of the world's urban centers, it is not only the interior design and level of finish and furnishings that determine the rent or "leaseability" of office space. The allocation of space within the structure itself and proportion of the gross to net areas that influence price are large factors in determining the competitive advantage integral to the building.

In the post-industrial era, where companies provide services but do not manufacture products, the cost of premises is the largest expenditure, second only to payroll. In this regard, the efficient use of space for a business has a significant impact on profitability.

In addition to the obvious commercial advantage of the best, most efficient use of space, space planning is often used to promote or discourage interaction among building occupants. Plans for laboratory research buildings include areas intended to promote casual interaction between researchers in different fields; for example, the chemist has the opportunity to talk informally with the botanist over coffee in the lounge that connects their respective laboratories. In this way, the space plan promotes the interaction of scientists in different fields and enhances research or product development. Conversely, in the design of a new embassy, space planning is one of the design tools which can be used to provide additional security. Adjacencies between secure and non-secure areas are carefully located to discourage the casual exchange of information.

As our ability to share program and design information electronically continues to grow, clients and architects will seek the services of those with the best expertise for the project, regardless of the geographic location of the project team and specialized consultants. While programming and space planning has historically been associated with the design process aligned with architects and engineers, we are finding that large consulting firms are offering these same services to corporate clients. It is not uncommon now to find a project program and space layout formulated by the same firm that provides the project pro forma financial analysis and financing. Additionally, we find that owners frequently commission space planners and programmers prior to hiring an architect and other design professionals. This pre-design service is key to setting the parameters for a successful design.

Bill Stinger
Senior Principal (HOK)

CHAPTER ONE

HISTORY AND OVERVIEW

*I*n attempting to study the early historical development and evolution of space planning and interior design, one needs to simultaneously draw upon and understand the interrelationships of other elements and disciplines, such as architecture and the decorative arts. This also includes ornamentation and furniture, which historically followed the development of architecture. This chapter should be used as a basis for a better understanding of the lines of development and evolution that led to the current status of our own development, and to correct our myopic vision regarding our design inheritance.

INTRODUCTION

Our civilization owes much to history. The vocabulary of design is constantly being reinterpreted, and in the context of the modern age, reflects new materials and new technologies. It is not possible to give more than a general overview of the major developments of interior design and space planning In a single chapter.

It is important to note that architecture, space planning, and the decorative arts are inevitably a reflection of a way of life. Before attempting to reconstruct ancient buildings and spaces, one must be aware of how these structures or spaces were used, and how man, woman, and society in general behaved in them. In ancient societies, the size of rooms and enclosed spaces were determined by several factors. These include engineering limitations and social-motivational factors.

ANCIENT MESOPOTAMIA AND EGYPT

In order to conduct foreign trade and build elaborate structures such as the Tower of Babel, the Pyramids, and the Parthenon, the ancients required a uniform system of measurement. The Mesopotamians invented a system of linear measurement over 6,000 years ago as a prerequisite for the construction of the many monumental buildings that the emerging epochs demanded, and this is easily recognizable as ancestral to our own imperial system.

The cubit was based on parts of the body (Figure 1.1), and was commonly used throughout the Near East with slight variations. The Egyptian cubit differed from the Sumerian (Mesopotamian) cubit and was rarely used outside Egypt. Just as a system of linear measurement was invented out of an urgent need to assist in the design and construction of temples and secular buildings, so too was writing invented out of a strategic need to control trade and the economy.

Today, we have basically two major systems of measurement: the Imperial system based on feet and inches as used primarily in the United States, and the Metric system which was developed much later using meters and centimeters, and which is widely used in Europe and much of the world. These two systems have displaced the cubit system used in antiquity.

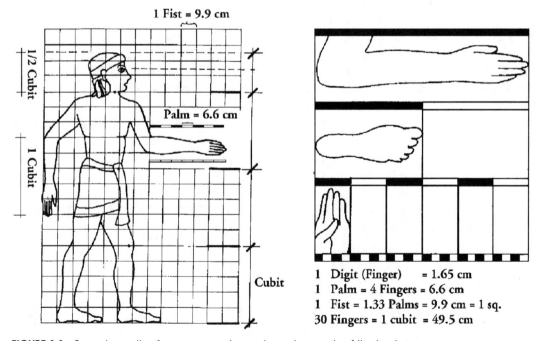

FIGURE 1.1 Sumerian units of measurement were based on parts of the body.

SPACE PLANNING, FURNITURE, AND DESIGN IN ANTIQUITY

To the people of antiquity, particularly as we approached the advent of written history, space planning, generically speaking, was a monopoly of temples and palaces. The chair was a status symbol for many centuries, used only by kings, nobility, and high officials. Moreover, the chair was prized by ancient monarchs because it represented the enemy's seat of authority, and its surrender indicated the enemy's subordination. This is clearly demonstrated by a relief discovered in Nineveh, northern Iraq (c. 704-681 B.C.), depicting Assyrian soldiers carrying away furniture seized as booty from a captured city (Figure 1.2).

The societies of early Mesopotamia and Egypt, which were the cradles of civilization, were highly stratified. At the top of the hierarchical scale was the king or pharaoh, whose powers were considered divine and absolute, and who represented God on earth. Next in line were the many princes, followed by priests, provincial governors, and the wealthy. Craftsmen were regarded as the lower echelon of society.

The first evidence of space planning as we know it can be found in Mesopotamia during the Early Dynastic Period (c. 3000 to 2350 B.C.). During this period, the ziggurat complex (overseen by a powerful priesthood), the monumental palace, and the administrative center all took shape. The temple, which was raised on gigantic bases, constituted the heart of the Mesopotamian city and for centuries constituted the hub of the city's economic system. In time, it lost some of its physical prominence to other points of the urban fabric—mainly the king's palace. By the Late Assyrian period, the ziggurat became a mere adjunct to the king's palace, which completely dominated the cityscape. What distinguished the ziggurat from the Egyptian pyramid is that the ziggurat was raised and reached by means of flights of stairs or spiral ramps (Figure 1.3). For the first time in history, we have evidence of the use of optical illusions in building by using the entasis principle, which was also used by the Greeks with the Doric column nearly a thousand years later. The Babylonians used this principle by incorpo-

FIGURE 1.2 Assyrian soldiers can be seen carrying furniture booty from a captured city.

rating a slight convex curving of the vertical and horizontal forms to overcome the optical illusion of concavity that characterizes straight-sided columns and walls. This made the ziggurats appear more solid from a distance.

It is clear that the Mesopotamian builders displayed an astonishing understanding of proportion and geometric principles in their architecture, as witnessed from their temples at Eridu VI, Songor b and other sites (Figure 1.4). The monumental buildings of this period appear to show an unusual grasp of harmonic proportions—the golden section and triangle, the Pythagorean

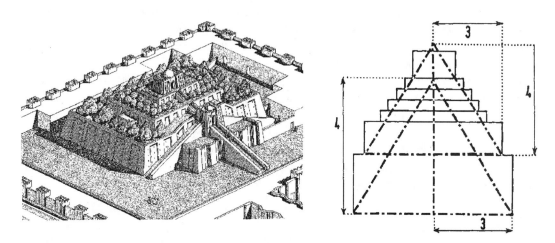

FIGURE 1.3 The ziggurat of Babylon as reconstructed by Stecchini (left). Reconstruction of the ziggurat of Ur built by Ur-Nammu and Shulgi, two Sumerian kings of the Third Dynasty (2113-2048 B.C.). It was constructed of mud-brick, reinforced with thick layers of matting and reeds (right).

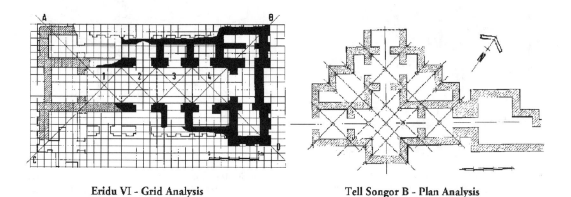

Eridu VI - Grid Analysis   Tell Songor B - Plan Analysis

FIGURE 1.4 Ancient Mesopotamian temples of Eridu VI (c. 3500 B.C.) (left) and Tell Songor B (c. 4000 B.C.) showing early use of harmonic proportions (right).

triangle (an unfortunate misnomer, since it was in use in Mesopotamia nearly 4,000 years before Pythagoras was born), and geometric progressions. A similar approach to design was used in much later ecclesiastical buildings like St. Michael's Church at Hildesheim (Germany), built some 5,000 years later (Figure 1.33).

With regard to early furniture design and manufacture, history shows that in the ancient civilizations of both Mesopotamia and Egypt, designers were well aware of the social and political implications of their furniture. They also had an intuitive understanding of ergonomics, as is clearly observed in their designs (Figure 1.5). In antiquity, the crafts of the carpenter, the metallurgist, and the ivory worker were often closely related to one another. This was necessary because the manufacture of royal furniture required the skill of all three craftsmen. The carpenter would build the frame, the metallurgist would gild and produce the other metal sections, and the ivory worker would carve the panels that decorate the furniture, if the furniture itself was not made of ivory.

Ancient seating habits also differed. A reconstruction of a chair depicted in the Royal Tombs in Sumer (c. 2600 B.C.) shows a chair with a low back which was used as an arm rest (Figure 1.6). The earliest representations of persons seated on a chair or throne are those of kings or gods (Figure 1.7). The ordinary citizen squatted on a matt or on baked brick benches (Figure 1.8). In southern Mesopotamia, the Sumerians used cane to construct their chairs and tables (Figure 1.9), as well as the spiny part of the fronds of date palm trees. These can still be found today in many village coffee-shops around the Middle East (Figure 1.10).

FIGURE 1.5 Mesopotamian chair from Ur III period (c. 2050 B.C.) showing that ancient cabinetmakers had an intuitive understanding of ergonomics and took into account the seating habits of the day.

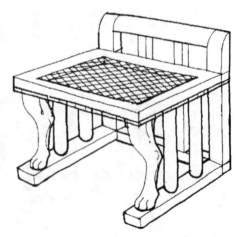

FIGURE 1.6 Illustration of low back chair with animal legs, used by the Sumerians during the Early Dynastic III Period (c. 2600 B.C.).

FIGURE 1.7 The earliest depictions of persons seated on a chair or throne are those of kings or gods. (Left) shows King Amenophis III of Egypt seated on a throne with elaborately carved side panels. (Right) shows King Hammurabi standing in front of the sun god seated on a throne with squared arches in its side panel (Old Babylonian period).

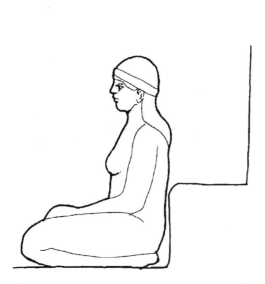

FIGURE 1.8 The common folk squatted on the floor as is still customary in many parts of the world today.

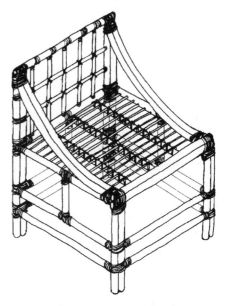

FIGURE 1.9 A reconstruction of a cane chair used by the early inhabitants of southern Mesopotamia.

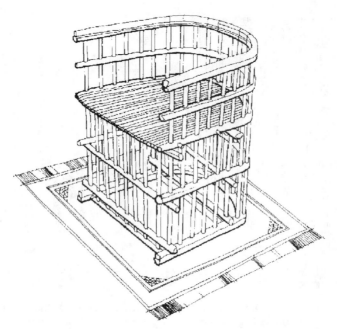

FIGURE 1.10 A reconstruction of a chair called *Kursi Jareed*, which is constructed from the spiny parts of the fronds of date palm trees. These chairs do not use any nails and can still be found in many village coffee-shops in the Middle East today.

Wood was the primary material used in furniture production, although ivory was used occasionally. Ancient Egyptian and Mesopotamian craftsmen had a wide variety of joint techniques at their disposal. Indeed, most of the woodworking techniques known to modern cabinetmakers were in use by the ancient woodworker. Dovetails, mitered corners, butterfly clamps, and scarf and half lap joints were common (Figure 1.11). Popular among ancient woodworkers was the use of complex mortise-and-tenon joints, sometimes secured by wet strips of leather wrapped around structural members and allowed to dry. Wooden dowels were also employed (Figure 1.12). Complex metal hinges and locking mechanisms that were initially utilized by the military also gained great popularity. The Egyptians used elaborate inlay and gilding (the application of very thin sheets of gold foil over an area) extensively on the more elaborate furniture pieces. Paint was also used for decorative effect by first covering the area with gesso. In many parts of the ancient world, including Egypt, Assyria, Babylonia, and the Levant, decorative textiles, pads, and cushions were also used for both seating and bedding (Figure 1.13).

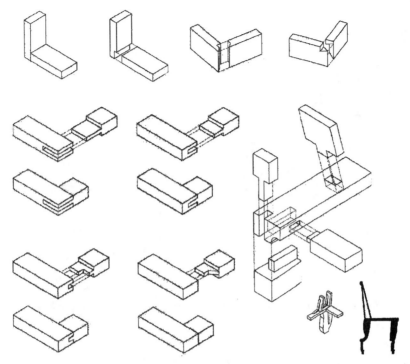

FIGURE 1.11 The ancient Egyptian and Mesopotamian cabinetmaker was well versed with many of the woodworking techniques used today. *(From Hollis S. Baker, Furniture in the Ancient World, The Connoisseur, London 1966)*

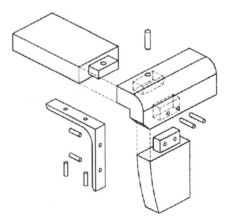

FIGURE 1.12 Detail drawing of furniture joinery used by ancient cabinet-makers. Wooden dowels were employed in the manufacture of furniture from an early date.

FIGURE 1.13   (Left) a chair with curved back and arched side panel depicted on an ivory plaque found in Assyria (c. 9th century B.C.) (Right) an Egyptian chair showing use of fabric in furniture.

The peoples of ancient Mesopotamia and Egypt also used tables, much as they are used today. In Figure 1.14 we see King Assurbanipaı seated on a banqueting couch dining with his queen. Many of the tables used by the ancients were of the folding type, some with only three legs to facilitate their use on uneven floors. A reconstruction drawing of the Pagoda table, a highly decorative three-legged inlaid Phrygian table that was recovered from Gordion, is shown in Figure 1.15.

In Figure 1.16, we see the Persian King Darius the Great seated on a high-backed throne dating from the 6th century B.C., with his feet on a footstool. Both throne and footstool show elaborate turned work which was popular at this time.

Timber of suitable quality for furniture production and building construction was not readily available in either Mesopotamia or in Egypt, and in both cases had to be imported. These regions obtained cedar, beech, ash, box cypress, elm, fir, oak, pine, and yew from Lebanon, Syria, and Turkey. From Sudan came African blackwood and from Ethiopia came ebony. Unlike Egypt, which had an abundance of stone for building its monuments, temples, and palaces—which has left lasting visual evidence—Mesopotamia had only mud for its base material. As we shall see, the limitations of indigenous materials available and in use at the time played a critical role in the ancient space planner's approach to architecture and design. Another fac-

FIGURE 1.14 Assurbanipal seated on a banqueting couch dining with his queen.

tor that greatly influenced exterior and interior architecture was the arid climate. In both Mesopotamia and Egypt, there was intense sunlight with minimal rainfall much of the year. This fostered the use of roof ventilators to direct cool air to the innermost rooms and interior courts. It also promoted the use of flat roofs, porticoes, loggias, and small inward looking windows placed high on the wall.

Throughout history, and up until recent times, religion was the principle motivator of most aspects of daily life. The gods, represented by the king or pharaoh, were responsible for the entire citizenry, both the humble and the high. Moreover, the early architect's and designer's experience of space was very different from our own. The Egyptians believed in the concept of ever-continuing life and appeared to have been preoccupied more with the correct orientation and alignment of religious and ceremonial structures in the cosmos than with enclosed space per se. Thus, Egyptian pyramids and temples were always built on a north-south or east-west axis due to magical connotations. This is also an ancient Mesopotamian tradition and there are many examples of ancient buildings, temples, ziggurats, and secular structures oriented towards the four cardinal points.

In ancient Egypt, the architect was referred to as "director of all the king's works," and during the Old Kingdom (2700-2200 B.C.), we witness a period of architectural grandeur, such as

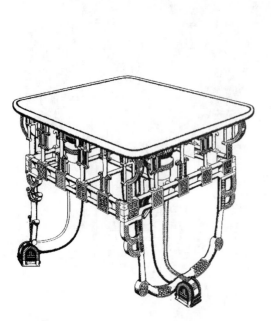

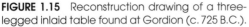

FIGURE 1.15 Reconstruction drawing of a three-legged inlaid table found at Gordion (c. 725 B.C.).

FIGURE 1.16 King Darius the Great seated on a high-backed throne with his feet resting on a foot-stool (6th century B.C.). Both throne and footstool display an early use of wood turning techniques.

the great pyramids of Dahshur and Giza. The construction of an Egyptian temple was an massive undertaking and required elaborate preliminary ceremonials before construction commenced. In designing an Egyptian temple, the architect, with a team of theologians, had to consider a number of complex issues. These included the nature of the principal god and co-deities for whom the sanctuary was to be built, along with all of their esoteric cult requirements. Upon completing an initial analysis and working out the plan's details, the plan was converted into drawings and presented to the pharaoh for approval.

In Egyptian domestic architecture, interior architectural detail and surface treatment were influenced by the hierarchical status of the owner as well as by economy. Floors were covered with a variety of materials; mainly mud plaster or mud brick, although stone and glazed tiles were also incorporated in the palaces. Walls were often surfaced with plaster applied to a base of brick or mud. When the owner was affluent, stone or glazed tiles were used to line the walls. Ornamental treatment for wall surfaces include painting, use of inlay, and relief carving (Figure 1.17).

Mesopotamia on the other hand was a clay civilization, and houses were usually simple, made of mud and inward looking with the main rooms placed around an open internal court (Figure 1.18). For temple construction the Mesopotamian builder had to conceive a highly original way of disguising the ubiquitous characteristics of the clay material he was forced to use. His method was basically to manufacture tens of thousands of clay nails about 4 inches (10 cm.) long that he baked in the sun. He then dipped them in different colored paint and left them to dry. Once dry, these brightly colored clay nails were inserted into the wet plaster to give a highly decorative effect (Figure 1.19). Ceilings were supported by walls, as well as by stone or wood columns. Many examples of ceiling patterns are attested to, which include geometric and religious themes as well as scenes from nature. Both the Egyptians and their Mesopotamian counterparts had a penchant for applying strong color in their decorative schemes.

FIGURE 1.17 Examples of Egyptian decorative motifs.

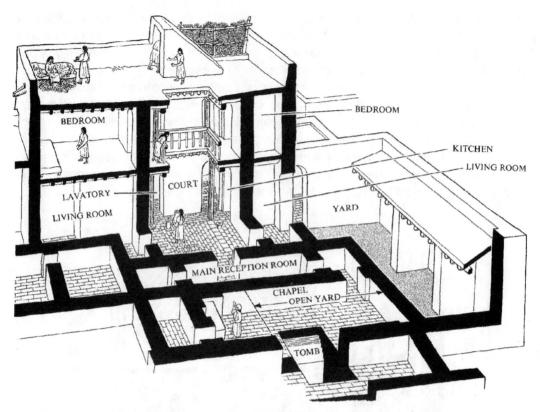

FIGURE 1.18   Ur: A sectional reconstruction of an affluent house of the time of Abraham, c. 2000 B.C. *(Helen and Richard Leacroft, The Buildings of Ancient Mesopotamia)*

GREECE

Excavations by Heinrich Schliemann and others clearly show that in their early stages, Egypt and Mesopotamia exercised a powerful influence on Greek art and—just as for their predecessors—art and architecture began in the service of religion. The Early Greek period (c. 750-500 B.C.) was one of transition, and Hollis Baker states, "The small city states of Greece with their ideals of democracy provided a very different background from that of the rich Oriental civilizations of Mesopotamia ruled by warlike kings, and the difference in the two cultures is apparent in the furniture that evolved."

Greek culture which centered on mainland Greece, as well as in Crete and an Aegean island group (the Cyclades), enjoyed it greatest prosperity between c. 500 and c. 330 B.C., which is an era historians term *classical* or *Hellenic*. When it came to design, the Greeks regarded

FIGURE 1.19 Brightly painted clay nails used by the Mesopotamian builders for decoration to hide the ubiquitous characteristics of the mud.

beauty as an attribute of the gods, and its conscious pursuit was a religious exercise. They typically preferred to develop form types, and then continue to refine them rather than create a multitude of new forms. During the Hellenistic period (c. 330 to c. 30 B.C.) that succeeded it, the emphasis was on the elaboration of basic forms, the characteristics of which the Romans later copied or adapted. Likewise, there was a greater emphasis on the interior of houses and palaces which became more impressive with rooms now taking on specific functions.

Under the leadership and rule of Pericles (443 to 429 B.C.), Athens' affluence reached its zenith, leading to unprecedented building activity and the highest achievements in Hellenic art and architecture of this period. During the reign of Alexander the Great (336 to 323 B.C.), lands under Greek control extended as far as Egypt and Syria. It was during this period that the Corinthian style was developed.

The Greeks, like the Romans, had a love for monumentality and grandeur, and marble which was in abundant supply in Greece, proved to be the perfect conduit to achieving their aspirations. Classical Greek and Roman architecture had a profound structural and decorative influence in subsequent periods, particularly from the Italian Renaissance onwards. Interpretations of classical architecture have been both literal translations and adaptations. Designers of later periods adopted and adapted from ancient Greece and Rome such features as axial planning, utilizing the colonnade as a space planning tool, using natural light as an effective design element, the atrium plan, among others. The classical architectural vocabulary was a source of inspiration as well as direct imitation during the centuries that followed, and classical motifs were used both structurally and decoratively. In interiors, they took the form of numerous moldings and pediments and other decorative effects and designs on walls and ceilings. Classical architectural motifs were also evident in furniture design.

Typically, the Greek temple was a simple, windowless, rectangular enclosure, whether surrounded by columns on all sides or with a front portico with columns of one of the three *orders* (Figure 1.20). The orders were important in Greek interiors not only to delineate a space, but also to give it scale. Thus as the order divided the spaces horizontally, it gave it direction and an axis. The decorative details in the capitals and entablature psychologically forced one's eye to move vertically upward and absorb the scale and monumentality of the structure.

The Greek classical orders typically consist of the column with a base (except for the Greek Doric column), shaft, capital, and entablature; each having its constituent components). These are classified by the capital as Doric, considered the oldest of the three styles, Ionic, and Corinthian. It should be noted that the Greek Doric column (Figure 1.21) typically had no base and stood directly on the *stylobate* (base platform). Its height measured between five and six times its diameter. The shaft tapered with a slight bulging to correct the optical illusion of an inward curve created by a straight column. This convex dilation, called *entasis*, made the Doric column appear more sturdy and robust from a distance. The Doric stylobate also billows slightly to counteract the illusion of a concave dip made by a flat base. It is probable that the concept of entasis was borrowed from the Babylonians who used it in the construction of their ziggurats, and whose culture Greek historians like Herodotus were certainly aware of.

The Doric column was never considered to be suitable for rich ornamentation. The Romans however, developed the Doric column by adding a base to it and modifying its proportions. In Greece the Doric was later partly superseded by the Ionic (Figure 1.22) which is thinner and more elegant, and whose capital is decorated with a scroll-like design (*a volute*). The last order to emerge was the Corinthian style (Figure 1.23). Its capital was decorated with acanthus leaves.

The beauty of Greek art is attributed to the exquisite proportions and graceful lines of its components. The Greeks were convinced that the secrets of beauty were ratios and proportions, which is why their temples were conceived in mathematical terms. Correcting optical illusions was a major consideration of the Greek architect. Proportions of the various structural and decorative elements including, columns, entablatures, moldings, and ornament varied among the orders. The module for heights of the various parts was determined by the column's diameter. The early Greeks found that rectangles with dimensions in the ratio of 2:3, 3:5 and 5:8 were most pleasing (whereas their Sumerian and Babylonian predecessors found the ratio of 3:4 to be more pleasing).

No nation has had a more consequential cultural influence on western civilization than ancient Greece. Many of the period styles that followed were influenced in one form or another by the characteristics observed in classical Greek and Roman pure and applied arts, including architecture, space planning, interior architecture, and furniture design.

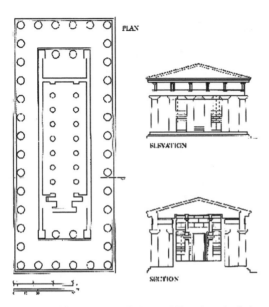

FIGURE 1.20 Temple of Hera at Paestum in Italy, built between 448 and 430 B.C. Plan, section, and elevation showing double colonnade of the cella. A prime example of the classic hexastyle temple. An enclosed sanctuary housed the image of the god. *(From Henri Stierlin, Encyclopedia of World Architecture, Van Nostrand Reinhold Co., 1983)*

FIGURE 1.21 Greek Doric structure of the Temple of Aphaea, Aegina (c. 500 B.C.)

Space Planning

The earliest known form of Greek temple was based on the Mycenaean *megaron*. The development of this simple plan type affected space planning into the Hellenistic period. It consisted essentially of three elements; a hall, a storeroom at the rear, and later, a porch. Palaces sometimes incorporated such megaron structures as independent units functioning as apartments. The Greeks, like many peoples in the region, preferred the courtyard layout in which the court was the focus of the plan and the various rooms were cuddled around it. The dining room was typically the largest room in the house, and where much of the daily activity took place. Also, it was usually richer in decoration than other rooms around the court and was often placed in the corner. Couches and furniture were usually arranged around the perimeter of the room, and as was the custom in ancient times, it was common to recline on these to eat. Situated around the court were other spaces, including the living room, kitchen, bathroom, and storerooms.

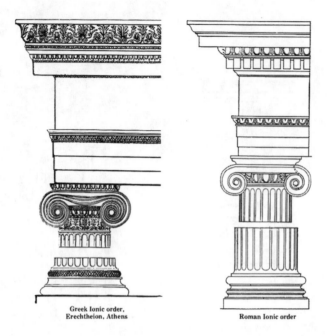

Greek Ionic order,
Erechtheion, Athens

Roman Ionic order

FIGURE 1.22   Ionic Order. (Left) Greek Ionic. (Right) Roman Ionic.

Greek Corinthian

Roman Corinthian

FIGURE 1.23   Corinthian Order. (Left) Greek Corinthian. (Right) Roman Corinthian.

Materials and Building Techniques

Early Greek construction techniques were strongly influenced by the Egyptian column and lintel form of construction. The Greeks were the first to use columns in a structural manner on the exterior of their buildings, as evidenced in the porticos and colonnades. Marble and limestone were indigenous materials and were used extensively for the exterior and interiors of many of their temples and secular buildings. Wood, clay, and thatch were also locally available. In domestic architecture, floor treatment varied according to the status of the owner, ranging from the simply utilitarian to the very decorative. Most houses used compacted earth floors, although wealthier homeowners of the classical period frequently used plaster, painting, or mosaic. Decorative floor treatment techniques included three principal methods of mosaic flooring using pebbles, glass, and stone set in a mortar. Walls in more modest residences were left unplastered mud; whereas in the more elaborate houses, plastering and painting were common. Fenestration was not a significant factor in wall design during the Greek period, particularly on the first floor, because like their Mesopotamian counterparts, Greek houses were inward looking.

Furniture and Decoration

The Greeks created various molding forms that, in addition to their aesthetic value, served to divide the surface into smaller parts and create interest and variety (Figure 1.24). By the late 7th and early 6th century B.C., Greek furniture of some sophistication began to appear, and

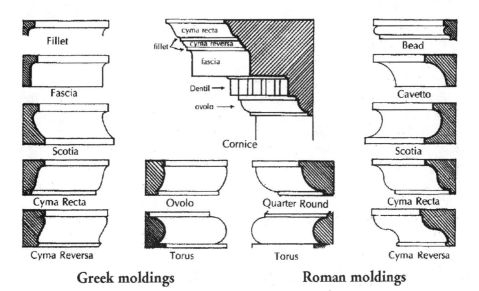

FIGURE 1.24 Examples of Classical Greek and Roman moldings. *(Courtesy, Sherril Whiton, Interior Design and Decoration, J.B. Lippincott Co.)*

by the 5th century B.C., most of the basic forms of Greek furniture were developed. Also during the 5th century B.C., there was an increase in the use of wood turning in furniture manufacture. The Greeks used marble, bronze, iron, and wood in the manufacture of their furniture. Decorative enhancements were achieved through relief carving and the use of inlay and painting. The Greeks used various materials in their inlay work, including imported woods, gold, ivory, and gems. Also practiced was painting popular design motifs on the furniture surfaces, giving a shining polychrome effect (Figure 1.25). The couch in ancient Greece served a dual function; in addition to being used as a bed for sleeping, it was used as a couch on which to recline when dining (Figure 1.26). This is reminiscent of the banqueting scene of Assurbanipal. This appears to have also been the custom on festive occasions throughout Greek and Roman history.

Types of Honeysuckle Borders

Fret Border

Kylix

Mosaic Pattern

Amphora

Acanthus Leaf

Guilloche

Antefix

Grecian Figure

Honeysuckle Band

Painted Bands from Vases

FIGURE 1.25 Examples of typical Greek decorative motifs.

FIGURE 1.26 Greek couch with cut-out legs and table painted on a vase depicting reclining male (530 to 510 B.C.). Compare with Figure 1.14, Assurbanipal dining.

In Figure 1.27a, we see an example of furniture form and motifs following those of architecture. The throne with cut-out legs (which lessened the strength of the legs) with volute capitals. In Figure 1.27b we see a chair with an unusual chair back with a palmette finial. During the Classical period, chair legs developed a more pronounced outward curve, and the back swept upward in a continuous line. During the early part of the 5th century B.C., the chair developed a broad horizontal back and a list at the top, establishing a fixed form for the classical chairs.

ROME

After their military conquest of Greece, the Romans became the immediate successors of Greek civilization, continuing the technical and stylistic tradition of ancient Greece and the Hellenistic period and making them their own. The energetic Romans initially found great difficulty in developing an independent art and architecture of their own, and were pressed to employ the Greek Orders, which they did with certain changes—especially in the Doric order, whose properties they modified. While the Romans adopted the three columnar orders of the Greeks, they seem to have had a strong preference for the richness of the Corinthian order, which they adopted and made the preferred form in the Roman design vocabulary (Figure 1.23b). They also added two other orders, the Tuscan (Figure 1.28), which is essentially a simplified Doric form developed from the Etruscan style with no flutings, and the Composite Order which had for the design of its capital the two rows of acanthus leaves of the

FIGURE 1.27a Vase painting, throne with cut-out legs and footstool (c. 470 B.C.)

FIGURE 1.27b Vase painting, chair with straight legs and chair back resembling a staff with a palmette finial (c. 460 B.C.)

Corinthian and the large volutes of the Ionic (Figure 1.29). The turning point came at the end of the Republican era, when its great generals, particularly Sulla, Pompey, and Julius Caesar, provided Rome with monuments worthy of a world capital. Buildings of colossal proportions were erected during the final period of the Western Empire (3rd and 4th centuries A.D.).

By the end of the first century B.C., the Romans developed a natural concrete which consisted of a volcanic sand mixed with lime. This new material revolutionized building construction and transformed classical architecture. Because this material was not suited to the beam and post system of Greek architecture, Roman architects extended the range of the architectural system to accommodate it. Massive edifices were erected for entertainment and the adornment of the city. Besides palaces, theatres, and temples (which were loftier and grander than their Hellenistic equivalents, and which generally followed the Corinthian style, being built on a raised base), new forms were introduced: the oval amphitheatre, grand basilicas, and the countless utilitarian structures and multi-storied residential and commercial blocks.

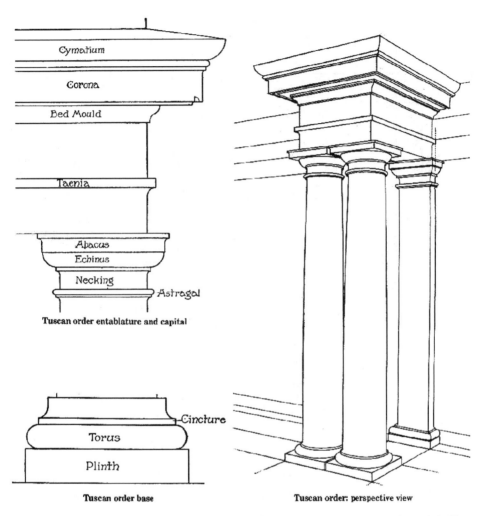

FIGURE 1.28 Tuscan order. A simplified version of the Roman Doric order, have a plain frieze and no mutules in the cornice. *(Courtesy, Cyril M. Harris, Ed., Historic Architecture Sourcebook, McGraw-Hill)*

It was with the enormous vaulted halls allowed by the introduction of concrete that Rome's architectural genius really shined (Figure 1.30). The Temple to the Pantheon of the Gods in Rome, built by the emperor Hadrian in A.D 120, is an impressive example of this. The dome's diameter of nearly 150 feet (43.3 m) forms a dramatic top-lit space that is decorated with rows of colored marble columns and arches. Other examples are the vast bathing establishments like that of the Emperor Caracalla built in A.D. 216 and which could house 1600 bathers. These vast public buildings required large roofed halls.

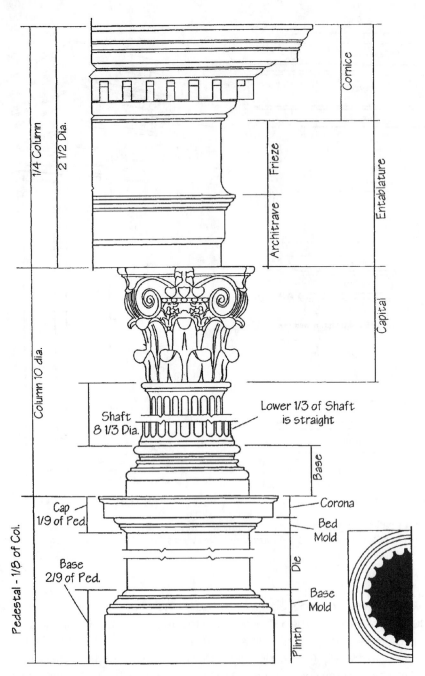

FIGURE 1.29 Composite Order. This is one of the fine classical orders, and is an elaboration of the Corinthian Order; essentially having the ancanthus leaves of its capital combined with Ionic volutes.

FIGURE 1.30 Reconstructed view of the interior of the Maxentius Basilica in Rome (307 to 312). *(Courtesy Boehthius Axel Ward-Parking, J.B., Etruscan and Roman Architecture, Penguin Books)*

The enormous energy, spirit, and spatial imagination of the Romans and their taste for monumentality—which is best illustrated by their architecture, particularly the imperial palaces—influenced and inspired many of the styles that followed, including Byzantium, the Renaissance, and above all, Baroque. They excelled at freeing up interior space, especially in secular and utilitarian architecture. Unlike the Greeks, the Romans often used the columns in a decorative and non-structural manner. Furthermore, the Romans gave greater importance to the design of the interior than their Greek counterparts, who possessed a preoccupation with the building's exterior. This emphasis on the interior is reflected not only in the lavish palaces and edifices Rome is famous for, but also to the majority of less pretentious dwellings, such as those at Ostia during the late Roman period (Figure 1.31).

Furniture

Documentary evidence reveals that the Romans relied on Greek furniture prototypes of the Hellenistic period for their inspiration. Furniture as a rule was sparse and limited to essentials, partly

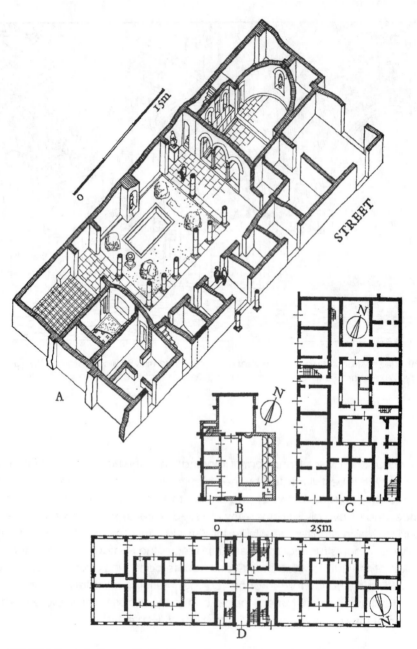

FIGURE 1.31 Late Roman, Ostia. Plans of houses and apartment houses. A) House of Fortuna Annonaria, late 2nd century, remodeled in the 4th century. B) House of Cupid and Psyche, c. 300. C) House of Diana, c. 150. D) Gordon House, 117-138. *(Courtesy Boehthius Axel Ward-Parking, J.B., Etruscan and Roman Architecture, Penguin Books)*

so as not to distract from the elaborate decoration of the walls. Furniture was made of wood, marble, bronze, iron, and precious metals, usually enriched with carving or relief ornament. The dining rooms were the most elaborate areas and contained couches placed around a low central table. The men dined in a reclining position, as did the Greeks and Assyrians before them, while the women sat on chairs. The couches were covered with cushions and tapestries embroidered with gold and silver thread imported from Babylonia or Egypt (Figure 1.32).

MIDDLE AGES

The fall and breakup of the Roman Empire and the rise of Christianity also marked the collapse of the Roman classical traditions of design. Weak central governments left Europe in a state of political confusion and social distress. Religion became a dominating focus and motivator in the life of the ordinary citizen. During this period, design was predominantly at the service of the church. The Middle Ages can be divided into four stylistic periods.

Early Christian Design (330 to 800)

Art and architecture continued to develop essentially under the aegis of religion, but with a strong Byzantine influence. The new art and architecture that developed amongst the Christian states that rose out of the ruins of the Western Roman Empire was unable to dispel the strong influence of the Eastern Roman Christian Empire. However, once Christianity gained official acceptance, a rejuvenated design vocabulary began to emerge, and churches developed into an important building type.

The early Christian church structure was an extension of those of Rome, and was modeled on two basic types of plans. The first was the Roman court building, or basilica, which was rectangular with colonnades separating a central space (the nave) from flanking aisles which were built lower to permit a clerestory to light the central space, as in St. Michael Church in Hildesheim, Germany (Figure 1.33). There was no vertical division into bays, and the axis was horizontal. A systematic analysis of the plan of the church reveals the architect's geometrical approach. The composition consists almost entirely of a combination of squares and diagonals, as was the case in the Mesopotamian temples. The second form type consisted of a circular or octagonal space surrounded by an ambulatory, and also had clerestory lighting. The style developed in central Italy and to a lesser degree in other countries bordering the eastern Mediterranean.

Byzantine Design (330 to 1453)

The Byzantine era of architecture and design was not ushered in until after Constantinople became the imperial capital of the Roman Empire in 330, and Emperor Constantine adopted

Roman bed

Roman Marble Table

White Marble Arm-Chair

Pompaian Table

Folding Stool

Roman Tripod

Bronze Seat

Roman Chair

FIGURE 1.32   Examples of Roman furniture.

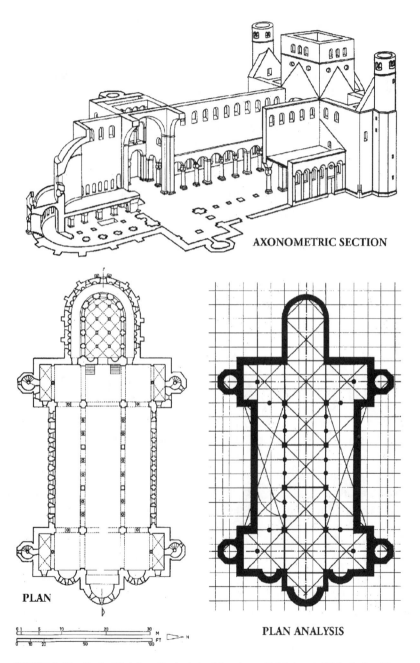

AXONOMETRIC SECTION

PLAN

PLAN ANALYSIS

FIGURE 1.33 Early Christian Period Architecture. St.Michael, Hildesheim (Germany). Planned in 993 and built in 1010-1033. Compare the plan analysis of this form of ecclesiastic architecture with that of early Mesopotamia temples (see Figure 1.4).

Christianity as the established state religion. It evolved largely from the Roman model, and by the 6th century, spread throughout the Empire, extending as far as North Africa. This was also primarily a church building development and Roman structural techniques remained in use, as were details, such as elaborate mosaic decorative art. Byzantine building includes major domed structures, such as the famous Santa or Hagia Sophia in Constantinople (532-537), whose dome spanned 100 feet (30m), buttressed by two half-domes, giving a total span of about 233 feet (70m.) without intermediate support (Figure 1.34). This marks the culmination of the dome formula. Decorative art reaches a level of elaboration and richness beyond the characteristic austerity of the Early Christian work.

The Byzantine style developed in Constantinople from the time it became the seat of the royal residence of the emperor Constantine and capital of the Eastern Roman Empire upon the death of Theodosius in 395, until its capture by the Turks in 1453. Sherrill Whiton describes the style as being, "characterized as a fusion between a debased Roman art and Oriental forms. Domed ceilings are typical." Interiors changed slowly as the basilica was adapted as a place of Christian worship. The vault was also developed during this period, but on a smaller scale. The square was the prevalent plan of the majority of Byzantine churches which contained three apses, preceded by a narthex and crowned with a central dome on a drum (Figure 1.35).

Romanesque Design (800 to 1150)

The Romanesque style developed from the Early Christian and Byzantine styles during the 9th to 12th centuries. However, it was only able to develop after it overcame the strong Byzantine and Classical influence. During the 10th and 11th centuries there was a sudden burst of ecclesiastical architectural activity with churches rising everywhere. Many of the Early Christian churches were destroyed by fire due to the use of wood in the construction of their roofs. Romanesque builders relied entirely on stone. The earliest styles, designed by amateurs who were primarily priests and monks, were developed in France and other Western countries. Although the Romanesque style was initially heavy, it later developed and attained certain refinements.

Romanesque stone structures were characterized by increasingly widespread use of the semicircular arch, the dome, and barrel-vault and groined vault, a remnant of Roman structural technique. The semicircular arched opening was one of the hallmarks of the Romanesque style and was used for doors, windows, and ornamental forms (Figure 1.35). Furniture during this period was minimal, partly due to undeveloped standards of comfort. Toward the end of the Romanesque era, larger churches began to apply increased elaboration to their decorative details, and continuous structural experiments in buttressed vaulting helped gradually usher in a new style of architecture, called Gothic.

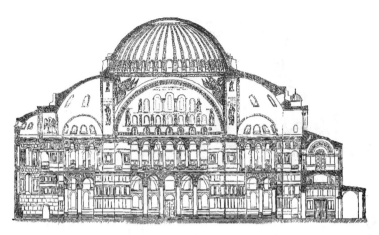

EAST WEST SECTION

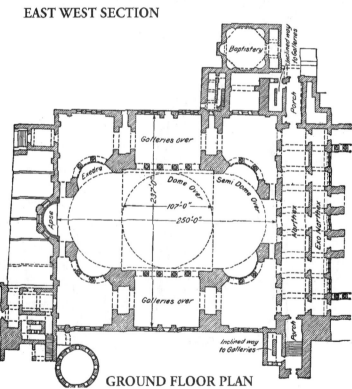

GROUND FLOOR PLAN

FIGURE 1.34 Byzantine Period. Plan and section of the Hagia Sophia in Constantinople built by Justinian 532-537. Plan shows the reconstructed atrium. This church which represents a totally new architectural development was designed by the architects Anthemius of Tralles and Isidore of Miletus. *(Courtesy Cyril M. Harris. (Ed.) Historic Architecture Sourcebook, McGraw-Hill)*

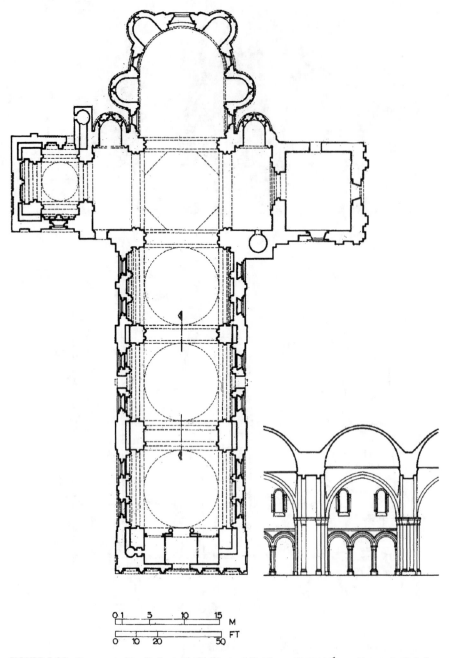

FIGURE 1.35 Romanesque Period. Cathedral of St. Pierre, Angoulíme (France). Building commenced in 1110 and consecrated in 1128. The nave is roofed by three domes in a row.

Gothic Design (1150 to 1500)

Gothic building developed from the Romanesque style and is widely regarded as one of the finest achievements of the Middle Ages. The transition from the Romanesque to the Gothic took place towards the early part of the 12th century in France, and reached its zenith during the 13th century in France and England. The plan form was typically in the shape of a Latin Cross. The main body of the building formed the nave, flanked on both sides by low aisles. Sometimes there were chapels dedicated to saints built off the aisles (Figure 1.36). The Gothic style is characterized by the use of the pointed arch (which was substituted for the semicircular arch), groin vault, buttress, tracery, and large windows, with a corresponding reduction in wall areas.

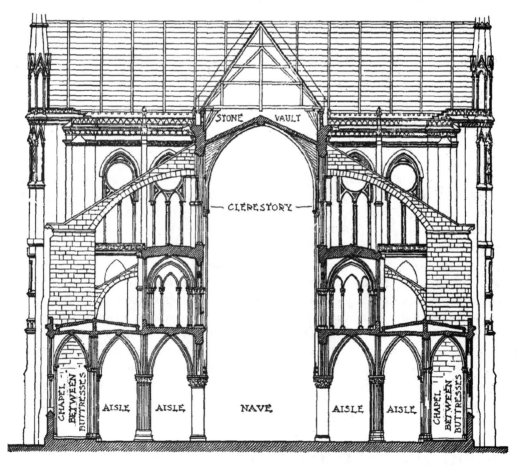

FIGURE 1.36 Gothic Period. Section through Cathedral of Notre-Dame, Paris. The cathedral was designed by Jean d'Orbais and started in 1211, with the main works completed in 1311. A prime example of French Gothic with its skillful use of flying buttresses. *(From Cyril M. Harris, Ed., Historic Architecture Sourcebook, McGraw-Hill Co., New York, 1977)*

Pointed arched ceilings supported by ribs carried down to slender clustered column supports, and the structure was dominated by equalizing the thrust and counterthrust. The characteristic features of the Gothic style are an accentuation of the vertical line, a constancy towards height and lightness while minimizing the role of the wall, which became thinner and very delicate, being broken up into tall bays. Structural strength was increased through the use of buttresses, and subsequently of flying buttresses, which removed the load-bearing structures to a position outside the actual building, thereby allowing the use of large windows. The final developments produced exquisite forms of lacelike stonework with intersecting ribs and beautiful intertwining tracery (Figure 1.37). From France, Gothic architecture and design spread throughout Europe, producing some local variations.

Gothic art in all its forms was conventional and idealistic. Almost all the furniture and woodwork of this period was in natural-finished oak, although walnut was used on occasion. The designs were heavy in their proportions and rectangular in shape. The parts were assembled with wooden dowels, mortise-and-tenon joints and hand-cut dovetails. Furniture designs and ornamentation were borrowed from architectural forms and motifs (Figure 1.38).

THE RENAISSANCE

As seen in relation to the Gothic style, the architecture of the Renaissance represents a complete break with tradition, even though the two styles coexisted for a long time. In Italy the memory of classical antiquity had never died and so it is not surprising that we should see in the early 15th century a rebirth of classical art and learning. Architects and designers sought to rediscover the essence of Roman architecture, both by looking at its monuments, and above all by studying Vitruvius's *Treatise on Architecture*.

The Renaissance blossomed and became a powerful artistic force, restating the significance of the module and rules of proportion, and giving new life to the classical orders. It was essentially the decorative language of antiquity that the Renaissance took as its model (Figures 1.39 and 1.40). The Renaissance produced a number of notable theoreticians, including Alberti, Serlio, Vignola and Palladio, all of whom pursued the mathematical structure of beauty by arithmetical, geometrical, and harmonic means. It was partially through their writings that the Renaissance style rapidly spread throughout Europe, while undergoing various modifications due to cultural and other differences. In France it became *le style classique*, whereas Italy and Germany gradually transformed it into the movement known as Baroque.

THE BAROQUE AND ROCOCO

The Baroque is a European style of architecture and decoration originally developed in the early 17th century in Italy and then spreading to the rest of Europe, developing new directions as it

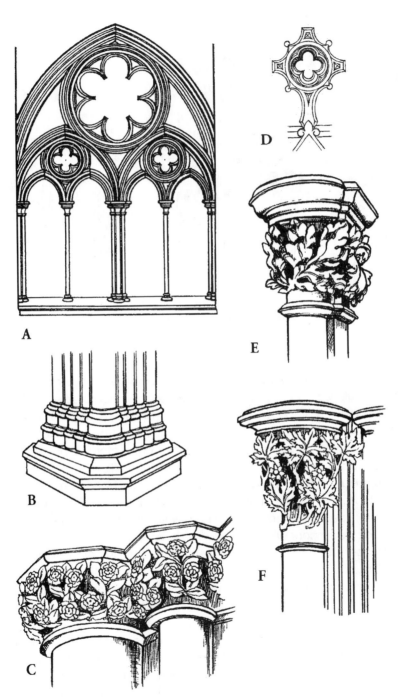

FIGURE 1.37 Examples of Gothic design elements and decoration.

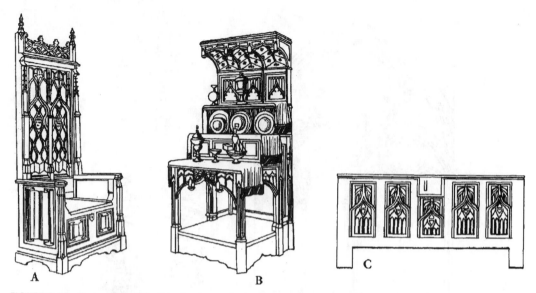

FIGURE 1.38 Examples of Gothic furniture displaying a characteristic emphasis on the vertical. a) Chair showing linenfold, tracery and buttresses. b) Credence. c) Oak chest with tracery carving.

went. Although the underlying vocabulary of the Renaissance remained in place, i.e. the orders, rhythms, and proportions of classical antiquity, the Baroque is characterized by the use of large scale, the interpenetration of spaces, sweeping curves, and lavish detail. Baroque architecture broke up the monolithic character of the facade, articulating it, and perforating it with bays.

Interiors were generally regal in their manner and characterized by formality of design, large-scale and elaborate details, and extravagance of workmanship and material. By the late 17th century, France dominated the arts in Europe, and became the source to which other countries looked for artistic inspiration. In the salons, the permanent elements of large rooms, such as walls, ceilings, doors, and windows, were important features of decoration. Furniture was regarded as secondary motifs and was placed against the walls, leaving the center of the room clear. The walls and ceilings were treated as one magnificent composition of decorative paintings, carvings, tapestries, paneling, and mirrors.

Baroque furniture and accessories displayed a richness of character equal to the room treatments (Figure 1.41), and in France, a special guild of cabinetmakers and apprentices was established by Lebrun, with quarters in the Louvre.

The late phase was called Rococo. In France the Rococo style was commonly known as Louis XV. The emphasis during the Rococo period was on interior applications rather than the exterior facade. And unlike the art of Baroque which was to glorify the king, the art of the Rococo was for everyone. Its features are essentially characterized by lightness and delicacy of line and structure, by asymmetry, and by the abundant use of foliage, curves, and scroll

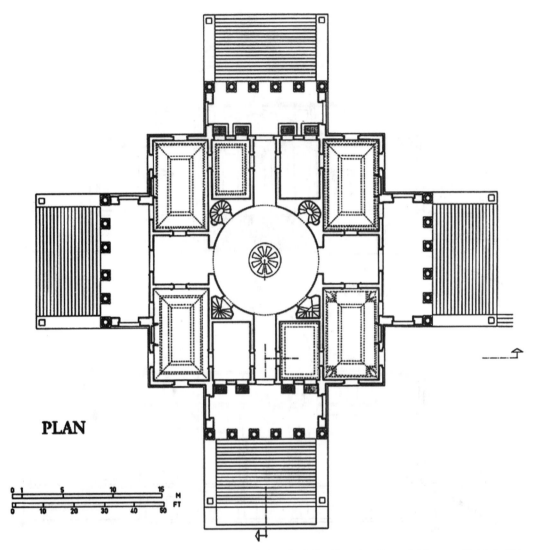

PLAN

FIGURE 1.39 Renaissance Period. Plan of the La Rotonda (Villa Almerico-Capra), Vicenza (Italy), built by Andrea Palladio in 1566. It has columned porches surmounted by pediments and a central domed hall. *(From Henri Stierlin, Encyclopedia of World Architecture, Van Nostrand Reinhold Co.)*

forms of decoration. The Rococo style often leaned to the extravagant ornamentation of surfaces. Furniture manufacturers during this period developed many new types, which were designed for comfort rather then pomp or pageantry. Furniture used the curvilinear form at all times, and especially the cabriole leg with a scroll foot instead of the goat's hoof (Figures 1.42a and 1.42b). Straight lines were avoided, as were the appearance of joints.

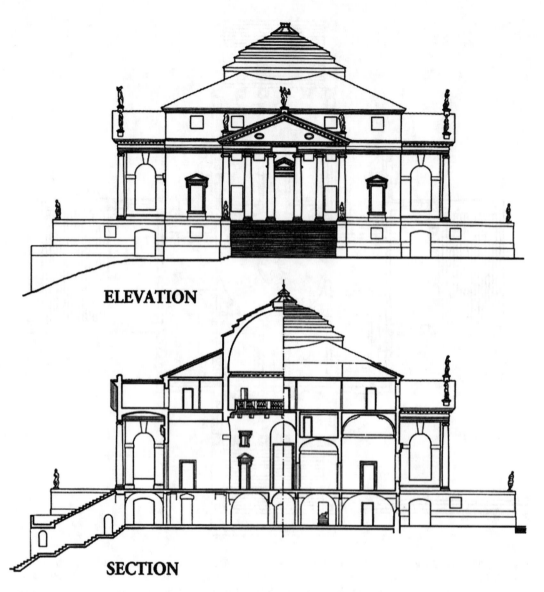

ELEVATION

SECTION

FIGURE 1.40 La Rotonda (Villa Almerico-Capra) showing section and elevation.

Carved Wood
Panel

Chair

Detail of Chapel Door
Versailles

Walnut Stool

Boulle Cabinet

Mantelpiece, Versailles

FIGURE 1.41 Baroque furniture and details.

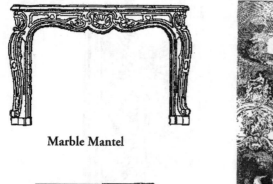

Marble Mantel

**Commode with
Ormolu Mounts**

Salon, Palace of the Archbishop of Speyer, Germany

FIGURE 1.42a Rococo furniture and details.

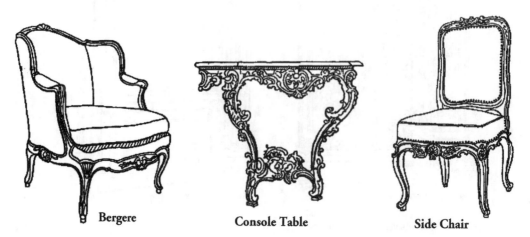

Bergere   **Console Table**   **Side Chair**

FIGURE 1.42b Rococo furniture and details.

NEOCLASSIC PERIOD AND 19TH CENTURY REVIVAL STYLES

The Neoclassic Period represents the last phase of European classicism in the late 18th and 19th centuries in Western Europe and the United States. The period is characterized by monumentality, sparing application of ornament and a stricter use of the orders (Figure 1.43). The movement was basically a reaction to Rococo and Baroque design, and was a period of reminiscence in which architecture and design turned to a variety of historical sources for inspiration—mainly Greek, Roman, and Egyptian forms during the Empire period (Figure 1.44).

Prominent artistic personalities of this period include architects like Robert and James Adam, Sir John Soane, and Sir William Chambers, and designers like Henry Holland. Adam collaborated with cabinetmakers such as Chippendale and Hepplewhite to produce furniture for his clients, and in the process had a significant influence on their design. The most characteristic ornaments popularized by Adam were the Grecian honeysuckle and fret, the fluted frieze or apron, the patera and rosette, and the husk. The 19th century revival styles reflected the enthusiasm of the period. Three furniture designers and manufacturers in particular stand out:

1. Thomas Chippendale II (son of Thomas Chippendale I) who in 1754 published, *The Gentleman and Cabinet-Maker's Director*, and manufactured his furniture in Mahogany.

2. Thomas Sheraton, who through his published work, *The Cabinet-Maker and Upholsterer's Drawing Book* in 1791 gained great recognition. His designs (particularly his chair backs) were greatly imitated by furniture manufacturers for many generations that followed.

3. George Hepplewhite, who popularized satinwood and painted motifs as a means of enrichment. Many of these cabinetmakers and others in England and their contemporaries on the continent, incorporated classical motifs.

In France, neoclassic interiors discarded the rococo curves, without sacrificing their charm and intimacy. Changes were principally in the forms and details. The Empire style became popular, and predominated after Napoleon become emperor in 1804. French cabinetmakers suddenly eliminated patterns and designs that referenced the old regime. While retaining the delightful lines and proportions of the monarchy, less carved ornament was used, reflecting difficult economic conditions of the time (Figure 1.45). Never before or since the Empire period has such an attempt been made to impose a decorative style upon a society by artificial methods, rather than allowing it to develop through natural evolution.

Furniture developed in the previous period continued to be made; proportions remained light and delicate, but the dominant line of design was straight and the shape took on a rectangular form. During this period, many books were published on Greek, Egyptian, and Etruscan art and architecture, and these had a major influence on artists of all mediums, including furniture design. Leading French cabinetmakers at the time include, Georges Jacob, Francois Jacob-Desmalter, Martin Eloy Lignereux, Barthelemy Rascalon, and Charles Burette. Charles Percier and Pierre-Francois-Leonard Fontaine established the Empire style in France.

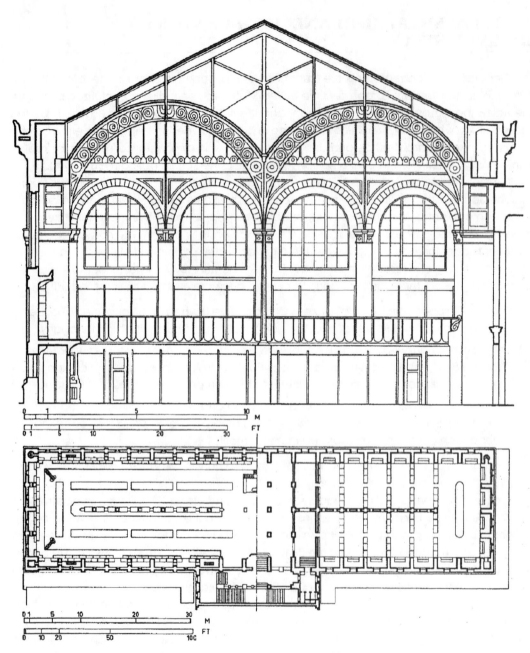

FIGURE 1.43a   Ste. Genevieve Library, Paris. Built in 1843-1850 by Henri Labrouste.

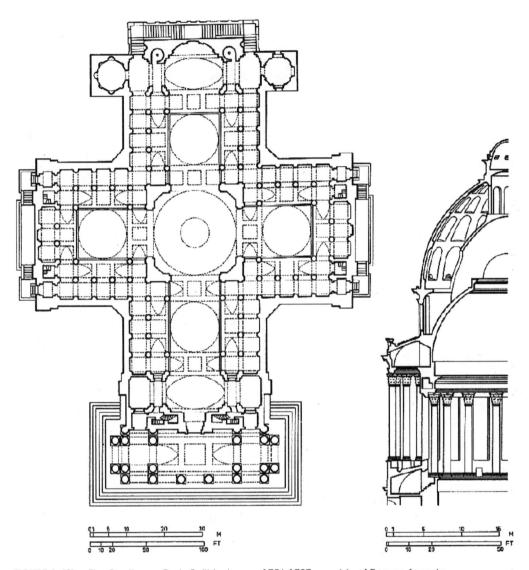

FIGURE 1.43b The Pantheon, Paris. Built between 1756-1797, consists of Roman facade.

Hepplewhite Sideboard

Mirror 1775

Philadelphia Highboy

Sheraton Armchair

Chippendale Sofa

Chippendale Chair

Goddard Type Desk

FIGURE 1.44 Neoclassic Period—Late Colonial and Early Federal furniture. *(Courtesy Sherril Whiton, Interior Design and Decoration, S.B. Lippincott Co.)*

During the late 19th century and well into the 20th century, the approach to the study of interior design was more imitative of earlier styles than innovative or original. The public enthusiasm for the Greek Classical look withered away towards the middle of the 19th century, and English furniture design also lost its luster and began to decline during the regency period (810-1820).

The American Periods

Perhaps the most important influence in the development of the industrial arts in America was the varied origins of its inhabitants, including the English, Dutch, French, German, Irish, Swedish, Spanish, and others. The English language became the common denominator. In Figure 1.46, we see furniture by Duncan Phyfe (1768-1854), who is one of the outstanding American cabinetmakers of the early 19th century.

Over-door Motif-Medallion   **Console**   **Commode**

Arabesque   **Arm Chair**   **Side Chair**   **Arm Chair**

FIGURE 1.44 Neoclassic Period—Late Colonial and Early Federal furniture. *(Courtesy Sherril Whiton, Interior Design and Decoration, S.B. Lippincott Co.)*

FIGURE 1.45 Examples of furniture and details from the Neoclassic period.

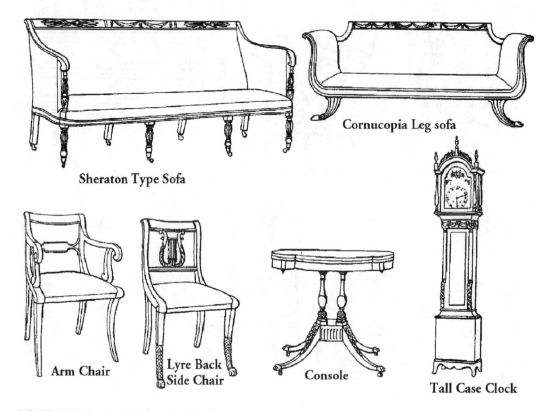

Cornucopia Leg sofa

Sheraton Type Sofa

Arm Chair

Lyre Back
Side Chair

Console

Tall Case Clock

FIGURE 1.46   Furniture by Duncan Phyfe.

RECENT HISTORY—THE LEAP FORWARD

The early 20th century was an age of contradictions, as well as great vigor and inventiveness. Industrialization brought mass production, removing form and emphasizing function. Art Nouveau was championed by Charles Rennie Mackintosh (1862-1928) and Antonio Gaudi (1852-1926), and was motivated basically by aesthetics and the seeking of a new style that was oblivious of the past. The Arts and Crafts movement, strongly propagated by William Morris (1834-1896) and others, revolted against the machine, advocating hand fabrication of products. Soon Art Deco came on the scene, dedicated to ending the conflict between art and industry. Creative design was adapted to suit mass production.

The famous Morris easy chair, being made of solid wood sections, symbolizes the arts and crafts furniture and marks the end of an era. In contrast, the antithesis to this approach is Breuer's Wassily chair, which is constructed of chrome-plated steel tube with a canvas seat.

The early 20th century also witnessed great architectural giants and visionaries like Frank Lloyd Wright, Auguste Perret (1873-1954), Adolf Loos (1879-1933), Peter Behrens (1868-1940) and Le Corbusier (1887-1968), Eliel Saarinen, Alvar Aalto, as well as leaders of the Bauhaus like Walter Gropius, Marcel Breuer and Mies van der Rohe.

In 1919, soon after World War I, Walter Gropius (1883-1969), founded the legendary Bauhaus school in Weimar, Germany. Gropius came from the Werkbund movement, which sought to integrate art and economics, and to add an element of engineering to art. The Bauhaus was founded by combining the Weimar Art Academy with the Weimar Arts and Crafts School. Students at this new school were trained simultaneously by both artists and master craftsmen, realizing the Gropius vision of familiarizing modern artists with science and economics to mold and unite creativity with a practical knowledge of craftsmanship, and thus to develop a new sense of functional design.

The practical innovations developed by the Bauhaus school, which is possibly the most influential school of its kind, came about like its contemporary Art Deco movement, in reaction to the florid, heavily decorative Art Nouveau furniture of the turn-of-the-century. It also revolutionized the architectural and aesthetic concepts and practices inherited from the Renaissance. But unlike Art Deco, which strived for handcrafted simplicity (Figure 1.47), the Bauhaus was totally modern. The profound impact of the Bauhaus stretches beyond our furniture and light fixtures, into the realms of architecture, theater, and typography, where the designs and style of the Bauhaus are still spoken of today. The school had three basic aims from its inception that remained unchanged throughout its life, even though the direction of the school often changed significantly. The first goal then, was to rescue all of the arts from the isolation in which each then found itself, and to encourage individual artisans and craftsmen to work together and combine their skills.

Secondly, the school set out to elevate the status of crafts, chairs, lamps, teapots, etc., to the same level enjoyed by fine arts, painting, and sculpting. The third aim was to maintain contact with industry leaders in an attempt to gain independence from government support by selling designs to industry. With these as its basis, the Bauhaus began and influenced our lives immensely in ways that most people probably take for granted. It's mission was always to provide an intellectual, reflective, yet functional approach to aesthetics. It put an emphasis on designer quality, mass-production, and machine-age materials. In Germany the Bauhaus became the focal point of the new creative forces accepting the challenge of technological progress.

This young and energetic movement that nurtured some of the 20th century's greatest architects and designers, lasted a mere 14 years due to the rise of Nazism in Germany. It sought to promote the philosophy of a free environment in which students are encouraged to create new forms of architecture and the arts. In the mid-1920s, the Bauhaus began to explore new technologies and ideas of mass production. The first public display of the Bauhaus's embrace of this technology was in 1923 at the annual government organized Deutscher Werkbund exhibition in Weimar, where a house designed by George Muche, a student, and Gropius' partner Adolf Meyer, was on display. The kitchen was designed by Marcel Breuer.

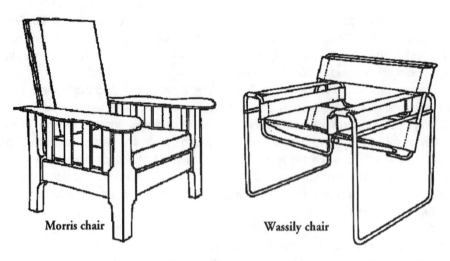

Morris chair   Wassily chair

FIGURE 1.47 Morris chair by William Morris and Wassily chair by Marcel Breuer (1925).

In 1924 funding for the Bauhaus was drastically cut at the instigation of conservative forces which forced it to move to Dessau, becoming the municipally funded College of Design. Almost all masters moved with it, while former students became junior masters in charge of the workshops. Dessau produced famous works of art and architecture and influential designs in the years between 1926 and 1932. Under pressure, Walter Gropius resigned as director on April 1, 1928 and was succeeded by the Swiss architect Hannes Meyer (1889-1954). Despite his successes, Hannes Meyer's Marxist convictions forced his departure and he was succeeded by Ludwig Mies van der Rohe (1886-1969). Under Mies, the Bauhaus developed from 1930 into a technical college of architecture with subsidiary art and workshop departments. After the Nazis became the biggest party in Dessau at the elections, the Bauhaus was forced to move in September, 1932 to Berlin. This fresh start in Berlin was short-lived, and it dissolved itself under pressure from the Nazis in 1933.

The Bauhaus's radical departure from convention, coupled by its inability to survive in the stymieing political and economic environment of the early 1930s in Nazi Germany, forced the legendary school to dramatically close its doors forever in 1933. Nevertheless, the Bauhaus language became an avant-garde dialect that was widely embraced. Many artists, architects, and designers involved with the Bauhaus had to flee the Nazi regime, and many sought refuge in the United States where their design philosophies found a receptive audience. Bauhaus ideals found a wide audience in the United States and throughout the world, and were expounded through various channels, like design periodicals and exhibitions, such as the Modern Movement Exhibition held at the Museum of Modern Art in New York City in 1932, which featured works by Le Corbusier, Walter Gropius, Mies van der Rohe, and others.

By the time the Nazis sparked the exodus of many of Germany's most talented designers and extinguished the Bauhaus's physical presence, it's ideas had already taken hold in the United States and other countries. Leaders of the movement had taken up important positions in prominent American universities, giving Bauhaus ideas an excellent forum and the momentum to go forward. Walter Gropius became a professor in the Graduate School of Design at Harvard. Ludwig Mies van der Rohe did the same at the Illinois Institute of Technology in Chicago. Laszlo Moholy-Nagy, who had headed the metal shop at the Bauhaus, was appointed Director of the New Bauhaus located in Chicago. It should be obvious to most architectural historians that the visionary ideals of the Bauhaus movement and many of its followers were at least 50 years ahead of their time, and these young visionaries launched the Modern Movement, which has shaped much of the art and architecture of the 20th century.

When Kathryn Hiesinger, curator at the Philadelphia Museum of Art, was asked which items stood out in her mind as design icons of the twentieth century, she said, "Furniture has gone through so many changes during this short 100 years, challenging our ideas over and over again of what a 'chair' is and what a 'couch' is, that I really have to look to that broad category as the source for my icon. Given that, if I had to name one period, I'd say the Bauhaus furniture of the 1920s and 1930s because it was so innovative in both its form and its use of materials."

Finnish architect Eliel Saarinen arrived on American shores in 1923, and while never formally a member of the Bauhaus, he strongly influenced modern architecture and design through his adaptations of Bauhaus theories. In 1932, he became President of the newly established Cranbrook Academy of Art in Bloomfield Hills, Michigan, which produced such legendary designers as Charles and Ray Eames (Figure 1.48), Harry Bertoia (Figure 1.49) and Florence Knoll.

FIGURE 1.48
Famous chair
and ottoman
by Charles
and Ray Eames.
(Courtesy Herman Miller, Inc.)

Cranbrook, which had much in common with the Bauhaus, also had a major impact on American design, art, and architecture of the 20th century. Saarinen's son Eero studied architecture at Yale and then went to Cranbrook to work with is father. In 1941, Eero Saarinen won first prize with Charles Eames in the International Functional Furniture Competition conducted by New York's Museum of Modern Art. Saarinen discounted the use of solid wood for furniture and experimented with man made materials (Figure 1.50).

The two primary pioneering industry leaders at the time that were renown for their innovative approach to furniture design and manufacture were Herman Miller (also from Michigan) and the Knoll company.

The Herman Miller company began in 1923 when its founder, D.J. DePree, his father-in-law, Herman Miller, and others purchased the Star Furniture Company in Zeeland, Michigan. From 1931 onward, DePree moved the company from manufacturing traditional home furniture to

FIGURE 1.49 Chair designed by Harry Bertoia.

FIGURE 1.50   Furniture designed by Eero Saarinen. Tulip tables, chairs, and stool. *(Courtesy Knoll, Inc.)*

innovative contemporary home and office furniture. Herman Miller hired talented Bauhaus-inspired designers like Charles Eames, and others. By the 1950s, while still a small company, Herman Miller had gained an international following for its modern furniture. Today the Herman Miller company is a leading global provider of office furniture and services that support work environments. If there was a furniture category for the Nobel prize, Herman Miller would be a prime contender for its first recipient.

Hans Knoll founded his H.G. Knoll Furniture Company in New York in 1938 at the tender age of 25, and only a year after immigrating from his native Germany. Hans's father was a pioneering German manufacturer of modern furniture. Knoll also built furniture designed by Bauhaus practitioners and other artists, and in 1947 Knoll produced Ludwig Mies van der Rohe's chrome and leather Barcelona Chair (Figure 1.51).

During the war, the ambitious Hans hired a young space planner and designer, Florence Schust, who he married in 1946, and who was pivotal in helping Knoll achieve his vision of

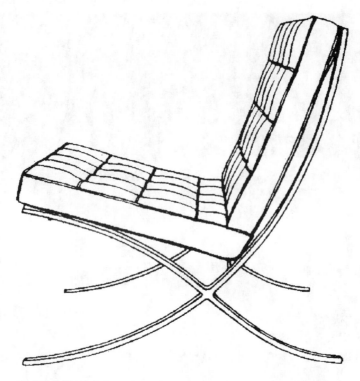

FIGURE 1.51   The Barcelona Chair by Mies van der Rohe, (1929).

modern furniture and interiors for modern buildings. Schust studied at Cranbrook, and at the Architectural Association in London. She later returned to the United States to complete her degree, and apprenticed with Walter Gropius and Marcel Breuer until she entered the Armour Institute (later called Illinois Institute of Technology) under Mies van der Rohe, who had a profound influence on her design approach.

Following their marriage, Florence and Hans also formalized their business partnership, and became known as Knoll Associates, Inc. Together, the Knolls championed the Bauhaus approach to furniture design and brought in talented designers like Eero Saarinen, Harry Bertoia, Isamu Noguchi, Jens Risom, and Franco Albini, to develop a collection of modern furniture now considered classics in the pantheon of modern design (Figure 1.52). The Knolls also used their extensive network of relationships with designers in Europe and America to expand the range of the firm's products, including the opening of a textile division. In the early 1950s, Knoll acquired a building in East Greenville, Pennsylvania which today serves as Knoll's headquarters.

Another industry leader, and one of the oldest in the furniture manufacturing business, is Steelcase Inc. Originally established in 1912 by Peter M. Wege, Sr., Walter Idema and ten other

FIGURE 1.52 Knoll furniture classics by: Jens Risom, 1941 (top left), Charles Ploock, 1965 (top right), Isamu Noguchi, 1955-1974 (bottom left), Franco Albini, 1958 (bottom right).

stockholders as the Metal Office Furniture Company in Grand Rapids, Michigan. Its first sale of desks was in 1915 when it furnished 200 fireproof steel desks for Boston's first skyscraper, the Customs House Tower. In 1937, it supplied oval-shaped desks, based on Frank Lloyd Wright's design vision, for the S.C. Johnson and Company building. Metal Office officially changed its corporate name to Steelcase in 1954. What is interesting about Steelcase is their innovative approach to space planning, in that they provide clients with services and products that help create high-performance working environments that integrate architecture, furniture, and technology.

The development of space planning emerged as a response to the needs of the time, particularly those of corporate growth. During the 1930s, there were only a handful of architects and designers who were outspoken on the inadequacy of how businesses were utilizing their office space. By the forties and fifties, these numbers multiplied and were joined by individuals and groups from other disciplines, including the two visionary manufacturers of contemporary furniture—the Herman Miller Company and Knoll Associates. The economic climate was favorable at the time and Herman Miller and Knoll made a conscious effort to educate their clients as well as the public. They used their showrooms as the main vehicle to attain this objective, which had an immeasurable impact on the future direction of design.

After the Second World War, there was a sudden expansion of businesses in the United States and throughout the industrialized world. This caused a massive building boom in homes and office buildings. The architects and designers of the Bauhaus were called in and commissioned to design much of corporate America. Also during the 1950s and 60s, the Knoll Planning Unit became an influential player in corporate design work. During this period of grandiose expansion, there was also a large influx of professionals, researchers, and scientists seeking employment and searching for the American dream. By the 1960s, the office workforce in the America was growing expeditiously at an unbelievable rate of 850,000 annually. This, along with the rapid expansion of businesses and the emerging technology presented by the computer and its practical application in the office environment, had a fundamental impact on the character of the office at the time. Additionally, office space suddenly became a valued commodity and rentals increased dramatically to keep pace with the growing demand.

In the Johnson Wax building (S.C. Johnson & Sons), Frank Lloyd Wright integrated the furniture with the design by painting the metal brick red—specifying the color of the brick Cherokee Red—and curving the forms. Although the design dates from 1939, it bridged the gap between the conventional office and the next development in office landscaping (Figure 1.53). It should be noted that Wright as early as 1904 recognized total office environments as having the potential to facilitate work processes, and he tried to attain this in the Larkin Company administrative building in 1904. This was the first entirely air-conditioned modern office building on record.

The office as we know it has a history going back nearly a century. Initially, it was a space housing perhaps a single person, devoid of typewriters, telephones, copiers, and other accouterments associated with the office of today. With the spread of industrialization, the office expanded and had to accommodate additional staff.

By the turn-of-the-century, experiments were taking place with new materials, and office buildings began using steel and iron. This inspired CEOs to take a whole new look at how the office space would best be utilized (Figure 1.54). Evolution of the office after World War II underwent several phases and transformations. Up to the 1950s, offices consisted of a few high-level executives or managers supervising large numbers of clerical employees.

Between the 1950s and early 1960s, the expansion of corporate businesses created an office building boom throughout the industrialized world. As businesses proliferated, large corporate America found itself with its management scattered in many locations. By the end of the 1950s, this management dislocation gave birth to a new phenomena; the development of corporate headquarters. Florence Knoll created an internal department called the Knoll Planning Unit whose role was to work with clients to identify their workplace needs and to customize interior architecture and furnishing solutions. This unit played a significant role in transforming the American business environment of the postwar years. Likewise, Florence Knoll's philosophy that architecture and interior design must be informed by functionality and work processes, as well as by aesthetics, is considered by some to have been a significant factor in the direction of today's approach to corporate interior design.

FIGURE 1.53 Johnson Wax building interior, 1939. (S.C. Johnson & Sons) by Frank Lloyd Wright. *(Courtesy Steelcase, Inc.)*

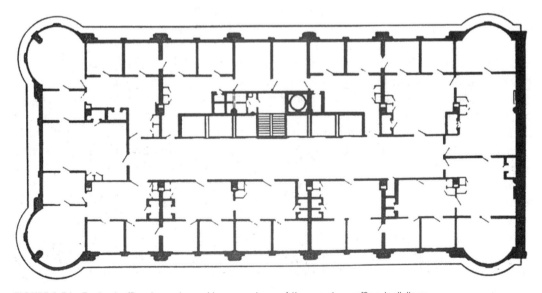

FIGURE 1.54 Typical office layout used in many turn-of-the-century office buildings.

The corporate headquarters amassed large numbers of people into one space. Prior to this, typical office building tenants occupied, at the most, several floors in that building. The new concept has an entire office building dedicated to housing one company. The rapid and enthusiastic development of corporate headquarters was also helped by new technological developments such as year around air conditioning and uniform lighting (ending dependence on natural light and ventilation), as well as the availability of materials. By the 1960s, the progressive character of the office worker was being altered by a variety of influences, primarily the absorption of a highly educated workforce pool, rapid expansion businesses, and the emergence of positive applications for the computer. Rising costs of rental office space to house these growing organizations prompted a search for improved office space efficiency. The development of space planning was born as a response to the problems of corporate growth.

By this time, the open bullpen concept was going out of fashion. The bull pen concept placed staff in open spaces with rigid grids of desks and aisles, and the executives were segregated to one or more sides in enclosed windowed offices (Figure 1.55). The executive core concept soon replaced it. This consisted of the staff being located around the building's perimeter, and the executives relocated their offices to the building core.

Office Landscape

The German term *Bürolandschaft* is translated into English as office landscape (commonly called open plan design), and is a term coined by journalists because of the large number of growing plants and openness of the first European installation. It is a system of office space planning and originated in Germany in 1959 by the brothers Eberhard and Wolfgang Schnelle, whose organization later became known as the Quickborner Team.

The Quickborner Team was a planning and management consulting group, and concluded that the typical existing office hindered rather than encouraged work productivity. They believed that office planning should be based on patterns of communication, and that other values like appearance, status recognition, and tradition, should be relegated to a minor role. They concluded that placement of work stations should be determined by the flow of communication, which is the primary part of daily office functioning.

Prior to developing the office landscape concept in 1959, Quickborner was a materials company specializing in paper related products, furniture and equipment, and filing systems for offices. The lack of harmony between products and systems instigated their move into investigating interdependencies within the office. They quickly realized that all elements of the office were interrelated and should be dealt with concurrently, and the physical setting of the office can have an impact on work processes. By eliminating partitions, they eliminated the enclosed office, the geometric grid and the space modules. This in turn led to the development of an approach to office planning later to be called office landscaping. Issues that had to be overcome included loss of privacy (due to elimination of partitions) and noise.

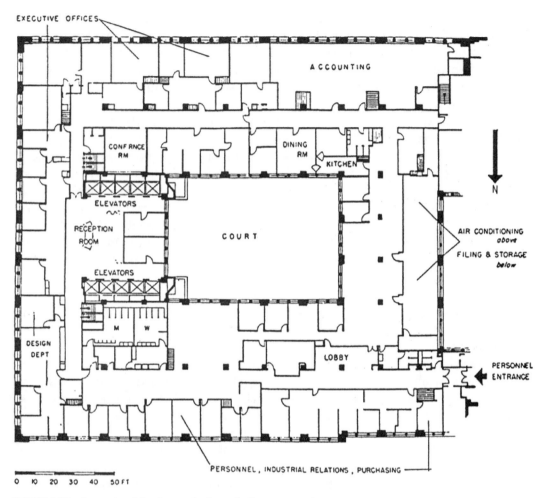

FIGURE 1.55 Example of the "open bull pen" office concept.

The new approach spread throughout Europe, with the first installation in 1960 for the Bertelsman Publishing Company in Gütersloh, West Germany. Soon, installations followed for other companies in Germany, such as Krupp, Ford, Deckel, Osram, Boehringer, Ninoflex, and Orenstein and Kippel. In the early sixties, the concept spread into other European countries. Office landscape projects were executed in Spain, the Netherlands, Scandinavia, and Britain.

During the early 1960s, while Robert Propst was developing the "Action Office" at Herman Miller Research, the Quickborner Team was also undergoing research into the corporate office in the United States. Office landscaping was first introduced into the United States in the fall of 1967, when Du Pont's Freon Products Division in Wilmington, Delaware moved into the first office landscape space outside Europe. Du Point retained the Quickborner Team to design their offices (Figure 1.56). Key to Quickborner planning is that it is based upon a systems analysis of work flow and communication—whether by conversation, written memos, or telephone. This data is then analyzed, leading to floor plans and furniture layouts that are free and non-rectilinear. People who are in frequent contact with each other are positioned adjacent, and those not needing frequent contact, are placed further apart.

The office landscape is a three-dimensional representation of the basic flow diagram. Spaces are more open than in conventional planning, and unlike in traditional offices, screens are usually four feet, six inches high rather than to the ceiling. This created acoustically problems that were offset by the use of carpet, plants, and acoustically treated ceilings. Clearly landscape planning had a strong impact in America and achieved great popularity because it was essentially efficient, flexible, open, and informal. However, because the approach did away with enclosed offices, including those of top executives, management in America often lacked enthusiasm for the new fashion.

Robert Propst, who was brought in by D.J. DePree to head Herman Miller's Research Center, believed that offices should be subservient to their occupants, and in some respects, his Action Office came to the rescue of the office landscape, mainly because the latter's approach left a number of outstanding issues such as acoustics unresolved. The Action Office was a radical new approach to office furniture. It was the world's first open plan office furniture system and was first marketed in 1964, although it was the revised Action Office system marketed in 1968 that received the greatest acclaim (Figure 1.57). The first installation of the product was in the Chicago offices of JFN Associates and had rave reviews. Since then, the system has been augmented with many modifications and additions, in response to the changing needs of the office. From the outset, Propst articulated a clear vision and coherent set of criteria for his open office design work. Judy Voss states that "like landscape planning, Action Office avoids the fixed partitions of conventional offices and substitutes movable screens." Propst's concept was a new emphasis towards ongoing change.

Computers have obviously had an enormous impact on space planning programs. Computerization both expanded the use of rectilinear, repetitive office layout patterns in the name of facilitating communications, and forced a rethinking of the design process to accommodate endless cords, cables, and electrical requirements.

The Environmental Movement

In recent years, environmental issues have played an increasing role in space planning and design, and today there is a growing cadre of environmentally conscious designers and space planners that are carrying the banner. However, two firms in particular, Hellmuth, Obata + Kassabaum (HOK) and Herman Miller have from the beginning, taken the lead in expounding the

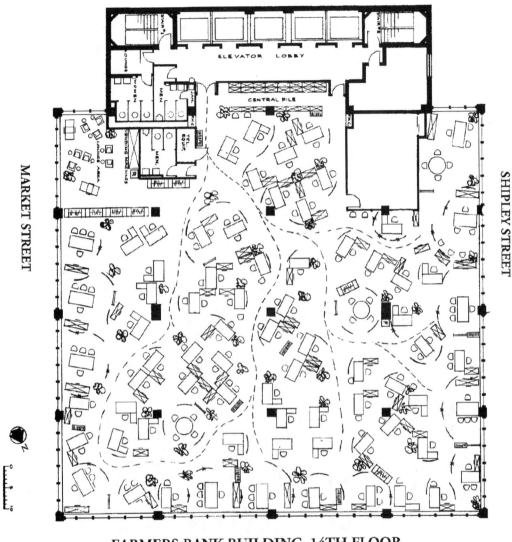

FARMERS BANK BUILDING, 14TH FLOOR

FIGURE 1.56 Office landscape designed by Quickborner for DuPont in 1967.

"Green" design approach. Buildings are known to have a tremendous impact on our environment—both during construction and through their operation. Green building is a growing network promoting the treatment of buildings as whole systems and is discussed in greater detail in Chapter 5.

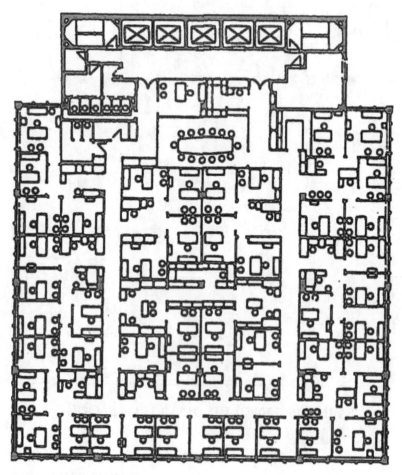

FIGURE 1.56 *(continued)* Office landscape designed by Quickborner for DuPont in 1967.

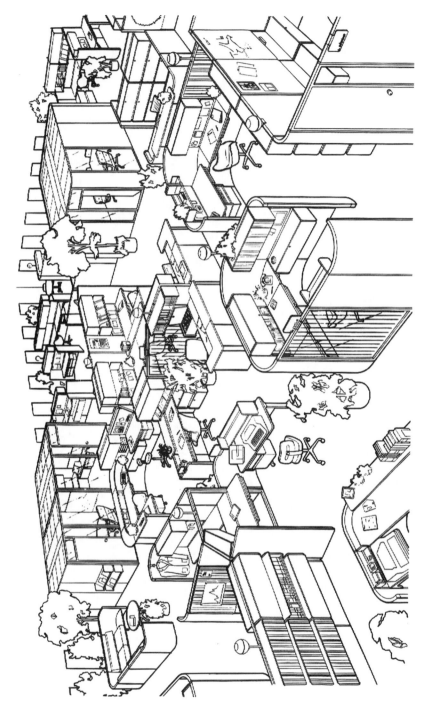

FIGURE 1.57 The Action Office System designed by Robert Propst. (*Courtesy Herman Miller*)

CHAPTER TWO

DESIGN METHODOLOGY

*T*oday's con-
temporary
office envi-
ronment is
often a sophisticated
and intricate eco-
system of many inter-
related elements and
sub-systems, in which
various individuals
occupy space. These
individuals have
special needs, and
the diligent space
planner is required to
address these needs.
In doing so, it is essen-
tial to recognize such
influencing factors as
evolving computer
and communications
technologies, psycho-
social elements of
the workplace and
planning for future
expansion and
growth.

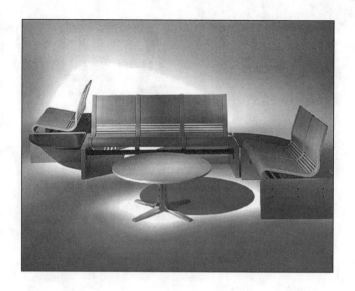

GENERAL OVERVIEW

Modern research shows that the physical work environment can often play a pivotal role in attracting and retaining personnel, which is why professional planners and designers expend so much effort trying to understand and resolve their clients' needs. A recently conducted survey of 200 corporate decision-makers for *Productive Workplaces* lists four major ways in which interior design impacts office productivity and efficiency. They are as follows:

- access
- comfort
- flexibility
- privacy

Design methodology is a structured process that outlines the parameters of generally accepted sequences of tasks that occur from the point at which a designer or space planner begins to work on a project to the point at which the project is complete and occupied. Additionally, the client may formally request a review of certain or all aspects of the project's performance, and commission a post-occupancy evaluation (POE). Such

POE feedback (conducted primarily for large corporations and institutions), provides strategic planners with reliable data on building performance and essential insight on positive and negative attributes of the building (Figures 2.1a, 2.1b).

Ideally, the space planner is an integral and contributing component of the design team from the outset of the design process. A space planner's early input could greatly enhance the final design by achieving a more satisfactory work setting solution. Customarily, however, the space planner is brought in after completion of the building shell and asked to work within the constraints of an existing space, or in the case of new construction, a shell. In either case, a comprehensive assessment of the space's prevalent features is necessary—both for traits worth preserving (e.g. good view, plentiful daylight, high ceilings and windows), and traits that need addressing (e.g. poor acoustics, small cellular rooms, embedded services, ducts and cabling, lack of natural ventilation). In the course of conducting such an evaluation, the planner should exploit these strengths and weaknesses to create an integrated high-performance environment solution that enhances productivity and efficiency.

A well-designed work environment is one that is dynamic and can be modified to address new conditions and work habits in line with the organization's continuous development and growth (or decline). The ultimate design solution should not only take into account existing circumstances, operational strategies, and factors like building code requirements and fixed elements within the space, but should also address important issues like the impact of change and evolution on the organization's futuristic needs resulting from increased mobile computing, wireless data networks, the demise of awkward desktop PCs, and the electronic meeting place. A designed space ultimately fails its objective if it is responsive solely to the needs of today while ignoring those of tomorrow. Likewise, successful space planning solutions can best be achieved when client organizations educate themselves to realize the need for an infrastructure planned to accommodate fast-paced change.

Typically, when clients engage the services of a professional designer, they have already researched their spatial and other needs in some depth, and may even have preconceptions of what the solution should be, though lacking the ability to translate this into a planning solution. Inexperienced clients often underestimate the complexity and analytical nature of the planning process, particularly where large projects are concerned. Furthermore, they may not be sufficiently aware of the need for new approaches and new solutions dictated by new technologies.

Despite variations in techniques and terminology, and despite the fundamental impact that new technologies have had on our perception of the modern workplace and how we communicate and process information, the design methodology process has remained intact, consisting essentially of seven sequential steps. These are:

1. Programming
2. Schematic design
3. Design development
4. Construction documents

5. Bidding (tendering) of construction documents.

6. Execution/supervision of project.

7. Post-occupancy evaluation.

PROGRAMMING PHASE: CREATING THE BRIEF OR PROGRAM

One of the first tasks in the design methodology sequence is invariably programming. Note that while many contracts do not include programming as part of basic services, the AIA/ASID Standard Form of Agreement for Interior Design Services does. Writing a brief or program,

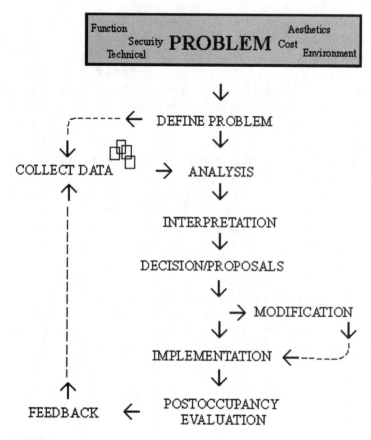

FIGURE 2.1a   The design methodology process and data analysis.

Planning Process Example

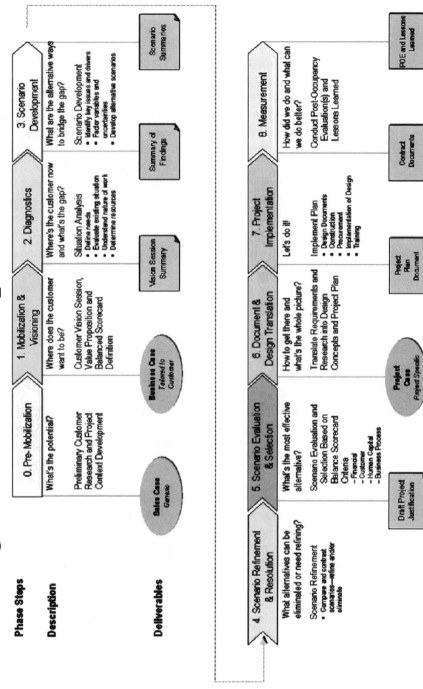

FIGURE 2.1b The planning process as seen through the eyes of the firm, Helmouth, Obatta + Kassalbaum. *(Courtesy HOK, Los Angeles)*

sometimes referred to as a project analysis report, project manual, or developmental planning report, defines the direction and basis of the proposed project.

Programming is a systematic approach to gathering information regarding goals, strategies, priorities, and existing problems within the organization, and then analyzing and interpreting this data to determine and define the client's goals, requirements, and objectives. Preliminary goals, priorities, and strategies will often require revisions after the data is analyzed. The final statement, which usually takes the form of a written document, creates the basis upon which the space planner can formulate a concept for the project, as well as a benchmark for both the decision making process and the evaluation of final solutions.

It is essential during this programming phase that the designer adequately consults with the owner to develop the applicable requirements of the project and studies the capability of meeting these requirements within the constraints of the owner's budget and site. Obviously, a clear and well-defined statement of a problem is fundamental to achieving an appropriate solution. If the objectives lack precision or clarity, an unsatisfactory solution would most likely result. Whether the space to be considered is residential, institutional, or commercial, the programming process customarily consists of the following elements.

Goal Definition

This phase is particularly important as it identifies and defines the client's strategic philosophy. For example, the client may opine that the company's corporate image should have precedence over its plan layout efficiency. The ramification of such a decision on the final solution could be enormous and may entail, among other things, increasing the project's budget. It may also necessitate increasing the space requirements initially programmed for the lobby and reception areas to portray a more impressive corporate image, than would have been required by its basic function.

It should be noted too, that the data needed for any in-depth analysis includes a comprehensive breakdown of personnel, equipment, and organizational and cultural requirements (Figure 2.2). The program brief should also track past and current organizational patterns and superimpose them on the organization's business plan as a means of attempting to project future trends in growth and operating procedures. The program should therefore be designed to accurately reflect the organization's needs not only at the time of occupancy, but for the duration of the occupancy. Unfortunately, however, one often finds that rapid project time frames coupled with tight budgets discourage future-oriented planning.

Nevertheless, rapid technological developments over the last few decades are imposing new challenges to our traditional perception of how we view today's office environment. The volatility of the global marketplace in the 21st century, with its eternal corporate mergers and acquisitions, makes even the most meticulous planning and forecasting problematic in attempting to predict future needs. Dynamic and creative solutions have become primary requisites for maintaining the validity of a program over time. This includes the incorporation of sufficient

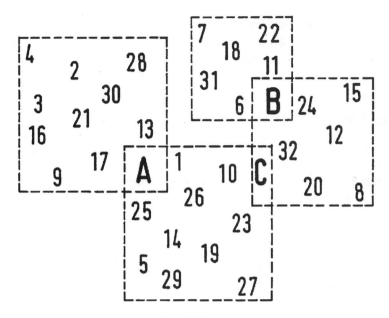

Problem defined and structured after analysis

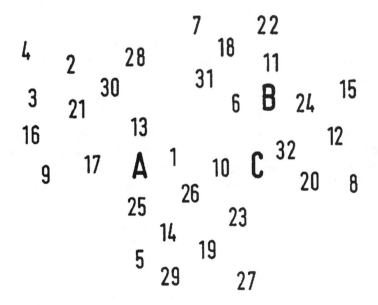

Data before analysis and structuring.

FIGURE 2.2 Diagrams showing one of the approaches used to define and structure collected data.

flexibility and adaptability into a design's infrastructure to be able to respond to changing conditions logically and promptly. In the absence of built-in flexibility and adaptability, any required spatial reconfiguration resulting from changes in business strategies, workforce composition and technology applications can be costly and disruptive.

Data Collection

Once the goals and objectives are defined, the planner proceeds with the task of information gathering. The collected data should be organized in a manner that is both methodical and easily accessible. A successful program needs the collection of information that answers pertinent questions about the following:

1. Personnel: what are the demographics of employees within the facility, what are their work habits, characteristics, and how do they interact with each other?

2. Work function: defining the tasks that are to be performed, and how they fit into the organization hierarchy. What are the needs for privacy? What special equipment is required to function efficiently, and are there specific criteria for individual workstations?

3. Departmental and interdepartmental communication: the primary focus is to establish spatial relationships or adjacency requirements between the various elements to determine placement in the space (Figure 2.3). The first task is to conduct a communication analysis starting with a study of individual communication patterns. This is then expanded into task-related groups, and then to larger groups or departments (Figures 2.4a, 2.4b). The analysis should determine the personnel relationships and priorities relevant to the work flow and the types of interdepartmental contacts required, whether contacts are made by telephone, in person, or in writing, their frequency of communication, and their need for shared facilities as shown in these examples.

4. Communication with the public: determine the frequency and nature of the contact, how much interaction there is with personnel, and whether there are special facilities or services needed for this contact such as waiting rooms, dining facilities, or auditoriums. Special facilities and services needed for contact with the public include easily understood graphics.

5. Communication and information relevant to paper flow: determine the procedure for document distribution, and the requirements for administrative personnel, typists, etc. to function efficiently (Figure 2.5).

6. Archives and record storage: determine the type and size of archive and record storage facilities needed, their preferred location, and whether any of these facilities will be shared.

7. Special facilities and equipment: determine what they are, what their primary function is, who uses them, and whether their function entails special requirements. Also, what furniture and equipment is needed for areas like mailrooms, conference rooms, lounges and

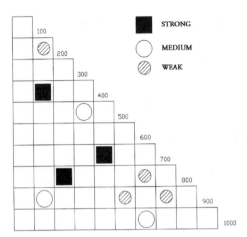

Sample Matrix of Interaction Intensity

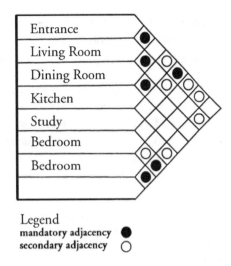

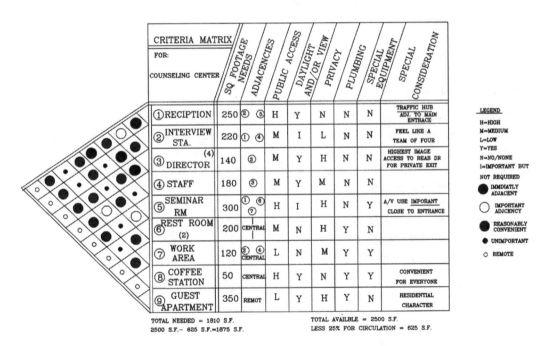

FIGURE 2.3 Adjacency matrix identifies proximity requirements for a residence and interdepartmental communications for a counseling center.

libraries. Also determine the spatial and technical requirements for items like vaults, computers, food service, and communications systems.

8. Existing equipment: prepare an inventory of all equipment and its condition for re-use.

The accumulated information should give the planner a comprehensive and pristine picture of the client's organization, culture and mode of operation. Additionally, it should clarify questions like the type of spaces envisaged, how they will be used, their relationships to each other, the number of people and equipment to be housed, code requirements, total budget available, building security needs, and the anticipated expansion rate of the company. Typical approaches to compiling information include the following.

Review of Existing Documents

In-depth reviews and analysis of relevant documents including organizational brochures, charts and records showing growth patterns, human resource and technology policies, business and management plans and vision gives planners the necessary insight into the organization's operating procedures, business strategies and objectives, and management style. It also puts the organization within a context for interpreting its past, present and future facilities needs.

Interviews and Field Surveys

The space planner is also required to conduct field surveys and interviews at different levels of key personnel within the organization, because the review of existing documents alone is rarely sufficient to achieve a satisfactory solution (Figures 2.6a, b, c). In addition, this type of data collection helps quantify and clarify the requirements for work flow, equipment, and special facilities. Questionnaires, personal interviews, and field surveys are vital investigative tools, and also help to identify problems possible solutions within an organization. Normally, an executive or senior staff member of the organization will accompany the interviewer on a guided walk-through of the facility.

A field survey of an existing building may consist of photographs and field measurements. The field measurements are used to prepare scaled drawings (preferably ¼ inch or ½ inch scale) that will form the basis for the final design. Where the building is still under construction, the information can be taken from the contract documents or, when the building is completed, from the as built drawings. Field surveys are an integral part of the programmatic process, especially where existing buildings are concerned, because they can furnish essential information including:

- Location and size of the various elements, both structural (exterior walls, columns, interior bearing walls, structural core), and non-structural (non-bearing partitions, built-ins)

PROJECT TITLE: Date:

EXISTING SPACE INVENTORIED

ITEM CODE	INVEN-TORY	ITEM DESCRIPTION	W	D	H	CONDITION
D-STL	101	DESK/LEFT	60"	30"	29"	Good
C-SP	102	CHAIR/TASK	24	24	36	Excellent
F-L3	103	LATERAL FILE/3 DRW	36	18	39	Good
D-DP	104	DESK/DOUBLE PED	72	36	30	Fair
C-ES	105	CHAIR/EXEC. SWVL	30	26	32	Good
C-SA	106	CHAIR/SIDE	20	18	32	Excellent
C-SA	107	CHAIR/SIDE	20	18	32	Good
O	108	BOOKCASE	36	12	72	Poor
O	109	CREDENZA	60	18	30	Good
O	110	STORAGE CABINET	36	18	60	Good
O	111	TERMINAL TABLE	36	24	29	Fair
O	112	COAT RACK	18	18	60	Good
O	113	PLAN FILE	54	42	36	Good
O	114	PLAN FILE	36	42	36	Good

CODES:

DESKS:
D-DP — DOUBLE PEDESTAL
D-SPL — SINGLE PEDESTAL (LEFT)
D-SPR — SINGLE PEDESTAL (RIGHT)

DESKS WITH RETURNS:
D-STL — SECRETARY TYPING (LEFT)
D-STR — SECRETARY TYPING (RIGHT)
D-EXL — EXECUTIVE (LEFT)
D-EXR — EXECUTIVE (RIGHT)

CHAIRS:
C-ES — EXECUTIVE SWIVEL
C-SP — SECRETARY POSTURE
C-S — SIDE
C-SA — SIDE WITH ARMS

FILES:
F-VLT4 — VERTICAL/LETTER (4 DRW)
F-VLG4 — VERTICAL/LEGAL (4 DRW)
F-L3 — LATERAL (3 DRW)
O — MISC/OTHER

FIGURE 2.4a Figures illustrate examples of taking inventory of existing space allocation and a statistical summary for a public relations office. *(From Julie K. Rayfield, The Office Interior Design Guide, John Wiley and Sons, Inc. 1994.*

PUBLIC RELATIONS OFFICE
PRELIMINARY SPACE REQUIREMENTS – STATISTICAL SUMMARY

	Space Type	Size (SF)	Qty	Staff	Area (SF)	Size (SF)	Qty	Staff	Area (SF)
		CURRENT SPACE REQUIRED				**FUTURE SPACE REQUIRED**			
OFFICE									
President/CEO	Ofc	400	1	0	400	400	1	0	400
Vice President	Ofc	400	1	1	300	300	2	2	600
Director	Ofc	175	6	6	1,050	175	7	7	1,225
Manager	WKST	100	5	5	400	100	7	7	700
Professional	WKST	80	7	7	560	80	5	5	400
Administrative	WKST	80	3	3	240	80	5	5	400
Subtotal: OFFICE SPACE & STAFF				22	2,950			26	3,725
SUPPORT FACILITIES									
Reception (Seat 2-3)		400	1	1	400	400	1	1	400
Small Conference (Seat 8)		510	1	0	1,020	510	2	0	1,020
Large Conference (Seat 20)		1,500	1	0	1,500	1,500	1	0	1,500
A/V Rear Screen Projection Room		400	1	0	400	400	1	0	400
Service Pantry		100	1	0	100	100	1	0	100
Coat Closets		30	1	0	30	30	1	0	30
Library		250	1	0	250	250	1	0	250
Employee Lounge		200	1	0	200	200	1	0	200
Copy/Work Room		250	1	0	250	250	1	0	250
Equipment Room		200	1	0	200	200	1	0	200
Printers-Shared		30	3	0	90	30	3	0	90
Supply Storage		60	1	0	60	60	1	0	60
Mail Room with Clerk		250	1	1	250	250	1	1	250
Bulk Storage Room		100	1	0	100	100	1	0	100
Central Archives		300	1	0	300	300	1	0	300
Vile Cabinets		14	10	0	140	14	10	0	140
Subtotal: SUPPORT FACILITIES				2	5,290			2	5,290

Subtotal: OFFICE & SUPPORT NET Square Feet 24	8,240	28	9,015
Corridors & Building Layout Factor – Estimated	3,300		3,550
Total Usable Area Required in Square Feet	11,540		12,565
Rentable Area Range:			
1. Core Factor @ 10%	1,154		1,257
Grand Total Rentable Area in Square Feet	12,694		13,822
2. Core Factor Estimated @ 15%	1,731		1,885
Grand Total Rentable Area in Square Feet	13,271		14,450

FIGURE 2.4b Figures illustrate examples of taking inventory of existing space allocation and a statistical summary for a public relations office. *(Courtesy of Herman Miller, Inc.)*

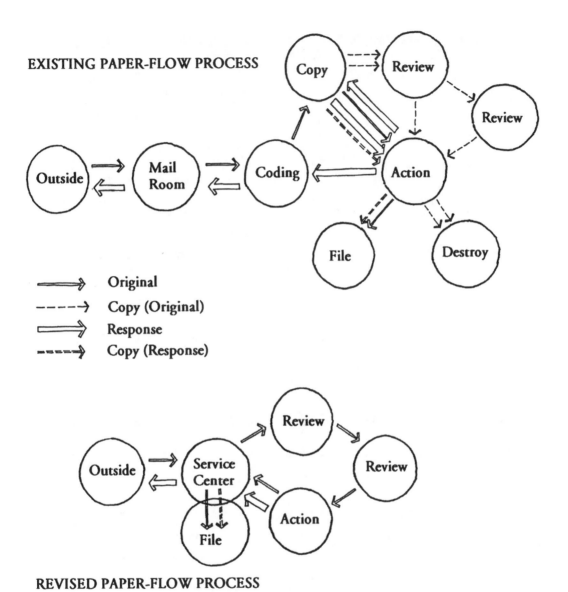

EXISTING PAPER-FLOW PROCESS

REVISED PAPER-FLOW PROCESS

FIGURE 2.5 Paper flow diagram. *(From Julie K. Rayfield, The Office Interior Design Guide, John Wiley and Sons, Inc. 1994)*

Topic	Question
Overall Organizational	
Mission and Goals	Provide and overview of your organization's mission and key goals.
Strategies	What are the primary strategies for achieving your goals?
Challenges	What are the most critical challenges facing your organization that need to be addressed to achieve your goals?
Metrics	How do you measure success in the following categories? 1) Financial 2) Human Capital 3) Customer 4) Business Process
Business Impact	What trends or factors may have a significant impact on your operations in the foreseeable future?
Best Practices	What organizations (private/public) do you aspire to be like? Why?
Political Considerations	Are there any political issues or sensitivities to be aware of?
Human Capital	
Culture	How would you describe the culture of your organization? Is it changing, or does it need to? If so, in what ways?
Retention	Are there issues or problems with attracting and retaining employees? Are there any concerns or initiatives you have in this area to increase employee satisfaction?
Business Process	
Organizational Structure	Does your current organizational structure support your mission? If not, how could it?
Technology – current	Does your current technology support your organization? If not, what would make a difference?
Technology – future	What future technologies may have an impact on your organization? What are the implications?
Customer	
Customers	Currently, how satisfied are they with your products and services? How could you serve them better?
Brand	Is it appropriate? How could it be improved?
Finance	
Economic Climate	What are the key financial opportunities and challenges facing your organization?
Financial Measures	Financial measures can by seen as either enablers of customer success or constraints within which the group must operate. How do you see yours?
Workplace	
Current Facilities / Workplace	What's working, what's not working and what's missing with your current facilities / workplace?
Project Success	What is your vision of success for this project? How would you measure it?

FIGURE 2.6a Vision Session Topic Menu: A key part of the workplace is the Vision Session—a dialogue between senior leadership, key shareholders, and the Planning Team that creates the context and goals for the project. *(Courtesy Hellmuth, Obata + Kassabaum, Inc. Architects, Planners, and Designers)*

INDIVIDUAL ASSESSMENT QUESTIONNAIRE

Name_____ Department_____

Manager or Team Leader_____ Dept. Number_____

Job Description_____

1. How many hours a day do you spend in your individual workspace? ____

2. What percentage of your day/job requires team meetings?
   1-5% ❑ 6 -10% ❑ 11-20% ❑ 21-30% ❑ 31-50% ❑ 50% or more ❑

3. Are the majority of your meetings planned or unplanned?
   mostly planned ❑ mostly unplanned ❑ some of each ❑

4. On a general basis, what **physical** activities do you perform per day at your
   workspace? Please give a percentage of your time, adding up to 100%:
   ___ reading   ___ collaboration with co-workers
   ___ phone work   ___ working with visitors to your space
   ___ writing   ___ keying or typing (on computer)
   ___ filing   ___ mousing (using mouse or input device)
   ___ retrieval of information   ___ collating documents
   ___ thinking   ___ other (describe)_____

5. What percentage of your day requires privacy or protection from distraction?
   1-5% ❑ 6-10% ❑ 11-20% ❑ 21-30% ❑ 31-50% ❑ 50% or more ❑

6. How many times a day are you interrupted?____

7. Are there tasks performed at your workspace that could be done elsewhere?
   yes❑ no❑ if yes, where?_____

8. Do other people need to access information stored in your workspace?
   yes❑ no❑ if yes, what?_____

9. Do you require additional layout/support space outside your own workspace?
   yes❑ no❑ if yes, describe_____

10. How often do you access hard copy files/records/documents in your workspace?
    1-5 times/day ❑ 6-10 times/day ❑ 11-20 times/day ❑ more than 20 times/day❑

11. Rank the following items for their importance to you: (number 1 to 13 with 1 being
    the most important)
    ___ workspace size   ___ environment (air circulation)
    ___ technology at your workspace ___ image (appearance of workspace)
    ___ adequate lighting   ___ natural light/view
    ___ acoustical privacy   ___ social areas for "brainstorming"
    ___ personalization (making the ___ visual communication with your
         space "yours")   co-workers
    ___ adequate storage   ___ minimizing distraction
    ___ ergonomics (comfort of chair, workspace)

12. Why is number 1 most important to you?_____
    _____

13. Describe what you like about your current workspace._____
    _____
    _____

14. Describe what you would change about your workspace:_____
    _____
    _____

FIGURE 2.6b Typical questionnaire form used in the information gathering process. *(Courtesy Herman Miller, Inc.)*

TEAM ASSESSMENT QUESTIONNAIRE

Team Name_____   Number of Team Members_____

Department _____

1. What percentage of time do you spend with your team?
   1-5% ❑ 6-10% ❑ 11-20% ❑ 21-30% ❑ 31-50% ❑ 50% or more ❑
2. What percentage of time do you spend outside of your workspace?
   1-5% ❑ 6-10% ❑ 11-20% ❑ 21-30% ❑ 31-50% ❑ 50% or more ❑
3. What type of team are you part of? (see "Team Types" Video or Handbook)
   linear ❑ parallel ❑ circular ❑ other_____
4. What is the primary method for team communication?
   face-to-face ❑ formal meetings ❑ unscheduled meetings ❑ E-mail ❑
   Voice mail ❑ teleconferencing ❑ fortuitous encounters ❑ telephone ❑
5. Do you have portable technology? (voice mail, pagers, laptop)
   yes ❑ no ❑ if yes, please list _____
6. Are there portions of your stored materials that could be centrally located and shared with
   your team? yes ❑ no❑
7. Is your team assignment temporary (under 1 year) or permanent (over 1 year)?
   temporary ❑   permanent ❑ if temporary, how long?_____
8. What of the following features are required by your team?
   ___ enclosed project room   ___ team library
   ___ flexible team meeting space   ___ presentation room
   ___ reception space   ___ team awards/celebration space
9. Please list team equipment (copier, fax, printer, etc.):_____
   _____
10. Does your team provide spaces for contract workers, auditors or others?
    yes ❑ no ❑ if yes, how many?_____
11. What is the goal of your team?_____
12. How often do you anticipate the physical needs of the team changing?
    weekly ❑ monthly ❑ quarterly ❑ yearly ❑ every 2 years ❑ 3-5 years ❑
13. Rank the following items for their importance to your team: (number 1 to 8 with 1
    being the most important)
    ___ group storage   ___ group meeting spaces
    ___ individual storage   ___ acoustical privacy
    ___ accommodation of technology ___ visual distraction
    ___ ergonomic accommodation   ___ movable furniture
        (adjustable surfaces, seating)
14. Does the team have members who:
    work in another time zone ❑ telecommute ❑ work at a customers site ❑
    travel more than 50% of the time ❑ work on flex hours ❑
15. Are there physically challenged team members who may require special   accommodation?
    yes ❑ no ❑
16. Does your team need to be positioned near any other team or particular space?
    yes❑ no ❑ if yes, what team(s) or space?_____
17. Is there any topic not previously covered that would improve your team space?
    _____

FIGURE 2.6c Typical questionnaire form used in the information gathering process.
(*Courtesy Herman Miller, Inc.*)

- Location and size of architectural elements like windows, doors, stairs

- Heights of ceilings, doors, windows, openings

- Location, configuration, and condition of electrical, plumbing, and mechanical outlets and systems

- Location and configuration of telephone lines and other communications outlets

- Amount of available natural light, views, and noise problems

- Potential environmental (asbestos, lead paint and radon) and other problems that may exist

- When existing furniture and equipment is to be reused, a detailed inventory and dimensioning is necessary

Observe the Prevailing Conditions

Analysis of existing conditions and space plans supplements and verifies information obtained from interviews, questionnaires, and field surveys. It also gives greater insight to the client's organization, facilitates, and corporate culture, identifying strengths as well as weaknesses within the organization and their impact on the final program. In addition to compiling information reflecting the organization's goals and objectives, the development of a set of preliminary space standards needs to be initiated and addressed at this point.

Data Analysis: Programmatic Concepts

Upon substantial completion of the data gathering process, one proceeds with a comprehensive analysis of the information collected. Conventional configurations of space criteria have changed dramatically over the years. Today, the most critical factors that impact the size and configuration of the space are area and spatial adjacencies. Another important factor is the influx of new technology, which has necessitated the provision of additional space for equipment. Other influencing factors include identifying future needs, defining working relationships, including traffic flow of personnel, visitors, and goods; grouping of various systems (plumbing, HVAC, electrical); need for natural light and ventilation; identifying public and private zones and functions; and other issues such as security, etc. The analysis process may require revising the existing organization charts, grouping of functions, and scheduling when the facility is to be used or moved into.

An organization's space needs may be determined in a variety of ways. The client may furnish the planner with a pre-prepared list of existing or perceived space needs. Such a list may be arbitrary and would be subject to on-going review and development, based on current corporate space standards. Space area requirements may also be determined by studying the numbers of persons to be accommodated and multiplying this number by the needs of a single person's requirements, the size of equipment needed, and the space needs for the activity being designed for.

General space standards guidelines have been developed and updated over time for different functions and activities, and are discussed in greater detail in Chapter Six. It is sufficient here to mention that computer software and computer programming now play a major role in programming analysis and data tabulations.

Interpretation of the Data: Articulating Client's Needs

Once the information is compiled, organized, and analyzed, the planner can begin to interpret the data for the final report. The client's needs are defined and balanced against the resources available for the project. This allows the planner to devise a budget that will accommodate as many of the client's needs as possible. Most CEOs recognize that space generally represents their second largest expenditure after staffing. Recent studies show that the average Fortune 500 company has approximately 25 percent of total assets tied up in real estate. It is not surprising therefore, that corporations are constantly looking for ways to reduce real estate costs by utilizing their existing space to the maximum.

While the effective use of space is essential, space flexibility and adaptability to change is becoming increasingly more important than space efficiency. The planner should ensure that the client is made aware that an office infrastructure which supports change can reap long term dividends for the firm.

Statement of Problem: Defining the Program

The final statement of the problem is the sum total of what is agreed upon by the client and the programmer, and reflects the most important aspects of the project, serving as the basis for initiating the design process. In small projects, the program document may be produced in an informal format that is mainly intended for use by the designer as an internal tool. However, particularly in larger and more complex projects where a formal designer/client relationship exists, the program is generally produced as a bound document and presented to the client for formal approval. Moreover, it serves as the criteria by which the results are evaluated. The program in its final form, should address issues like:

- Goals and objectives of the organization. These consist of both functional goals (e.g., greater operational efficiency, or a larger space), and aesthetic goals (e.g., enhancing corporate image).

- Organizational structure, including primary, secondary, shared and part-time activities such as conference/meeting rooms, copy areas, kitchen/tea areas and reception areas.

- User requirements, including determination of user characteristics and demographics (age, sex, physical disabilities), number and function of employees and groups—current and future—personal preferences and location of user or activity space.

- Square footage requirements. Space is an increasingly valuable and costly resource. Space allocation and square-footage needs should be determined by activity areas for each user group, equipment, and type of support function, as well as for non-assigned space needs (circulation space, storage rooms, toilets and other amenities). These space standards should reflect flexibility and be driven by technology and new work habits, but when you plan for technology, you plan for change (Figure 2.7). Offices today may include various types of work stations, These can vary from static and cluster formations to high-churn, flexible team or mobile temporary environments. This mix typically evolves as the organization itself evolves.

- Adjacency requirements (and degree of adjacency). Spatial relationships for employees, user groups, and support activities (zoning of related activities, functional groups and departments, where close proximity to one another enhances efficiency) are defined.

- Staffing needs. Current and projected staffing needs are established, based on projected company growth and the impact of advances in communications technology.

- Revision of traditional design standards for various activities, support functions, and equip-ment, taking into account emerging trends in communication technologies and its impact on the individual's needs and work habits (Figure 2.8).

- Furniture and equipment requirements: these should be carefully selected to incorporate built-in mechanisms that give it flexibility, and adaptability. Good seating is essential to high performance. Furniture should also be capable of reconfiguration when required, and equipment should include upgrading options whenever possible (Figure 2.9).

- Sound control, taking into account the result of emerging voice recognition technologies on reporting and communication procedures and the effect of noise on privacy and pro-duction levels (Figure 2.10).

- Environmental requirements for the design of electro-mechanical systems such as lighting, acoustics, ventilation, heating and cooling.

- Security issues and requirements. The importance of security has increased dramatically following the 1995 Oklahoma City bombing and the September 11, 2001 terrorist attacks on the World Trade Center and the Pentagon, with new security guidelines now in place. Security related issues are discussed in some depth in Chapter Twelve. It should be noted, however, that traditional office buildings rarely address security needs adequately. More-over, lobbies and entrances, particularly those of the federal government and other insti-tutions, were not designed to accommodate the cumbersome security equipment that current circumstances dictate, and which is likely to be with us for the foreseeable future. The planner can capitalize on evolving advances in technology to make security stations less imposing and more reassuring. The need for increased security should be balanced and not hamper a building's efficiency.

- Aesthetic objectives, and goals. The internal aesthetic requirements as seen by employees from within the organization are not identical to those viewed by visitors and clients from without. Surveys have consistently shown that aesthetics can significantly impact an employee's health and emotional well being within the workplace; on the other hand, the primary importance of a firm's corporate image is reflected in how the public perceives the corporation.

SCHEMATIC DESIGN PHASE: CONCEPT DEVELOPMENT

As we proceed to design for today's working environment, we often find new criteria evolving in tandem with traditional ones. The global competitive marketplace coupled with rapidly rising real estate costs is placing increasing pressure on many American and European firms to reorganize, downsize, and maximize space and, in the process, formulate new space standards. In practice, this has resulted in a more innovative approach to space planning, witnessing a general departure from the historically closed space environment to a greater acceptance of open space work and multi-functional environments that downplay office hierarchies and instill a sense of community in its members, while simultaneously allowing for better communications and encouraging the continuous flow of ideas and creativity. This has been further facilitated by the fact that open spaces offer greater flexibility and are generally easier to handle than cellular or partitioned ones.

During the earlier programming phase, data was collected, analyzed, interpreted, and finally executed in the form of a written project brief that was approved by the client. Functional solutions reflecting the client's needs and goals are clearly articulated in this document. This facilitates the transition from gathering and analysis of data to its utilization in the development of a schematic design, which can now begin. It should be noted that this phase of the space planning process is actually a two and three-dimensional translation of the project program. During this phase of the project, a schematic space plan is developed in parallel with the interior designer's preliminary design concepts for finishes and furniture. If the project is not very large or complicated, the same individual (or team) can do both the schematic space plan and the schematic design.

The first task is to generate an environmentally friendly layout that effectively addresses the client's previously stated needs, goals and objectives. Regardless of the complexity of the program, there is a methodical approach to the development of a space plan which is generally achieved through the following:

Selecting and Evaluating the Space

Many preliminary space planning decisions are developed within the context of the organization's prevailing conditions. Diagrams showing the general functional relationships required

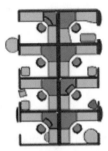

STATIC

Static environments become dynamic with the addition of mobile Quick Shift Tables and active storage. Each workstation can be configured as individual needs require.

HIGH CHURN

High-churn work areas, characterized by frequent changes in organizational structure or personnel, require furniture that can be adjusted and positioned to meet personal needs. These areas also require panels and screens that can be easily moved to change workstation size without disruption. Active storage components move easily from the workstation to a conferencing area. Mobile tables move where and when they are needed.

TEMPORARY/FLEXIBLE

Each workstation combines worksurfaces, storage and meeting tables to accommodate the people who use them. Mobile components enhance flexibility and can be reconfigured by the hour, the day or as needed.

MOBILE/TEMPORARY

Freestanding, mobile furniture creates a worksetting that adapts quickly to new needs, and is especially appropriate to team-based projects. Mobile screens divide space to define conference areas. The Scout provides a plug-in source for power and data in freestanding environments.

FIGURE 2.7 An example of workstation flexibility in today's office environment. *(From TeKnion Corp., Furniture for the Future of Business)*

EUROPEAN SPACE STANDARDS

City	Average Space per Employee	
Central London	181 sq. ft.	16.8 m^2
Frankfurt	274 sq. ft.	25.5 m^2
Amsterdam	258 sq. ft.	24.0 m^2
Brussels	258 sq. ft.	24.0 m^2

U.K. office standards are quite similar to the U.S. and tend to be smaller than on the European continent.

TYPICAL SPACE STANDARDS IN THE U.K.

Function	Type of Space	Typical Office Size	
Senior Manager/Director	Private Office	215 – 323 sq. ft.	20-30 m^2
Manager/Head of Dept	Private Office	161 – 215 sq. ft.	15-20 m^2
Manager/Professional	Private Office	108 – 161 sq. ft.	10-15 m^2
Professional	Group Room/Open Plan	97 sq. ft.	9 m^2
Secretarial/Administration	Open Plan	97 sq. ft.	9 m^2
Clerical	Open Plan	75 – 97 sq. ft.	7-9 m^2
Dealer (Trader)	Group Room/Open Plan	65 – 97 sq. ft.	6-9 m^2

In the U.S., offices are trending towards downsizing for professional and managerial job grades per the most recent IFMA surveys.

U.S. SPACE STANDARDS

Job Function	Space per Employee – 1994		Space per Employee –2002	
Upper Management	289 sq. ft.	26.9 m^2	275 sq. ft.	25.5 m^2
Senior Management	200 sq. ft.	18.6 m^2	190 sq. ft.	17.7 m^2
Middle Management	151 sq. ft.	14.0 m^2	140 sq. ft.	13.0 m^2
Senior Professional	115 sq. ft.	10.7 m^2	115 sq. ft.	10.7 m^2
Technical/Professional	90 sq. ft.	8.4 m^2	95 sq. ft.	8.8 m^2
Senior Clerical	81 sq. ft.	7.5 m^2	85 sq. ft.	7.9 m^2
General Clerical	69 sq. ft.	6.4 m^2	75 sq. ft.	7.0 m^2

FIGURE 2.8   Evolving space standards and square footage criteria.

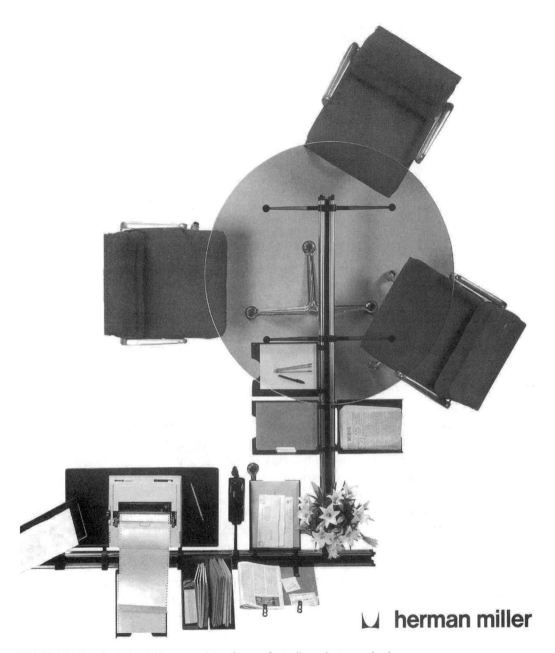

FIGURE 2.9 Furniture should be capable of reconfiguration when required.

SOME FACTORS THAT INFLUENCE THE
ANNOYANCE QUALITY OF NOISE

Acoustic factors	Sound level
	Frequency
	Duration
	Spectral complexity
	Fluctuations in sound level
	Fluctuations in frequency
	Risetime of the noise
Nonacoustic factors	Past experience with the noise
	Listener's activity
	Predictability of noise occurrence
	Necessity of the noise
	Listener's personality
	Attitudes toward the noise source
	Time of year
	Time of day
	Type of locale

FIGURE 2.10 Noise factors that affect privacy and production levels. *(From Mark S. Sanders and Ernest J. McCormick, Human Factors in Engineering and Design, McGraw Hill, New York, 1987)*

by the project are now prepared, and preliminary space allocation plans showing partitions, furnishings, equipment, lighting, and other pertinent planning ideas, are developed (Figure 2.11). Most contemporary businesses in this age of rapidly advancing technology are designed to accommodate complex systems of computer networks and equipment necessary to run the business.

Space requirements for floor loading, cabling, HVAC, electrical and acoustical considerations, should be determined at this stage. The designer/space planner also prepares studies to establish the design concept of the project including types and qualities of materials, finishes, and furniture. This may include color and material sample boards and preliminary selection of furniture types as appropriate. A preliminary statement of probable project cost is also prepared based on the design concept, furnishings, fixtures and equipment, and on comparison with current costs for other projects of similar scope and quality. As with all budgets, the designer is not responsible for final project cost.

Special requirements for floor loading, cabling, HVAC, electrical and acoustical considerations should be determined. In addressing the needs of the modern workplace, the design should take into account, not only functionality, ergonomics, and the physical environment but also psychological and social considerations as well.

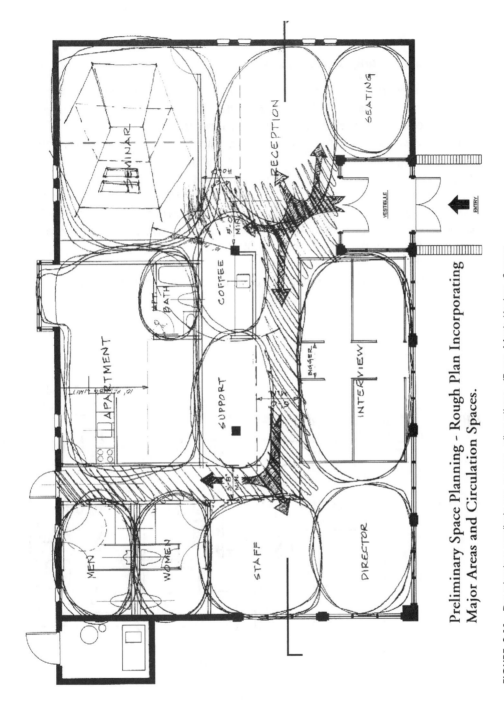

Preliminary Space Planning - Rough Plan Incorporating Major Areas and Circulation Spaces.

FIGURE 2.11 Developing preliminary space allocations. *(From Mark Karlen, Space Planning Basics, John Wiley and Sons, Inc., New Your, 1993)*

Bubble and Blocking/Stacking Diagrams

The schematic space plan takes the bubble and blocking/stacking diagrams to the next level of detail and sophistication (Figures 2.12, 2.13). When the area assignment is complete, the space planner proceeds to develop a space layout that reflects the program's stated requirements and objectives. Functional elements are located within the space in a format consistent with the program's goals and objectives while retaining the desired adjacencies and functions. While the schematic space plan is being developed, the design team simultaneously works on preliminary design concepts for interior architectural elements, finishes and furniture. This is outlined in greater depth in Chapter Three. It should be noted that blocking/stack plans lack detailed information regarding the activities and space layout within the organization. This comes at a later stage in the development of the design. Upon completion of the schematic design, it should be presented to the client for review, modification and final approval (in writing), before proceeding to the next phase, of design development.

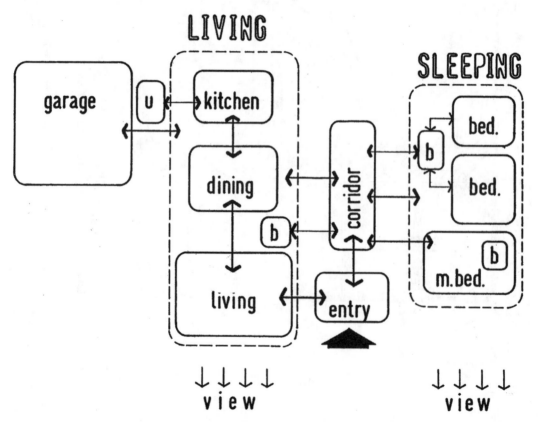

FIGURE 2.12 Bubble diagram for showing functional relationships and approximate space allocation.

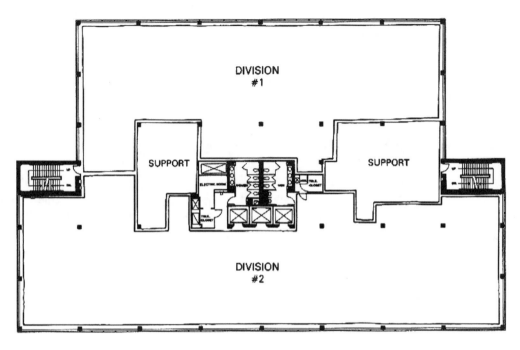

A. Blocking Plan

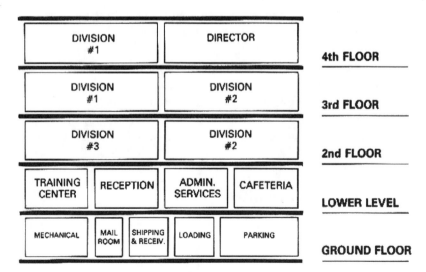

FIGURE 2.13   a) Block plans locate support areas in close proximity to allow maximum flexibility for space planning the divisions. b) Stacking plans locate service areas on the ground level for access and structural capacity on grades. *(From Julie K. Rayfield, The Office Interior Design Guide, John Wiley and Sons, Inc. 1994)*

DESIGN DEVELOPMENT PHASE

During the design development phase, the planner refines the approved schematic design so that the size, scope, and character of the project are generally fixed. Drawings, color boards, samples, furniture selections, and other specifics of the job are presented to the client for final approval or modification before starting work on the contract documents phase.

Design development documents usually include detailed plans showing partition and door locations, furniture and fixture layout, lighting design, sketches of special built-in cabinetwork and furniture, and other elevation or three-dimensional drawings sufficient to describe the character of the design (Figures 2.14a, 2.14b). In some cases, outline construction specifications may also be developed. Again, at the end of this phase, the client must review and approve the final scheme before proceeding further. The designer also submits another estimate of project cost for approval, reflecting the changes and specific decisions made since the schematic design phase.

CONSTRUCTION DOCUMENT PHASE

During this phase of the operation, all the necessary documents needed to execute the project are prepared, and upon getting approval for the design development submissions, the designer is responsible for preparing detailed drawings, specifications, and other documents necessary to construct the project. Products that vendors need to supply are also defined in this phase. The contract documents may include the work for both construction and furniture purchasing, or they may be developed separately so individual contracts can be let for construction and Furniture, Fixtures, and Equipment (FF&E). The AIA/ASID standard form states that separate documents are to be prepared. This is usually preferred because interior construction contracts differ from furniture and equipment contracts. Nearly a third of the designer's costs normally go into producing these documents so it is vitally important to be as efficient as possible to maximize profits. Errors or omissions require changes, which will increase project costs.

Construction Documents Required

The basic document package includes all the construction drawings (layout plans, elevations, sections, reflected ceiling plan details, cabinet details, finish and hardware schedules, construction details, furniture plans, and other miscellaneous drawings). As part of the design team, the planner's drawings must also be coordinated with those of other consultants including mechanical, electrical/telephone, plumbing, and fire protection, as well as the architect and interior designer (if applicable). The number of drawings that make up the contract document package depends largely on the size and complexity of the project (Figures 2.15a, b, c).

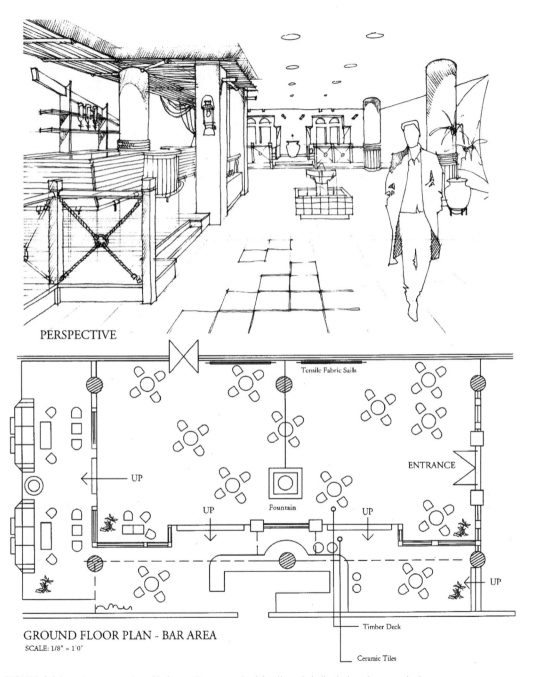

PERSPECTIVE

Tensile Fabric Sails

UP

ENTRANCE

UP

UP

Fountain

UP

Timber Deck

GROUND FLOOR PLAN - BAR AREA
SCALE: 1/8" = 1'0"

Ceramic Tiles

FIGURE 2.14a An example of information needed for the detailed development phase.

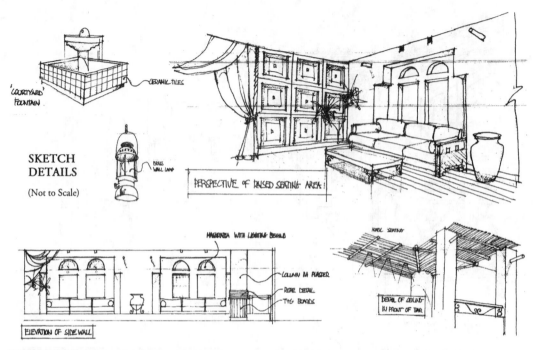

'COURTYARD'
FOUNTAIN

CERAMIC TILES

SKETCH
DETAILS

(Not to Scale)

BRASS
WALL LAMP

PERSPECTIVE OF RAISED SEATING AREA !

MAGNERABRA WITH LIGHTING BEHIND

COLUMN IN PLASTER
ROPE DETAIL
TILE BOARDS

WOOD SEATING

DETAIL OF CEILING
IN FRONT OF BAR

ELEVATION OF SIDE WALL

FIGURE 2.14b   An example of design development details that help explain the concept.

Construction drawing documents are increasingly being prepared through the use of sophisticated CAD software programs like AutoCad, Microstation, and VersaCad, which are discussed in greater detail in Chapter 10. The advantages of using computer drafting are many, including greater representational accuracy, the ability to reuse standard details, and the capability of depicting the actual furniture to be used (from furniture manufacturers' libraries). The designer should immediately advise the client of any adjustments made to the previous project cost estimates based on changes in the scope of work made during document preparation.

BIDDING (TENDERING) PHASE

Once the contract documents are completed, the designer assists the owner in the preparation of the bidding package. This consists of construction drawings, specifications, the necessary procurement forms, general conditions of the contract, and forms of agreement between the owner and the contractor as well as any other special project provisions specifically listed

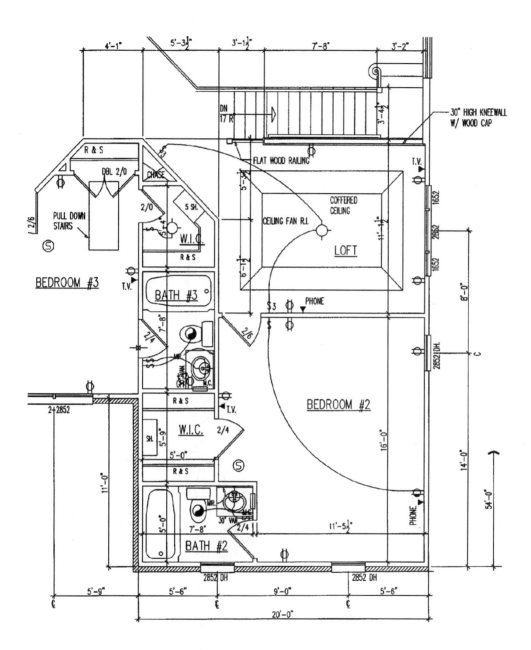

PART OF SECOND FLOOR PLAN

Scale: 1/4" = 1'-0"

FIGURE 2.15a An example of construction document electrical layout details.

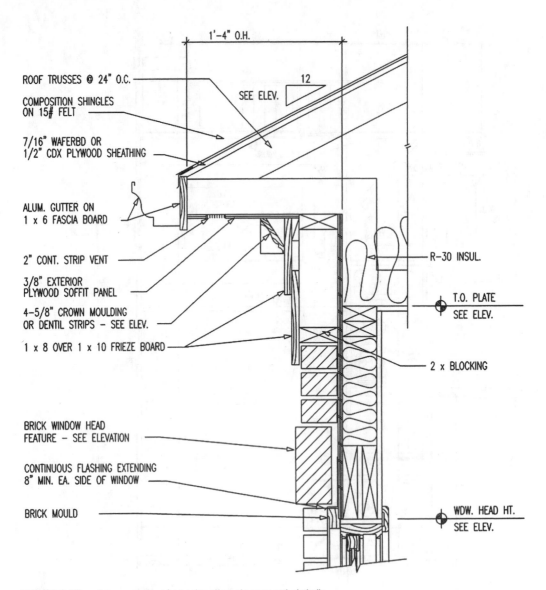

ROOF TRUSSES @ 24" O.C.

1'-4" O.H.

SEE ELEV.

12

COMPOSITION SHINGLES
ON 15# FELT

7/16" WAFERBD OR
1/2" CDX PLYWOOD SHEATHING

ALUM. GUTTER ON
1 x 6 FASCIA BOARD

R-30 INSUL.

2" CONT. STRIP VENT

T.O. PLATE
SEE ELEV.

3/8" EXTERIOR
PLYWOOD SOFFIT PANEL

4-5/8" CROWN MOULDING
OR DENTIL STRIPS - SEE ELEV.

1 x 8 OVER 1 x 10 FRIEZE BOARD

2 x BLOCKING

BRICK WINDOW HEAD
FEATURE - SEE ELEVATION

CONTINUOUS FLASHING EXTENDING
8" MIN. EA. SIDE OF WINDOW

BRICK MOULD

WDW. HEAD HT.
SEE ELEV.

FIGURE 2.15b   An example of construction document details.

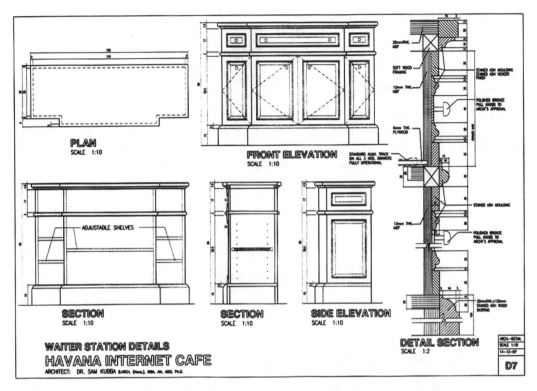

FIGURE 2.15c An example of construction document details. *(Courtesy Ibtesam Sharbaji, Kubba Design)*

in the agreement. Note that the term *tender* is used in lieu of bidding in many countries around the world, including Canada and Great Britain. A bid package may be required for either furnishings or construction, or both. Sometimes negotiation on the client's behalf may replace the bidding process. If, for any reason, the final costs significantly exceed the budgeted costs for the project, a redesign may be required in order to remain within the budget.

Bidding Procedures

Typically, the owner (with the help of the designer/planner), puts the project out to bid. This usually entails inviting several contractors to bid on the project as defined by the contract documents. After an analysis of the bids, the designer submits recommendations to the owner, who makes the final decision in awarding the contract. The award would be based on the contractor's price, experience, execution time, etc.

Many owners prefer competitive bidding procedures for construction and for the FF&E (when applicable), because this most often results in the lowest price and best value for money. For the majority of public agencies, bidding is, in fact, mandatory. Competitive bidding procedures are defined in greater detail in AIA document A771, *Instruction to Interior Bidders*, which contains instructions bidders need to follow in preparing and submitting their bids.

Prequalification of Contractors

Bidding can be either open or by special invitation. Open bidding is usually solicited through advertising in newspapers and trade journals, as is the case in the majority of public work. Sometimes, the owner will pre-qualify a number of contractors to whom he will send out invitations to bid. It is preferable to have several bidders to encourage competitiveness. Sometimes the owner will want to negotiate a price with only one or two contractors.

Bidding Documents

Bid documents are usually made available through the planner's office. Each contractor will receive a complete bid package consisting of: contract drawings, specifications, bidding documents, bid forms, and other documents pertaining to the job. A deposit is typically taken for each set of documents which may be later returned upon return of the bid package in good shape. On occasion, the contractor must purchase the documents with no refunds.

Instructions to Bidders and Pre-bid Conference

With larger projects, it is useful to hold a pre-bid conference. This is attended by the bidders, the owner, and his design team, who respond to questions asked by the bidders and also discuss the bid package. This meeting also provides an opportunity for the owner to discuss any issues of concern, respond to questions asked by bidders, and to give clarification and instructions as needed. This meeting should be documented and the minutes distributed to all prospective bidders.

Evaluating the Bids and Awarding of the Work

The designer normally assists the owner in filing documents required for various governmental approvals. Notice that the designer's responsibility is to assist the owner and not to perform all this work alone. After the necessary documentation is prepared, the designer assists the owner in obtaining bids (or negotiated proposals, if the project is not bid) and evaluating the bids (tenders), and assists in preparing contracts for interior construction and for FF&E. The designer is responsible for providing coordination of all these activities. After receiving the bids, the designer reviews the pricing and recommends a contractor to the owner. They then proceed to negotiate a final price for the work. The lump-sum contract is the most common form of construction contract. Another popular type is the cost-plus or construction management type.

CONTRACT ADMINISTRATION: EXECUTION
AND SUPERVISION PHASE

The primary objective of this phase is to ensure the project is completed on time, according to the contract specifications, and within the stipulated budget. In the AIA/ASID standard form of agreement between owner and architect for interior design services (Form B171), the scope of the designer's services during the contract administration phase is extensive. The agreement may specify that the services provided are to be over the entire course of the contract, or only during the period of construction and installation. In the first instance, the services provided are more numerous and comprehensive, and the planner's duties would additionally include administrative services such as project documentation and analysis of consultants' agreements. In the latter case, the planner is not concerned with pre-construction services. In either case, the planner/designer acts as the owner's representative and advises and consults with the owner. Instructions to the contractors are forwarded through the designer, who has the authority to act on behalf of the owner, but only to the extent provided in the contract documents. In this document, the owner rather than the designer has the authority to reject goods.

The designer assists the owner in coordinating the schedules for delivery and installation of the various portions of the work but is not responsible for neglect or malfeasance of any of the contractors or suppliers to meet their schedules or perform their contractual obligations (Figures 2.16a, 2.16b).

The signed agreement with the client will stipulate that, as part of the monitoring process, the designer will visit the project periodically (or as necessary) during the execution period to determine whether construction and installation are proceeding in accordance with the contract documents, and also to keep the owner informed of any defects or deficiencies that may occur in the work of the contractors. The designer, however, is not required to make exhaustive or continual inspections.

One especially important provision is that the designer is not responsible for the means, methods, techniques, sequences, or procedures of construction. Nor is the designer responsible for fabrication, procurement, shipment, delivery, or installation of construction or furnishings. Moreover, the designer is not responsible for job site safety or for the acts or omissions of the contractors, subcontractors, or suppliers.

During the construction and installation phase, the designer also determines the amounts owed to the contractors and suppliers based on observations at the project site and on evaluation of the contractors' applications for payment. In the majority of cases, the contractor will, during the execution of the contract, submit requests for *change orders*. Change orders consist of work that deviates from the construction documents; they are usually either requested by the owner or by the designer. In some cases, problems arise or the drawings are inaccurate or unclear. More often than not, change orders will impact the budget, and sometimes the contractor will request an extension of the contract time. However, the client or

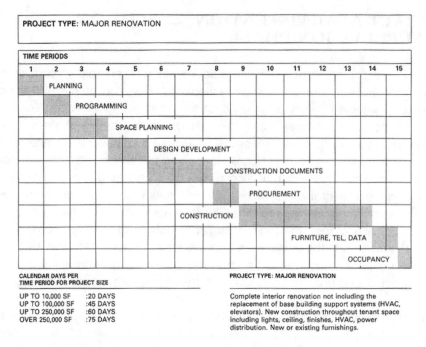

PROJECT TYPE: MAJOR RENOVATION

TIME PERIODS

1	2	3	4	5	6	7	8	9	10	11	12	13	14	15

PLANNING

PROGRAMMING

SPACE PLANNING

DESIGN DEVELOPMENT

CONSTRUCTION DOCUMENTS

PROCUREMENT

CONSTRUCTION

FURNITURE, TEL, DATA

OCCUPANCY

CALENDAR DAYS PER
TIME PERIOD FOR PROJECT SIZE

UP TO 10,000 SF   :20 DAYS
UP TO 100,000 SF :45 DAYS
UP TO 250,000 SF :60 DAYS
OVER 250,000 SF   :75 DAYS

PROJECT TYPE: MAJOR RENOVATION

Complete interior renovation not including the
replacement of base building support systems (HVAC,
elevators). New construction throughout tenant space
including lights, ceiling, finishes, HVAC, power
distribution. New or existing furnishings.

Schedules Produced by the Space Planner or Architect

PROJECT SCHEDULE: **DATE:**

TASKS	MONTH 1	MONTH 2	MONTH 3	MONTH 4	MONTH 5	MONTH 6	MONTH 7	MONTH 8	MONTH 9
PROGRAMMING									
SCHEMATIC DESIGN									
DESIGN DEVELOPMENT									
CONTRACT DOCUMENTS									
BUILDING PERMIT									
FURNITURE ORDER									
CONSTRUCTION									
FURNITURE INSTALLATION									
DATA & COMMUNICATION									
MOVE IN									

FIGURE 2.16a Typical schedules for different types of projects. *(From Julie K. Ray-field, The Office Interior Design Guide, John Wiley and Sons, Inc. 1994)*

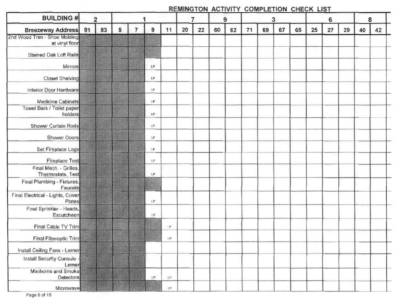

Part of an Activity Chart for a Housing Development

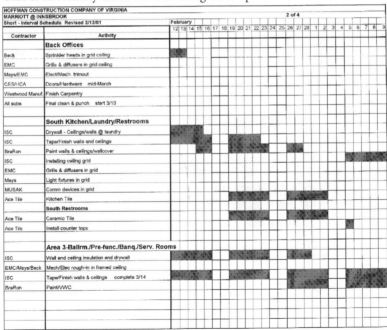

Section from a Construction Schedule for a Hotel

FIGURE 2.16b Typical schedules for different types of projects. *(Courtesy Inspection and Valuation International, New York)* designer may order minor changes in the work not involving an adjustment in the contract sum or an extension of the contract time. The contractor may also request funds for materials stored on or off site. After studying contractors' applications, the designer issues certificates for payment, usually monthly. In most cases, a single form is used as the application and certificate for payment.

The designer is considered the interpreter of the requirements of the contract documents and is expected to be an impartial judge of performance by both the owner and the contractors. Any decisions made should be consistent with and reflect the intent of the contract documents and be reasonably inferable from them. The designer's decisions concerning aesthetic judgments are final if they are consistent with the intent of the contract documents.

Part of the designer's day-to-day contract administration activities includes reviewing contractor's submittals of samples and shop drawings and then taking appropriate action. Shop drawings are the documents from which subcontractors actually build, which makes the submittals of particular importance because they determine whether the drawings and samples correctly interpret, and are consistent with, the construction documents. When the designer reviews shop drawings, it is mainly for conformance with the design concept expressed in the contract documents, but also to ensure that the details work. The contractor is responsible for determining the accuracy and completeness of dimension, details, quantities, and other aspects of the shop drawings.

When the job is substantially complete (i.e. sufficiently complete to allow occupancy), and the contractor submits for final payment, the designer tours the project and prepares a *punch list* (Figure 2.17). This list identifies deficiencies and substandard or incomplete work, and a copy is given to the contractor for correcting. When the punch list items are all reportedly resolved, the designer undertakes a final review and inspection to determine the status of the project, and to ensure that the final placement of all items is complete, the work has been correctly implemented, and that all items have been supplied, delivered, and installed according to the contract documents.

The designer's responsibilities do not include the receipt, inspection, and acceptance on behalf of the owner of FF&E at the time of their delivery and installation. Nor is the designer authorized to stop the work, reject nonconforming work, or terminate the work on behalf of the owner. Instead, the designer can recommend to the owner that nonconforming work be rejected.

Before the client or tenant can move into the space, a *certificate of occupancy* must be obtained. Theoretically, this is the contractor's responsibility, although the planner and owner sometimes assist in this. The certificate of occupancy is the last requirement in the approval process, and represents a governmental approval stating that the space in question was inspected and built as per the approved construction documents and in compliance with all relevant codes. The move-in should be well planned and coordinated.

ARCHITECT'S PUNCH LIST

WORLDGATE 3 OFFICE BUILDING   March 24, 2002

ABC Architects & Space Planners

First Floor:

1. Replace broken vision glazing panel - S wall.
2. Flash patch at C.O. and at interior glass doors joint to granite floor (typical)
3. Install door to exit corridor from lobby.
4. Clean drywall dust and mud at intersection of C.W. and wall (NE corner of W lease area).
5. Finish caulking floor control joint (E lease area).
6. Replace doors which we incorrectly prepped.
7. Install mini-blinds.
8. Finish final cleaning floors, doors, etc. (typical)
9. Install sprinkler head escutcheons (typ.)
10. Loading Area

    a. Touch up paint at double doors to corridor
    b. Touch up paint at walls.
    c. Trim out walls at joint to door frames.
    d. Install door stops.

11 Switchgear Room

    a. Touch up paint at walls.
    b. Remove paper from all wall fixtures, etc.
    c. Install door stop.

12. Pump Room

    a. Touch up paint on door.
    b. Remove paper from all fittings, etc.
    c. Install door stop.

13. Engineer's Office

    a. Install transition strip at VCT floor under door.
    b. Install door stop.
    c. Install outlet cover plate.

14. Exit Corridor

    a. Clean off base
    b. Touch up paint at walls.
    c. Repair gyp. board around electric outlet

FIGURE 2.17 Example of punch list items for an office building.

FEEDBACK AND POST-OCCUPANCY EVALUATION

The space planner will often return to the site after the client has occupied it for a time to evaluate the building's performance. In most instances, this is an informal review undertaken at the designer's own time and expense. At other times, the client may hire the designer to do an extensive formal post-occupancy evaluation (POE). Formal POE feedback is now most frequently used by large corporations and the institutional sector (such as school districts, state government and federal agencies) in an attempt to evaluate and improve upon building performance, particularly where there is a program for recurring construction programs or repetitive building types. In either case, the exercise provides valuable information on design procedures, materials, construction details, and user satisfaction. This knowledge should be documented and continuously updated. It should also be put at the disposal of researchers and design professionals to facilitate and assist in producing better solutions.

POE is one of the most methodical and effective diagnostic tools available at our disposal to assess a building's performance in meeting the immediate and long-term goals and objectives of the client. In carrying out the POE, there are various conventional data collecting tools available to the planner, including, interviews, personal observation, photography, analysis of various aspects of the building's performance, surveys, etc. To that end, the POE should be able to provide answers to some or all of the following questions:

- Does the final space layout satisfy the original and current program requirements?
- Is the design image consistent with the stated goals of the client?
- Is adequate flexibility and expandability provided and consistent with the original needs of the client?
- Are rooms and spaces of adequate size for their intended function, and can they be adapted to differing functions?
- Were all adjacencies provided for?
- Are any materials and finishes providing unexpected maintenance problems?
- Are construction details well designed and adequate for their purpose?
- Does the furniture and fixtures meet the functional and design criteria established during programming?
- Is the furniture selected adequate for the functional requirements of the space and the type of use it receives?
- Is the lighting adequate for the space?
- Are there any ergonomic problems with the furniture selected?
- Are there any problems with the HVAC systems?
- Was adequate power and communication provided for?

- How did the contractor, subcontractors, and other suppliers perform?
- Is the client satisfied with the project?
- Are the actual users satisfied with the performance and appearance of the finished space?
- What problems have arisen that may be covered by product or contractor warranties?
- Is the circulation and relationships between various spaces satisfactory?

ADDITIONAL SERVICES

The specific services that the space planner agrees to perform should be itemized in the scope of work. Many of the additional services not normally included in a contract are listed in the AIA/ASID standard form of Agreement (Form B171). Defining these services helps avoid potential disputes with the client at a later date.

CHAPTER THREE

SPACE PLANNING AND DESIGN FUNDAMENTALS

*T*he search for beauty probably begins with the story of mankind itself, yet undertaking the design of an office or departmental interior today can be a daunting task. Any decisions we make concerning layout, color, wallpaper, flooring, furnishings or lighting could have a lasting effect on an organization and its people.

It is not surprising, therefore, that as space planners and designers, we shoulder a heavy burden of responsibility; we owe it to our clients to give them the best possible solutions that fulfill their needs.

GENERAL OVERVIEW

The hallmark of a good space planner/interior designer is the ability to create a space that is both functional and aesthetically pleasing. As discussed in the previous chapter, the design process is usually very methodical and often extremely time consuming, with frequent infusions of creativity.

The designer/space planner proceeds from a basic idea to a final solution, beginning by studying the space to be designed. Where existing floor plans can be found, all well and good; where none exist, a survey needs to be conducted and the relevant areas drawn to an appropriate scale.

For a small project such as a residence or small retail outlet, a scale of ¼ inch = 1 foot (1/50) would probably be acceptable. For a larger complex, like a shopping mall, office building or factory, a ⅛ inch = 1 foot (1/100) scale may be more appropriate for the overall plan, and a larger scale, such as ½ inch = 1 foot (1/25) for smaller spaces within the overall plan. A detail for a door or coving on the other hand may require an even larger scale like one quarter full size (Figure 3.1).

scale: ⅛"=1'0"

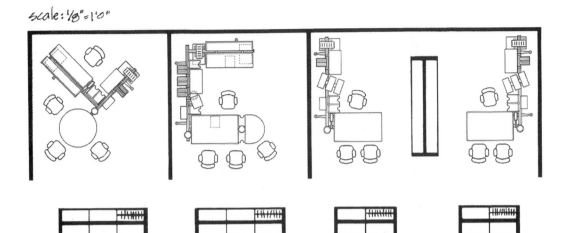

FIGURE 3.1a Illustration showing Burdick Group Furniture by Herman Miller at ⅛ inch (1/100) scale.

scale: ¼"=1'0"

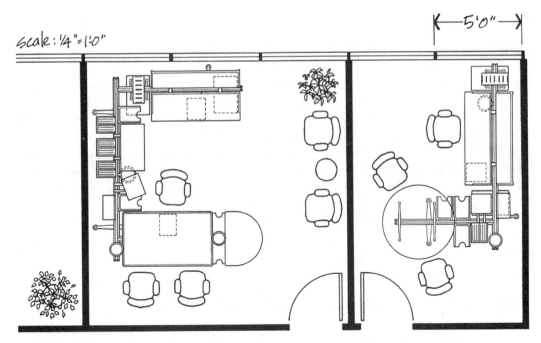

FIGURE 3.1b Illustration showing Burdick Group Furniture by Herman Miller at ¼ inch (1/50) scale.

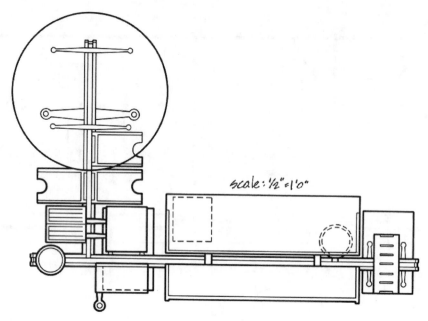

scale: ½"=1'0"

FIGURE 3.1c   Illustration showing Burdick Group Furniture by Herman Miller at ½ inch (1/25) scale.

The planner should include as much relevant information on the drawings as possible, including door locations and swings, window and partition locations, heights of ceilings, windows and door schedules, electrical outlets, and proposed and existing finishes.

Modern technology is basically utilitarian, so the question for corporations and other clients is how to integrate the needs of technology with those of the organization. The physical relationship between workers and their machines will continue to be an issue as people spend increasing amounts of time dealing with each other through machines. Improving the comfort of sitting at computers for long hours would be best dealt with as a combined effort between corporations and manufacturers. Modern interior spaces have incorporated and integrated new technologies as they become available.

FUNCTIONAL ASPECTS

Design Process and Investigation Techniques

Most buildings are designed for people, and since people's needs change with the times, location, and tradition, the criteria for designing a home, office, restaurant, or commercial space will vary as well. This is particularly true when it comes to planning interior spaces. In the Middle East, for example, space standards are generally more generous then those of the United States and Europe. As discussed in the previous chapter, the first step in the design process is to determine the client's precise needs. A number of questions need be answered that will provide an insight to the client's functional, aesthetic and psychological needs (Figure 3.2).

CLIENT PREFERENCE CHART QUESTIONNAIRE

NAME: **OCCUPATION:**   **AGE:**

LOCATION
- ☐ City (Urban)
- ☐ Suburb
- ☐ Development
- ☐ Country (Rural)
- ☐ Other

TYPE OF HOME
- ☐ Single Story
- ☐ Split-Level
- ☐ Two Story
- ☐ Apartment/Condo
- ☐ Other

STYLE OF HOME
- ☐ Contemporary
- ☐ Colonial
- ☐ Ranch House
- ☐ Spanish
- ☐ Other

WORKING HABITS
- ☐ Works at Home
- ☐ Works Occasionally at Home
- ☐ Never Works at Home
- ☐ Other

ROOM NEEDS + DIMENSIONS
- ☐ Separate Living Room
- ☐ Separate Dining Room
- ☐ Living/Dining Room
- ☐ Separate Kitchen
- ☐ Kitchen/Dining Area
- ☐ Open Plan
- ☐ Family Room
- ☐ Den (Rumpus, T.V.)
- ☐ Home Office/Study
- ☐ Separate Bedroom
- ☐ Bedroom with Bath
- ☐ Other

FURNITURE STYLE
- ☐ High Tech
- ☐ Contemporary
- ☐ Modern
- ☐ Period
- ☐ Mixture
- ☐ Art Deco
- ☐ American Colonial
- ☐ Neo Classical
- ☐ Spanish
- ☐ Empire/Directoire
- ☐ Oriental
- ☐ Other

LEISURE HABITS
- ☐ Internet/Computer
- ☐ Gardening
- ☐ Painting
- ☐ T.V.
- ☐ Reading
- ☐ Sports
- ☐ Photography
- ☐ Music
- ☐ Sewing
- ☐ Handicrafts
- ☐ Other

ENTERTAINING
- ☐ Formal Dinners
- ☐ Intimate/Informal Dinners
- ☐ Buffet Suppers
- ☐ Cocktail Parties
- ☐ Teas
- ☐ Barbecues
- ☐ Other
- ☐

COLLECTIONS
- ☐ Books
- ☐ Stamps
- ☐ Guns
- ☐ Apartment/Condo
- ☐ Silver/China
- ☐ Records/CDs/DVDs
- ☐ Videos
- ☐ Art
- ☐ Other

FABRICS
- ☐ Velvet
- ☐ Silk
- ☐ Wool
- ☐ Satin
- ☐ Cotton
- ☐ Chintz
- ☐ Polyester
- ☐ Acrylic
- ☐ Other

COLORS/PATTERNS
- ☐ Tints (Light)
- ☐ Shades (Dark)
- ☐ Warm Colors
- ☐ Cool Colors
- ☐ Combinations
- ☐ Specific Colors
- ☐ Small Patterns
- ☐ Bold Patterns
- ☐ Specific Patterns

ADDITIONAL REMARKS & COMMENTS:

FIGURE 3.2 Typical questionnaire for a private residence.

The next step is to ensure the best possible inter-relation between the various functional areas. More often than not, the space planners will be handicapped because the various areas and their correlation will be predetermined by the architect or by existing spaces. Nevertheless, designers and space planners often have to knock down walls and put up new ones as required.

A space planner must first get a feeling for the spaces he plans to design. A *bubble* diagram helps determine the best relationship of the various areas (Figure 3.3). A space that serves no physical (utilitarian) or psychological function should be eliminated because it is wasted space.

The bubble diagram should also reflect the relative sizes of the various spaces. A designer should always start with an overall concept or theme and work towards the details (i.e. from the general to the particular). This is true whether we are designing a multistory skyscraper, a bungalow or a simple piece of furniture.

The large interior space should, whenever possible, be revealed in stages and not all at once. The designer should allow the eye to be led through the space to experience it gradually (Figure 3.4).

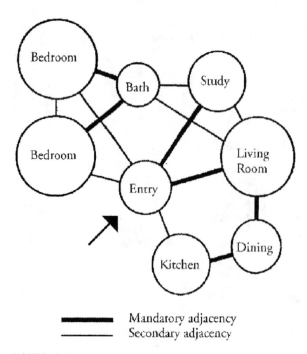

——— Mandatory adjacency
——— Secondary adjacency

FIGURE 3.3 A bubble diagram helps the designer achieve the best solution possible from a functional standpoint.

FIGURE 3.4 Upon entering the Sears Boise reception area, the visitor gets a glimpse of the Teknion work stations in the adjoining space. *(Architects HOK; Photograph by Hedrich Blessing, 1998 Photographers)*

AESTHETIC ASPECTS

The aesthetic aspects of space planning and interior design consist essentially of Principles (Unity and Harmony, Balance, Proportion, Scale, Rhythm, Emphasis, Variety and Contrast), and Elements (Space, Form, Line, Texture, Pattern, Light, and Color). These two fundamental design ingredients are essentially the same as those of many other design disciplines, particularly architecture and painting, and have changed little over the years. Each contributes in one way or another to the perception and success of the overall design; the whole equals more than its individual components. Most designers today would agree that no matter how aesthetically pleasing a design is, the real and final test is how well it functions.

DESIGN PRINCIPLES

Unity and Harmony

We are surrounded by both unity and discord. In nature we find mostly unity; in man made objects, mostly discord. Every design requires a unifying theme to hold it together. When choosing furnishings, colors, and materials, you should be consistent and try to make certain everything blends. Elements should not appear to be a mere afterthought.

For example, it is unlikely you would include a polished contemporary acrylic coffee table in a reception area where the overall theme is early 18th century provincial. It should be emphasized, however, that these are only general guidelines. When the designer/planner feels confident enough, he or she may well break these rules and get away with it. In many respects, because it encompasses and blends the other principles into a unifying whole, the principle of unity and harmony is the most important of all the principles, without which the design would fall apart. Unity and harmony can be achieved by various means, which include:

- Having a central theme and consistency of style throughout the design always helps in unifying the various components of the design (Figure 3.5).

- Using the elements of repetition and uniformity. For example, the walls can be painted in a single color (or harmonious color scheme) or similar light fittings can be used in a number of areas. Likewise, using similar materials and finishes helps create a feeling of unity and harmony. Lack of unity makes a space seem smaller (e.g. using a different wallpaper pattern on each wall of a room).

- Having a strong focal point in a space so that the space revolves around it, such as a round conference table with a pendant light fitting hanging over the center of the table (Figure 3.6). Alternatively, one could create a strong focal point by incorporating a fireplace or hanging a large painting. Even the way furniture is laid out can impact the perception of unity and harmony of a space. Furniture should seem to belong. It should reflect and blend with the character of the space and its purpose. Colors should be sympathetic to the furnishings and harmonize with them.

Balance

When we talk about balance in space planning and interior design, we are mainly concerned with visual weight (as opposed to actual weight), coordinated in such a way so as to create a sense of equilibrium. Equilibrium is a fundamental force in everyone. This sense of equilibrium produces a psychological impact on our brain cells. Thus, how important or heavy a form appears to be, as opposed to its actual weight, is what concerns us. Generally speaking, and with all other things being equal:

- A large object or shape has more visual weight than a smaller one.
- A small, dark shape can be equal to or greater than a larger, lighter one.

FIGURE 3.5 Design by the author for a living room showing how a central theme can be achieved by using one basic style of furniture, in this case manufactured by Ethan Allen.

FIGURE 3.6 The circular suspended ceiling echoes the circular rug and creates a strong focal point. IBM eBusiness Services, Santa Monica, CA. *(Courtesy HOK Architects)*

- Warm, intense, advancing colors have more weight visually than do cool, dull, receding ones. Thus, you can alter the visual weight of an object by altering its color.

- Surfaces that are textured, rough or patterned have more visual weight than smooth, plain ones.

- Irregular shapes have more weight visually than simple geometric ones.

- The more light in an area, the more weight visually it will have.

- A form that blends with its surroundings has less visual weight than one that contrasts with it. Curtains having an identical pattern to that of the wall appear "lighter" than ones that contrast with the wall.

One should note that the equilibrium of a room could change constantly during the day due to many factors—the amount of sun entering different parts of the room at different times of the day; the opening and closing of curtains or blinds; the use of artificial light at night or when reading; the viewing of television; the presence of people in a room, or merely the placing of a book or vase of flowers on a table. While this shifting of balance is inevitable, nevertheless, we should attempt to control these factors when ever possible.

There are three basic types of balance, symmetrical, asymmetrical, and radical.

Symmetrical Balance

Sometimes referred to as formal, symmetrical balance (Figure 3.7) is formal in character and is achieved when identical elements are arranged similarly on either side of an imaginary center line. Symmetrical balance can often be seen in traditional and classical architecture and in "period" interiors. Symmetrical balance is also frequently encountered in nature—in man, animals and insects—and we find it in such man-made objects as furniture, clothing, and buildings.

When properly executed, designs using symmetrical balance can suggest a feeling of repose and dignity. However, unless one is careful, the resulting design could appear rigid, inert and boring. When used in interior design, symmetrical balance will usually focus around a dominant architectural feature such as a fireplace or window.

Asymmetrical (Informal) Balance

In asymmetrical balance, visual weights are equal but not identical (Figure 3.8). This type of optical balance or equilibrium is much more casual, subtle and interesting than its symmetrical counterpart, but it requires much more skill to achieve. To achieve a successful asymmetric arrangement, designers must rely on their own judgment and instincts because there are no definitive rules to follow. Here we can employ elements of every size, shape or form as well as color in a multitude of ways to achieve the required balance. A grouping of small objects can be made to balance a larger one. Likewise, a small dark colored object can be perceived to balance a larger light colored one.

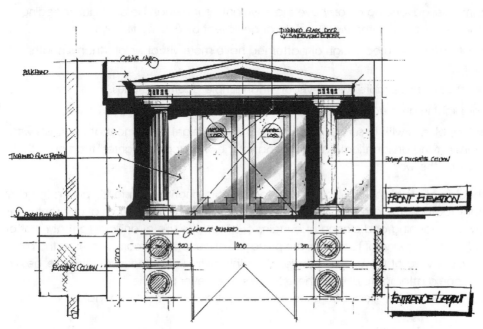

FIGURE 3.7   A classical design for an office entrance by the author showing the use of symmetrical balance.

In asymmetrical balance, there is more freedom and flexibility and no obvious center line dividing the design as in the symmetrical arrangement. Instead, there is the juxtaposition of various elements of different weights arranged around a balancing point or fulcrum to achieve balance. Because of their informal nature, asymmetrical designs frequently are found in modern interiors and modern architecture.

Radial Balance

Radial balance is not used as extensively as asymmetrical or symmetrical balance, but it is nevertheless important. As the name implies, it is based on a circular arrangement. All elements of the design radiate from or around center point or focus (Figure 3.9). Typical radial designs are a circular dining table with a floral arrangement in the center and chairs arranged around it, or a spiral staircase revolving around a central post.

Rhythm

Rhythm is the repetition of an element in a regular sequence; it directs the eye and helps it to move about a space. Rhythm is essentially a disciplined movement and can be either passive or dynamic. There are essentially four types of rhythm:

22-6549
BREAKFRONT CHINA
70"W x 17"d x 82"h
TWO ADJUSTABLE GLASS SHELVES
LIGHTENED INTERIOR. PANELLED
GLASS DOORS, ADJUSTABLE SHELF
BEHIND TWO CENTER DOORS

WALL DECOR

22-9500
PEDIMENT MIRROR
29"W x 49"H
BEVELED GLASS
FINISHES: 252, 254

WALL DECOR

41-3RT1
TRADITIONAL DESK CLOCK
ANTIQUED DARK CHERRY

22-6540
CHIPPENDALE SIDE
CHAIR
21¼"W x 23"d x 40"h

22-6544
DOUBLE PEDESTAL TABLE
OPENS TO 126"W W/3 APRONS
LEAVES: 46"L x 2"L x 29½h

CERAMIC VASE

CERAMIC VASE

22-9505
BOW FRONT CHEST
38½"W x 19"d x 32"h
FINISHES: 252, 254

RECTANGULAR CARPET

FIGURE 3.8   Asymmetric balance is attained by having one large picture on the left side of the cabinet balanced by the smaller ones on the right side.

1. Rhythm created by repetition is the most common and can be seen everywhere, particularly on fabrics, plates, wallpaper, and in nature. It can involve color, line, texture, pattern, or form. Repetitive rhythm is achieved by repeating a color or pattern on a wall, on curtains or even in a painting. This type of rhythm is passive and must be handled sensitively or it becomes boring (Figure 3.10).

2. Progressive rhythm is an ordered, gradual change in the size, direction, or color of an object or space (Figure 3.11). It is more subtle, dynamic, and inventive than simple repetition and can be achieved by succession in size from large to small (or vice versa) or in color by succession from dark to light (and vice versa).

3. Rhythm by alternation or rhythm by line is the regular, undulating, and continuous flow of a line or space (Figure 3.12).

4. Rhythm by radiation is created when an object's lines or motifs extend outward from a central axis, in a light fixture (Figure 3.13).

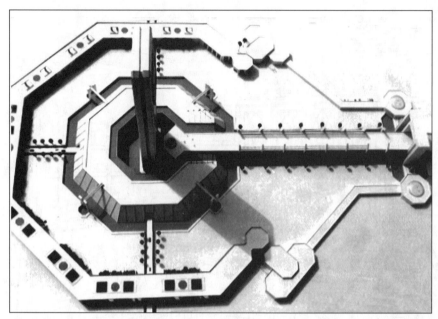

FIGURE 3.9
A design by the author for a proposed 600 foot high unknown soldier monument. The inner octagon shell contains parking, museum, retail and support facilities. The outer octagon contains offices, parking and other facilities.

FIGURE 3.10   This layout of Castelli 3D workspaces by Haworth shows several types of rhythm.

FIGURE 3.11   A staircase design example of progressive rhythm.

FIGURE 3.12
Rhythm by line is attained in the floor treatment.

FIGURE 3.13   An example of rhythm by radiation. *(Courtesy Steelcase, Inc.)*

Scale

Scale is a relative quality. It is the relation of the size of an element to that of another element within the same perceived space. When dealing with furniture, interior design, and architecture, the human being makes an excellent unit of measurement. Scale thus becomes the relation of an element's size to that of an average human being. Color, texture, and pattern must also be considered as they have a direct bearing on scale. Strong colored, large patterned and coarse textured objects will appear larger than objects of soft, light colors, small patterns and smooth textures. Furniture designed for adults would be out of scale in a child's play room, just as a child's chair would be out of scale in an adult's living room (Figure 3.14). Designers should give scale careful consideration when purchasing furniture or designing a space. Large bulky furniture can make a small room appear even smaller by emphasizing its smallness. Likewise, small furniture or accessories in a large space will make the furniture and accessories appear smaller and the space larger.

The scale of different elements within a room or space should be harmonious within their context. All the elements of a design should be in scale with each other, otherwise the design tends to appear uncomfortable and fragmented. A single, small painting hung over a large table would appear weak and out of scale with the furniture (Figure 3.15). Since we perceive objects in relation to their surroundings, a large double bed in a small room would appear too big for the room—and out of scale with it. Likewise, a large table lamp placed on a small, delicate table would look bulky and out of scale with the table.

FIGURE 3.14
Furniture for children differs in scale from that used by adults.

FIGURE 3.15   The small painting on the left (behind the table) is too small, out of scale, and distracting.

Scale can help in the creation of unity and harmony. This can be achieved through similarity or contrast. Scale is the relative proportion that the representation of an object bears to other objects. It is also the relationship of the various elements in space to each other and to the whole. These elements include the width and height of openings, doors and their moldings, windows and their surrounds, a fireplace, furniture, and rugs. The size of a room has a strong bearing on the scale of furniture, its relation to the walls and to other furniture and other elements such as pictures, mirrors, drapes, rugs or lamps. These must all be related to each other and to the average human being, the standard unit of measurement.

Emphasis

Emphasis relies on the principle of dominance and subordination. This concept (sometimes referred to as the center of interest), is used by the designer to focus attention on a particular area or object in a given space. If we desire to give this object or space a feeling of prominence, we should place great emphasis on it. It would then become a dominant feature (Figure 3.16). On the other hand, if we want to subordinate it to another element, we would decrease the emphasis.

FIGURE 3.16 A visual expression that depicts three approaches to increasing the emphasis and importance of the bed by making it a focal point in the room.

Essentially, each room or area should have only one dominant element, with all others elements subordinate to it. This will give it a feeling of unity and order. A lack of emphasis in a room makes it monotonous and boring. Emphasis is a vital element to the success of an interior. An interior that is thoughtfully arranged will immediately tell you where the most important feature lies and which features are less important. For our purposes there are three basic types of emphasis:

1. Dominant emphasis.
2. Subdominant emphasis.
3. Subordinate emphasis.

Initially, you must decide exactly what it is you want to emphasize and the level of emphasis. It could be a fireplace, an empty wall, a treasured piece of furniture, or a beautiful view from your living room (Figure 3.17). After deciding on the degree of visual dominance you want to give the object, you must take into consideration the effect of people on the space their presence or absence. Dominance can be achieved in several ways. These include:

1. *Size:* The larger the object in relation to its surroundings, the more dominant it appears (Figure 3.18).
2. *Lighting:* Can be used to focus attention on an area or object (e.g. a painting) (Figure 3.19). Directing the light on the Monster's Board lettering increases the emphasis on it.
3. *Contrast:* You can also gain dominance by contrasting a textured surface against a smooth one, or a strong color against a light color (Figure 3.20).
4. *Furniture Arrangement:* In this illustration at the offices of Monster.com, the staff meeting space is emphasized by the use of furniture arrangement and the red carpet (Figure 3.21).
5. *Accessories:* When thoughtfully arranged, they add to an element's importance (Figure 3.22).

It is unfortunate that many of today's designers and space planners do not give emphasis sufficient consideration in their designs, thereby ending up with uncoordinated spaces with competing elements.

Contrast

Contrast is one of the essential principles of design, yet too great a contrast can destroy the unity of a scheme. Contrast is obtained by the juxtaposition of two or more dissimilar or opposing elements or qualities (e.g. light colored objects set against a dark wall, or a circular dining table in a square room). Contrast can be achieved through various means.

- Contrast of line, obtained when lines vary in their direction. For example, horizontal lines versus vertical or diagonal lines, or straight lines versus curved lines.

FIGURE 3.17 The presence of the two paintings on the vertical panel adds emphasis to it.

- Contrast of form, such as a circular lamp and lamp shade on a square coffee table.
- Contrast of color is achieved when a dark color is used simultaneously with a light color; for example, a dark upholstered piece of furniture sitting on a light beige rug. Contrast can also be achieved by using complementary colors such as purple against yellow.
- Contrast of texture, such as a rough surface placed adjacent to a smooth surface, or a hard surface against a soft surface.

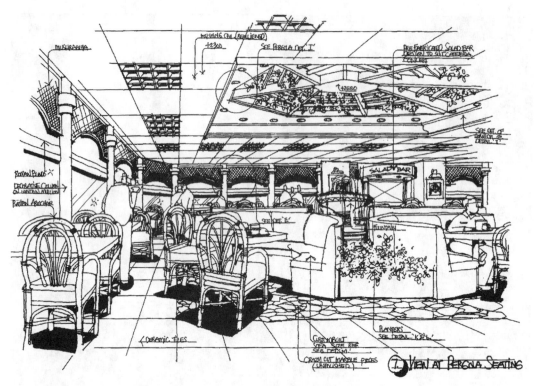

FIGURE 3.18 The pergola seating area is enhanced by the inclusion of a water fountain and the decorative treatment above it, which also increases the emphasis on it. *(Ibtesam Sharbaji, Architect)*

FIGURE 3.19
By directing light on the *Monster Board* lettering, we increase the emphasis on it.

FIGURE 3.20 This shows how a space planner can emphasize a space by the use of contrasting materials and shapes. IBM eBusiness Services, Santa Monica, CA. *(Courtesy HOK Architects)*

FIGURE 3.21   The staff meeting space at the offices of Monster.com achieves emphasis by the use of furniture arrangement and the circular red carpet.

FIGURE 3.22
Accessories like art work can add to a space's importance. *(Courtesy David-Carter-Scott, architects)*

Proportion

Proportion and scale are two distinct terms. Unfortunately, many people, even designers, do not differentiate and use the two interchangeably. When we think of proportion, we think of good and bad whereas scale implies large or small. Scale generally refers to the human being as a unit of measurement or to a part of an element as related to another part or to the whole. Moreover, the casual observer in a room or building does not often notice harmonious proportions. An object can be of beautiful proportions in itself, yet totally out of scale with its surroundings. A typical example is a small painting whose measurements fit the Golden Section (i.e. 5:8), yet is out of scale when hung by itself on an empty wall.

Proportion is, in a sense, a composition of parts of an element or elements. It refers to the mutual relationship of these parts to the whole. There have been persistent attempts through history to find a method of measuring beauty. Many architects, painters, and designers have tried to formulate definitive and precise rules to achieve ideal proportions. However, these attempts to rationalize proportion display an inherent rigidity and if adhered to too closely, a design may lose its spontaneity. Moreover, these rules are usually impractical when dealing with free form designs.

The Babylonians (c. 2500 BC) found proportions in the ratio of 3:4 to be pleasing, while the early Greeks found that rectangles with dimensions in the ratio of 2:3, 3:5 and 5:8 were most pleasing. The Greeks for some reason disliked the square which architects and designers often use today with great success and enthusiasm. Thus, one can see the difficulty in defining proportion because there are no precise guidelines. However, one can achieve a feeling for pleasant proportions by close observation and developing a discerning eye.

The sense of proportion is largely an intuitive judgment and, as such, presents several problems. It is easily affected by environmental influences like lighting and shadow placement. The eye is attracted to the light source and sets up an independent movement of its own. In the same room, a dark floor and light ceiling give a totally different spatial perception than a light floor and dark ceiling. Also, its findings do not offer proof to the intellect; an individual's assertion that the shape of an object is pleasing can be confirmed only by exposing other individuals to the same object with identical results. These individuals should preferably be of varying cultures, different age groups, and of both sexes.

It is sometimes argued that our concept of proportion is based on what we have been taught since early childhood. However, this does not explain why certain aesthetic judgments are almost universally valid, thereby allowing us to enjoy art by totally alien cultures and civilizations.

It is interesting to note that Fechner, in his study of proportion, found that when observers were asked to choose between rectangles of different shapes, a preference emerged for proportions approaching that of the golden section (i.e. 5:8). Yet when he measured the proportions of hundreds of museum paintings, he found that on average a shorter rectangular shape was preferred, i.e. 5:4 for upright pictures, and approximately 4:3 for horizontally extended ones.

This clearly indicates that when a rectangle is perceived on its own, the proportions of the golden section appear to work well. But when a rectangle is read as part of a pictorial composition in which every part is related to every other, then the golden section formula does not work well. Balance and equilibrium appear to be at the root of this sense of proportion. It is essential therefore, to remember that when designing an object or space, it must not be conceived in isolation, but as it relates to its surroundings.

ELEMENTS OF INTERIOR DESIGN

Space

Space is the distance, interval, or area between, around, or within things, and is either two or three-dimensional. It is the most essential element in space planning. There are basically three kinds of space: flat space, perceptual or implied space, and actual space. Flat space is an implied two-dimensional space, consisting of height and width. It is ideally suited to two-dimensional expression where there is no illusion to depth (Figure 3.23).

Perceptual space is also an implied space frequently used in two-dimensional expression (as well as three-dimensional) such as photography, where the space is an illusion. We can create, control and vary the depth of perceptual space by various means. These include: shadows, color, mirrors, line, perspective, and overlapping (depth of field). Shade and shadow suggests substance to an object as well as volume. Furthermore, shadow automatically implies light (Figure 3.24).

Perceptual space is affected by color contrast. Lighter values appear to recede; darker values appear to advance. By the use of reflective surfaces such as mirrors, one can increase the visual perception or the apparent size of a space. Non-reflective surfaces can make a space appear smaller than the same space using reflective surfaces. Likewise, transparent materials like glass help increase the apparent size of a space (Figure 3.25). Thus, a small room

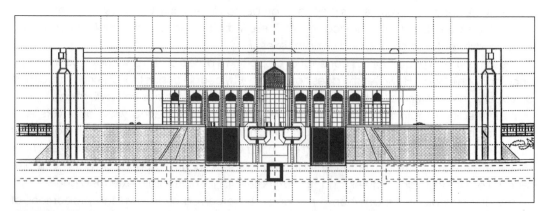

FIGURE 3.23 Flat space is ideally suited where there is no illusion of depth.

FIGURE 3.24 Shade and shadow suggests volume as well as substance. Compare this illustration with Figure 3.5, a line drawing with no shade or shadow.

with a large window would appear larger and less confined than the same size room with no windows at all.

Line can be a very potent force in interior design. Horizontal lines make a space appear longer. Vertical lines make it appear higher. By the judicious use of line, a designer can create an illusion of depth or height. Linear perspective is another means of creating perceptual space. When drawing an interior of a typical room, we know that the room has a floor, ceiling and four walls. Yet it would be difficult for us to see all the different planes simultaneously. Our main concern is to show how the room appears visually—not physically. Therefore, nearby objects will appear larger than distant objects, all else being equal (Figure 3.26).

A method to achieve an illusion of space that was used by the ancient artists (who were unfamiliar with perspective), is to use the technique of overlapping or depth of field. By suggesting that an object is behind another object, you imply depth and, therefore, space. Ideally, you should have a foreground (that nearest to the observer), a middle ground (between the nearest and the farthest part of the plane), and the background.

FIGURE 3.25 The use of transparent materials and reflective surfaces increase the perception of a space. *(Courtesy Steelcase, Inc.)*

The designer should have a complete understanding of the dynamics of perceptual and actual space and the difference between them, even though it may seem pretty obvious. The former is an illusion; the latter is a fact. But actual space can also be manipulated to create illusions by using other design elements like light, color, texture, line and reflected surfaces.

Form

It is impossible to separate form from space because one creates the other. Like space, form can be two-dimensional or three-dimensional. As designers, our main emphasis will be on the three-dimensional aspects because these make up our main environment. Paintings and photographs are examples of two-dimensional form, which often depicts recognizable objects that have the perception of depth, height and width.

The importance of form in architecture and interior design is obvious—everything we feel, see, or touch is a manifestation of one type of form or another. But three-dimensional form

FIGURE 3.26 Nearby objects appear larger than distant objects. The hanging light in the foreground appears larger than the one further back.

consists of more than the outline shape of an object: It also contains the object's inner part as well, and also its apparent weight. Form is the antithesis of space, i.e., if form is considered to be a positive mass, then space would be considered negative. Forms can be either straight, curved, or irregular (Figure 3.27).

Line

Line is one of the most fundamental elements of design because it can enclose space and convey form through outline and contour. Without line, which in theory has only one dimension and technically consists of a series of points, we cannot perceive form or shape.

There are basically two types of lines: straight and curved. Straight lines can be either horizontal, vertical, or diagonal. Psychologically, straight lines can portray an impression of strength, firmness and simplicity. Lines of transition tend to lead the eye from one point to another. Lines also express direction, create pattern and can connote texture. They can also

FIGURE 3.27   Illustration depicting various types of form within a space.

create emphasis or subordination; for example, the direction of a carpeted staircase can be emphasized by incorporating a six inch border in a stronger or lighter tone than the main stair carpet. The way lines are used can have a dramatic effect on how we perceive a space. Lines can also imply qualities evoking an emotional response from an observer.

Horizontal lines (parallel to the horizon) tend to suggest repose and tranquility, and also make a room appear wider. (Figure 3.28a). Diagonal lines suggest motion and energy, activity, dynamism and restlessness. Diagonal lines also have a tendency to lead the eye upward (Figure 3.28b). Strong vertical lines can have an uplifting quality and tend to suggest strength, aspiration and dignity. They also express masculinity and formality. Vertical lines have a tendency to lead the eye upward to create an illusion of increased height (Figure 3.28c).

Line can alter the apparent proportions of an object or an entire room. Two identical rectangles, one divided vertically and one horizontally give very different perceptions of space and form. A careful balance of line quality and direction is imperative to a room's feeling of comfort and harmony.

Texture

Texture is a term that refers to the surface quality of an object, i.e. its roughness or smoothness, coarseness or fineness. A distinction should be made between actual tactile textures and visual textures. Actual texture can be felt by touching. By contrast, visual textures are simulated textures. They have a uniform surface to the touch, yet the material reveals a textural pattern

FIGURE 3.28a
This image Illustrates a bedroom with a horizontal emphasis.

FIGURE 3.28b
This image employs diagonal lines to suggest motion, energy and dynamism.

FIGURE 3.28c   This image shows how the use of vertical lines increases the perception of height. *(Courtesy HOK Architects)*

below a relatively smooth surface. Here, texture is the result of the brain translating this visual perception to texture. Visual texture also plays a vital role in the pictorial arts such as painting and photography, where the eye can distinguish between lustrous, shiny, dull, rich or weak surfaces that cannot be experienced by touch alone.

Texture plays an increasingly important role in contemporary interior design by creating contrast and variety. We are conscious of several texture sensations in architecture and interior design, four of which are:

1. Totally smooth surface, such as worktops, painted walls, ceilings, windows and built in furniture (Figure 3.29a).
2. The rough textures associated with concrete and brick, stucco and stone (Figure 3.29b).
3. The soft sensation of a pillow, a plush pile carpet or gentle upholstery or curtains (Figure 3.29c).
4. The delicate and sensuous texture of live objects such as human skin or leaves and flowers, and even the kinetic texture of rippling water.

FIGURE 3.29a Shown here is a smooth surface coupled with light, shadows, and reflections.

FIGURE 3.29b
An example
of a rough tex-
tured surface.

FIGURE 3.29c
Example of a
soft textured
surface.

Texture can affect us in many ways. It gives us a physical impression of what we touch; it also affects the amount of light a surface will reflect. Smooth surfaces will reflect more light than coarse surfaces.

Texture adds beauty and interest to our lives. Smooth surfaces like glass, stainless steel and polished marble suggest a feeling of luxury and formality. On the other hand, rough surfaces like stucco, brick and stone tend to suggest a feeling of solidity, masculinity, and informality. The designer should refrain from using too many different textures of a similar nature side by side because the end result is usually discordant. Contrasted textures are usually more appealing than a combination of like textures. For this reason, it is generally unwise to use brick and stone or even different types of brick in the same field of vision, unless a particular statement is to be made, e.g. where a dark colored brick is used to delineate a wall or an outline course of lighter colored brick.

Texture is also be used by the designer to create illusions, e.g. rough surfaces can reduce the apparent height of a ceiling or reduce the apparent distance of a wall and make colors appear darker and heavier. Smooth surfaces, on the other hand, have the opposite effect. Rough textures also contribute a sense of warmth, whereas smooth textures generally feel cold. Most people prefer living in an environment of varying textures. Shiny surfaces of brightly polished materials are easier to clean than coarse materials such as masonry. The textures of materials chosen by the designer should be appropriate to the desired effect—whether aesthetic or functional.

Pattern

Pattern as opposed to plain design is the easiest way of designating surface enrichment. It is closely related to texture and form, and is a repetition of a motif (Figure 3.30). Pattern is formed by the use of line, form, light and color.

The use of pattern should be controlled. Too much pattern can break up a room, making it appear very busy and uncomfortable. At the same time, a room with no pattern at all can be dull and lack character. The total arrangement of the various components of a room creates an overall pattern. For example, groupings of furniture or paintings on a wall create pattern. Pattern can be seen everywhere—on man made objects like fabrics and wallpaper, and in natural forms like leaves and flowers.

Pattern is a subjective word and is suggestive of being decorative. It can be an applied design to an objects surface or can emerge from its structure. Correctly used, it can unify a composition; improperly used, it can destroy it. But decorating success lies with the distribution as well as the choice of pattern.

Pattern, in essence, is created by the juxtaposition of related positive and negative visual elements in a given space. It works best with the element of color. When working together, they act as an accent to catch the eye. When pattern is blended with color, they work in harmony. Pattern helps create instant visual impact and mood. Texture can add another dimension,

FIGURE 3.30 Surface enrichment is achieved by use of graphic pattern on the walls of the Monster.com cafeteria.

that of depth, as well as tactile interest. The basic sources of pattern are textiles, wall coverings, floor coverings (e.g. rugs and tiles), and nature.

Pattern can strongly affect the appearance of a room or space. For example, a wallpaper with a vertical design will make a ceiling appear higher, whereas one with a strong horizontal emphasis will make a room appear wider and the ceiling lower. The ceiling will also appear lower if wallpaper is used on it. Likewise, a large strong pattern could look out of place in a confined space, just as a very small pattern in a large room becomes insignificant. Too much pattern tends to make a small room appear cluttered, and reduces the amount of furniture needed to fill it. Pattern is also used frequently to disguise unpleasant design features or defects like uneven walls.

Today, many wallpaper and textile manufacturers have a large selection of coordinated fabrics and wall coverings in an infinite range of patterns and colors. This is a great boost to creating a unified and controlled design. Certain patterns are associated with definite periods.

Light

From the earliest times, seeing has been part of the wonder of life. The magnificent spectacle of the universe itself can only be fully appreciated through the eyes. Two thirds of the information received comes through vision, and the eyes are second only to the brain in complexity. They are the window to the universe.

Lighting serves two basic needs—to illuminate a task and to establish a mood. It shapes the look and feel of a space by highlighting certain areas and playing down others. The sun is still the primary source of light and natural lighting is preferred because of its soft and changing qualities, as well as a point of reference to tell the weather and time of day. Some of the factors in the emotional impact of light are:

- Darkness brings fear to many.
- Everyone can feel blue at times.
- Bright colors and images can lift our spirits.
- Dark colors can be depressing—or soothing.

Technically, when we speak of light, we are talking of visible light in the middle of the spectrum. Newton showed that a glass prism breaks up white light into a colored spectrum, and that if the color passes through a second prism, it becomes white light again. There are four psychologically pure hues: blue, yellow, green and red. Tints are a hue plus white, or desaturated hues, like pink.

Color

There is a gradual but steady movement of people out of the natural environments and into the man-made ones. People are leaving the wide, open spaces—the large house with its rose garden—to move into a crowded multistory apartment complex, somewhere in the middle of a plethora of multi-story box-like structures. With the increasing complexity of modern civilization, architects and designers, those responsible for meeting our environment will have to make a greater effort at understanding the psychic makeup of people.

Color is a potent psychological force and is often utilized in hospitals and other institutions for specific effects. At the University of California, San Francisco Medical Center hospital, intensive care units that were painted in bright yellows and oranges were found to make patients feel better and instill a desire to recuperate faster. Blue, on the other hand, is used in hospital recovery rooms following surgery because it is an emotionally sedative color. Color also has many applications in education settings.

Guidelines for Creating a Color Plan

To create a successful color plan for an interior space, the designer should work in a methodical way consistent with his or her personality. But whatever method of work the designer may choose, certain principles must be adhered to. These principles are listed below.

Analysis of the Problem

In the initial analysis the interior designer must determine the following:

1. How the space will be utilized. Whether it will be used for sleeping, relaxing, reading or eating. What length of time it will be in use. Will the space be used during the day or in the evening and by whom? If the space is to be used mostly by young children, your choice of colors would be different than if it was to be used by elderly persons.

2. What is the size and shape of the room or space? The designer must determine whether there are any unusual features that require special emphasis, or whether there are any elements such as columns or pilasters that need to be subdued. Are the ceilings too high or the room too narrow?

3. What is the room's orientation? If the windows are facing north, then there won't be any sunlight. You may decide to compensate for this by introducing warm colors.

4. What are the client's color preferences? If it is a family, do they all share the same preferences? If not, how will you cater to the conflicting tastes? How will this effect your proposed solution? Is it compatible with your own analysis and findings? If not, what modifications are necessary?

5. How will the existing colors of adjoining areas affect the design? Does the client have any existing furniture or furnishings he is adamant on keeping and which need to be considered? How will they affect your proposals?

Solution Phase One: Available Options

Designers have at their disposal numerous color harmonies. A detailed analysis is not within the scope of this study, but some of the more popular color harmonies used are:

1. Achromatic color harmony
2. Monochromatic color harmony
3. Analogous color harmony
4. Analogous with complementary accent
5. Complementary color harmony
    a. Direct
    b. Split
    c. Double
    d. Tetrad
6. Triad color harmony
7. Other color scheme

Before deciding which of the above color schemes will be most suitable, the designer must take into consideration all of the elements of the proposed space, including structural elements such as walls, floors, and ceilings, as well as non-structural elements such as furniture and furnishings, rugs, and paintings.

CHAPTER FOUR

FOUR

COMMUNICATION AND DRAFTING METHODS

Although today's design office relies less on manual drafting than it did in the past, the ability to prepare drawings manually remains an integral part of the design process, essential to a designer's growth. Indeed, those who master the language of drawing will likely find themselves capable of communicating with their clients and peers with greater spontaneity, expressiveness, confidence and sophistication.

GENERAL OVERVIEW

Drawing is a creative and cognitive process involving perceptive observation and thinking in images. The purpose of this chapter therefore, is to encourage readers, whether professional space planners, designers, architects or aspiring students, to achieve these goals, as well as attain a fluent command of the language of architectural drafting.

Drafting Equipment and its Uses

Although in the final analysis, it is the designer's own hand and mind that determines the finished drawing, the use of appropriate equipment and materials can go a long way to facilitate achieving quality results.

Drawing Boards and Tables

The size of architectural drawings will vary depending on the size of the job. Often they will be 24 inches to 48 inches long by 24 inches to 36 inches wide, which means a large drawing board is needed. The board should have a smooth and flat drawing surface, and the edge guiding the T-square must be straight and true. A board's surface is very important for good drafting, and it is desirable for the board to have an inclination of 10 or 15 degrees for better drafting. Many types of drafting boards and tables are available in today's marketplace (Figure 4.1). Many designers prefer using boards that incorporate a parallel bar. The bar is kept parallel by braided wires attached to the board at the corners, and the bar runs on pulleys.

Pens, Pencils, Leads, Erasers, Erasing Shield

Most ink drafting is done with technical pens. Technical pens typically have tungsten carbide or jewel points that last longer and are suitable for use on films. They are also capable of precise line widths, and can be used for both freehand and drafted ink drawings. Technical drafting pens come in a variety of point sizes. A starting set should include the following point sizes: 0.1 mm (3 x 10), 0.2 mm (2 x 10), 0.4 mm (1) and 0.8 mm (3). For very thick lines, a 2 mm (6) can be used. Technical pens need considerable maintenance and cleaning, and care must be taken not to allow the ink to clog up. An alternative to the technical pen is the disposable drafting pen that is available in a fine to broad felt-tip point.

FIGURE 4.1 A designer using a typical drawing board and T-square and other instruments. *(Muller, Edward J., et al, Architectural Drawing and Light Construction, 5th Ed., Prentice Hall, 1999)*

Lead holders and mechanical pencils are often preferred to the traditional wooden pencil or the technical drafting pen. The wood pencil needs to be continuously shaved back to expose about ¾ inch of the lead shaft, and the technical drafting pen, while capable of producing better quality drawings than the lead pencils, requires greater skill to use. Mechanical pencils are available in a variety of point sizes, and are capable of precise line widths. A sharp lead point is essential to good line quality (Figure 4.2).

Lead, whether for the lead holder, for the mechanical pencil, or the common wooden pencil, also comes in various degrees of hardness, from 9H (extremely hard) to 6B (extremely soft). Before making a determination on the most appropriate lead for the job, the designer should decide on the desired sharpness of lines and the opaqueness of the lead for reproduction. The most common and recommended lead weights are:

- 4H (hard and dense), for accurate layouts, but not satisfactory for finished drawings as it doesn't print well
- 2H (medium hard), hardest grade recommended for finished drawings. Will not erase easily if pressed too firmly.
- F and H (medium), recommended for finished drawings and lettering
- HB (soft), for dense, bold line work and lettering. Erases easily, prints well, but smears easily.

Erasers typically consist of a rubber or synthetic material and are used to erase errors and correct drawings. Block erasers such as art gum, white plastic, or soft pink are effective in removing pencil and plastic lead from tracing paper and film. Ink erasers are generally too abrasive for drawing surfaces and should be avoided. Electric erasing machines are also available which can save the designer much valuable time.

Erasing shields are thin metal or plastic instruments with pre-punched slots and holes of various sizes used to protect some portion of a drawing while erasing others. To erase with the shield, select the hole or slot that best fits the line or area to be erased and hold the shield down firmly on the drawing. Then rub the line with the appropriate eraser. Erasing shields with square holes are preferable as they allow you to more precisely erase the areas of a drawing that need eradication.

Triangles, Templates, Irregular Curves

Triangles are three-sided guides used to draft vertical lines or diagonal lines at 30 degrees, 45 degrees, or 60 degrees, usually in conjunction with a T-square. The 30 degree/60 degree and 45 degree/90 degree triangles are basic equipment. They are usually made of transparent acrylic plastic about 0.06 inches thick with true, accurate edges. They also come in various sizes, from extremely small ones used for detailing or lettering, to very large ones, used for large drawings, perspective, and so on (Figure 4.3).

The adjustable triangle is a very useful tool, and is used for general drafting as well as for sloping lines and odd angles such as those found in roof slopes and stair risers. It contains a

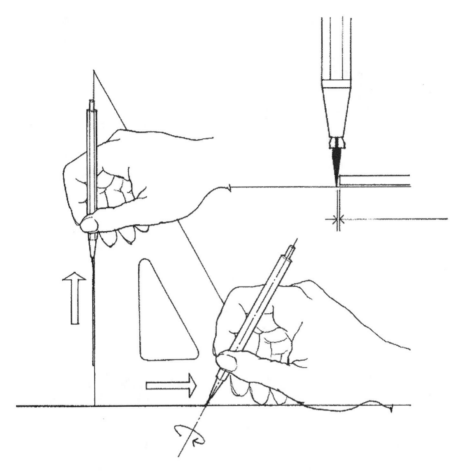

FIGURE 4.2 The procedure for drawing vertical and horizontal lines. For vertical lines, draw the line upward, rotating the pencil slowly between the thumb and forefinger. For horizontal lines, lean the pencil in the direction of the line at an angle of about 60 degrees with the paper and draw the line from left to right. *(From Ching, Francis D.K., with Juroszek, Steven P., Design Drawing, Van Nostrand Reinhold, New York, 1998)*

protractor scale adjustment from 0 degrees to 45 degrees from the horizontal or base line, and thus replaces the need for a protractor when drawing odd angle layouts. The required angle can be achieved by loosening or tightening a setscrew, that also serves as a convenient lifting handle. An adjustable triangle with a 6 inch to 8 inch leg is adequate for most jobs.

Templates are made of thin plastic with variously sized or scaled pre-punched openings cut in the sheet. Templates are time saving devices, and generally used for drawing different shapes commonly found in architectural plans. Specialty templates are available for drawing furniture, trees, electrical and plumbing fixtures, mechanical equipment, geometric shapes (circles, squares, rectangles, triangles, ovals, hexagons), and standard symbols (such as arrows, door swings, electrical, etc). Some of the larger sanitary, appliance and furniture manufacturers have templates specific to their own lines of production (at various scales), and are given free upon request.

Irregular curves (sometimes referred to as French curves) are used to draw uneven radii and non-uniform curvature, and are usually made of clear acrylic. Where considerable curved work is involved, the designer may prefer to use an adjustable curve. The adjustable curve consists of a flexible metal core covered with a rubber or metal ruling edge, and can be bent to the desired curvature before the line is drawn.

Scales

Most construction drawings are drawn to specific scales and the majority of architectural drawings are done using an architect's scale. Scales are measuring devices calibrated in a variety of scales to allow the translation of large objects (in this case, buildings or spaces) into a small proportional drawing. For example, for large building projects, one-eighth of an inch to equal one foot is the usual scale used for drawing plans, elevations and sections, whereas for smaller buildings such as residences, one-quarter of an inch to equal one foot is typically used. Larger scales are used such as one-half of an inch up to three inches to equal a foot for sections of a project and for details (such as construction and furniture details).

Scales require distinct machine-divided markings coupled with sharp edges to achieve accurate measurements. Architectural scales are usually flat or triangular in shape and in several lengths—the 12 inch (30 cm) triangular shape being the most popular. Below are listed the most relavent scales found on the triangular architect's scale with their approximated metric equivalents:

- $\frac{1}{32}$ inch = 1 foot (1/400 metric scale equivalent—often used for site plans–actual 1/384)
- $\frac{1}{16}$ inch = 1 foot (1/200 metric scale equivalent—often used for large projects and small site plans—actual 1/192)
- $\frac{1}{8}$ inch = 1 foot (1/100 metric scale equivalent—actual 1/96)
- $\frac{1}{4}$ inch = 1 foot (1/50 metric scale equivalent—actual 1/48)
- $\frac{3}{8}$ inch = 1 foot (no precise metric equivalent—actual 1/32)
- $\frac{1}{2}$ inch = 1 foot (1/20 or 1/25 metric scale actual 1/24)
- $\frac{3}{4}$ inch = 1 foot (no precise equivalent—actual 1/16)
- 1 inch = 1 foot (one-twelfth size—approximate equivalent 1/10)
- 1½ inch = 1 foot (one-eighth size)
- 3 inches = 1 foot (one-quarter size)

Accuracy in using the scale when preparing architectural or technical drawings is of the utmost importance to maintain quality control and avoid possible confusion.

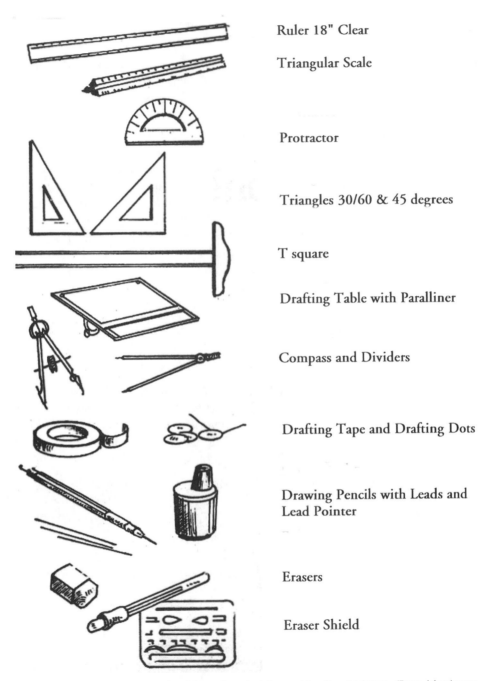

Ruler 18" Clear

Triangular Scale

Protractor

Triangles 30/60 & 45 degrees

T square

Drafting Table with Paralliner

Compass and Dividers

Drafting Tape and Drafting Dots

Drawing Pencils with Leads and Lead Pointer

Erasers

Eraser Shield

FIGURE 4.3 Some of the tools, aids and materials used by the designer. *(From Montague, John, Basic Perspective Drawing: A Visual Approach, 3rd Ed., John Wiley and Sons, Inc., New York, 1998)*

LETTERING

Drawings are a means of communication of information to others, and generally contain two basic types of information, graphic or artistic and text in the form of notes, titles, dimensions, etc. Legibility and consistency are the key ingredients to good lettering. Lettering should enhance a drawing by making it easy to interpret and pleasant to look at; it should not detract from the drawing or be illegible and unsightly to look at.

Skill in freehand lettering adds style and individuality to a designer's work, but in any style of lettering, uniformity is important. This applies to height, proportion, inclination, strength of lines, spacing of letters, and spacing of words. Letters should be spaced by visually equalizing the background areas between the letterforms and not by mechanically measuring the distance between the extremities of each letter (Figure 4.4). The use of light horizontal guidelines (using a hard lead such as a 4H) should be practiced to control the height of letters, while light vertical or inclined guidelines are required to keep the letters uniformly vertical or inclined. Words should be spaced well apart, while letters should be spaced closely within words.

If one examines the alphabets and typefaces in use today, it becomes apparent that the vast majority of them fit into one of the following four basic classifications (Figure 4.5):

- Roman: Perfected by the Greeks and Romans and later modernized in the 18th century. The Roman alphabet displays enormous grace and dignity and is considered our most beautiful typeface family.

- Gothic: This alphabet is the base from which our single-stroke technical lettering has evolved, and is the primary style used by most designers today. It is an easily read and simply executed letter that has been in use for many years as a commercial, block-type letter. Its main characteristic is the uniformity in width of all of the strokes. Modifications of this letter include inclined, squared, rounded, boldface, lightface, and the addition of serifs.

- Script: Script alphabets are cursive in nature and resemble handwriting. The lowercase letters are interconnected when used within words or sentence beginnings. Their characteristic free-flowing strokes impart a sense of delicacy and personal temperament, and are not suited for general use in technical drawing.

- Text (Old English): Originally used by the central European monks for recording religious manuscripts. This alphabet is characterized by the use of strokes of different width, due to the original employment of a flat quill pen. This alphabet is unsuitable for technical drawing because it is difficult to read and draw, and is not much used in modern works.

All of the above typefaces can be produced in *italic* (having inclined, lightface, and curved characteristics). The character of the typeface used should always be appropriate to the design being presented. Today there is an overwhelming body of well-designed typefaces available in the form of pressure-sensitive, dry transfer sheets as well as the computerized typography. There are also several excellent books available that deal with basic lettering practice.

TYpogRaphY

abcdefghijklmnopqrstuvwxyz

0123456789

abcdefghijklmnopqrstuvwxyz
0123456789

ABCDEFGHIJK

lmnopqrstuvwxyz

0123456789

SPACING
Correct spacing of equal areas

SPAC
Incorrect spacing of letter forms

SERIFS Serifs

FIGURE 4.4 Examples of various typefaces in current use.

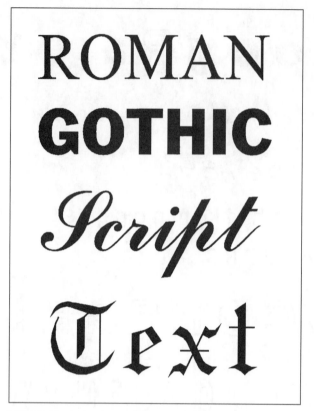

FIGURE 4.5 Most alphabets currently in use can be classified into four basic categories: Roman, Gothic, Script, and Text.

TECHNICAL DRAWING AND DRAFTING TECHNIQUES

Pragmatically, architectural drawings are essentially one of two types. The first type is a technical format, e.g. working drawings (also called construction or production drawings). The second type of drawing is graphic and artistic in nature and tends to be more creative, such as design, presentations or concept drawings. Working drawings will typically contain much more data and information than graphic drawings (Figure 4.6). Such information would likely include dimensions, material and finishes data, interior and exterior details, as well as structural, mechanical, electrical, plumbing and other information—in fact, everything a contractor would need to build the project.

Design and presentation drawings serve a totally different purpose or function, generally to sell the scheme, and are typically produced during the initial developmental stages of a project (for client approval) or for competitions. These may include color, shadow, and anything that would enhance the project's appeal to the client (or jury). Design drawings are also likely to include perspective sketches or renderings of the project where this adds to the projects understanding or appeal. Figure 4.7 shows a presentation drawing of a week-end villa for a Middle Eastern client by Ibtesam Sharbaji. The ink drawing includes suggested furniture layout and other pertinent information to sell the scheme to the client.

Paul Laseau in his book, *Architectural Representation Handbook*, rightly points out that conventions play an essential role in the realm of architectural representation within the context of common perceptions and understanding. They basically reflect a common language that permits us to mentally organize what is being communicated. Laseau says, "Conventions have evolved from historically practical needs within the design process, such as the ability to establish scale, proportion, dimension; the need to identify parts, or portray the views one might see when moving through an environment; and the need to evaluate a building design qualitatively and quantitatively. The terms elevation, section, plan, and perspective each have a commonly understood meaning and represent a shared expectation among designers and the people with whom they work." There are three basic types of convention: 1. Orthographic projection, 2. Paraline projection, and 3. Perspective projection.

Orthographic Drawing and Projection (Two-Dimensional Drafting)

Common types of orthographic drawings include plans, elevations and sections. The most obvious attribute of orthographic drawings is its constant scale, that is, all parts of the drawing are represented without foreshortening or distortion, retaining their true size, shape, and proportion. Thus, a four foot square window will always be drawn to be four feet, no matter how far it is from our viewpoint (Figure 4.8).

Plans are orthographic views of an object as seen directly from above. Floor plans are the most common form of plans and depict the layout of a building. A floor plan is represented by a horizontal section taken through the building or portion of a building just above the windowsill level. In addition to the arrangement of rooms and spaces, floor plans should show the location of various architectural elements such as stairs, doors, and windows, and also details like wall and partition thickness. The greater the scale of a drawing, the more detail that is to be included in it (Figure 4.9). Thus, a drawing of ¼ inch = 1 foot scale will typically contain more information and show greater detail than a drawing of ⅛ inch = 1 foot scale. Other types of plans include site plans which typically show the layout of a site, and reflected ceiling plans which are normally used to locate light fixtures and a ceiling's design features.

Reflected ceiling plans are actually another variation of a section, representing an orthographic view of the ceiling of a room or space. Normally, the reflected ceiling plan is identical to the floor plan, and theoretically shows construction elements that touch the plane of the

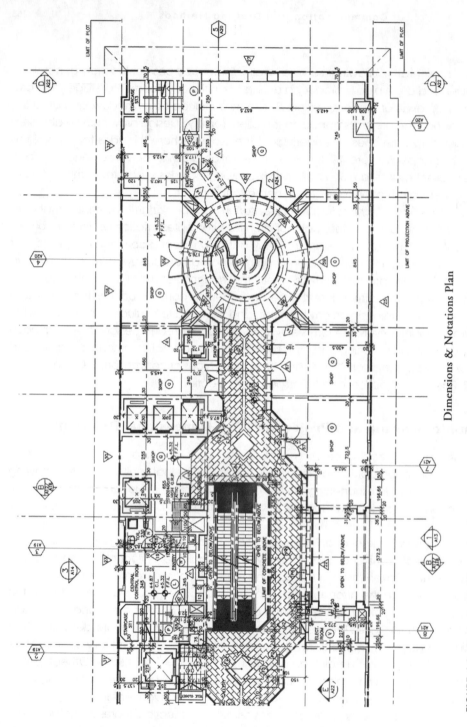

FIGURE 4.6 Part of a first floor plan for a shopping mall, showing some of the information a general contractor or builder would need to have on construction documents in order to build the project.

Dimensions & Notations Plan

154

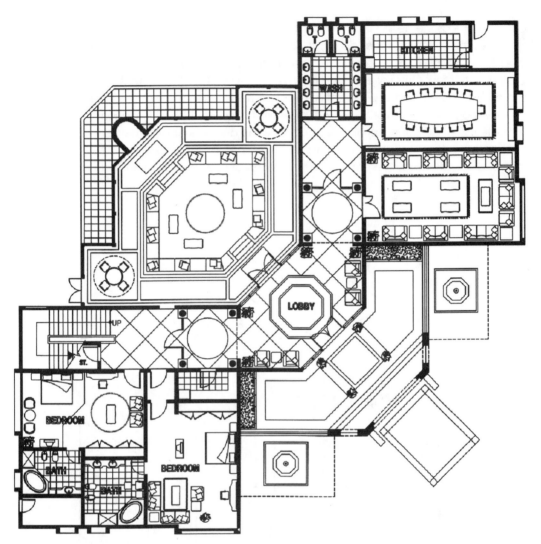

GROUND FLOOR PLAN

FIGURE 4.7 Example of a design drawing (as opposed to a working drawing) of a ground floor plan for a residence by Ibtesam Sharbaji.

ceiling, as well as the ceiling itself and fittings in the ceiling. Designers often take liberties and sometimes show elements that do not touch the ceiling (e.g. doors and cabinets) to make it easier for the contractor to follow the plans. Elevations are vertical views of the exterior of a building or its interior. Interior elevations consist basically of a vertical front view of walls, partitions, etc. without the use of perspective (Figure 4.10). Elevations are necessary because plans can only show the dimensions of length and width, and not height. Elevations can also communicate essential information like type of materials and finishes and their extent.

Sections are also orthographic views of an object, and supplement the information on plans and elevations. As the term implies, a section depicts a vertical cut through a structure

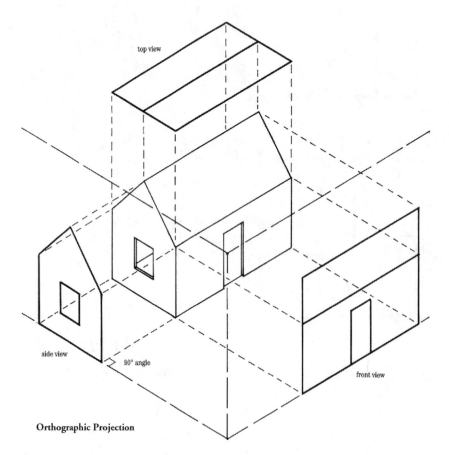

FIGURE 4.8 An example of orthographic projection depicting the roof (top view), and two elevations. In orthographic projection, all elements are shown in their true relationship with each other. *(From Ballast, David K., Interior Design Reference Manual, Professional Publications, Inc., Belmont, California)*

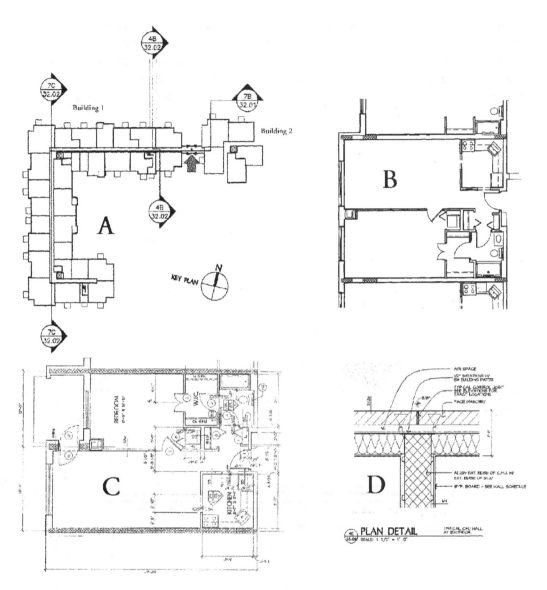

FIGURE 4.9 Drawings drawn in different scales: A. 1/500 scale; B. ⅛ inch = 1 foot ; C. ¼ inch = 1 foot and D. 1½ inches = 1 foot. Notice that the 1/500 scale drawing is basically a block plan and incorporates very little detail, and thus cannot be built from, unlike the 1½ inch = 1 foot drawing which gives the information necessary for its purpose.

or portion thereof, offering clarification to aspects of a design, in addition to essential information which plans and elevations alone cannot furnish, such as heights of doors, windows and ceilings, or floor and foundation construction details, location and depth of recesses, etc. (Figure 4.11). In addition to the above, designers often need to furnish other types of drawings with adequate details and specifications so that the contractor can build the project as originally conceived.

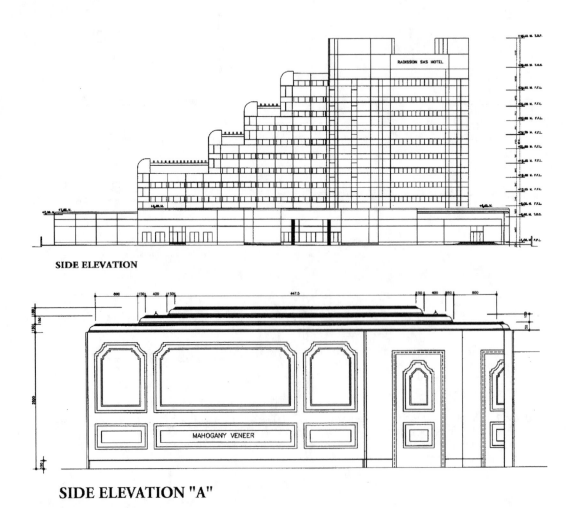

SIDE ELEVATION

MAHOGANY VENEER

SIDE ELEVATION "A"

FIGURE 4.10 An example of an exterior elevation of a hotel originally drawn to ⅛ inch = 1 foot scale, and an interior design elevation of a wall, originally drawn to ½ inch = 1 foot scale.

Paraline (Pictorial) Drawings and Projections

Paraline drawings are used to communicate a sensation of three-dimensional space in a single image. However, they differ from perspective drawings in one important aspect, mainly: all parallel lines in reality remain parallel in paraline drawings, whereas in perspectives they converge to a vanishing point.

Designers regard paraline drawings as a form of shorthand for the creating a credible three-dimensional image of a space, and because of their ease of construction, they have enjoyed considerable popularity amongst designers for presentations. Designers are also attracted to paraline drawings because of their constant scale, which makes them especially useful in taking advantage of today's technological revolution including the rapid duplication capabilities of modern computer graphics. Paraline drawings are also used extensively in catalogs, in general sales literature as well as in technical work.

There are several classifications of paraline drawings and projections, each named after the method of projection that is used to make them. The most important ones for space planners and designers include three basic types: axonometric, plan oblique, and elevation oblique.

Legend

1. Grad Student Offices
2. Lab
3. Faculty Offices
4. Light Court
5. Main Entrance
6. Sylvan Grove

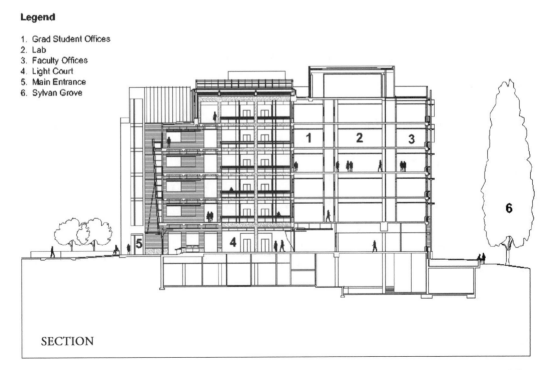

SECTION

FIGURE 4.11 An example of a typical design section through a building. *(Courtesy Department of Computer Science and Engineering, University of Washington)*

Axonometric Drawings

An axonometric drawing is one that is accurately scaled and depicts an object that has been rotated on its axes and is inclined from a regular parallel position to give it a three-dimensional appearance (Figure 4.12). The principal advantage of axonometric is that one can use an existing orthographic plan to start a drawing without any redrawing. The plan is simply tilted to the desired angle. In much of Europe, an axonometric drawing means that the axis is at a 45 degree angle, and for an isometric drawing, the axis is 30 degrees/30 degrees or 30 degrees/ 60 degrees.

Axonometric drawings can take on one of several forms, the most common being *isometric, diametric,* and *trimetric.* Figure 4.13 illustrates the different types of paraline drawings.

Isometric Drawings

Isometric drawing render a three-dimensional view of an object in which the two sets of horizontal lines of the object are drawn at equal angle and all vertical lines are drawn vertically. The resulting drawing has all three angles equally divided about a center point, and all three visible surfaces have equal emphasis. Orthographic drawings cannot be used in isometric drawings.

One can use any angle to draw an isometric, but the most common one is 30 degrees because it is a standard triangle and gives a reasonably realistic view of an object. Isometrics are easy and quick to draw and can be measured at any convenient scale

Dimetric

A dimetric projection is an axonometric projection of an object placed in such a way that two of its axes make equal angles with the plane of projection, and the third axis makes either a smaller or a greater angle.

Trimetric

A trimetric projection is an axonometric projection of an object so placed that no two axes make equal angles with the plane of projection, so that each of the three principal axes and the lines parallel to them, respectively, have different ratios of foreshortening (and therefore drawn at different scales) when projected to the plane of projection. The wide angle choice gives the designer considerable flexibility and control of the pictorial view.

Plan Oblique (Plan Projection)

Ching states that "a plan oblique orients a horizontal plane or plan view parallel to the picture plane and therefore reveals its true shape and size." A 45 degree/45 degree oblique has a

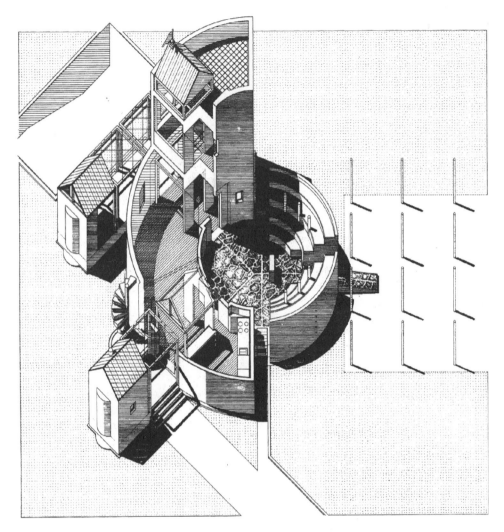

FIGURE 4.12 An example of an axonometric drawing by Brian Healy. *(From Laseau, Paul, Architectural Representation Handbook, McGraw-Hill, New York)*

higher angle of view than an isometric, giving more emphasis to horizontal planes. A 30 degree/60 degree oblique also has a high angle of view with one vertical plane receiving more emphasis than the other. Plan obliques are constructed by projecting vertical elements up from an orthographic plan. This facilitates showing the true form of horizontal planes as well as in depicting horizontal circular planes. In plan oblique, all vertical and parallel lines remain parallel and can be drawn to scale (Figure 4.14).

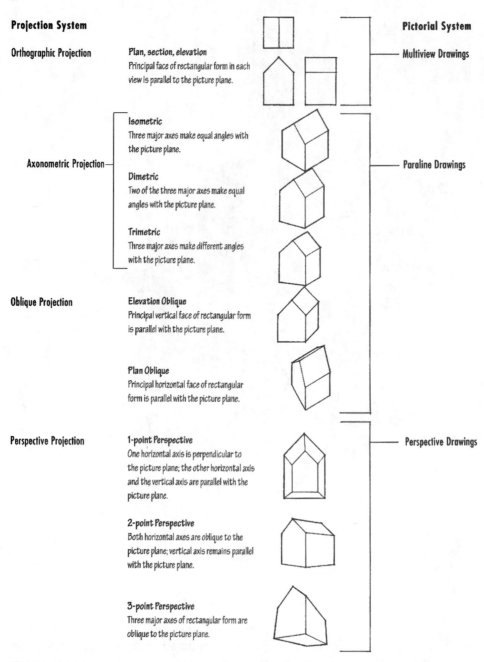

Projection System

Orthographic Projection

    Plan, section, elevation
    Principal face of rectangular form in each
    view is parallel to the picture plane.

Axonometric Projection

    Isometric
    Three major axes make equal angles with
    the picture plane.

    Dimetric
    Two of the three major axes make equal
    angles with the picture plane.

    Trimetric
    Three major axes make different angles
    with the picture plane.

Oblique Projection

    Elevation Oblique
    Principal vertical face of rectangular form
    is parallel with the picture plane.

    Plan Oblique
    Principal horizontal face of rectangular
    form is parallel with the picture plane.

Perspective Projection

    1-point Perspective
    One horizontal axis is perpendicular to
    the picture plane; the other horizontal axis
    and the vertical axis are parallel with the
    picture plane.

    2-point Perspective
    Both horizontal axes are oblique to the
    picture plane; vertical axis remains parallel
    with the picture plane.

    3-point Perspective
    Three major axes of rectangular form are
    oblique to the picture plane.

Pictorial System

Multiview Drawings

Paraline Drawings

Perspective Drawings

FIGURE 4.13 Diagram depicting the various pictorial and projection systems used by designers. *(From Ching, Francis D.K., with Juroszek, Steven P., Design Drawing, Van Nostrand Reinhold, New York, 1998)*

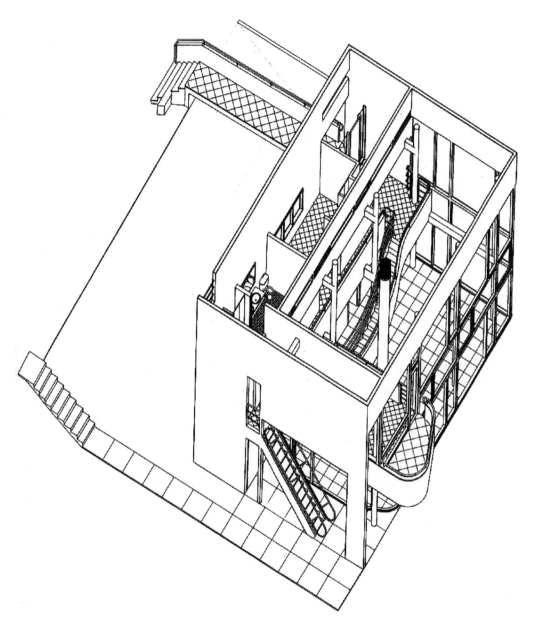

FIGURE 4.14 An example of a plan projection drawing by Richard Meier of Shamberg House. Plan projection is the most commonly used form of paraline drawing. *(From Laseau, Paul, Architectural Representation Handbook, McGraw-Hill, New York)*

Elevation Oblique

Elevation oblique rotates the principal vertical face to be parallel to the picture plane to reveal its true shape and size, which in turn allows us to directly construct an elevation oblique from an elevation view of the principal face. This face is usually the longest, most important façade of the object. Oblique drawings reflect the true shape of planes parallel to the picture plane, and rather than fixing the viewer in one position, this drawing allows the viewer the choice of many observation points.

PERSPECTIVE DRAWING

Perspective drawing is a system for representing three-dimensional space on a flat surface. The general principle behind it is simple, and shares many features with the way people actually perceive space and objects in it. It depends essentially on four interconnected criteria that will invariably affect the final image: the level of our eyes when viewing the scene or object, and thus determining the *horizon* line, the distance from the picture plane to the object, the distance from the station point to the object and cone of vision, and the angle of object to the picture plane (Figure 4.15).

The law of perspective—parallel lines that lie in the same plane will appear to converge at a point on the horizon (at the eye level). The point of apparent convergence is called the vanishing point (VP). This is true whether we view an object placed at an angle, such as a building seen from the corner or look into a space, such as a room, (Figures 4.16, 4.17). In essence, there are three basic forms of perspective drawings, they are:

- One-point perspective
- Two-point perspective
- Three-point perspective

One-Point Perspective (Parallel Perspective)

The one-point perspective depicts a building or interior space with one side parallel to the picture plane (perpendicular to the observer's line of sight). All vertical and horizontal lines within these planes remain vertical and horizontal, while the receding parallel sides are formed by converging lines to a single point, called the vanishing point (VP), which is usually positioned within the view. Illustrations in Figures 4.18 and 4.19 are examples of typical one-point perspectives.

To set up a one-point perspective, connect the corners of the elevation to the vanishing point and mark off the depth via the lines of sight in the plan. One-point perspectives are often used to draw interiors, as they give an accurate depiction of the facing wall, in addition to observation of both receding side walls.

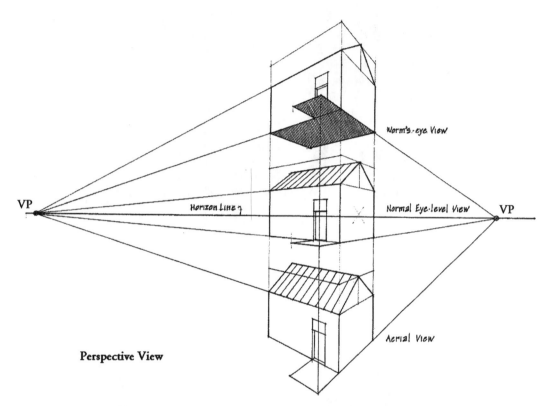

FIGURE 4.15 Perspective drawing depends essentially on the level of our eyes when viewing a scene or object (the horizon), and our distance from the object. When viewing an object that is below the horizon line, the top side of the object will be visible. When viewing an object that is divided by the horizon line, neither top nor bottom will be visible. Where the object is above eye level, the bottom of the object will be visible. *(From Ching, Francis D.K., with Juroszek, Steven P., Design Drawing, Van Nostrand Reinhold, New York, 1998)*

Two-Point Perspective

In two-point perspective, the verticality of vertical lines is maintained, but both major sets of horizontal lines are oblique to the picture plane, and both sets have their own vanishing points (Figure 4.20). Our distance from an object seen at an angle determines where the vanishing points lie on the horizon. To set up a two-point perspective, connect the corner height line to the right and left vanishing points and with the lines of sight in the plan, mark off the depth of the object. Constructing a two-point perspective view is basically the same as that for a one-point perspective except that you're required to establish two vanishing points. Shade and shadow are often used in perspective drawings to give us a better perception of the depth and form of a space or object. The drawing of shadows and reflections both follow the same immutable rules of perspective.

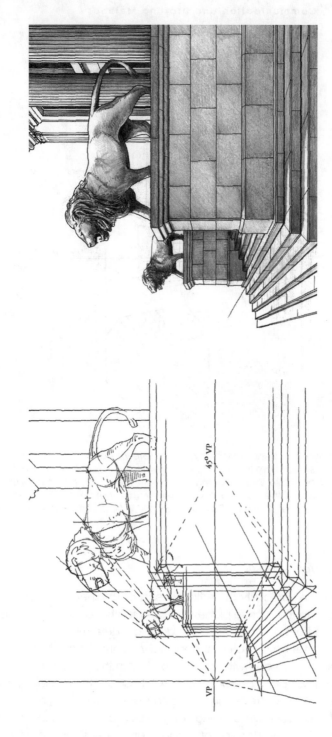

FIGURE 4.16 Lines that are parallel to each other in a scene converge toward a common point at eye level. The point at which these lines converge is called the Vanishing Point. *(From Montague, John, Basic Perspective Drawing: A Visual Approach, 3rd Ed., John Wiley and Sons, Inc., New York, 1998)*

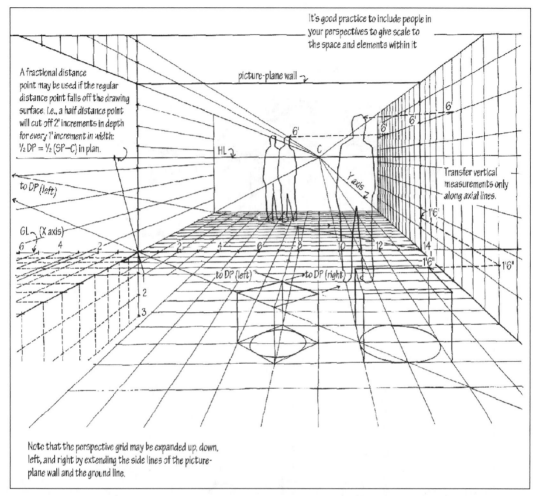

It's good practice to include people in your perspectives to give scale to the space and elements within it

picture-plane wall

A fractional distance point may be used if the regular distance point falls off the drawing surface. I.e., a half distance point will cut off 2' increments in depth for every 1' increment in width: ½ DP = ½ (SP–C) in plan.

HL

C

Y axis Z

Transfer vertical measurements only along axial lines.

to DP (left)

6'

GL (X axis)

6   4   2   2   4   6   8   0   12   14

to DP (left)   to DP (right)

1'6"

1'6"

2

3

Note that the perspective grid may be expanded up, down, left, and right by extending the side lines of the picture-plane wall and the ground line.

FIGURE 4.17 The height of the station point determines how a building or object is seen. *(From Ching, Francis D.K., with Juroszek, Steven P., Design Drawing, Van Nostrand Reinhold, New York, 1998)*

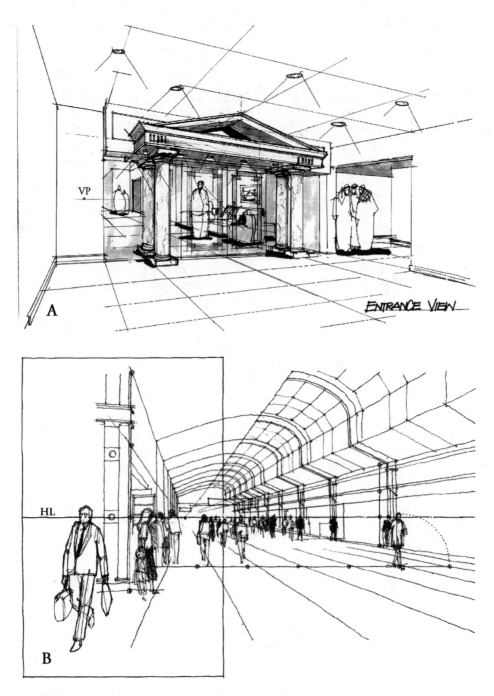

FIGURE 4.18 Two examples of one-point perspective. *(Drawing 4.18B from Ching, Francis D.K., with Juroszek, Steven P., Design Drawing, Van Nostrand Reinhold, New York, 1998)*

FIGURES 4.19 Two examples of one-point perspective. *(Drawings by Ibtesam Sharbaji, Kubba Design)*

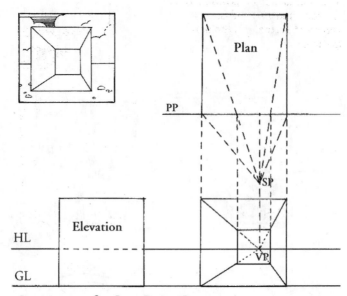

Setting up of a One-Point Perspective

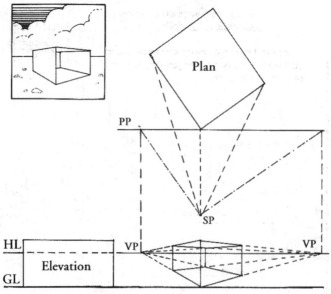

Setting up of a Two-Point Perspective

FIGURE 4.20 General procedure for setting up of a one-point and two-point perspective. *(Based on a drawing by Montague, John, Basic Perspective Drawing: A Visual Approach, 3rd Ed., John Wiley and Sons, Inc., New York, 1998)*

Three-Point Perspective

The observer's central axis of vision is horizontal and the picture plane vertical in both one-point and two-point perspective. In three-point perspective the object is either tilted to the picture plane or the spectator's central axis of vision is inclined upward or downward and the picture plane is tilted (Figure 4.21). Three-point perspective usually indicates that the spectator is very close to the object, or that the object is very large, and is not widely used in architectural presentation.

FREEHAND SKETCHING

To be able to sketch out one's visual ideas accurately and rapidly is a powerful creative and communication tool that only comes with continuous practice. Figure 4.22 shows the practical use of annotated freehand sketches in the design development of computer tables for an internet café. Moreover, freehand sketches are often helpful not only in developing one's drawing skills and awareness of the environment (Figure 4.23), but also facilitate analyzing many of the esthetic aspects of a project prior to and during the design development stage, as well as presenting preliminary design concepts to the client.

PRESENTATION TECHNIQUES

Presentations as used by space planners, architects and designers are either to persuade a potential client to commission a project, or to get approval for design work already carried out. In the first instance, the prospective client has no obligation to the designer. Here, the presentation may be of a speculative nature, with no contract or fee, basically in an effort to obtain a commission.

The second type of presentation relates to a project that is authorized by the client, and for which the space planner or designer is seeking approval for ideas and concepts that are developed or completed for a particular phase before proceeding further. This type of presentation is the designer's tool and means of communication (Figure 4.24).

Francis Ching, a well known educator and author, points out that an effective presentation possesses several key characteristics:

- A vision or point of view: Ching says that a presentation "should communicate the central idea of a design scheme—graphic diagrams/abstractions/overlays are effective means of articulating the various aspects of a design scheme, especially when they are visually related to the more common architectural drawings."

FIGURE 4.21   Three-point interior perspective by Paul Stevenson Oles. Republic Bank Tower Proposal, Dallas, TX. Skidmore Owings and Merrill—Chicago, Architects. *(From Laseau, Paul, Architectural Representation Handbook, McGraw-Hill, New York)*

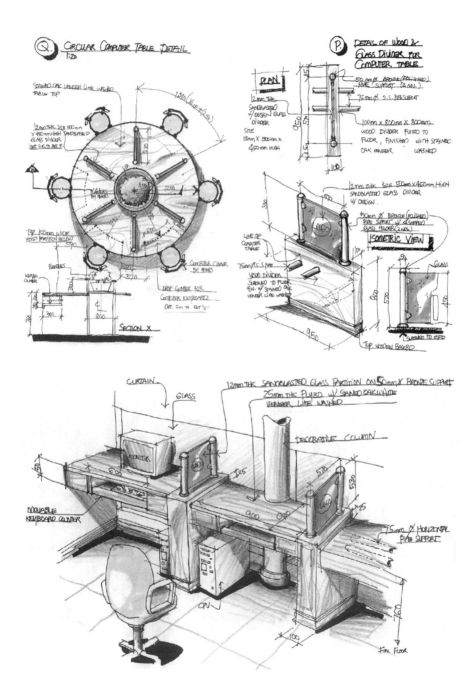

FIGURE 4.22 The use of freehand sketches in the development of design details. Note that the sketches are fully dimensioned (in metric) and annotated and could be used to manufacture the items.

Paul Laseau - Place des Vosges, Paris

Mohammed Bilbeisi- St. Paul's Cathedral, London

Brian Crumlish - Piazza di Spagna, Rome

FIGURE 4.23   Examples of freehand sketches by three different architects. *(From Laseau, Paul, Architectural Representation Handbook, McGraw-Hill, New York)*

Cabinet of Ministers design proposal - Reception Area

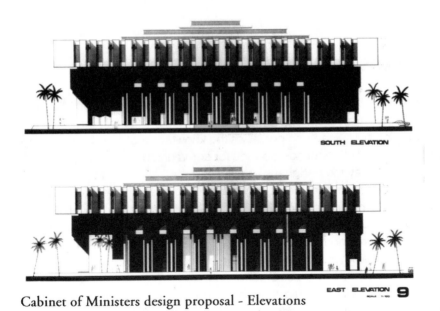

SOUTH ELEVATION

EAST ELEVATION **9**

Cabinet of Ministers design proposal - Elevations

FIGURE 4.24 Presentation can play a critical role in winning competitions and in convincing clients of the virtues of a design. The above design by the author won first prize in an international competition for the design of the Cabinet of Ministers complex in Abu Dhabi.

- *Unity:* Effective presentations are harmonious and have a unified and homogenous concept, with no individual part detracting from the whole. Sheet and board format should be uniform in size, and the color and texture of paper or board should be coordinated. Lettering and titles should be neat, appropriate, and consistent throughout.

- *Continuity:* "Each segment of a presentation should relate to what precedes and what follows it," says Ching, thereby reinforcing all the other segments of the presentation.

- *Efficiency and Economy:* "Less is More" is the famous phrase of Mies van der Rohe and it certainly applies to presentation techniques. Good presentations are organized in a logical and chronological way, for clarity as well as appearance. Boards should never appear crowded.

Such presentations assist clients in visualizing and understanding the design intent and solutions proposed. The participation of clients in the design process can be very beneficial. However, intelligent participation by the client can be achieved only if there is an in depth understanding of what is proposed. Design presentations vary considerably from one firm to another in their format and sophistication. Likewise, there are no set rules and the type of presentation chosen will depend on several factors including the size of the project, its purpose, and whether the targeted audience is a single individual, a board of directors, or a committee. One must also bear in mind that presentations are only a means to an end; they should not obscure the main objective, which is presenting the design concept.

RENDERINGS

Michael Doyle, in his book *Color Drawing*, says, "As buildings are built with the use of a variety of materials, so too can drawings of buildings—whether exteriors, interior spaces, or landscaped views—be built when one possesses the knowledge of how to draw these materials" (Figures 4.25, 4.26, 4.27). Renderings are tools for communicating and should therefore, clearly and accurately convey the designer's intentions.

Before a rendering is made, the designer should discuss with the relevant party (i.e. client, jury, or committee) what information needs to be shown and at what level of detail is required. This conversation would bring to light the specifics of the project, details as to whom the images will be shown, and most importantly why the images are needed. This information is invaluable as these elements affect what type of images to produce.

There are many types and styles of rendering, and successful renderings are executed in almost all of the different art media. The most popular are pencil, pen and ink, colored pencil, watercolor, gouache, tempera, acrylic, pastel, and charcoal pencil. Good renderings require considerable training and practice, as well as a basic understanding of perspective, color, shade, shadows and reflections. Increasingly, however, designers are moving towards digital graphics as a means to produce images. Small practices often prefer to employ professionals for their renderings, especially for important presentations. There are many excellent books on the subject, and the reader would be well advised to consult them.

BUILDING MODELS

Models typically fall into two main categories: the study model and the presentation model. The purpose of this chapter is more to give an overview of model making and their relevance to the space planning process than to explain in detail how they are constructed.

The study model is made to help clarify and define spatial relationships, as well as how a building project relates to the site. It is a creative tool and is made more quickly and with inexpensive materials.

Presentation models, on the other hand, are usually made for clients, juries or exhibitions. They may be simple or elaborate, but are nearly always meticulously constructed (Figure 4.28). The intention is to sell the project.

Models are normally seen below eye level, which in a way is unfortunate, because buildings are rarely seen that way. This gives a disproportionate emphasis on the roof area and upper parts of the model. To compensate for this, one needs to lift and rotate the model (when possible), to view it from different angles. Moreover, models are typically made to a specific scale that is determined by the project's size, and the model's purpose. For example, a block model may be constructed to a ¹⁄₃₂ inch (1:400) scale and would show little detail other than the overall form (Figure 29); a building may be constructed to ⅛ inch (1:100) scale, and a room to ½ inch (1:20) scale. The smaller the model's scale, the less specific detail that can be shown, and vice-versa.

Modelmaking Materials and Equipment

The materials and equipment needed would usually depend on the type of model to be constructed. Some professional presentation models may require specialized equipment, but for the average model, the following would be needed:

- Utility, craft and retractable blade knives, and hand-held board cutter and beveler.
- Metal ruler, scales and dividers.
- Triangles (30/60 degree and 45/90 degree) and circular templates.
- Adhesive—white glue, rubber cement or spray adhesive.
- Illustration board, poster (Bristol) board, foamcore (foamboard), balsa wood, basswood, and chipboard (pulpboard).
- Scaled objects, e.g. trees, vehicles, people, finishes (brick, stone, etc.).
- Miscellaneous materials, including paint, sandpaper, plastic (clear and colored).

Two proposals for Marriott Hotel in Abu Dhabi

FIGURE 4.25
Two renderings reflecting different architectural treatment for the same building which the author submitted to the Marriott Hotel Group for a proposed hotel in Abu Dhabi. Often the designer is required to submit more than one proposal.

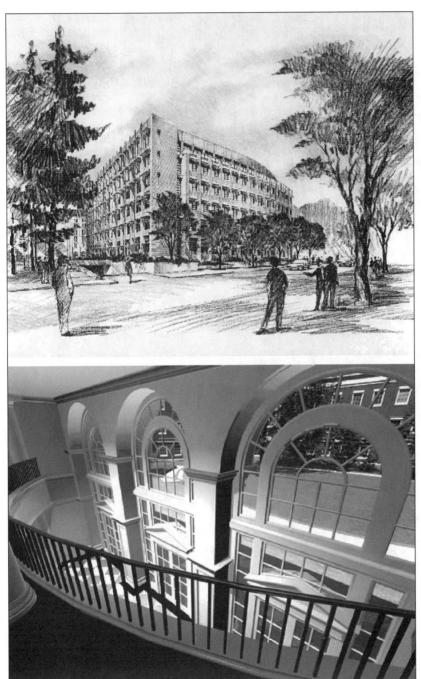

FIGURE 4.26
Two renderings reflecting different techniques. Upper rendering is the CSE Building, University of Washington. *(Courtesy Department of Computer Science and Engineering, University of Washington)* Lower rendering is of an interior stairway at Shelby Hall, University of Alabama. *(Courtesy of architects Hellmuth, Obata, and Kassabaum, Inc.)*

FIGURE 4.27
Upper illustration is to demonstrate interior lighting. *(Courtesy Crane Digital, Fort Collins, Colorado).* Lower rendering is of Marina Towers. *(Courtesy John Stuart Pryce)*

FIGURE 4.28
Examples of
professionally
made presen-
tation models.
*(Courtesy
Howard Mod-
els, Toledo,
Ohio)*

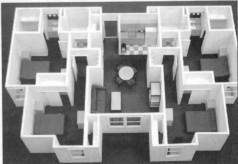

Top Model: Brooklyn, New York

Left Model: Daewoo Center, Poland

Right Model: Callaway House Dorms,
San Antonio, Texas

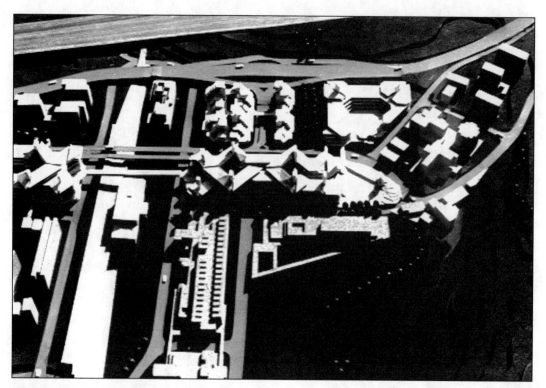

FIGURE 4.29 A simple block model by the author for a competition in Perugia, Italy. Balsawood was used for the proposed buildings, painted thin card for the roads, and cork for the site contours and existing buildings.

Most architectural models require a base; this represents the site or part thereof. With level sites, the model could sit on a flat piece of board with streets, pathways, people, landscaping and other features represented (Figure 4.30). With space planning models, the model may consist of floor layouts and therefore the site may not be shown, as the exterior walls depict the parameters of the model.

Contoured bases are more difficult to construct, depending on the complexity of the site's topography. Where the topography of a site is characterized by a gentle slope, the slope can be incorporated into the base. A site's slope refers to its rise (height in feet or meters) and its run (horizontal distance in feet or meters). This basically means that a site having a one-in-ten slope rises one foot to every ten feet of horizontal distance. There are several ways to construct sloping sites and these are shown in Figure 4.31. Complex contours can be built up of layers of illustration board, cardboard or other material that approximates the thickness, to scale, of the rise in contour. Thus, a ⅛ inch illustration board is the correct thickness for the con-

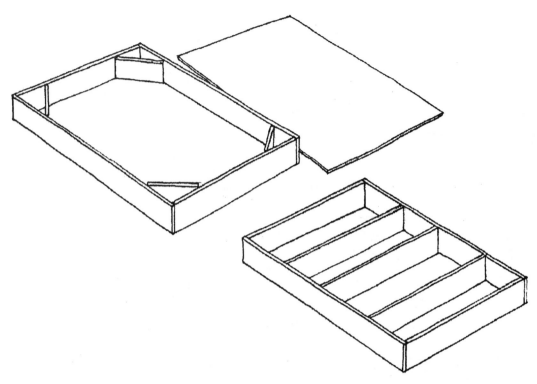

FIGURE 4.30 How to construct the base of a simple level site. *(From Martha Sutherland, Modelmaking: A Basic Guide, W.W. Norton and Company, Inc., New York, 1999)*

tours of a ⅛ inch = 1 foot scale model where the rise is in 1 foot increments or multiples thereof. Contour lines are generally labeled according to their elevation in feet (or meters) above sea level. The information is derived from topographical maps or from a survey.

To construct a contoured base you will need one or two copies of the original contour drawing printed to the required scale. These will then used as a pattern to construct the contours as shown in the illustrations. The base can be solid-core or hollow base type. In the solid-core type, contours are cut so that they cover the whole base behind the contoured edge. This arrangement gives maximum strength and does not require additional support underneath. The contour layers are essentially glued in place after being cut to the required patterns. The hollow base technique is sometimes used to minimize cost and reduce the model's weight, using much less material. This method of construction uses piers to support the contours as shown in the illustrations. Figure 4.32 is an example of a simple model that can be made by the designer.

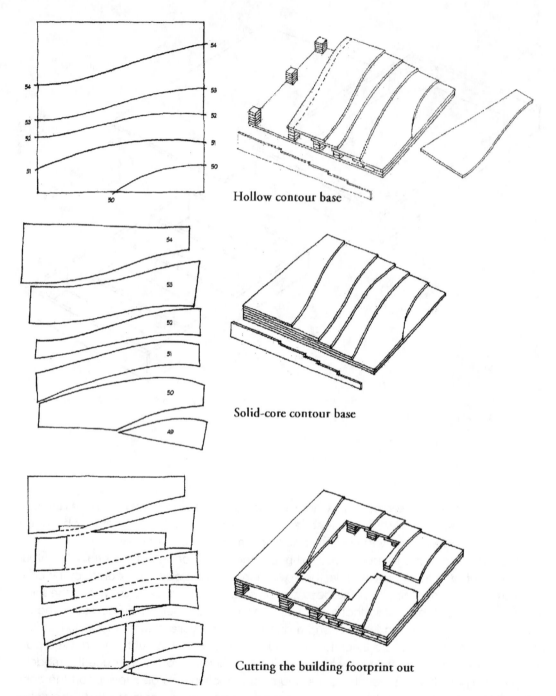

Hollow contour base

Solid-core contour base

Cutting the building footprint out

FIGURE 4.31   How to construct contour models. *(From Martha Sutherland, Modelmaking: A Basic Guide, W.W. Norton and Company, Inc., New York, 1999)*

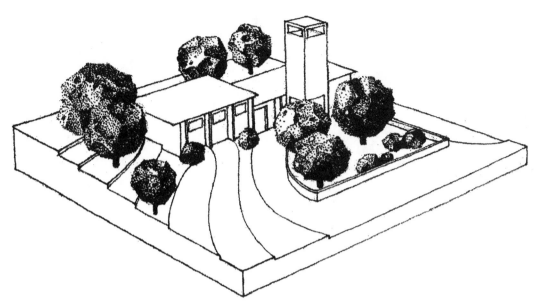

FIGURE 4.32 A simple model upon completion. *(From Martha Sutherland, Modelmaking: A Basic Guide, W.W. Norton and Company, Inc., New York, 1999)*

Entourage and Other Elements

The word *entourage* refers to almost everything excluding the land or the building itself, and can be realistic or abstract. Architects typically prefer abstraction to attain consistency and so as not to divert from the project's main focus, that of the building itself.

Trees and shrubbery are easy to make (or realistic looking miniature trees can be purchased to various scales and types at many crafts stores), depending on the model constructed. Sponge, cotton wool, styrofoam, and wire are the favorite materials. Figures and vehicles are useful elements in a model because they give scale and a feeling of movement. Again, the final choice depends on the model's scale and purpose. Other elements such as texture and changes in material (for example, grass as opposed to concrete or asphalt) can be achieved by the use of textured materials painted to the desired color, or plastic, mirror, etc. There are also numerous specialty papers that are printed to look like wood, stone, marble and water.

CHAPTER
FIVE

HUMAN,
SOCIAL, AND
PSYCHOLOGICAL
FACTORS

*O*ver the last few decades, there has been a serious push towards a user-orientated design approach that emphasizes human needs as much as aesthetics. Indeed, a lot has changed over the last few decades. Today's working environment is increasingly computer-driven, while office workers confront much greater complexity in their tasks. Added to this, we find workers are increasingly conducting their business from a home office, on the road, and on short-term projects in collaborative work environments.

GENERAL CONSIDERATIONS AND CORPORATE IMAGE

Many of today's offices and the furniture in them fail to reflect or fully support these evolving work styles and technologies. If we examine the root cause of increased employee absenteeism and turnover in today's workplace, we will discover a glaring link between worker satisfaction and job performance. At the same time, environment behavior researchers have also evidenced a direct correlation between worker satisfaction with their physical environment and their perception of the quality of worklife. Moreover, these studies clearly indicate that the physical environment of the office is a critical ingredient in job satisfaction and productivity.

The enormous new challenges facing corporate America in the new millennium, created by radically changing job requirements, among other things, necessitates not only a realignment of tasks, but also a social readjustment on the part of employees. This human response to new work strategies and evolving demands plays a pivotal role in a corporation's ability to compete viably in the global marketplace. Corporations by necessity are changing organisms, and the measure of their success hinges upon their ability to seamlessly adopt to the process of continual change. The bottom line, therefore, in determining the office set-up is to create a physical environment that fully supports these changes.

It has become prudent for today's space planners to benefit from the large body of research by social scientists to become acquainted with the psychological and anthropological implications of space and environment. This could also herald in a new, additional role as an environmental design researcher.

Traditionally, interior designers and space planners have maintained a one-to-one relationship with their clients. Now, the design professions suddenly find themselves thrust into an unfamiliar territory. Designers can no longer seek design solutions based on the traditional process—to understand and then design for the corporate culture—for today's needs and the projected life cycle of these institutions, but are now required to look at a company's profile from both the perspective of spatial problem-solving, as well as a social organization with particular needs that must enter into their design calculations (Figure 5.1). In the current global climate, where fastidious corporations and designers alike are seeking the competitive edge, increasingly more and more, designers are exploring and investigating the impact of these social issues on the design process and the proposed solution.

A workplace that looks inviting is vital in attracting and keeping people. Space planning is essentially based on the physical size of people and their physiological and psychological needs, and any final solution must reflect these needs.

ENVIRONMENTAL CONSIDERATIONS AND HUMAN COMFORT

Optimum comfort is subjective, and the criteria for achieving it varies from person to person and culture to culture. Nevertheless, these criteria are all interlinked and share basic environmental factors that include:

- Air temperature
- Relative humidity
- Air movement
- Sound and noise control
- Ventilation
- Thermal radiation and surrounding surface temperatures
- Sustainable building

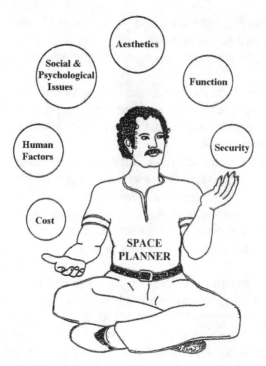

FIGURE 5.1 The space planner trying to juggle some of the many issues and disciplines that need to be considered for their impact on the design process.

Air Temperature

Our body's metabolism is fueled by the food we eat which in turn, produces heat that we need to dissipate at a certain rate to maintain our comfort level. Physical exertion increases the metabolic heat to be lost, whereas inactivity reduces it. We can lose heat in one of three ways: by convection (heat is transmitted by the flow of a liquid or gas), by radiation (transfer of heat energy through electromagnetic waves from one surface to a colder surface) and by evaporation (absorbed by perspiration). Air temperature is one of several primary factors that determine the sensation of thermal comfort (Figure 5.2).

Relative Humidity

Relative humidity is another important comfort parameter, and is defined as the percentage of moisture in the air compared with the maximum amount of moisture the air can hold at a

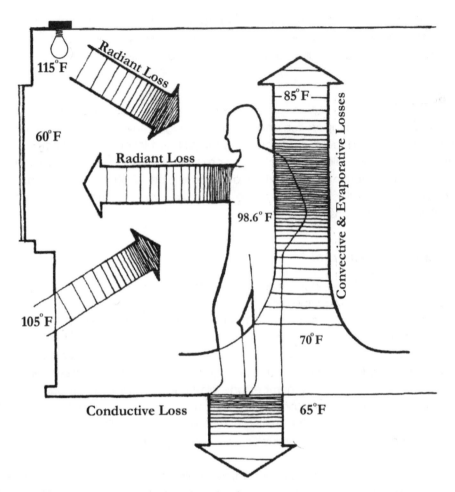

FIGURE 5.2 Types of heat loss and heat gain.

given temperature without condensing. High levels of humidity increase the discomfort levels in an overheated space. Esmond Reid in his book *Understanding Buildings—A Multidisciplinary Approach*, says, "In a cold room, dampness is an adverse factor in that it reduces the insulation of our clothes, albeit the effect is slight. More significantly, our ability to perspire relies on there being a vapor pressure drop between our skin surface and the surrounding air. At 21 degrees Celsius, 50 per cent RH would be comfortable but 80 percent would feel clammy." Comfortable relative humidity levels range between 30-65 percent, and tolerable ranges between 20-70 percent.

The above shows that relative humidity and our related ability to perspire and cool are highly significant in the overheated environments. This is why hot humid climates are much more uncomfortable and difficult to deal with than hot arid ones.

Air Movement

Air movement increases evaporation and heat loss through convection, reducing the comfort level in an under-heated room and increasing the comfort level in an overheated room. In rooms that are too warm, air movement would help maintain our comfort level by increasing the rate of heat convection from our skin and facilitating perspiration evaporation. This is why a breeze reduces the effective temperature, and makes you feel more comfortable under high temperature conditions.

Sound and Noise Control

As we witness the rapid disappearance of the traditional workplace, many companies are now scrambling to encompass the new trends that have emerged, such as downsizing, outsourcing and the open plan environment. This rapid transformation from a traditional closed office setting to an open plan office environment in corporate America has created new and unprecedented challenges for the space planner like the presence of increased noise that negatively affects worker productivity (Figure 5.3). In fact, some industry observers cite noise and poor office acoustics as the number one obstacle to improving productivity in open offices. Noise reduction relates, in part, to the emotional aspect of creating a comfortable, healthy and safe work environment. Limiting unwanted noise and distraction while increasing privacy helps improve employee productivity by creating a more comfortable work environment (Figure 5.4).

Trying to achieve an appropriate acoustical environment in buildings that have open offices can be a daunting challenge for the space planner. To successfully meet this challenge in achieving noise reduction, one needs to consider several aspects including:

1. Modifying floor plans to minimize auditory or visual distractions, and increase the amount of personal space.

2. The use of carpet, appropriate system furniture and ceiling systems to increase acoustics control and minimize conversational noise and other auditory distractions. The use of sound masking technology and equipment may also be required to prevent conversational speech from being a distraction in the work environment. Acoustical needs should be addressed according to the specific tasks to be performed in a particular area.

3. Design spaces to provide the appropriate level of privacy based on the task to be performed, even to the point of providing special rooms for tasks that involve increased concentration or confidentiality, and require the highest degree of privacy.

A professional paper from the ASID (and others), *Sound Solutions*, concludes that, "...properly designed offices—whether closed, open, or mixed plan—can be designed to support a broad range of individual and team workspace acoustical requirements. Such support requires attention to the mix and range of worker tasks, to the special needs of worker using advanced technology, to space planning issues, to the choice of architectural finishes and elements, to the choice of furniture elements, and to the ambient sound in the workspace." It goes on to say that, "The incorporation of appropriate strategies and products for reducing noise in the workplace will continue to be an important part of designing and creating work environments where productivity is supported and enhanced."

Ventilation

Although vital to breathing, the first consideration for ventilation is not providing oxygen and removing carbon dioxide. It is generally the needs for cooling and the removal of humidity, odors, and contaminants. The amount of ventilation required in a room or space depends on several factors, including the size of the room, its function, and whether people smoke in the room. For example, a bar (where smoking takes place) needs a higher ventilation rate than a library (where smoking is not permitted). Relevant building codes should be consulted as they stipulate the minimum ventilation requirements for different types of occupancy, typically by stipulating minimum operable window areas, and/or minimum mechanical ventilation and exhaust rates. Capacity is measured either in terms of fresh air circulated in cubic feet per minute, or for exhausting of air using mechanical systems, in terms of complete air changes per hour.

Mechanical systems are designed to filter and recirculate much of the conditioned air, and introduce a certain percentage of outdoor air along with the recirculated air. In situations where exhausting of air is required, such as in toilet rooms, kitchens, and places where noxious fumes are present, ventilation systems must exhaust directly to the outside; none of the exhausted air can be recirculated (Figure 5.5).

A toilet room exhaust fan, for example will be connected to a duct that leads to the exterior without connecting in any way to the building's ventilating system. Local building codes should always be referenced. Typical examples of the number of air changes per hour are: office floors 2-6; classrooms, 3-4; restaurants, 10-15; kitchens, 20-40. Public places such as auditoria and dance halls, are often measured in terms of the number of occupants to be served, 30 m^3/person/hour, for example.

Thermal Radiation and Surrounding Surface Temperatures

Radiation is the transfer of heat energy by electromagnetic waves, and therefore does not involve matter. All bodies emit radiation at various wavelengths, including those of visible light and heat. The intensity of radiant heat increases or decreases with the temperature of the

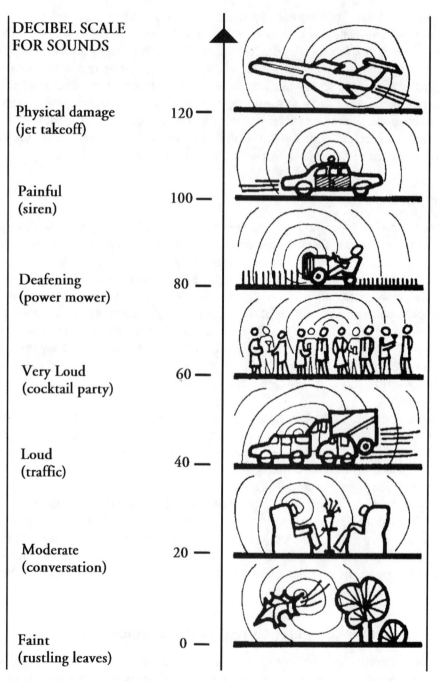

FIGURE 5.3 Decibel scale for noise levels. *(From De Chiara, Joseph, Panero, Julius, Time-Saver Standards for Interior Design and Space Planning, McGraw-Hill, New York, 2001)*

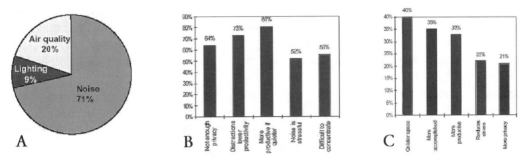

FIGURE 5.4 Graphs indicate: A) Contributing factors to workspace distractions overall. B) Workplace perceptions and attitudes. C) Workplace perceptions and attitudes after noise reduction techniques were implemented. *(From ASID, et al, Research Paper, Sound Solutions, 1996)*

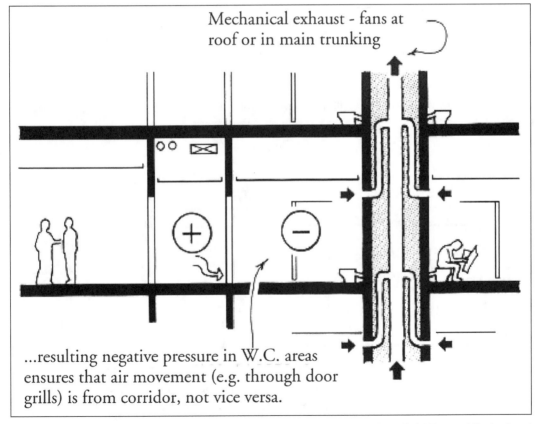

FIGURE 5.5 A typical mechanical extract and natural inlet application. *(From Reid, Esmond, Understanding Buildings—A Multidisciplinary Approach, MIT Press, Cambridge, Massachusetts, 1999)*

source. Surrounding surface temperatures affect radiant losses from, or gains to, the body. If the surrounding area is colder than the surface temperature of the skin (typically around 85 degrees Fahrenheit), the body will lose heat through radiation; if it is warmer, the body will gain heat. For example, cold windows will reduce the comfort level of a room that would otherwise be within the comfort zone.

The mean radiant temperature (MRT) reflects the value used to ascertain this aspect of comfort. The MRT is a weighted average of the temperatures of the different surfaces in a room or space, the occupant's angle of exposure to these surfaces, and quantity of sunlight present, if any. The MRT is an important factor in achieving a satisfactory comfort level in cold rooms and in the winter because as the air temperature decreases, the body's heat loss through radiation increases, and decreases by evaporation (Figure 5.6).

Sustainable Building

Demands for sustainable building are increasing, particularly in population centers suffering from environmental hazards where the most efficient building methods tend to concentrate. Firms like Hellmuth, Obata and Kassabaum (HO+K), Herman Miller, and Kone have taken an active leadership role in their respective professions to promote sustainable design. In addition, we now have the LEED (Leadership in Energy and Environmental Design) Green Building Rating System, giving us another powerful tool to help us face the growing environmental challenges that were ushered in with the new millennium. For a sustainable design strategy to succeed, it is necessary to demystify and simplify the process

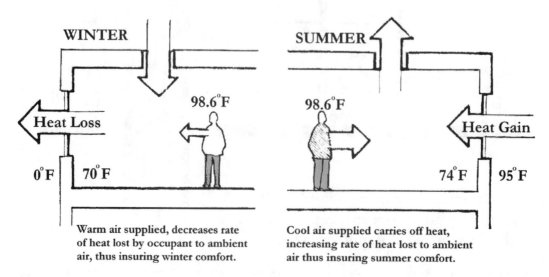

FIGURE 5.6 Heat flow during summer and winter seasons.

Sandra Mendler, coauthor of *The HO+K Guidebook to Sustainable Design*, has done this by developing a simple list of ten basic, yet fundamental, steps towards achieving a sustainable design strategy. They are:

1. *Designing for flexibility.* By designing in flexibility through the use of modular planning, future renovations can limit waste. Considering future needs and designing for ease of expansion also conserves resources.

2. *Maximizing the use of natural daylight.* Develop space planning to maximize access to natural light, avoid closed spaces such as walled offices at the perimeter. Consider light colored finishes to maximize daylight distribution. Specify internal shading devices at windows that contribute to energy-efficiency and daylighting strategies.

3. *Setting high lighting efficiency standards.* You can dramatically reduce energy use with high efficiency lamps, reflectors, and ballasts, a combination of task and reduced ambient lighting, and smart controls such as occupancy sensors and daylight dimming. Specify light-emitting diodes (LED) exit lights. Incorporate daylight in building interiors as a source of ambient light.

4. *Designing for good indoor air quality.* Ventilation rates are determined by the design of the base building HVAC system however, interior designers should explore opportunities to upgrade systems where necessary to meet current standards. Develop space planning to isolate potential sources of contamination such as print rooms and food service areas. Carefully select building materials to limit the introduction of pollutants into the building (see #5).

5. *Reusing existing materials, use less materials, and specify environmentally responsible building materials.* Evaluate life cycle environmental impacts to select environmentally preferable options. Specify quantifiable improvements such as low VOC requirements, minimum recycled content, and avoidance of toxic materials and/or admixtures. Consider use of refurbished furniture, carpet, and systems furniture instead of new.

6. *Specifying energy-efficient and water saving appliances.* Encourage the use of EPA Energy Star copiers, fax machines, computers, and printers. Specify energy and water efficient dishwashers and refrigerators.

7. *Using water efficient plumbing fixtures.* The minimum standard should be the low-flow fixture requirements that appear in the 1993 Energy Policy Act. Use of aerators and self-closing or electronic faucets for lavatories can further reduce water usage.

8. *Designing for ease of maintenance and the use of environmentally friendly cleaning products.* Select materials that are low maintenance and that have compatible maintenance requirements. Consult with cleaning specialists during the design process to develop a plan for future cleaning procedures that use non-toxic, low VOC cleansers. Accommodate needs for proper storage of chemicals and equipment.

9. *Making room for building recycling facilities.* Provide facilities for recycling at the point of use on each floor (e.g. galleys and copy rooms). Consider the use of recycling chutes in multi-story buildings. Common recyclables are white paper, newspaper, glass, aluminum and plastic. Other potential recyclables include cardboard, mixed paper, and organic waste (food and soiled paper). Staging areas need to be provided at the loading dock and a compactor for cardboard may be desirable.

10. *Recycling demolition and construction waste.* During demolition recycle steel studs, metal from ceiling grids, ductwork, metal frames, doors, and carpet. Salvage cabinets, plumbing fixtures, hardware, and equipment by donating them to Habitat for Humanity or other local nonprofit. Use construction waste specification that mandates recycling of concrete, wood, metals, plastic containers, and cardboard and encourages recycling of other materials.

LIGHTING

Light is a fundamental element in architecture and interior design. While 80 percent of our impressions of the world are visual, 100 percent of those impressions are dependent on light and, therefore, lighting. Lighting serves two primary objectives—illuminating a task and creating a mood. It is an essential ingredient to establishing a comfortable interior environment because nearly all office tasks are visually oriented. While people typically prefer natural lighting because of its soft and changing qualities, artificial lighting is unfortunately the norm for most workers. Also, it should not be assumed that all lighting is fundamentally the same. Too many facility managers make this fundamental error. Lighting that is ideally suited for white-paper tasks in an office space, is totally different from the lighting needed to perform computer tasks within the same space.

Research has shown that the cumulative effects produced by working in an uncomfortable lighting environment can significantly impact performance in a negative way. Furthermore, the unique challenges created by computers in the workplace, has inspired the Illuminating Engineering Society of North America (IESNA), and the American National Standards Institute (ANSI), to combine their efforts to develop an industry Recommended Practice (RP) lighting standard for offices with computers or other video display terminal (VDT) systems. By focusing on ways to make lighting more effective, building owners can reduce energy costs, increase safety and do much more.

Natural Light—Daylight

Daylight encompasses all natural light that is available during the day and originates from the radiation of the sun in the visible spectrum. What we perceive as light is the visible portion of the electromagnetic spectrum (consisting of a very narrow band of electromagnetic energy), ranging from approximately 380 nanometers to 770 nanometers. Only wavelengths in this range stimulate the human visual system (receptors in the eye that permit vision). These wavelengths are called *visible* energy, even though we cannot actually see the energy. When a light source emits radiant energy that is relatively balanced in all visible wavelengths, it appears white in color.

The main reason that we continue to incorporate natural light in modern buildings is because we find it comforting and it increases our psychological well-being. This is true even though natural light is less predictable and more difficult to control than artificial light. Very often, natural light will be used to supplement artificial light particularly in adverse climatic conditions and in the evenings. Where natural light is the prime source of day-time lighting, it will inevitably influence a building's shape and orientation. Designers of large buildings must consider the building's plan depth and its ramification on light penetration. Space planners should normally consult with a lighting and environmental engineer, particularly when designing a building of more than one story in height.

Artificial Light

Gary Gordon , a lighting consultant, says that, "The initial step in planning light for a space is to establish an appropriate emotional environment for the activity that will take place there. Lighting can affect impressions of spaciousness, relaxation, privacy, intimacy, and pleasantness; it can produce a festive, carnival-like atmosphere or a quiet place for contemplation (Figure 5.7); it can create cold, impersonal public spaces and warm, intimate, private ones. Light can have a strengthening or reinforcing effect in creating a suitable psychological setting, similar to that provided by background music."

The second step in the lighting design process is to estimate the amount of light required for the activity that will take place in a given space. Gary Gordon says that in general, "The light needed for visibility and perception increases as the size of details decreases, as contrast between details and their backgrounds is reduced, and as task reflectance is reduced." Our visual perception of space depends upon both incident light and surface finish. When designing a lighting system, therefore, it is essential to understand the impact and ramifications of reflected light (Figure 5.8). Color perception is yet another factor important to the appraisal and performance of a visual task. Color characteristics of light can significantly alter a person's perception of an object.

In lighting design, we use the color temperature of lamps to categorize them as warm, neutral or cool sources. The terms are not directly related to temperature; instead, they describe how the light source appears visually. The color temperature of the lamp will affect the visual appearance not only of the lamp itself, but more importantly, objects in the room. Lamps with a warm color temperature, for example, produce light that is saturated with red and orange wavelengths, producing a richer appearance of red and orange objects and lending a reddish tint to whites, while darkening blues and greens.

FIGURE 5.7 The Golden State Museum, Sacramento. Lighting helps establish an appropriate emotional environment for the activity that is to take place, and can affect impressions of spaciousness. *(Courtesy Gallegos Lighting Design, Los Angeles)*

Craig DiLouie, a lighting consultant, says, "Warm light sources are traditionally used for applications where warm colors or earth tones dominate the scene, and where we want to impart a feeling of comfort, coziness and relaxation. Applications include the home, restaurants, lobbies, and private offices. Neutral light sources are traditionally used for applications where we want to enhance all colors equally, such as supermarkets and stores. Cool light

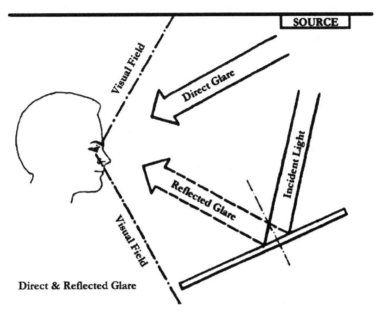

FIGURE 5.8 Direct and reflected glare.

sources are traditionally used for applications where we want to enhance blues or stimulate the occupant to alertness and activity, such as offices and hospitals."

For illuminance, ANSI/IESNA recommends a maximum of 50 foot candles (500 lux) of general lighting on the work plane for areas combining paper and screen-based tasks. When the work load consists mainly of screen-based tasks, or where supplemental task lighting is provided for paper-based work, then lower general illuminance may be acceptable.

In a workplace environment, glare can be minimized by correctly positioning the monitor in relation to the space's light sources. Most current guidelines recommend placement of monitors at right angles to windows and also perpendicular to linear light sources, such as fluorescent tubes. Glare can also be controlled by using a polarizing filter attached to either the screen or the light source.

Artificial Light Sources

There are three basic types of artificial light sources, they are: incandescent, fluorescent, and high-intensity discharge. In addition, to the three basic types of lighting, we have neon and cold-cathode lamps.

Incandescent Lighting

Incandescent lamps are the oldest and most popular light source because of their low cost, rich color rendering (which complements and flatters the complexion), and wide range of sizes and wattage (Figure 5.9). In addition, they are easily dimmed, giving them a longer lamp life. Halogen lamps are a particular type of incandescent lamp that is filled with gas. The gas allows it to burn with a greater intensity and a whiter light.

Tungsten-halogen is a type of halogen lamp that is energy-efficient, is smaller in size, has a long life, and maintains its bright-whiteness throughout its life. They come in standard voltage (120) and low-voltage lamps. Low voltage incandescent lamps (they require a transformer), are increasingly being used. They have the advantage over standard incandescent lamps because they are smaller, have a more precise beam (bulbs come in spot and flood form), and a whiter light.

Fluorescent Lighting

Fluorescent lamps are generally far more efficient than standard incandescent lamps and last 10-20 times longer. Most fluorescent lamps are white when not lighted, and variations in their phosphor composition produces differences in the color of emitted light. Essentially, two degrees of whiteness are possible in a space illuminated with fluorescent lamps: cool lamps are compatible with the environmental effect of daylight, and warm lamps produce an atmosphere similar to that associated with incandescent lamps.

Fluorescent lamps have lower wattage rating than incandescents because they are designed to consume less electricity. Moreover, they light as brightly as incandescents, because their light output (in units Lumen) is equal to incandescents. With the advent of improved color-rendering characteristics, the use of fluorescent lighting in domestic applications has increased dramatically. Likewise, recent industry developments in fluorescent lighting fixtures now completely eliminate glare by redirecting it away from the viewer's eye level to offer a more comfortable and more attractive work environment.

High-Intensity Discharge Lighting

High-Intensity Discharge (mercury lamps, metal halide, or high sodium) lamps (HID) is the generic term for a family of lighting types that are more lumen-efficient than either incandescent or fluorescent, and produce peaks of energy at specific wavelengths. The clear mercury lamp produces a very cool white light of predominantly blue and green energy. The lack of energy at the warm (red) end of the spectrum results in particularly poor color rendering qualities.

Metal halide lamps are similar in construction to mercury lamps, except that various metal halides have been added. These halides produce additional wavelengths that increase the mercury lamp's spectral distribution, resulting in a whiter light and truer color rendering than the mercury lamp.

Neon and Cold Cathode Lighting

Physically, neon and cold cathode lamps are equal in all aspects except size. But while a lighting system's primary purpose is to generate a high amount of light efficiently, a neon sign's main function is to transmit a message via light. Neon and cold cathode lamps can be formed into an unlimited number of shapes, which is why they are used for signage and specialty accent lighting. Many people associate neon solely with signage and, therefore, rarely realize that cold cathode or "big tube" neon, is a versatile light source that's used in numerous applications (Figure 5.10).

Today, even as new lighting solutions offer lighting designers an increasing number of system options, neon remains a popular choice, particularly when it comes to nightlife. It offers an endless array of shapes, colors and animation possibilities, and lighting engineers and electric-sign companies continue to search for new and innovative ways to apply this lighting medium to commercial applications. Modern cold cathode systems utilize lamps which provide beautiful and quite, seamless lighting effects, dimming illumination for indirect illumination, long life and a wide array of colors and high color rendering shades of white.

Fiber Optic Lighting

Fiber optic lighting is another option that offers new opportunities for creativity, design and application. Exciting atmospheres and particular special effects can be produced as well as functional and technical solutions. Essentially, you start with a light source (sun, light bulb, etc.) The fiber optic wire is then placed in front of the light source and light is conducted through the fiber optic wire and carried anywhere you wish it to. The intensity and glow of the actual fixture depends on the wattage of the bulb and the amount of fiber in the wire going to the fixture. The possibilities are almost infinite.

Furthermore, unlike standard lighting, fiber optic lighting enables you to change the color of light without changing light bulbs. A simple flicking of the switch will rotate a color wheel (which is located between the light source and the fiber optic wire) and change the color of light in the fixtures, without the need to change any light bulbs. Using multiple light sources will give you more options than a single light source.

There are possible applications in every area of lighting, from showcases to interior and exterior lighting. Also, as fiber optic lighting components transmit light (instead of electricity), there is no risk of fire or electric shock. Furthermore, light conducted by fiber-optic cables is dust-free, does not contain any ultraviolet rays, does not generate heat, and has no visible lighting elements because the light box is hidden.

Another benefit of fiber optic lighting, in addition to the wide variety of design and safety, is its long maintenance. Problems associated with the changing or servicing of lamps in light sources in inaccessible locations do not arise when fiber optics are used. The light source can be located in an easily accessible place where it can power a great number of lightpoints. Still, there is only one lamp to replace if needed.

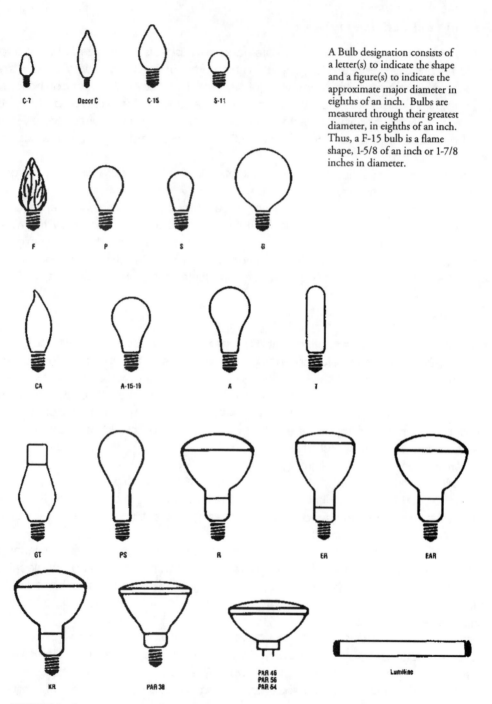

A Bulb designation consists of a letter(s) to indicate the shape and a figure(s) to indicate the approximate major diameter in eighths of an inch. Bulbs are measured through their greatest diameter, in eighths of an inch. Thus, a F-15 bulb is a flame shape, 1-5/8 of an inch or 1-7/8 inches in diameter.

FIGURE 5.9 Types of incandescent lamps.

FIGURE 5.10 The use of cold cathode lighting in a municipal building in Toronto, Ontario. *(Courtesy Cathode Lighting Systems Inc., Maryland)*

Types of Lighting

Lighting designers wield considerable leverage and power over how a space is viewed by choosing the right light source. Placement and position of light sources depend to a large degree on the direction and distribution of the light decided upon. A light scheme can dramatically alter the visual perception of surface textures and sculptural form. Lighting can be classified into several types, depending on its function. These include the following:

- Task or local lighting provides the right level of illumination for specific surfaces or areas for a wide range of visual tasks or activities, from reading and writing to making-up and shaving. The task light source is usually placed in close proximity to the task surface (either above or beside), enabling the available wattage to be used more effectively than with general lighting. For example, in general living areas, task lighting could be provided by a table or floor lamp. In domestic kitchens, task lighting is needed at the counter, the sink, and the stove. Often, task lighting is combined with general (ambient) lighting for greatest efficiency.

- Ambient or general lighting illuminates a room in an overall, generally uniform manner. The dispersed quality of the illumination can effectively reduce the contrast between tasking lighting and the surrounding surfaces of a room. Ambient lighting is furnished in most positions of a space by the reflections of light directed to the walls and furnishings. It also helps bring the various sections of a space together, by softening shadows, smoothing out and expanding the corners of a room, and providing a comfortable level of illumination that allows ease of movement and general maintenance.

- Accent light is a form of directional local lighting used to create focal points, by emphasizing a particular object, draw attention to a specific part of a space, or create rhythmic patterns of light and dark within a space. Accent lighting is often used to relieve the monotony of general lighting, as well as adding drama to a space.

Lighting Fixtures

Lighting fixtures are usually categorized by how individual fixtures (luminaries) are mounted (Figure 5.11). These include the following:

- Suspended or pendant fixtures relate to luminaires dropped below the level of the ceiling. They vary widely in design, price and the quality of light they produce. Some diffuse light evenly in all directions, while others (depending on the shade used) are directional, and tend to direct light downwards. Often they are mounted on rise and fall fixtures. These can include direct incandescent or fluorescent fixtures, chandeliers, track lighting, and other types of specialty lights. Fixtures should be located far enough below the ceiling to allow for the proper spread of light to bounce off the surface. Designers sometimes use pendant mounting to put the source of light closer to the task area where the ambient light is insufficient. Sometimes, designers use suspended specialty fixtures for strictly aesthetic reasons.

- Freestanding fixtures help to raise the general level of illumination as well as provide local task lighting for reading or other activities. Floor lamps are the most common type of freestanding light fixture. These are available in countless styles and sizes and can be custom designed and manufactured if needed (say to a particular design for a hotel or restaurant). Freestanding lights that direct most of their output to the ceiling are called torchières.

- Wall mounted fixtures also come in a variety of styles, are adjustable or nonadjustable, and can provide indirect, direct-indirect, or direct lighting. However, they are best used for directional lighting, reflecting light off ceiling or walls, and for lighting objects, or surfaces. For general illumination, sconces can be used to direct most or all the light toward the ceiling. Sconces are often used as decorative elements as well as light sources. Cove lighting is another form of wall mounted fixture that can be mounted near the ceiling and will indirectly light either the ceiling or the wall depending on how it is designed.

- Accessory lighting fixtures includes table lamps and neon lights and are intended mainly for decorative lighting rather than for task or ambient lighting. They too are available in an almost unlimited number of styles and shapes.

- Furniture-mounted lighting is typically used with task ambient systems, in which the lights are built into the furniture as part of the design, or alternatively, furniture mounting fixtures are utilized. In both cases, they are normally mounted above the work surface to provide adequate task illumination, with uplighting being provided by lights either built into the upper portions of the furniture or as freestanding elements.

ANTHROPOMETRICS

The famous Greek mathematician Pythagoras once wrote that, "Man is the measure of all things." This was restated many years later by Euclid in a mathematical formula, and later illustrated by Leonardo Da Vinci in the 15th century with a diagram of a man's body inside a circle and square, and became known as *The Golden Rule* (Figure 5.12). Indeed, if an object, an environment or system is intended for human use, then its design should be based on the characteristics of its human users. This is where anthropometrics comes in.

Anthropometrics is the branch of ergonomics that deals with measurements of the physical characteristics of human beings, particularly their sizes and shapes. A large amount of research has been conducted over the last few decades that has established the range of human dimensions from foot length to shoulder width. These dimensions have been established for a variety of population groups, ages, and sex, and include percentile distributions showing what percentage of the population falls within various measurement limits.

We also now have at our disposal a large body of knowledge relating to the minimum or optimum dimensions needed for a human being to perform general activities. Widths of rooms, heights of shelving, and clearances around furniture are examples of dimensions that are set by space planners and interior designers and which must relate to the physical sizes, needs, and limitations of people (Figures 5.13 through 5.16). The fallacy of the "Average Man" has clearly been established, and depending on the nature of the design problem, the solution should normally be conceived to accommodate the 5th or the 95th percentile, thereby allowing the greatest segment of the population to be served.

Track Lighting   Ceiling Fixture   Recessed Low Voltage   Recessed Fixture

Wall Mounted Fixture   Aquarium Lamp   Pendant Light   Pendant Track Lighting

Ceiling Mounted Fixture

Picture Light   Tiffany Lamp

Torchiere Floor Lamp   Mini Accent Light   Landscape Lighting   Floor Lamp

FIGURE 5.11 Various types of light fixtures.

πάντων χρημάτων
μέτρον ἄνθρωπος

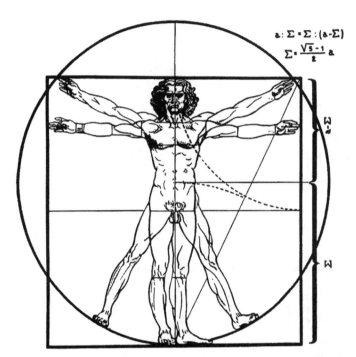

FIGURE 5.12   "Man is the measure of all things." *(From Panero, Julius, Anatomy for Interior Designers, Whitney Library of Design, New York, 1977)*

When planning for accessibility, the space planner should also take ADA factors into consideration such as the attitude at which the wheelchair approaches the desired object. The reach limits for frontal and side reach should be plotted, and elevation targets representing the maximum height at which controls requiring manual dexterity should likewise be located (Figure 5.17).

ERGONOMICS

Ergonomics is the science of making the work environment safer and more comfortable for workers using design and anthropometric data. It is basically a user-centered approach that

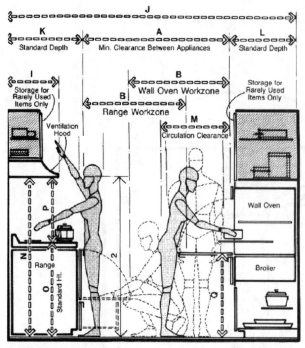

RANGE CENTER

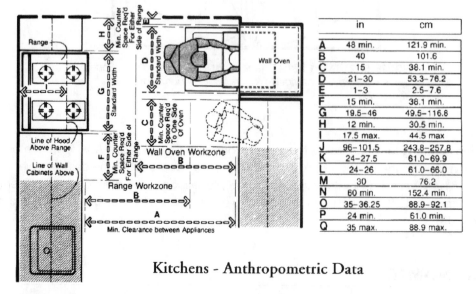

	in	cm
A	48 min.	121.9 min.
B	40	101.6
C	15	38.1 min.
D	21–30	53.3–76.2
E	1–3	2.5–7.6
F	15 min.	38.1 min.
G	19.5–46	49.5–116.8
H	12 min.	30.5 min.
I	17.5 max.	44.5 max
J	96–101.5	243.8–257.8
K	24–27.5	61.0–69.9
L	24–26	61.0–66.0
M	30	76.2
N	60 min.	152.4 min.
O	35–36.25	88.9–92.1
P	24 min.	61.0 min.
Q	35 max.	88.9 max.

Kitchens - Anthropometric Data

FIGURE 5.13 Anthropometric data—kitchen clearance dimensions. *(From De Chiara, Joseph, Panero, Julius, Time-Saver Standards for Interior Design and Space Planning, McGraw-Hill, New York, 2001)*

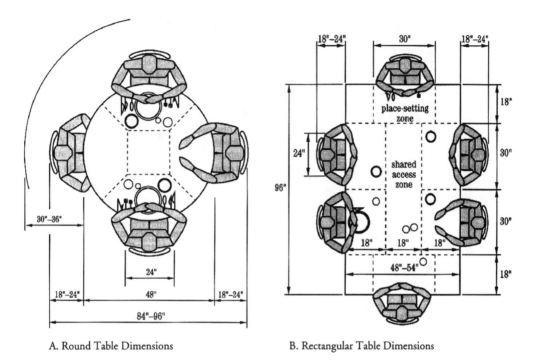

A. Round Table Dimensions   B. Rectangular Table Dimensions

FIGURE 5.14 Minimum dimensions needed for dining. *(From Ballast, David K., Interior Design Reference Manual, Professional Publications, Inc., Belmont, California, 1998)*

aims to ensure that people's capabilities and limitations are taken into account, and to fit the workplace to the worker, rather than vice versa. Ergonomics also studies the relation between human physiology and the physical environment, emphasizing the importance of the interaction of all component parts, which is why it is sometimes called Human Factors. Ergonomics uses the information developed by anthropometrics, and then applies it in studying how humans interact with physical objects like chairs, tables, control panels, and the like, to ensure that the product is fit for use by the target users. As the American workforce continues to get older, ergonomic needs become even more critical. David Gilmore et al make the point that human factors research requires:

1. Demands together with the technological requirements.

2. The boundaries between which issues are defined as "technical" and "organizational" are not fixed and need to be negotiated.

3. New applications of technology should be seen as the development of permanent support systems and not one-off products which finishes with implementation (i.e. the way in which technological change alters the organization needs to be considered).

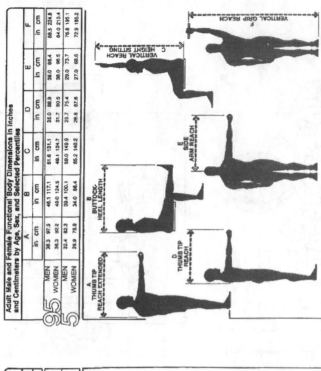

Adult Male and Female Functional Body Dimensions in Inches and Centimeters by Age, Sex, and Selected Percentiles

	A		B		C		D		E		F	
	in	cm	in	cm	in	cm	in	cm	in	cm	in	cm
95 MEN	38.3	97.3	46.1	117.1	51.6	131.1	35.0	88.9	39.0	88.4	88.5	224.8
95 WOMEN	36.3	92.2	49.0	124.5	49.1	124.7	31.7	80.5	38.0	96.5	84.0	213.4
5 MEN	32.4	82.3	39.4	100.1	59.0	149.9	29.7	75.4	29.0	73.7	76.8	195.1
5 WOMEN	29.9	75.0	34.0	86.4	55.2	140.2	26.6	67.6	27.0	68.6	72.9	185.2

A THUMB TIP REACH EXTENDED B BUTTOCK-HEEL LENGTH C VERTICAL REACH SITTING D THUMB TIP REACH E SIDE ARM REACH F VERTICAL GRIP REACH

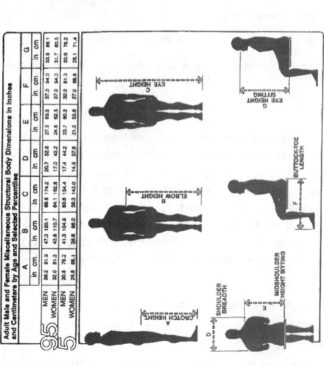

Adult Male and Female Miscellaneous Structural Body Dimensions in Inches and Centimeters by Age and Selected Percentiles

	A		B		C		D		E		F		G	
	in	cm	in	cm	in	cm	in	cm	in	cm	in	cm	in	cm
95 MEN	36.2	91.9	47.2	120.1	68.6	174.2	20.7	52.6	27.3	69.3	37.0	94.0	33.9	86.1
95 WOMEN	32.0	81.3	43.6	110.7	64.1	162.8	17.0	43.2	24.6	62.5	37.0	94.0	31.7	80.5
5 MEN	30.8	78.2	41.3	104.9	60.6	154.4	17.4	44.2	23.7	60.2	32.0	81.3	30.0	76.2
5 WOMEN	26.8	68.1	38.8	98.0	56.3	143.0	14.9	37.8	21.2	53.8	27.0	68.6	28.1	71.4

A CROTCH HEIGHT B ELBOW HEIGHT C EYE HEIGHT D SHOULDER BREADTH E MIDSHOULDER HEIGHT SITTING F BUTTOCK-TOE LENGTH G EYE HEIGHT SITTING

FIGURE 5.15 Anthropometric data relating to the 5th and 95th percentiles for men and women. *(From De Chiara, Joseph. Panero, Julius. Time-Saver Standards for Interior Design and Space Planning. McGraw-Hill, New York. 2001)*

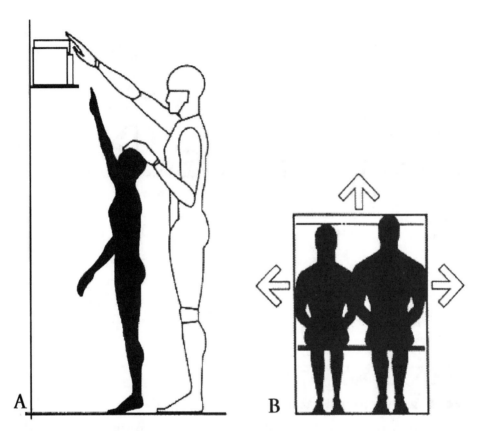

FIGURE 5.16 A. Persons of smaller body dimensions and therefore, within the lower-range percentile data should be used to determine dimensions where reach is the determining factor. B. For larger-size persons, the high percentile range data should be used in establishing clearance dimensions. *(From De Chiara, Joseph, Panero, Julius, Time-Saver Standards for Interior Design and Space Planning, McGraw-Hill, New York, 2001)*

4. Humans should be seen as the most important facets of an information systems and should be "designed in."
5. The people context of information systems must be studied and understood for it is clear that dimensions such as gender, race, class, power affect people's behavior with respect to technologies.
6. Design by doing, user participative design.

Recently promulgated ergonomic regulations and standards by the U.S. Government's Occupational Safety and Health Administration (OSHA) are designed to significantly impact workplace injury awareness and safety. The main objective for the standards, which took

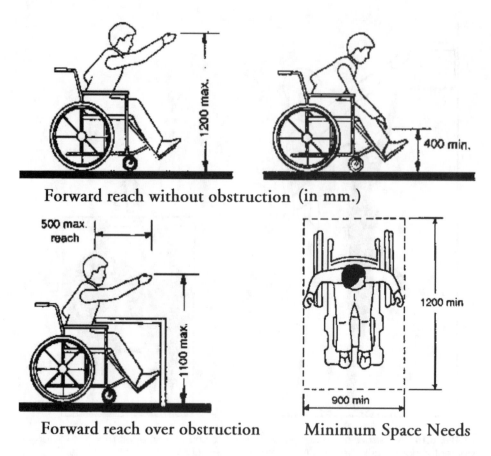

Forward reach without obstruction (in mm.)

Forward reach over obstruction   Minimum Space Needs

FIGURE 5.17 A. Establishing dimensions where reach is the determining factor, people of smaller body dimensions and, correspondingly, the lower range percentile data should be used. B. Establishing clearance dimensions, larger-size people and correspondingly, the high percentile range data should be used. *(From De Chiara, Joseph, Panero, Julius, Time-Saver Standards for Interior Design and Space Planning, McGraw-Hill, New York, 2001)*

effect January 16, 2001, is to regulate work-related musculoskeletal disorders (MSDs) ranging from lifting, pulling and pushing to computer keyboarding and mousing. MSD is the term used to describe a variety of physical conditions including back pain, neck tension and carpal tunnel syndrome. Judy Leese, senior ergonomic program manager at Herman Miller says that, "Although OSHA has not set specific standards for office workstations, assembly lines and other work areas, the new rules take affect whenever injuries can be connected to the workplace." Several leading office furniture manufacturers, like Herman Miller and Haworth, market ergonomically oriented products including seating, height-adjustable tables and other computer support products and accessories.

The issue of proper posture by computer users is not complex, nor difficult to achieve. The feet should rest flat on the floor, with the knees bent at a 90 degree angle. The upper body should be bent 90 degrees relative to thighs. Hands on the keyboard should form a straight horizontal line from the wrists to the elbows, which in turn should be bent 90 degrees relative to the upper arms. In the sitting position, the top of the computer monitor should be roughly 15 degrees below eye level, and at a distance approximately twice the width of the screen. Thus, if a 15-inch cathode ray tube monitor is about 11 inches wide in viewable area, the required distance is 22 inches (Figure 5.17).

The reality is that cost and its justification has always been a major factor in the decision on whether to proceed or not with ergonomic improvements to the work environment. It should be noted that the cost of correcting ergonomic design at the initial part of a design project is estimated to be approximately 10 percent of the cost that will be incurred later. Moreover, the steps involved in the cost justification process should be an integral part of the design process, and are:

- Predicting potential injuries/illness. This requires monitoring and reviewing past medical records/OSHA logs to look for patterns and to determine how many MSDs occurred over the last year or years.

- Estimating the full cost of an injury/illness. Again this may not be straightforward and means tracking medical expenses, workers' compensation, and other indirect costs such as productivity loss.

- Achieving the appropriate ergonomic solution and estimating its cost. There are several approaches to determine the cost effectiveness of a solution, but one of the more popular methods used by ergonomists is the cost/value matrix, which fundamentally compares the cost of the solution with the effectiveness of the solution, based on their empirical and professional experience.

- Choosing the appropriate cost justification technique. The three techniques that are most often used to cost justify ergonomic changes in the work environment are based on: 1. Benefit/Cost Ratio (comparing the cost of ergonomic-related injuries to the cost of implementing the ergonomic solution), 2. Payback Period (the length of time it will take to recover the costs of improvements), and 3. Losses vs. Goods Sold (the sales volume that is needed to offset the cost of an injury; this provides a dollar figure that the firm should be willing to spend to implement an ergonomics solution).

- Performing the calculations to evaluate the value of the benefits and costs over the life of the project, taking into consideration the reduced liability risks the company will enjoy by addressing the ergonomic issues.

- The final step in the process is the analysis of the above data and making a recommendation.

Dr. Teresa Bellingar, corporate ergonomist at Haworth, Inc. says that, "Until companies start realizing what affect ergonomic-related injuries have on the bottom line, it will remain difficult for some companies to justify spending money to make changes in the work environment—even if they believe it's the correct thing to do."

PSYCHOLOGICAL AND SOCIAL SETTINGS

Innovative space planning and interior design should offer solutions that enhance communication and teamwork, support business processes and improve staff welfare and morale. Indeed, well-designed interior spaces should respond to the psychological, social and physical needs of the people using them. Often, a basic understanding of these human needs are easily determined and action taken to achieve a design solution. In other cases the particular needs are determined during the programming process by identifying the precise needs of the users.

There has been much research in the field of environmental psychology, in an effort to predict human behavior and designing spaces that enhance people's lives. But even though environmental psychology is not an exact science, designers and space planners should attempt to develop a realistic model of both the people who will be using the designed environment and the nature of their activities. This model can then serve as the foundation on which to base many design decisions. The following concepts are some of the more common psychological and social influences that impact the design process.

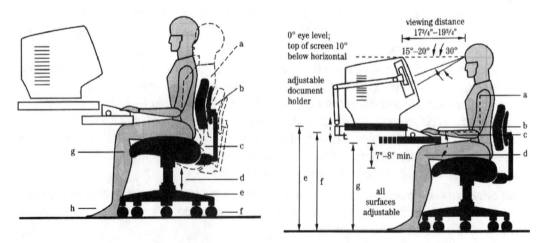

FIGURE 5.18   a) Chair design criteria for workstations. b) Computer workstation dimensions. *(From Ballast, David K., Interior Design Reference Manual, Professional Publications, Inc., Belmont, California, 1998)*

Behavior Settings

Seven trends within the changing workplace have been identified that are expected to place a greater emphasis on human behavioral adaptation in the future. These are:

- Continuous technological advances will facilitate the creation of diverse human work behaviors.
- Socialization will be a prime organizational objective in the future.
- Tacit knowledge sharing, team and communities of practice will grow.
- With information becoming increasingly available, learning and the pursuit for knowledge will increase.
- Maintaining people emotionally connected to each another will be one of the major challenges for organizations in the new millennium.
- Emotional intelligence will be an important quality in attaining competency for leadership.
- Human relationships will play a greater role in achieving business success.

Proxemics and Territoriality

Edward T. Hall, an anthropologists and the father of proxemics, states that this branch is particularly important for interior designers because it seeks to identify the hidden rules governing the use of space and the unstated rules of distancing and screening for different activities like talking, working, or making love. Hall observed that there are specific distances used by humans in their transactions with other human beings, and that these distances vary from culture to culture. He further states that there are four zones of territorial distance, which determine how near or far from others we wish to be in a given situation (Figure 5.19). These distances are:

- Intimate Distance (close phase and far phase): This invisible sphere extends about 1½ feet (45 cm) out from our bodies. This reflects the distance in which we can touch and be touched and is reserved for our most intimate relationships; when others invade this zone, we tend to back away.
- Personal Distance: can either be close—1½ feet (45 cm) to 2½ feet (about 75 cm)—or far—to 4 feet (about 1.20 m)—phases. The close phase is still for special relationships; while the far phase is a bit more formal and is used for conversations of personal interest and involvements.
- Social Distance: is also divided into close—4 to 7 feet (1.2 to 2.1 m)—and far—7 to 12 feet (2.1 m to 3.6 m)—phases. These phases are normally used for impersonal business: the close phase usually reserved for those we work with; the far phase for others.
- Public Distance: According to Hall, "Several important sensory shifts occur in the transition from the personal and social distances to public distance, which is well outside the circle of involvement."

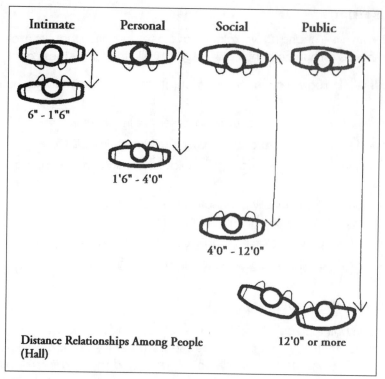

FIGURE 5.19 Distance relationships among people. *(From De Chiara, Joseph, Panero, Julius, Time-Saver Standards for Interior Design and Space Planning, McGraw-Hill, New York, 2001)*

These distances are generally applicable to "non contact middle-class Americans" and less to cultures whose population traditionally like contact, such as Latin Americans, Middle Easterners, and Pakistanis. It is also unlikely to apply to young children. Casual and friendly conversations usually take place at closer distances, without fixed barriers; the executive's sofa area, the cafeteria, and hallways are all places where personal distance is possible. Understanding the concept of territorial distances and their existence should increase our capacity to design buildings and spaces that work, as the advantages and/or restrictions of the setting often determines the tone of the involvement.

Another area where territorial distance should be considered is in the conference room. Conference rooms are frequently designed to fit the conference table, without adequate consideration to the number of potential users. Where rectangular tables are used, the greater the territorial distance between the head person and others, the more formal the conference will be. Where a company wants maximum participation in a meeting, the group should be limited to seven members or less, preferably seated at a round table, 60 inches in diameter. When attendance consists of more than seven members, participation dialogue becomes concentrated among a few.

Personalization

People will almost always consciously or unconsciously modify the space they use. David Ballast points this out and says, "One of the ways territoriality manifests itself is with the personalization of space. Whether it happens in one's home, at the office desk, or in a waiting lounge, people will often arrange the environment to reflect their presence and uniqueness. The most successful designs allow this to take place without major adverse effects to other people or to the interior as a whole." By entering a person's home, you almost immediately get a glimpse of their personality. In the office, you almost always find personal family photos and other personal items—whether on the CEO's desk, or the typist. The measure of a design's success is how well it adapts to its users.

Group Interaction

Environment is an important factor in human interaction and can be either conducive to it or hinder it. Groups are generally predisposed to act in a particular way, and if the setting does not facilitate the activity, they will either modify it or try to adapt to it to make it work. Where the setting is totally incompatible with the activity, stress and other adverse reactions will result.

Seating arrangements are typically used to facilitate group interaction. People usually seat themselves at a table in a manner compatible with the nature of the relationship of those around them. Figure 5.20 shows three classical seating positions around a table. Position (a) indicates the existence of intimacy, whereas position (b) suggests formality, and possible competition. Position (c) on the other hand, indicates a lack of desire for contact, by the avoidance of direct eye contact.

When considering seating arrangements, it has been found that round tables tend to promote greater cooperation and equality among those seated around them. Rectangular tables are more suitable for formal settings and larger groups, where the senior person usually sits at the end as this is considered a more superior position. Also, group interaction studies show that for spaces designed for informal activities, it makes more sense to use tables that will accommodate say, four persons than large tables designed for larger groups. A fundamental understanding of the basics of group interaction will assist the space planner in achieving the right solutions.

Status

Status has been an important design consideration from prehistoric times, and in many cultures today, the physical environment still holds much symbolism. Some people like houses in certain

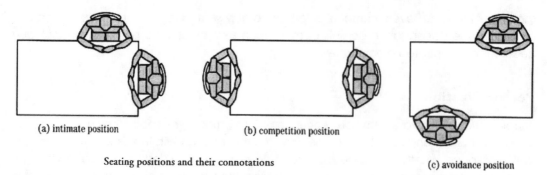

(a) intimate position   (b) competition position

Seating positions and their connotations

(c) avoidance position

FIGURE 5.20   Distance relationships—table seating. *(From Ballast, David K., Interior Design Reference Manual, Professional Publications, Inc., Belmont, California, 1998)*

styles because that reflects status. Marble floors and walls have traditionally indicated status (this may be partially due to the fact that it is so expensive), which is why it is often used in banks and prestigious offices and some custom homes. Status is also expressed in other inexplicable ways. For example, in the United States and many European countries, a corner office carries more status with it than one in the middle of a string of offices. In many cultures office size is also equated with status, with the desk located as far from the door as possible. This gives the person behind the desk greater psychological authority. It is up to the designer to investigate the requirements and implications of status and determine what the goals of the client are in this respect.

Color Psychology

Color can be used decoratively, symbolically, or therapeutically, and designers should not under-estimate the psychological effect of color on human beings. Laboratory tests as well as practical experience clearly indicate the existence of radiant energy in color. This radiant energy force can affect our health and happiness. It can generate a sense of well being or discomfort, vigorous activity or subdued passivity.

Color scientists have known for some time that colors can make a space appear stimulating or depressing, warmer or cooler. Certain colors like green are found to be relaxing, while others, like red, invigorate and excite, while still others can create anxiety, irritation and physical discomfort. B.J. Kouwer says, "Color perception is not an art involving only the retina and 'consciousness' but the body as a totality."

Color preference gives us a clue to a person's personality. Persons with an easy going personality are likely to prefer simple colors; those with a complex and discriminating personality will probably show a greater preference for subtlety. Taylor Hartman, author of *The Color Code* says, "Personality is not black and white. Personality is a kaleidoscope," and "Some people see the world through rose-colored glasses. Others see it through dark glasses."

Hartman believes that your personality determines whether you are easily depressed, casual, formal, careful, or carefree, and whether you are passive or assertive. Furthermore, studies have shown that normal persons with extrovert personalities are generally quite fond of color, particularly the warmer hues, whereas persons with introvert personalities lean towards the cooler colors of the spectrum. They are also, generally, less responsive to color.

Many tests have been undertaken to determine how people react to certain colors. The heart beat, blood pressure and respiration were measured under different colored rays of projected light. We also know that color can make an object appear heavier (using dark or strong colors) or lighter (using weak colors).

In his book, *Color and Human Response*, Faber Birren, a well-known color theorist, discusses various ways the human brain responds to color, and these are outlined below:

Biological Response

The area of the electromagnetic spectrum that is visible runs the gamut from red through orange, yellow, green, blue, and violet. In the main, there are different biological reactions to the two extremes of the spectrum, red and green or blue, and according to Dr. Thomas R.C. Sisson, "Light does not merely lend illumination to human existence but exerts a powerful physical force, affecting many compounds within the body, some metabolic processes, the life and generation of cells—even the rhythms of life. Light is ubiquitous, it can be manipulated, and it is not entirely benign." Many scientists have now concluded that environmental light can penetrate the mammalian skull in sufficient quantity to activate photoelectric cells imbedded in the brain tissue, which makes light essential to living a healthy and normal life.

While light is essential to human existence, so too are rhythms of light and dark. Lightness and darkness cause different physiological actions in the body, such as a change in body temperature. In humans, Birren says that, "red tends to raise blood pressure, pulse rate, respiration, and skin response (perspiration) and to excite brain waves. There is noticeable muscular reaction (tension) and greater frequency of eye blinks." Blue, on the other hand, has a reverse effect, lowering blood pressure and pulse rate. The green segment of the spectrum is roughly neutral. Reactions to orange and yellow are similar to reaction to red, but less pronounced.

Visual Response

Artificial environments today often expose people to unbalanced light sources. Incandescent light is almost completely lacking in ultraviolet wavelengths. Some mercury sources, rich in ultraviolet, lack red and infrared frequencies. Clear mercury lighting is unsuitable for domestic and the office because of the distortion of colors in an environment and the unflattering appearance of the human complexion. James P.C. Southall wrote, "Good and reliable eyesight is a faculty that is acquired only by a long process of training, practice and experience. Adult vision is the result of an accumulation of observations and associations of ideas of all sorts and is therefore quire different from the untutored vision of an infant who has not yet learned to focus and adjust his eyes and to interpret correctly what he sees. Much of our young lives is unconsciously spent in obtaining and coordinating a vast amount of data about our environment, and each of us has to learn to use his eyes to see just as he has to learn to use his legs to walk and his tongue to talk."

Glare is inimical not only to clear vision, but to physical, mental, and emotional comfort, and over a period of time can aggravate muscular imbalance, refractive difficulties, nearsightedness, and astigmatism. The eye is generally quick in adjusting to brightness, and slow in adjusting to darkness.

Emotional Response

Research in the field of psychology is always difficult, and often subject to dispute. Kurt Goldstein, a researcher writes, "One could say red is inciting to activity and favorable for emotionally-determined actions; green creates the condition of meditation and exact fulfillment of the task. Red may be suited to produce the emotional background out of which ideas and action will emerge; in green these ideas will be developed and the actions executed."

There are strong emotional relation ships between color and music, and many have written about it. In experiments conducted in Germany, it was found that colors that stimulated alertness and creativity (light blue, yellow, yellow-green, and orange), could raise a person's IQ by as much as 12 points.

Aesthetic Response

Man's early use of color was not essentially concerned with aesthetics, but more with symbolism, and our current attitude towards color as an aesthetic tool dates more or less from the Renaissance. It is interesting to note that about eight percent of men have some color deficiency in vision, but less than one-half percent of women. The usual deficiency is to red or green or both. Brown and olive green, for example, may look the same.

Psychic Response

Psychic response deals mainly with emanations, visible and invisible, with auras, the astral body, corona discharge, bioplasma body, and with modern terms such as electrodynamics, psychotronics, and biodynamics, which have become matters of serious scientific investigation and popular exploitation, but which are outside the scope of this work.

CHAPTER SIX

PROJECT COST ANALYSIS

*C*ost estimating is one of the most important aspects of project management, as it determines the base line of the project cost at different stages of development. Establishing a budget early in the programming or design process can be critical to the project because it influences many of the design decisions and assists in deciding whether the project is even feasible.

GENERAL OVERVIEW

Building projects are typically developed with a ceiling placed on construction costs. The cost may be a fixed limit of an amount predetermined from the beginning, as with public buildings financed from appropriations or bond issues. Alternatively, the ceiling may be established during the design development phase when the scope of the client's program as well as the quality of construction, equipment, and materials are considered relative to the amount of money he is willing or able to spend. This approach requires that anticipated costs schedules be prepared at various intervals. These schedules function as economic controls in balancing the three interdependent factors of scope, quality, and cost. Both methods put a high premium on accuracy on the estimates produced by the space planner, architect, and engineer.

During the early phases of design development, preparing a prebid cost estimate with a high degree of precision is usually very difficult to achieve. The reason for this is that market and competitive forces in the industry at the time of bidding are major factors in determining the level and quality of proposals received. Because of this uncertainty, a bidding contingency should be established whenever a fixed limit of cost is put in as a condition of the professional services contract or when such a limit is implied by a final estimate agreed on by client and space planner or designer prior to calling for bids. Although the amount allocated for the bidding contingency will vary depending on the circumstances, it is not often less than 10 percent of the estimate. The percentage of contingency can be reduced upon establishment of a definitive estimate based on the quotations received from the contractors.

It is also important that the extent of the space planner's responsibility be defined when no bids are received within the costs limits specified for the project. Many contracts incorporate a provision that require consultants, at their own expense, to revise the plans and specifications so that an acceptable facility may be built within the cost limitations initially set out. In private work, such a provision would stipulated that such services are the limit of the consultant's responsibility in this connection and that upon completion of the revised design and documents the consultant will be entitled to the fees established in the professional services contract.

FACTORS THAT INFLUENCE PROJECT COSTS

There are a number of important factors that influence a project's final cost, not just construction costs and furnishing expenses (Figure 6.1). The client often prepares a budget that includes anticipated cost schedule. Below are some of the major elements that will impact the projects final costs.

Construction Costs

- *Building Type:* The type of occupancy is considered one of the major cost variables. It defines what features the building is likely to have. For example, a townhouse has entirely different cost characteristics from a hospital. The usual basic classifications are 1. Residential, 2. Commercial, 3. Industrial, 4. Educational, 5. Institutional, 6. Religious, 7. Recreational. These classifications in themselves are of little value if we are using the cost per square foot method to arrive at our costs (Figure 6.2).

- *Building Complexity:* A building's complexity is an important factor in its total final cost. A warehouse will obviously cost much less than, say, a biometric research facility. Likewise, the complexity or otherwise of a building's exterior and interior elements can have a detrimental impact on its overall cost. Curves, recesses, and cantilevers add to a building's cost. Building systems also vary depending on their complexity or simplicity. For example, a complex cladding exterior wall system will cost more than a simple stucco finish (Figure 6.3).

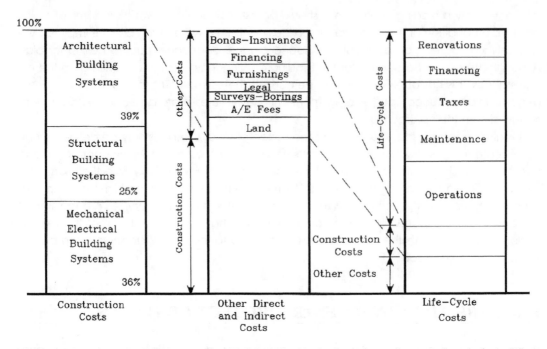

FIGURE 6.1   Diagram illustrating the various elements that typically make up the overall cost of a building.

- *Building Quality:* The quality of building materials and systems will greatly impact building cost. Marble is more expensive than brick or stucco. Certain types of mechanical systems are more costly than others. The aesthetic quality of a building's design also impacts its value (Figure 6.4).

- *Building Size and Shape:* Obviously, all things being equal, the larger the building's size, the more it will cost to construct. However, economies of scale can reduce costs for larger projects, resulting in a lower unit cost. Unit cost is also reduced when there is repetition. For example, it is cheaper to build a row of 15 townhouses than it is to build two. A building's size is determined by estimating the net square feet required to satisfy predetermined requirements and criteria. Also, the ratio of net square feet to the gross square feet needed to enclose them is a design decision and can significantly impact the overall construction cost. Low-rise buildings utilize different types of foundations and construction and mechanical systems than high-rise buildings, which in turn impact the overall costs in different ways (Figure 6.5).

- *Building Location:* There are numerous site and location factors that directly impact the cost of construction. The size and shape of the site, its topography, soil, geology, and climate are obvious physical factors that affect the cost of construction. Irregularly shaped sites may require special consideration when designing or during construction. Steep slopes as well as those with poor soil or unstable geology conditions will typically require more engineering and foundation work, as well as additional utility service connections for the structure. Both direct and indirect construction costs are also affected by location. An identical building constructed in different regions (or different countries) will have differing costs due to variations in the costs of labor, material and services in each locality (Figure 6.6). For example, cost of materials for a dense urban area may be higher due to traffic and site storage limitations.

- *Other Factors:* There are numerous other factors that impact construction costs, including: productivity, weather conditions and season of year, safety requirements, environmental considerations, availability of adequate energy, skilled labor and building materials, etc.

17100 | S.F., C.F. and % of Total Costs

		17100 | S.F. & C.F. Costs		UNIT	UNIT COSTS			% OF TOTAL			
					1/4	MEDIAN	3/4	1/4	MEDIAN	3/4	
010	0010	**APARTMENTS** Low Rise (1 to 3 story)	R17100 -100	S.F.	45.50	57	76				010
	0020	Total project cost		C.F.	4.08	5.40	6.70				
	0100	Site work		S.F.	4.08	5.70	9	6.80%	11%	14.10%	
	0500	Masonry			.84	2.21	3.62	1.50%	4%	6.50%	
	1500	Finishes			4.79	6.25	8.05	9%	10.70%	12.90%	
	1800	Equipment			1.48	2.19	3.25	2.70%	4%	6.20%	
	2720	Plumbing			3.50	4.55	5.75	6.70%	9%	10.10%	
	2770	Heating, ventilating, air conditioning			2.26	2.78	4.09	4.20%	5.80%	7.70%	
	2900	Electrical			2.62	3.43	4.68	5.20%	6.70%	8.40%	
	3100	Total: Mechanical & Electrical		▼	9.05	11.55	14.50	16%	18.20%	23%	
	9000	Per apartment unit, total cost		Apt.	42,000	64,000	95,500				
	9500	Total: Mechanical & Electrical		"	7,900	12,600	16,500				
020	0010	**APARTMENTS** Mid Rise (4 to 7 story)	R17100 -100	S.F.	59	72	88				020
	0020	Total project costs		C.F.	4.71	6.50	8.90				
	0100	Site work		S.F.	2.41	4.78	8.60	5.20%	6.70%	9.10%	
	0500	Masonry			4.01	5.55	7.85	5.90%	7.60%	10.60%	
	1500	Finishes			7.60	9.70	12.30	10.50%	13.10%	17.70%	
	1800	Equipment			1.98	2.83	3.70	2.80%	3.50%	4.70%	
	2500	Conveying equipment			1.37	1.68	2.06	2%	2.30%	2.70%	
	2720	Plumbing			3.54	5.65	6.30	6.30%	7.40%	10%	
	2900	Electrical			4.16	5.70	6.60	6.70%	7.50%	8.90%	
	3100	Total: Mechanical & Electrical		▼	12	16.25	19.95	18.80%	21.60%	25.10%	
	9000	Per apartment unit, total cost		Apt.	68,000	80,500	133,500				
	9500	Total: Mechanical & Electrical		"	12,600	15,100	19,100				
030	0010	**APARTMENTS** High Rise (8 to 24 story)	R17100 -100	S.F.	68.50	82.50	101				030
	0020	Total project costs		C.F.	5.80	8.15	9.90				

FIGURE 6.2 Part of a table giving square foot and cubic foot costs for different building types. In the *Building Construction Cost Data for 2002* by RS Means, there are 59 separate categories for costing buildings.

Top: South Pointe I Office Building, Herndon, Virginia, HOK Architects
Bottom: Montpelier II Offices, Columbia, Maryland, Morgan Gick & Asso, Architects.

FIGURE 6.3   Two different types of building envelope are illustrated. The building in the top illustration will cost more than the one in the lower illustration. *(Courtesy Inspection and Valuation International, New York)*

ONE STORY AVERAGE

LOW

SQUARE FOOTAGE	1500	1750	2000	2250	2500	2750	3000
COSTS							
FRAME	39.99	39.19	38.39	38.19	37.23	36.28	35.90
INTERIORS	41.80	40.97	40.13	39.92	38.92	37.92	37.53
OVERHEAD & PROFIT	9.09	8.91	8.72	8.68	8.46	8.24	8.16
TOTAL	$90.88	$89.06	$87.24	$86.79	$84.61	$82.44	$81.58

MEDIUM

SQUARE FOOTAGE	1500	1750	2000	2250	2500	2750	3000
COSTS							
FRAME	43.98	43.11	42.23	42.01	40.95	39.90	39.49
INTERIORS	45.98	45.06	44.14	43.91	42.81	41.72	41.28
OVERHEAD & PROFIT	10.00	9.80	9.60	9.55	9.31	9.07	8.97
TOTAL	$99.97	$97.97	$95.97	$95.47	$93.07	$90.69	$89.74

HIGH

SQUARE FOOTAGE	1500	1750	2000	2250	2500	2750	3000
COSTS							
FRAME	45.98	45.06	44.14	43.91	42.81	41.72	41.28
INTERIORS	48.07	47.11	46.15	45.91	44.76	43.61	43.16
OVERHEAD & PROFIT	10.45	10.24	10.03	9.98	9.73	9.48	9.38
TOTAL	$104.51	$102.42	$100.33	$99.81	$97.30	$94.81	$93.82

FIGURE 6.4 The quality of building materials and systems can have a significant impact on the final cost of a project as depicted in this table for an average one story dwelling. *(From Home Builder's Costbook, Bni Building News)*

S.F. & C.F. Costs | R171 | Information

R17100-100　Square Foot Project Size Modifier

One factor that affects the S.F. cost of a particular building is the size. In general, for buildings built to the same specifications in the same locality, the larger building will have the lower S.F. cost. This is due mainly to the decreasing contribution of the exterior walls plus the economy of scale usually achievable in larger buildings. The Area Conversion Scale shown below will give a factor to convert costs for the typical size building to an adjusted cost for the particular project.

Example: Determine the cost per S.F. for a 100,000 S.F. Mid-rise apartment building.

$$\frac{\text{Proposed building area} = 100,000 \text{ S.F.}}{\text{Typical size from below} = 50,000 \text{ S.F.}} = 2.00$$

Enter Area Conversion scale at 2.0, intersect curve, read horizontally the appropriate cost multiplier of .94. Size adjusted cost becomes .94 x $72.00 = $67.70 based on national average costs.

Note: For Size Factors less than .50, the Cost Multiplier is 1.1
For Size Factors greater than 3.5, the Cost Multiplier is .90

The Square Foot Base Size lists the median costs, most typical project size in our accumulated data and the range in size of the projects.

The Size Factor for your project is determined by dividing your project area in S.F. by the typical project size for the particular Building Type. With this factor, enter the Area Conversion Scale at the appropriate Size Factor and determine the appropriate cost multiplier for your building size.

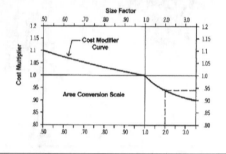

FIGURE 6.5　Square foot project size modifier illustrating the impact of size on the overall cost of a building. *(RS Means Company, Inc., Building Construction Cost Data, 2002)*

Most costbooks in the United States use costs that represent national averages. However, costs will vary from region to region, and state to state. In order to more closely approximate the probable costs for specific locations, a location factor is used. Below is a typical example from a Home Builder's Costbook.

Geographic Cost Modifiers

ALABAMA			FLORIDA			LOUISIANA	
BIRMINGHAM	0.79		JACKSONVILLE	0.80		BATON ROUGE	0.84
HUNTSVILLE	0.77		MIAMI	0.86		LAKE CHARLES	0.82
MOBILE	0.81		ORLANDO	0.80		MONROE	0.78
MONTGOMERY	0.75		TAMPA	0.82		NEW ORLEANS	0.86
TUSCALOOSA	0.75		WEST PALM BEACH	0.84		SHREVEPORT	0.78
			GEORGIA			**MAINE**	
ALASKA			ATLANTA	0.83		AUGUSTA	0.85
ANCHORAGE	1.30		AUGUSTA	0.75		BANGOR	0.83
JUNEAU	1.33		COLUMBUS	0.75		LEWISTON	0.87
FAIRBANKS	1.37		MACON	0.77		PORTLAND	0.89
NOME	1.43		SAVANNAH	0.79			
						MARYLAND	
ARIZONA			**HAWAII**			ANNAPOLIS	0.92
FLAGSTAFF	0.91		HILO	1.31		BALTIMORE	0.90
PHOENIX	0.89		HONOLULU	1.25		HAGERSTOWN	0.88
PRESCOTT	0.91		MAUI	1.28		ROCKVILLE	0.95

FIGURE 6.6　Construction costs of identical buildings located in different regions will vary. When estimating, this should be taken into account.

Furniture, Fixtures, and Equipment (FF&E)

On the majority of building projects, the furniture, fixtures and equipment (FF&E) budget is separate from the construction budget. This is because the method by which they are specified, purchased, and installed differs from that of construction items. Some of the items that normally form part of the FF&E budget include:

- Furniture
- Appliances
- Accessories
- Artwork
- Rugs and mats
- Interior plants and planters
- Free-standing equipment (e.g. vending machines and library bookshelves)
- Window coverings
- Lamps

Contractor's Overhead and Profit

The contractor is entitled to add a reasonable amount for overhead and profit when bidding a job. This could be submitted as part of the bidding procedure. Overhead and profits could be listed as a separate work item and proportionally billed each month to progress as the job proceeds. Alternatively, it can be submitted using a front end loaded schedule of values (this means raising the values of work performed early in the job and lowering the values of work done later).

Professional Fees

Space planners and professional consultants deliver a service to a client for a fee, and unenlightened clients may at times look at professional fee arrangements with a jaundiced eye. Professional fees for other consultants involved in the project may include architects, interior designers, mechanical and electrical engineers as well as legal, testing and others.

While there is no hard-and-fast rule on calculating a consultant's fee for services rendered, there are four methods or approaches that are used most frequently. These methods have been developed over time to satisfy the many conditions under which buildings are designed. The four approaches are:

- Percentage of construction costs
- Professional fee plus expenses
- Multiple of direct personnel expense
- Fixed fee (lump sum)

Taxes

Taxes can be defined as charges levied upon persons or things by a government. There is a legal obligation to pay taxes associated with owning property or earning income. Taxes that need to be considered include sales tax paid on furniture and other purchased items. Some jurisdictions collect taxes on professional services, in which case the space planner would normally include such tax in the professional fees category. Should it be necessary to appear as a separate line item, it can be placed under taxes. The general contractor and the subcontractors are required to pay taxes on materials used in construction and these are included in the total construction budget.

Moving Costs

A fair percentage of clients prefer to include moving costs in their total building budget. Moving costs are comprised of monies needed to physically relocate and may also include miscellaneous items like the cost to reprint stationery and downtime caused by the move. In the case of large companies and certain types of organizations such as medical facilities, moving costs can be substantial.

Telephone, Data Systems, and Security Equipment Installation

As telephone and data systems (computers, local area networks, and the like) are purchased separately and installed by specialty companies, the costs for these systems should be kept separate. Frequently, the client will coordinate these items separately without involving the space planner. However, the designer may need to coordinate the work with the suppliers of these services to provide space for equipment, proper location of outlets and conduit, and other required mechanical and electrical support services.

Insurance, Bonding, and Permits

Insurance policies are policies that guarantee compensation for losses from a specific cause. There are various types of insurance cover including against fire, flood, earthquake, liability, etc. The owner is responsible for purchasing and maintaining owner's liability insurance, boiler and machinery insurance, and property insurance.

Bonding is an agreement insuring one party against loss by actions or defaults of another. A performance bond, also known as a completion bond, is given by a contractor and issued by an insurance company to guarantee the completion of contracted work. Public authorities often require a performance bond prior to granting a contract for work to be completed. Performance bonds for contractors and subcontractors are typically issued by insurance companies. The owner has the right to stipulate that the contractor furnish a performance bond and payment bond, both in the full amount of the contract. Such bonds should be incorporated into the contract sum. If the bond requirement is imposed after the contract sum has been determined, the premium will be added to the contract sum.

A permit is a document, issued by a government regulatory authority, which allows the bearer to take some specific action, such as constructing a house. It is important that the work of the contract does not start prior to the effective date of all insurance and bonds or prior to the imposition of lenders' liens. Furthermore, all governmental approvals and permits must be in place prior to commencement. After these preliminary essentials are in place, the owner should give written notice to the contractor to commence construction.

Contingency Fund

A contingency fund is money set aside for possible loss due to unforeseen conditions that may arise during construction. A contingency should always be added to the budget to account for unforeseen changes by the client and other conditions that will add to the total cost of the job. For an early project budget, the percentage of the contingency should be higher than contingencies applied to later budgets, because there are more unknowns at the beginning of a project. The amount of allocated contingency depends on the type of project but normally ranges from 5 to 10 percent of the total budget. Renovating older structures typically requires a higher contingency than building a typical low-rise office building, for instance. You may also have a separate contingency for construction and one for furniture, fixtures and equipment.

METHODS OF ESTIMATING

There are numerous methods to develop a preliminary budget and estimate for the cost of a project. But one must remember that cost estimates are just that, *estimates*. Bids usually received for the construction of a project, and based on identical contract documents, will vary in price by 5 to 10 percent and sometimes more. One approach to the classes of estimates is shown in Figure 6.7.

The Square Foot or Comparative Method

The square foot or comparative method directly compares a building of known cost with the proposed building. Construction costs are reduced to an average cost per square foot of floor area (a cubic foot is sometimes used). By definition, a square foot estimate, due to the limited amount of detail required, involves a relatively lower degree of accuracy than a more detailed unit price based estimate. However, square foot costs make a useful starting point and are useful in the conceptual stage of a project when there is a lack of details. Square foot estimates are also useful after the bids are in and the costs can be worked back into their

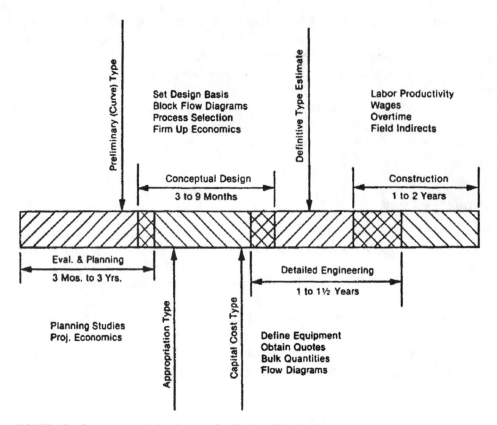

FIGURE 6.7 One approach to classes of estimates (timeline).

appropriate units for information purposes. The square foot approach should be discontinued, however, once details become available for the project design, as the project can then be priced according to its particular components.

For an estimate based on this method to be useful, the building used as the cost basis must be similar to the building for which the cost is to be estimated. To meet the test of similarity, the building should be intended for the same type of occupancy, be roughly equal in size, be of like construction, and be approximately of the same quality of construction.

The base cost per square foot is calculated by dividing the total known cost by the square footage of the building. Building size is computed from exterior dimensions; multiplying the length by the width gives you the area . Where buildings are not rectangular, draw a plat of the building with measurements, and then divide the plat into sections, to allow you to calculate the area. If some of the walls do not form right angles, calculate the area by forming triangles, or by some other logical process.

The cost must reflect current building prices. Firms like R.S. Means Company, Inc., Craftsman Book Company, and BNi Building News publish updated construction cost books as well as estimating software packages. Means Contractor's Price Guide—Residential Square Foot Costs for example, organizes pricing into two major estimating sections: Square Foot Costs—with more than 30 square foot cost models for different types of residential construction , and Assemblies Costs—with approximately 100 commonly used residential construction systems with a wide variety of alternative specifications and prices. In addition there are extensive location factors that enable you to adjust material and labor costs for all U.S. zip codes and Canada. The costs used by these publishers represent U.S. national averages and are given in U.S. dollars. The location factors/city cost indexes must be used to give a more accurate estimate of the project you are costing. For example, if you estimate the cost of a small commercial building to be $1,500,000 using the cost figures from a costbook which is based on the national average, and your project is in New York, then you would multiply the $1,500,000 by the location factor given in the costbook which let us say is shown as 1.3. This would give you a modified estimated cost of $1,950,000 to build the project in New York.

A variation of this approach that is more accurate is the breaking down of the building into different types of areas with estimated costs given to each area. This may be the best method of establishing a preliminary budget for a project. It should be noted when calculating areas that gross square feet is not the same as usable square feet. Usable square feet is basically the net square feet or the total gross square feet minus that occupied by corridors, lobbies, rest rooms, kitchen, etc. (Figures 6.8a, 6.8b).

The Parameter or Unit-in-Place Method

As the design develops and the space planner and client have a firmer idea of the exact scope of the work, and the detailed design is in progress, the budget can be refined. Once the essential features of the facility are identifiable, a different procedure is used to determine the estimated costs. The most commonly used method at this time is the parameter or unit-in-place method, which involves the breaking down of the project into an appropriate hierarchy of levels, each level with an detailed itemization of construction quantities and furnishings and assigning unit costs to these quantities (Figure 6.9). In preparing these estimates, the estimator will include anticipated amounts for contractors' overhead and profits.

For example, wall and ceiling finishes can be broken down into paint, wallpaper, ceramic tile, marble, mirror, and so forth. The areas are multiplied by an estimated cost per square foot and the total budget for wall covering is developed. If the design has not progressed to the point of selecting individual wall finishes, an average cost of wall covering can be estimated and assigned to the total area of the project. Furniture can also be estimated using this method. If no decision has been taken regarding the final manufacturer and fabric of a seating group for example, the costs for typical sofas, chairs, and coffee tables based on the estimator's experience can still be totaled to arrive at a working budget number.

Using this method of budgeting, the cost implication of each building component can be evaluated, allowing decisions to be taken concerning both quantity and quality of the components to meet the original budget estimate. If floor finishes or wall covering are over budget, the space planner and the client can review the unit cost estimate and decide upon action to be taken. For example, the client may decide to replace the expensive mirror or marble component with textured paint. Similar decisions can be applied to any of the budget parameters.

Unit cost or parameter line items are based on commonly used units that relate to the construction element or cost item under study. For instance, a gypsum wallboard partition would have an assigned cost per square foot or cost per linear foot (for a specified height) of a complete partition of a particular construction type, rather than itemized costs for studs, gypsum board, screws, and finishing. This simplifies the procedure to calculate the linear footage of partitions (even when based on a preliminary space plan) and multiply by a unit cost. Executive chairs, on the other hand, would be budgeted on a per unit basis because the number required can be easily determined. The unit cost for each element in the bill of quantities is assessed in order to compute the total construction cost.

Detailed Quantity Survey or Takeoff Method

Developing an estimate is an exacting and demanding professional task, but it is not an actual science. The most precise method used to develop a budget is by measuring actual quantities of materials and furnishings and multiplying these quantities by firm, quoted costs. These detailed estimates cannot be utilized until late in the design and construction document phase of a project. The quantity survey or *takeoff*, on which every construction estimate is based on, is an extraction from the drawings and specifications of all the labor and material required for the project. A good takeoff shows everything necessary to prepare an accurate estimate for the project.

When projects are negotiated with a selected contractor, that contractor will take the construction documents and specifications and prepare a precise estimate, including overhead and profit. Sometimes, the quotation is too high, or more than the client has budgeted. In this case, the client will usually sit with the space planner and contractor and try to find ways to modify the quantities or qualities of materials or the entire scope of the job to meet the specified budget. When a project is given to several contractors to bid, a final quotation of costs is not known until bids are in. Where a developer doesn't maintain a staff capable of preparing accurate estimates, the client may hire an independent cost estimator to develop such a budget.

The interior designer or space planner calculates the furnishing costs by developing itemized lists of the various types and number of furniture to be purchased in addition to other items such as window coverings, artwork, light fixtures, accessories, and anything else that is being specified by the designer/planner. The manufacturers and model numbers are known

Owner's Overall Budget

Project: _____ **Date of Estimate** _____

A. Land Acquisition, Feasibility, and Financing Costs

1.	Land cost	$ _____
2.	Rights-of-ways	_____
3.	Title report	_____
4.	Real estate appraisal	_____
5.	Financing costs and loan fees	_____
6.	Bonds and assessments	_____
7.	Community development fees	_____
8.	Legal and accounting fees	_____
9.	Topographic, boundary, and aerial surveys	_____
10.	Geophysical investigation and report	_____
11.	Environmental impact report	_____
12.	Feasibility studies	_____
13.	Sales, leasing, and advertising costs	_____

                                      A. Total .... $_____

B. Design Costs

1.	Architectural and engineering fees	$ _____
2.	Landscape architectural fees	_____
3.	Interior design, graphics, and color consultation	_____
4.	Special engineering (solar, acoustical, etc.)	_____

                                      B. Total .... $_____

C. General Building Construction Cost

1.	_____ square feet @ $ ____ per square foot =	$ _____
2.	_____ square feet @ $ ____ per square foot =	_____
3.	_____ square feet @ $ ____ per square foot =	_____

                                      C. Total .... $_____

D. Other Construction Costs

1.	Off-site development (utilities, streets, curbs, gutters, sidewalks, fire hydrants, street trees, etc.)	$ _____
2.	On-site development (grading, retaining walls, fences, walks, paving, etc.)	_____
3.	Landscaping, planting, and irrigation	_____
4.	Recreational Features (swimming pool, tennis court, etc.)	_____

                                      D. Total .... $_____

E. Construction-related Costs

1.	Cost estimating	$ _____
2.	Permit fees	_____
3.	Construction taxes required by various government agencies	_____
4.	Insurance and bonds	_____
5.	Materials testing and inspections	_____
6.	Property taxes during construction	_____
7.	Utility costs during construction	_____
8.	Construction funds disbursement service	_____
9.	Construction Management	_____
10.	Auditing of construction costs	_____

                                      E. Total .... $_____

F. Furnishings

1.	Interior finishes, flooring, blinds, and draperies	$ _____
2.	Furnishings, fixtures, appliances, and equipment	_____
3.	Graphics	_____

                                      F. Total .... $_____

               Total of A, B, C, D, E, and F ...... $_____

**G. Contingency for estimating errors, design errors, and
   unforeseen conditions** .... $_____

                    New Total .... $_____

H. Adjustment for inflation (to date:_____) x _____ % ....$_____

                    Total Overall Budget ....$_____

FIGURE 6.8a A preliminary construction budget format based on the square foot method. *(From Arthur F. O'Leary, A Guide To Successful Construction, BNi Publications, Inc., California)*

SCOPE OF CONSTRUCTION	AREA (SF)	APPROX COST/SF	EXT COST
REFURBISH EXISTING Existing office space to remain. Modify Elec/Mech systems to meet requirements. Minor Arch changes: replace carpet, ceiling, paint. Cost ranges between $10 and $14/SF.	17,400 SF	$ 12	$208,800
NEW ENCLOSED AREAS Demo existing partitions, reconfigure as necessary. Modify Elec/Mech systems to meet requirements. Replace carpet, ceiling, paint, etc. Cost ranges between $28 and $32/SF.	4,350 SF	$ 30	$ 130,500
NEW OPEN AREAS Demo existing partition layouts. Modify Elec/Mech systems to meet requirements. Replace carpet, ceiling, paint, etc. Cost ranges between $18 and $22/SF.	21,750 SF	$ 20	$ 435,000
VENDING / FOOD SERVICE	2,500 SF	$ 75	$ 187,500
COMPUTER ROOM	2,000 SF	$150	$ 300,000
MAIN RECEPTION / SUPPORT / MAIL	1,500 SF	$ 45	$ 67,500
CONSTRUCTION TOTAL	**49,500 SF**		**$1,329,300**

FIGURE 6.8b A preliminary construction budget depicting estimated costs for modifications to existing space and new construction. *(From Julie Rayfield, The Office Interior Design Guide: An Introduction for Facility and Design Professionals, John Wiley and Sons, Inc.)*

or easily ascertained, along with color and fabric selections, applicable discounts, delivery costs, and taxes to be paid. On smaller projects, the designer may be requested to supply the furniture and other items, but for large commercial projects, furniture is typically purchased through recognized dealers who prepare the purchase orders and present precise costs to the client. In both cases, the final cost to the client is easily calculated (Figures 6.10, 6.11).

Life Cycle Costing

Life cycle costing (LCC) is a method for evaluating all relevant costs over time of alternative building designs, including systems, components, materials, and practices. The LCC method takes into account first costs, including the cost of planning, design, purchase, and installation, future costs, including costs of fuel, operation, maintenance, repair, and replacement, and any resale or salvage value recovered during or at the end of the time period examined.

CSI #	CATEGORY	UNIT COST	QTY	ESTIMATE	QTY	ALLOWANCE	QTY	DIFF	BUDGET	FORECAST	DIFF
10	General Conditions										
	Allowance	500,000	1	500,000	0	0	1	500,000	500,000	500,000	0
10	Subtotal			500,000		0		500,000	500,000	500,000	0
20	Sitework										
	N/A	0	0	0	0	0	0	0	0	0	0
20	Subtotal			0		0		0	0	0	0
30	Concrete										
	Allowance	100,000	1	100,000	0	0	1	100,000	100,000	100,000	0
30	Subtotal			100,000		0		100,000	100,000	100,000	0
40	Masonry										
	Allowance	100,000	1	100,000	0	0	1	100,000	100,000	100,000	0
40	Subtotal			100,000		0		100,000	100,000	100,000	0
50	Metals										
	Allowance	100,000	1	100,000	0	0	1	100,000	100,000	100,000	0
50	Subtotal			100,000		0		100,000	100,000	100,000	0
60	Wood & Plastics										
	Allowance	500,000	1	500,000	0	0	1	500,000	500,000	500,000	0
60	Subtotal			500,000		0		500,000	500,000	500,000	0
70	Moist Thermal Control										
	Allowance	250,000	1	250,000	0	0	1	250,000	250,000	250,000	0
70	Subtotal			250,000		0		250,000	250,000	250,000	0
80	Doors/Windows/Glass			1,165,000		1,845,000		(680,000)	(605,000)	(605,000)	0
90	Finishes			6,378,445		4,190,725		2,187,720	2,550,000	2,550,000	0
100	Specialties			4,349,875		0		4,349,875	4,730,000	4,730,000	0
120	Furnishings			370,000		90,000		280,000	287,500	287,500	0
130	Special Construction			250,000		0		250,000	250,000	250,000	0
140	Conveying Systems			250,000		0		250,000	250,000	250,000	0
150	Mechanical			2,425,000		1,800,000		625,000	650,000	650,000	0
160	Electrical			4,892,250		1,472,500		3,419,750	3,622,500	3,622,500	0
170	Special Areas			13,276,900		0		13,276,900	13,925,000	13,925,000	0
	FIT UP TOTAL			34,907,470		9,398,225		25,509,245	27,210,000	27,210,000	0
	Furniture			18,127,500				18,127,500	19,652,500	19,652,500	0
	Equipment			7,050,000				7,050,000	7,640,000	7,640,000	0
	FURN/EQUIP TOTAL			25,177,500		0		25,177,500	27,292,500	27,292,500	0
	Arch/Eng Services			3,450,000		0		3,450,000	3,450,000	3,450,000	0
	Contingency			5,774,300				5,774,300	6,264,500	6,264,500	0

FIGURE 6.9 An estimated relocation budget based on program requirements. *(From Julie Rayfield, The Office Interior Design Guide: An Introduction for Facility and Design Professionals, John Wiley and Sons, Inc.)*

Budget for Headquarters Remodel
Project #330

Section	Item	Quantity/Unit	Unit Price	Amount	Subtotal
100	Demolition				
100.01	partitions	3600 SF	2.00	7200	
100.02	ceilings	3700 SF	0.25	925	
100.03	carpet	3700 SF	0.25	925	
100.04	relocate entry	1 allowance	7200.00	7200	
					16250
200	Partitions				
200.01	full height	225 LF	27.00	6075	
200.02	partial height	24 LF	21.00	504	
200.03	partial glass	44 LF	100.00	4400	
200.04	operable partitions	50 LF	175.00	8750	
200.05	drywall facing	124 LF	20.00	2480	
					22209
300	Doors/Frames/Hardware				
300.01	entry	5 EA	600.00	3000	
300.02	interior—singles	3 EA	500.00	1500	
300.03	interior—pairs	2 EA	900.00	1800	
300.04	sliding	4 EA	800.00	3200	
300.05	closet-pairs	5 EA	1000.00	5000	
					14500
400	Finishes				
400.01	walls—paint	(included in partitions)		0	
400.02	walls—fabric tack panels	130 SF	6.00	780	
400.03	walls—wall covering	1 allowance	2000.00	2000	
400.04	floor—carpet	450 SY	22.00	9900	
400.05	floor—vinyl tile	140 SF	1.50	210	
400.06	floor—inset carpet	1 allowance	1000.00	1000	
400.07	ceiling	3740 SF	2.25	8415	
400.08	window coverings	342 SF	3.25	1112	
					23417
500	Millwork				
500.01	kitchen cabinets	28 LF	350.00	9800	
500.02	mail counter & boxes	14 LF	400.00	5600	
500.03	office alcoves counters	130 LF	100.00	1300	
500.04	wall storage	86 LF	150.00	12900	
500.05	president's office	9 LF	250.00	2250	
500.06	workroom	30 LF	200.00	6000	
500.07	display	21 LF	300.00	6300	
500.08	shelving	30 LF	50.00	1500	
500.09	admin. assistant	35 LF	300.00	10500	
					67350
600	Electrical				
600.01	fluorescent lighting	67 EA	175.00	11725	
600.02	incandescent downlights	7 EA	125.00	875	
600.03	wall outlets	36 EA	150.00	5400	
600.04	dedicated wall outlet	1 EA	250.00	250	
600.05	floor outlets	4 EA	300.00	1200	
600.06	telephone outlets	9 EA	100.00	900	
600.07	fire/security system	1 allowance	10000.00	10000	
600.08	upgrade power panel	1 allowance	3500.00	3500	
600.09	undercounter lights	47 EA	100.00	4700	
600.1	exit lights	6 EA	100.00	600	
					39150
700	Plumbing				
700.01	kitchen sink	1 EA	3000.00	3000	
					3000
800	Heating/Ventilating/A.C.				
800.01	additional roof unit	1 allowance	5000.00	5000	
800.02	secondary distribution	1 allowance	3000.00	3000	
800.03	controls	1 allowance	500.00	1000	
					9000
900	Equipment				
900.01	refrigerator	1 EA	600.00	1000	
900.02	microwave	1 EA	400.00	400	
900.03	garbage disposal	1 EA	300.00	300	
900.04	water heater (insta-hot)	1 EA	300.00	300	
900.05	dishwasher	1 EA	400.00	500	
900.06	projection screen/motor	1 EA	1600.00	1600	
					4100

Subtotal $	199476
10% for contingency	19948
10% contractor's overhead and profit	21942
TOTAL $	241366

FIGURE 6.10 A preliminary budget based on the Parameter Method. *(From David Ballast, Interior Design Reference Manual, Professional Publications, Inc., CA)*

SCOPE OF FURNITURE	QUANTITY	UNIT COST	EXT'D COST
OFFICE FURNITURE			
VP/Director - Private Office	9	$12,000	$108,000
Manager - Private Office	28	$ 7,100	$198,000
Professional - 9'x 9' Workstation	94	$ 4,700	$441,800
Technical/Consultant - 7'x 9' Workstation	57	$ 3,200	$182,400
Clerical - Freestanding Furniture	23	$ 5,000	$115,000
Files - 5 Drw Lateral / 3' Wide	150	$ 680	$102,000
CAFETERIA FURNITURE			
Chairs	70	$ 250	$ 17,500
Tables	18	$ 450	$ 8,100
RECEPTION AREA FURNITURE			
Sofas	2	$ 4,000	$ 8,000
Lounge Chairs	4	$ 1,200	$ 4,800
Occasional Tables	2	$ 800	$ 1,600
CONFERENCE ROOM FURNITURE			
Tables	6	$ 3,000	$ 18,000
Chairs	72	$ 400	$ 28,800
FURNITURE TOTAL			**$1,234,800**

FIGURE 6.11 A preliminary furniture budget can be developed by estimating quantities and unit pricing. *(From Julie Rayfield, The Office Interior Design Guide ; An Introduction for Facility and Design Professionals, John Wiley and Sons, Inc.)*

Estimate Cost Control

It is necessary for both the owner and the contractor to adopt some base line for monitoring the project and impose cost control during the construction process. For the owner, a *budget estimate* must be adopted early enough for planning long term financing of the project. Cost control is necessary to establish budget estimates for financing, budgeted cost after contracting but prior to construction, and estimated cost to completion during the progress of construction. Consequently, the detailed estimate is often used as the budget estimate since it is sufficiently accurate to reflect the project scope and is available long before the consultant's estimate. As the work progresses, the budgeted cost is typically revised periodically to reflect the estimated cost to completion. A revised estimated cost is necessary either because of change orders initiated by the owner or due to unexpected cost overruns or savings.

The contractor will normally use the bid estimate as the budget estimate, which will also be used for control purposes as well as for planning construction financing. The budgeted cost should also be updated periodically to reflect the estimated cost to completion as well as to insure adequate cash flow for the completion of the project.

COMPUTER AIDED COST ESTIMATION: ESTIMATING SOFTWARE PACKAGES

The possibilities for automating and controlling your estimating spreadsheets are unlimited, and there are many tools that developers and contractors can use to estimate more effectively and efficiently. Moreover, there are currently many computer aided cost estimation software systems on the market. These range in sophistication from simple spreadsheet calculation software packages to integrated systems involving design and price negotiation over the Internet. While these proprietary packages involve some investment to purchase, maintain, and train (assuming you already have adequate computer hardware), significant efficiencies usually result. In particular, cost estimates may be prepared with greater accuracy, more rapidly and with less effort. Below is a list of the more popular packages that are available today to developers and contractors:

- ACEIT (Automated Cost Estimating Integrated Tools) helps analysts store, retrieve, and analyze data; build cost models; analyze risk; time phase budgets; and document cost estimates. It is a generic, flexible, Windows-based system you can use to estimate virtually any task on any type program. The result of government sponsored efforts, the ACEIT suite of applications is available to U.S. Government organizations with no charge for use.

- BEST ESTIMATE: Estimator for renovators and remodelers, general contractors, design/builders, architects and designers.

- Bidworx: Takeoff and estimating software for construction management.

- BSD SoftLink products, by Building Systems Design, enable users to perform cost management, cost engineering, value analysis, and construction specifications.

- CD Estimator for Windows allows you to customize prices, descriptions, and markup. Includes training video and Job Cost Wizard, which allows you to take estimates from your estimator and export them into QuickBooks Pro or create your own billing.

- COCOMO: In 1981 the Constructive Cost Model (COCOMO) was published in the book *Software Engineering Economics* by Dr. Barry Boehm. There are several tools that implement the model available via the Internet.

- COSMIC has over 810 computer programs that were originally developed by NASA and its contractors for the U.S. space program.

- Cost Analysis Strategy Assessment (CASA) is a Life Cycle Cost (LCC) decision support tool. CASA can present the total cost of ownership depending on user selections, including RDT and E costs, production costs, and operating/support costs. CASA covers the entire life of the system, from its initial research costs to those associated with yearly maintenance, as well as spares, training costs, and other expenses.

- Cost Estimating Guides—Labor and material cost guides. Most come with a CD and include a stand-alone estimating program, National Estimator, with a multimedia tutorial.

Also included is a job costing program, Job Cost Wizard, that lets you turn estimates into invoices and export your estimates to QuickBooks Pro.

- Cost Xpert software costing tool calculates information including project costs, schedules, tasks, deliverables, maintenance, and support requirements.

- COSTIMATOR: Computerized cost estimating and process planning for manufacturing.

- CostTrack is an integrated cost/project management software package.

- Crystal Ball—Choose a range for each uncertain value in your spreadsheet. Crystal Ball uses this information to perform hundreds of what-if analyses. These analyses are summarized in a graph showing the probability for each result.

- DeccaPro activity based cost estimating software.

- ECOS European Space Agency (ESA) Costing Software.

- ECOM European Space Agency (ESA) Cost Modeling Software.

- EMQUE's Perfect Project integrated accounting, estimating, cost and project management software for the construction industry.

- Decision by Life Cycle Cost (D-LCC) is a software package for automated life cycle cost evaluation and cost effectiveness analysis.

- DecisionTools Suite (@RISK, PrecisionTree, TopRank, BestFit, and RISKview) provides a suite of integrated decision analysis programs running from a common toolbar in Microsoft Excel.

- D4COST is a conceptual cost modeling system that provides the tools to produce building cost estimates. It contains a database of over 900 construction projects that includes total building costs, materials and labor, contract requirements, general requirements, and site costs.

- DOD Tools and Models Index: This index contains abstracts of tools and models that are currently used in the U.S. Department of Defense and have the potential for wider application.

- ForecastX, available in an ActiveX control, cross-platform libraries and Java, allows you to add business forecasting, time series forecasting, demand and inventory planning, data mining, sales forecasting, optimization and statistical algorithms to your client server and web-based applications.

- JPL's Project Design Center Tools and Models: Include many engineering, cost estimating, and management tools used in the design and development of spacecraft.

- KAPES (Knowledge Aided Planning and Estimating System) is a knowledge-based computer system which can be used to control purchasing and outsourcing costs, the generation of bid cost estimates, and the improvement of shop floor efficiency.

- Means DemoSource allows you to download free estimating software demos and product information that you can use to make construction estimating software decisions for your organization.

- • G2 Estimator: project estimating and management and control systems.

  - • Timberline Software Corporation's Precision Collection of estimating software covers the entire estimating process, from conceptual estimate to final bill of materials. Offers analytical capabilities, pre-built databases and links to AutoCAD and scheduling.

- Micro Estimating Systems, Inc.

  - • Machine Shop Estimating is an engineering based, computer-aided, estimating system.

  - • FabPlan is an engineering based, computer-aided, processing planning and estimating system.

- National Construction Estimator is designed for building costs of residential, commercial, and industrial construction. Provides manhours, recommended crew, and gives the labor cost for installation.

- Optimize allows managers to forecast the effort, cost and resources required for object-oriented and component-based software development. Optimize is UML based and can be used standalone or in conjunction with CASE tools and Microsoft Project to help transform modeling data into scheduling information.

- PACES (Parametric Cost Engineering System) is a military construction cost estimating system.

- PCM Parametric Cost Model from Parametric Consultants: The cost calculation within this model is driven by a mass and a complexity factor. The complexity factor is derived by a reverse calculation with a similar type of equipment where the costs are know. ECOM is linked to these different parametric models in the simple way of exchanging data via files. Since the user has no access to the formulae, this method can be considered as a black-box approach, where just the supplier takes care about the maintenance of the internal calculation process. This requires an experienced estimator in order to receive reliable cost figures.

- Primavera Systems, Inc.

  - • TeamPlay: Enterprise-wide project portfolio management for IT and application development projects.

  - • Concentric Suite—an integrated way to manage people, teams, and projects.

- Pulsar, by Estimating Systems, is a PC-based construction cost estimating package that uses the R.S. Means Cost Data. It is designed for commercial, government and facilities estimating.

- R.S. Means Preliminary Project Cost Data is a parametric resource based on data from R.S. Means that allows users to select from approximately 60 building types in any location in the United States (and 33 locations in Canada) and obtain a cost estimate for building the project in that market. The service is available for free to registered users (registration is free, as well).

- RACER (Remedial Action Cost Engineering and Requirements System) will estimate costs for studies, remedial design, remedial action, and related site work at environmental restoration projects.
- RAPIDCOST: Manufacturing cost estimating system for Windows.
- Resource Calculations, Inc. (RCI): Software tools for management of software development.
- Success4: Commercially available Windows-based estimating and cost management software system.
- Timberline Software offers sophisticated analytical capabilities, pre-built databases and links to AutoCAD and scheduling.
- TRACES (Tri-Services Automated Cost Engineering Systems) provides cost engineers with tools to prepare budgetary, Government estimates, and current working estimates in support of the DOD military program and the Corps of Engineers Civil Works program.
- Video Estimator lets you draw on pictures to estimate material. It combines elements of CAD, spreadsheet and database software into a cost estimating program.
- Visual Estimator: Construction cost estimating and bidding system for Windows
- Welcom
  - Cobra is a cost management system designed to manage and analyze budgets, earned value, actuals, and forecasts.
  - Open Plan is an enterprise-wide project management software system that supports multiple projects.
  - Spider is a Web-based statusing tool for remotely viewing and updating project data from Open Plan, Welcom's enterprise-wide project management system.
  - WelcomHome is a virtual project office that provides a process-driven approach for distributed team members. It can be used both independently and in conjunction with scheduling and cost management tools such as Microsoft Project, and Welcom's Open Plan and Cobra.
- WinEstimator, Inc. is the producer of several Windows-based cost estimating software products for use in the construction industry.
- WinRACE: Rapid Access Cost Estimating for general construction and process plant construction.

The more common features most computer estimating software have include:

- Databases for unit cost items such as worker wage rates, equipment rental and material prices. These databases can be used for any cost estimate required.
- Databases of anticipated productivity for various components types, equipment and construction processes.

- Import utilities from computer aided design software for automatic quantity-take-off of components. Alternatively, special user interfaces may exist to enter geometric descriptions of components to allow automatic quantity-take-off.

- Export utilities to send estimates to cost control and scheduling software. This assists management of costs during construction.

- Version control to allow simulation of different construction processes or design changes for the purpose of tracking changes in anticipated costs.

- Provisions for manual review, over-ride and editing of cost elements resulting from the cost estimation system.

- Flexible reporting formats, including provisions for electronic reporting rather than simply printing cost estimates on paper.

- Archives of past projects to allow rapid cost-estimate updating or modification for similar projects.

CHAPTER SEVEN

FURNITURE AND FURNISHINGS: ASSESSMENT AND PROCUREMENT

*T*he workforce is changing under the onslaught of modern technology, and with it the office landscape. As we settle into the information age, the increase in population of white collar workers continues to outpace that of other segments of the labor force. The higher level of training required for these upper-level positions has manifested itself in an increase in employee absenteeism and turnover. This is beginning to pose serious financial and productivity problems to the corporate world.

GENERAL OVERVIEW

Many designers are now seeking office systems that support a work environment that integrates technology in a constantly evolving workplace. What is configured today can be reconfigured tomorrow without losing any data. Generally, the planning of the workplace environment should facilitate greater interaction between people and their support facilities. Space planners should avoid having the design layout dictated by the furniture /people. Instead, they should undertake a strategic review of a client's goals and corporate objectives to create an innovative, flexible, and effective solution that enhances communication, teamwork, supports business processes and improves staff efficiency and morale.

MAIN FURNITURE STYLES

Over the millennia, civilizations have witnessed many epochs and styles in both architecture and furniture. Today, as in the past, designers will use a particular style to reflect a client's desired personal or corporate image. Space planners, architects, and interior designers therefore need to have a basic understanding of the main attributes and characteristics of these styles in order to better serve their clientele. Of note, style determination is not always clear-cut, and often a piece of furniture (or architecture for that matter) will display more than one influence (Figures 7.1 through 7.3). What follows is a summary outline of the major relevant styles and periods relating to furniture.

- *Adam Style:* A British Neo-Classical style in furniture and interior decoration dating from about 1760 to 1790, named after its creator and principal exponent, Robert Adam, a prominent architect and designer of the period. The style was characterized by the liberal use of classical motifs in painted or inlaid decoration on rectilinear forms with slender, elegant proportions. Much of the furniture during this period was executed in satinwood. The style mixes well with Hepplewhite, Sheraton, Phyfe, Empire, Louis XIV and Chippendale.

- *Art Deco:* Popular decorative style of the 1920s and 1930s. The name is taken from the title of the 1925 Paris World's Fair, L'Exposition Internationale des Arts Décoratifs et Industriels Modernes, where such work was first exhibited. It is characterized by a restrained, stylized use of ornament, simple furniture shapes, an emphasis on fine craftsmanship and an opulent use of precious and exotic materials. Its emergence was a reaction to the excesses of its predecessor, Art Nouveau.

- *Art Nouveau:* This is a European design reform movement of the 1890s and early 20th century with an elaborate curvilinear design style having developed from it. Abstract and organic motifs were the basic characteristics of the style. Different interpretations of the style developed in different European countries.

- *Arts and Crafts Movement:* Based on the ideas of John Ruskin and William Morris which emphasized simple, functional design, a lessening of excessive decoration, and the use of traditional materials.

- *Baroque Furniture:* European furniture of the 17th and early 18th centuries that is characterized by bold detail and highly ornamented sweeping curves. The Louis XIV Style is the French version of the Baroque (see Chapter One).

- *Bergère:* Originally an 18th century French furniture form, the bergère sometimes took the form of a wing chair or had a low back that merged into the arms. It was first manufactured in the Louis XV style.

- *Biedermeier Style:* A furniture style that was popular in northern Europe from about 1800 to 1850, characterized by functionality, simplicity of form, and restrained decoration. The style mixes well with both provincial French and American pieces and with 18th century formal styles.

- *Chinese Furniture:* The history of Chinese furniture stretches back several thousand years and was characterized by its conservatism. Traditional Chinese furniture is also characterized by its reliance on crafted joinery in construction, to the complete exclusion of nails and screws and with only occasional use of glue and dowels. Many of their later chairs featured a cubical frame below the seat, composed of the legs and a low box stretcher whose front element served as a footrest. The upper parts varied. Lacquering techniques were perfected during the Ming period.

- *Chippendale Style:* A British Rococo furniture maker whose work can be divided into three main periods: French, Chinese and Gothic. The furniture was generally rich, graceful, refined, substantial, but not heavy. Early Chippendale pieces have cabriole legs and other features common to early 18th century furniture. Fretwork is extensively used as are

Chippendale
Arm Chair

Italian Renaissance Credenza

Sphinx Supports

Bergère
(Rococo)

Shaker Rocker

FIGURE 7.1 Furniture of different styles and periods.

motifs like the acanthus, shells, acorns, roses, dolphins and scrolls. The style mixes well with Early Georgian, Hepplewhite, Sheraton and Adam style pieces. Chinese Chippendale can also be used with contemporary, Chinese Modern, and Swedish Modern.

- *Contemporary Style:* A British furniture style of the 1950s. The Contemporary style was characterized by light, elegant pieces with long, low profiles. It is essentially an outgrowth of the International style of the 1930s. In the United States, the term is used more loosely to describe postwar smooth-lined furniture that reflects simplicity, lightness and elegance of design.

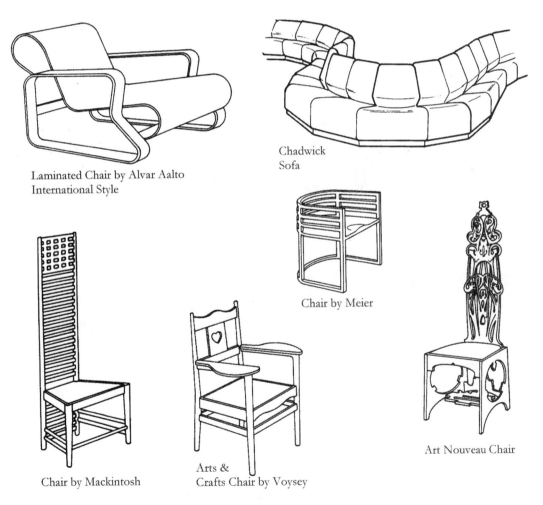

Laminated Chair by Alvar Aalto
International Style

Chadwick
Sofa

Chair by Meier

Chair by Mackintosh

Arts &
Crafts Chair by Voysey

Art Nouveau Chair

FIGURE 7.2 Furniture of different styles and periods.

CAMEL BACK   CHESTERFIELD   COGSWELL   TUB   LAWSON

SETTEE   TUXEDO   FANBACK   CHARLES OF LONDON   SHELL

CHARLES OF LONDON   LAWSON   COCKFIGHT   OPEN ARM PULL-UP   CORNER

DRUM   GATE LEG   TILT TOP   WINDOW SEAT   TETE-A-TETE

NESTED TABLES   DAVENPORT   CLOSED ARM OCCASIONAL   BANK OF ENGLAND

CONSOLE   FIRESIDE   BARREL

PEMBROKE   TRESTLE   CLUB   WING

Shape Identification of Chairs, Sofas and
Occasional Tables

FIGURE 7.3 Furniture is produced in many shapes and forms. Many types have identifying names as can be seen from this illustration.

- *Egyptian Style:* European decorative style of the 18th and 19th centuries that used motifs taken from ancient Egyptian furniture and art (including the sphinx, lotus, blossoms, winged disks, obelisks, etc.), and is primarily associated with the French Empire and British Regency styles of the early 19th century.

- *Empire Style:* French Neoclassical style of the early 19th century, and is associated with France's First Empire under Napoleon Bonaparte.

- *Federal Period Style:* Essentially covered the period from the 1780s to 1830s and is characterized by the Neoclassical style.

- *Gothic Furniture:* Characterized by a strong vertical emphasis in its structure, and a pronounced naturalism in its decorative elements.

- *Hepplewhite (1770—1786):* This is a style of the Georgian period of the 18th century. Hepplewhite's book, *Cabinet-maker and Upholsterer's Guide*, strongly influenced cabinetmaking in Britain, northern Europe and America. The Hepplewhite tradition exemplified the neoclassical style and was characterized by graceful, refined slender lines and proportions. Mahogany is the favored wood, with satinwood, birch, sycamore and rosewood also used.

- *International Style:* The style originated in Europe during the 1920s and 1930s (inspired by the Bauhaus), and is characterized by clarity of structure, simplicity of line and a minimum of decoration. Its leading formulators were Walter Gropius, Marcel Breuer, Ludwig Mies van der Rohe, and Le Corbusier.

- *Louis XV Style:* Represents the French furniture style of about 1730 to 1765, the second phase of rococo furniture. Furniture became ornate, luxurious, and more feminine. It was smaller in scale and the term *Rococo* became synonymous with the Louis XV style. The flower was the favorite motif. The furniture was characterized by its curved lines, straight lines being used only when necessary. Many woods were used, including oak, rosewood, mahogany, walnut, beech, ebony, holly, tulipwood, and maple.

- *Louis XVI Style:* Often considered the "golden age of cabinetmaking," the style was both a reaction to the rococo style that reached its zenith during the reign of Louis XV, and to a resurgence of interest in classical forms. The Louis XVI style was characterized by an emphasis on straight lines and geometrical shapes and by a restrained use of classically inspired decorative motifs. The style mixes well with Adam, Sheraton, Hepplewhite and Directoire styles.

- *Medieval Furniture:* Lasted from about the 5th century to the 16th century and was roughly contemporary with Byzantine furniture but was much cruder in design and construction. The range of furniture forms was limited, and tended to be simple and utilitarian. It often took the form of miniature buildings, due to the use of arcading and pilasters.

- *Neoclassical Style:* The British Adam style and the French Louis XVI style were the dominant modes of neoclassical furniture in the late 18th century, the period with which the term neoclassical is most closely associated.

- *Duncan Phyfe (1768-1854):* New York's leading cabinetmaker during the first half of the 19th century. Creator of American Empire style and exponent of Directoire Style.

- *Pop Art Furniture:* Stylistic trend of the 1960s inspired by the Pop Art movement in painting and sculpture. It was a reaction against the prevailing tastes of the 1950s.

- *Post-Modern Furniture:* Style is associated with Post-Modern architecture, and arose in the late 1970s. It reflects general dissatisfaction of many architects and designers with functionalism and the European International Style. Its forms, shapes and decoration are drawn from the historical styles, particularly from the neoclassical period.

- *Queen Anne Style:* The furniture of this period originated during the reign of William and Mary and proceeded into the early Georgian era. It is noted for its charming simplicity, delicate proportions, graceful curving lines and veneered walnut surfaces. Carved decoration was minimized, and the principal motif was the shell, although the honeysuckle, rosettes and husk were also used. Queen Anne furniture mixes well with contemporary and 18th century walnut pieces.

- *Regency Style:* Late neoclassical style of British furniture, popular during the first four decades of the 19th century. The style was characterized by a pronounced eclecticism, and was in essentially an archaeological revival, being strongly influenced by a mixture of Egyptian, Greek, Roman, and Chinese furniture. It was a style of simplification and functionalism, and furniture pieces were scaled down to smaller, more intimate sizes. Mahogany is the favored wood but rosewood and satinwood were also used. The style mixes well with Adam, Hepplewhite, Sheraton, French Empire, Biedermeier, Duncan Phyfe, and American Empire.

- *Renaissance Furniture:* Domestic furniture became more sophisticated, although still bulky, with greater elaboration of carving.

- *Rococo Furniture:* The style was promoted by Louis XV's craftsmen, and owed much to the influence of oriental art. It is characterized by an excessive use of curves, with asymmetrical surface carvings of rocks, shells and waves.

- *Scandinavian Modern:* Style of furniture designed and manufactured in Scandinavia during the 20th century. The furniture is characterized by the use of traditional materials and excellent craftsmanship.

- *Shaker Furniture:* Furniture designed and built by the Shakers, an American religious community, and first came into fashion in the 1860s. Their furniture was inexpensive, simple, and unornamented, based on the philosophy that "beauty rests on utility."

- *Thomas Sheraton (1751-1806):* Chair design reached its peak during this period, and his *Cabinet-maker's and Upholsterer's Drawing Book,* which was produced between 1791 and 1794 filled the gap between the Neoclassical and Regency periods. Sheraton worked mainly with mahogany.

- *Spanish Colonial Furniture:* Furniture made in Spain's American colonies between the 17th and 19th centuries. It was generally European in structure and form, but decoration was influenced by local traditions. Early work followed the Spanish Mudéjar and Plateresque styles, but by the mid-17th century evolved into distinct colonial styles. By the 18th century, local motifs and schemes were increasingly frequent, although furniture remained greatly influenced by the Spanish baroque.

THE STATE OF THE FURNITURE INDUSTRY TODAY

In today's highly competitive business environment, leading furniture manufacturers are continuously seeking innovative ways to address the complex range of workplace criteria and the challenges of the rapidly evolving office, including supporting the integration of people and technology, facilitating productivity, and creating a flexible environmentally attractive workplace. For many, these are indeed challenging times.

Many furniture manufacturers, like Herman Miller, offer sophisticated products for the contemporary technology-driven office. Firms like the ones discussed below and others have become international in character, employing thousands of people and offices worldwide. Among the more prominent manufacturers of furniture and office systems competing in today's market are:

Herman Miller

Herman Miller, Inc., is a Zeeland, Michigan, based firm, and is a leading global provider of office furniture and services that support work environments. Its rise to acknowledged international leadership in the production of progressively designed furniture began in 1946, when its design director George Nelson recruited Charles Eames. The firm has been one of the dominating forces in the international furniture market over the last thirty years and has contributed greatly to the widespread popularity of modern design today.

Herman Miller is reputed to have developed the world's first open plan office furniture system, The Action Office. It revolutionized office design and the way people work. Based on a vision of planned non-obsolescence, the system's components have been updated regularly to meet the changing needs of the workplace. Today, many U.S. businesses use open plan offices, and Herman Miller has one of the largest installed bases in the industry (Figure 7.4).

Another Herman Miller product in long-term production is the Ethospace system (1984), another first in office architecture systems. This unique frame-and-tile system was developed by Bill Stumpf, Jack Kelley, and an internal Herman Miller design team, mainly in response to the evident needs of a complex and changing workplace (Figures 7.5, 7.6a, 7.6b).

Herman Miller's seating products also demonstrate their leadership in problem solving design. With the Ergon chair (1976), Herman Miller applied modern ergonomic design to office seating (Figure 7.7). This was followed by the Equa chair (1984), which also set new standards for comfort and ergonomic support. In 1994, Herman Miller introduced a major breakthrough in work chair design. the Aeron chair (Figure 7.8), widely lauded for its innovative design and now included in the permanent collections of museums worldwide.

The Equa and Aeron chairs have each been given the prestigious title, "Design of the Decade"—Equa by *Time* magazine in the 1980s, and Aeron as a "Design of the Decade" Gold Winner in the 1990s by *Business Week* magazine and the Industrial Designers Society of America. (More information is available at www.hermanmiller.com.)

Herman Miller designed Resolve, another breakthrough systems product which was unveiled at NeoCon '99, winning the gold award for systems as well as the "Best of Competition" award. Nature and geometry is said to have inspired Herman Miller's new Resolve office system which designer Ayse Birsel brought to life. But extensive research and testing helped fine tune Resolve and confirmed the viability of what Herman Miller describes as "the biggest

FIGURE 7.4 The Action Office Series 2 with curved worksurfaces and panels with Aeron chairs and Meridian files. The Action Office was originally designed by Robert Propst, former director of Herman Miller's Research Center. *(Courtesy Herman Miller, Inc.)*

Phone Kiosk

Coffee Bar

Kitchenette

Butterfly Reference Table

Storage Pantry

Exercise Area

FIGURE 7.5 The Ethospace System by Herman Miller, first introduced in 1984.

FIGURE 7.6a
The Ethospace System by Herman Miller.

FIGURE 7.6b
The Ethospace System by Herman Miller.

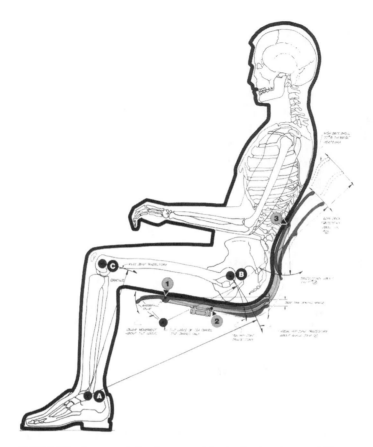

FIGURE 7.7 Ergonomic/anthropometric studies by Herman Miller.

breakthrough in office systems since 1968," when they introduced Robert Propst's Action Office, the original panel-based furniture system that first established open office design.

The results of the research generally confirmed Resolve's position as an acceptable alternative to traditional cubicle office systems, particularly for companies that operate in collaborative, high tech environments. Several test site participants said that the openness of Resolve's infrastructure contributed to a "freer, lighter, energetic, and creative environment." It appeared that the system encouraged increased employee collaboration, particularly around the computer. This reinforced the Resolve design and research teams' contention that the system is ideal for many of today's high tech, team oriented companies with flatter hierarchies (Figures 7.9a, b,c).

The Resolve system is an innovative new product that is designed to meet the needs of companies that are technologically advanced, fast moving, and collaborative in nature. It is also

FIGURE 7.8   Aeron chair by Herman Miller.

designed to help companies respond quickly and inexpensively to high churn rates, reduce real estate costs, accommodate new and emerging technologies, and develop a sense of community among employees. However, the Resolve system is not suitable for all work situations.

Knoll

Knoll, Inc., another global leader in the design and manufacture of office furnishings, offers elegantly conceived, creative products for office and residential use. Knoll sought the finest living designers of the 20th century, producing their designs with both full credit and royalties. Knoll acquired the rights to produce the Barcelona, MR and Brno designs of van der Rohe, and the seminal Wassily chair of Breuer. To that list of fine designers, they added such noted artists as Risom and Noguchi, and famous Finnish architect Eero Saarinen. Saarinen (who lived from 1910 to 1961) was an architect whose seminal modern designs in the 1950s set the scene for the contemporary designs that are the vivid reminders of the 1960s.

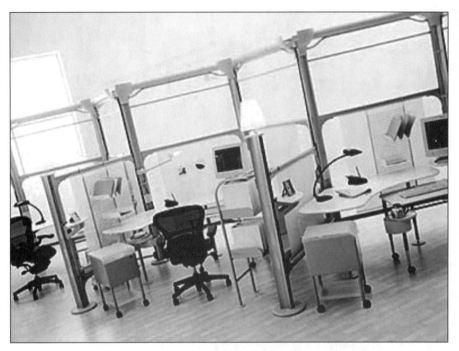

FIGURE 7.9a
The Resolve
Office System
by Herman
Miller.

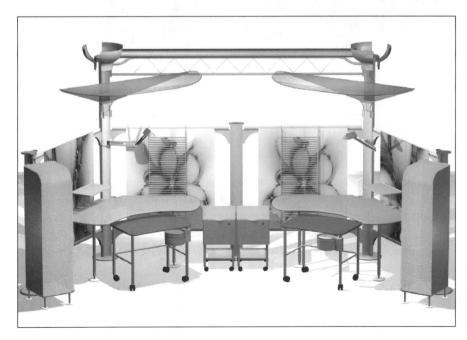

FIGURE 7.9b
The Resolve
Office System
by Herman
Miller.

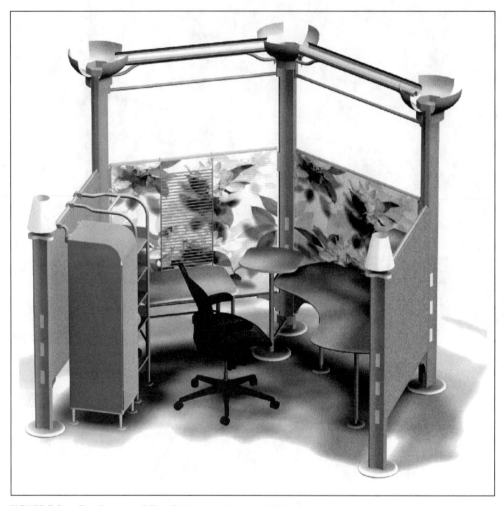

FIGURE 7.9c   The Resolve Office System by Herman Miller.

The Knoll Planning Unit played a pivotal role in transforming the American business environment of the postwar years. An internal department that worked with clients to identify their workplace needs and to customize interior architecture and furnishing solutions, the Knoll Planning Unit followed Florence Knoll's philosophy that architecture and interior design must be informed by functionality and work processes as well as by aesthetics. (More information is available at www.knoll.com.)

Knoll's philosophy is to combine solid workplace research with innovative thinking to create distinctive, high performance working environments that address the unique and ever-changing needs of businesses (Figures 7.10 through 7.13).

FIGURE 7.10
Knoll Inter-
action
Tables with
Morrison
Panels.
*(Courtesy
Knoll, Inc.)*

FIGURE 7.11
Knoll Bulldog
Management
Chairs with Pro-
peller Table.
Options include
upholstered
outer shell,
arms, armless,
glides, low/high
seat height
cylinder. *(Cour-
tesy Knoll, Inc.)*

FIGURE 7.12
Knoll Equity
System with
curved glazed
panels and
adjacent
workspaces.
*(Courtesy
Knoll, Inc.)*

FIGURE 7.13
Knoll Free-
standing
Reff Private
Office in
light maple
veneer,
can-
tilevered
desk and
office
tower.
*(Courtesy
Knoll, Inc.)*

Steelcase

Steelcase is another Michigan furniture manufacturer that started from humble beginnings. Today, it is a public company with over 20,00 employees worldwide. From the mid 1950s onwards, the company embarked on a strategy of expansion and today is the largest manufacturer and supplier of system office furniture in the world. Its products and services are designed to enable customers and their consultants to create work environments that harmoniously integrate architecture, furniture and technology.

Steelcase broke new ground with the introduction of Pathways®, a portfolio of products that integrate furniture, worktools, technology products, and interior architectural products. It is considered to be the most ambitious new product introduction in the company's 86 year history (Figures 7.14 through 7.21). The Pathways portfolio consists of various elements including a modular post and beam product for open environments, a building wall treatment product that adds performance and features to existing walls, and a system of portal doors and sidelights that provide entry, access and security to enclosed areas. Steelcase also has an impressive array of office systems, interior architecture systems, seating products, and desks and tables. (More information is available at www.steelcase.com/en/findex.jsp.)

FIGURE 7.14 Steelcase Leap® Chair Coach® Edition. *(Courtesy Steelcase, Inc.)*

FIGURE 7.15 Steelcase Pathways post and beam detail. *(Courtesy Steelcase, Inc.)*

FIGURE 7.16
Steelcase
Werndl
EmergeTM
Desk by
Vecta.
*(Courtesy
Steelcase,
Inc.)*

FIGURE 7.17
Steelcase
Pathways
Conjunc-
tion®,
teaming
area.
*(Courtesy
Steelcase,
Inc.)*

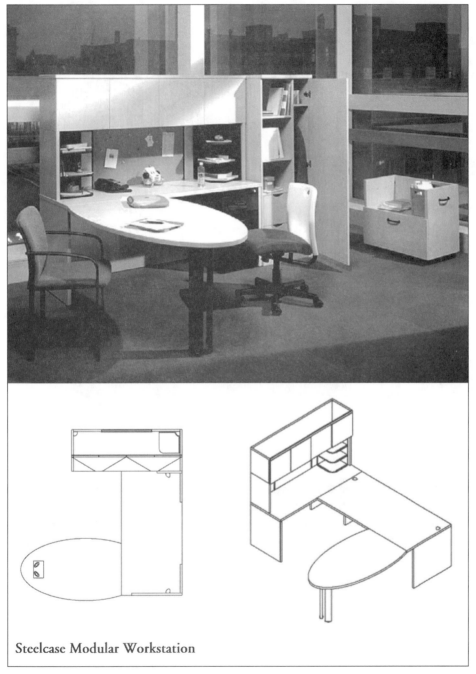

Steelcase Modular Workstation

FIGURE 7.18 Steelcase Reply™, an adaptable desk system by Turnstone. *(Courtesy Steelcase, Inc.)*

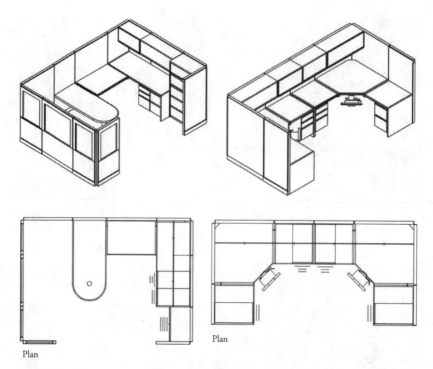

Plan

Plan

FIGURE 7.19 Steelcase Series 9000®, line drawing of manager's workstations. Dimensions are 12 feet 10 inches deep by 9 feet 2 inches wide. (*Courtesy Steelcase, Inc.*)

Haworth

Haworth, now the second largest designer and manufacturer of contract office furniture in the world, produces and markets its products under approximately 20 principal brands, including Haworth, Haworth Ten, Castelli, Comforto, Kinetics, Röder, and United Chair. For many years, Haworth has been among a handful of manufacturers that have redefined and impacted the industry with inventions like the universal panel hinge, the acoustic panel, the pre-powered modular panel, and the adjustable keyboard pad.

Today, Haworth offers a broad range of products, including modular panel systems furniture, task and lounge seating, storage products, wood and metal casegoods (desks, credenzas, storage), mobile furniture, a complete line of tables, and ancillary office furnishings. Addressing the way we work today and how we'll work tomorrow, Haworth offers its customers "furniture for what's next." Moreover, Haworth's innovative inventions helped to move the company into the international marketplace (Figures 7.22 through 7.28). For more information go to www.haworth.com/index_fhome.asp.

FIGURE 7.20 Steelcase Series 9000®, individual workstations. Dimensions are 6 feet 6 inches deep by 7 feet 8 inches wide. *(Courtesy Steelcase, Inc.)*

FIGURE 7.21 Steelcase Pathways Secant® adjacent work station. *(Courtesy Steelcase, Inc.)*

FIGURE 7.22 Haworth's Profile product line for conference areas. *(Courtesy Haworth, Inc.)*

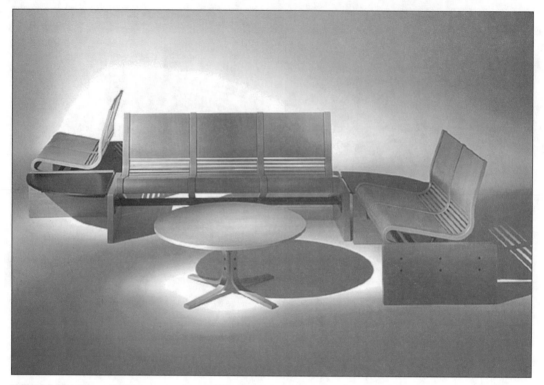

FIGURE 7.23 Haworth Alliance contoured European bench seating with freestanding coffee table. *(Courtesy Haworth, Inc.)*

FIGURE 7.24 Haworth X99 is a complete seating system incorporating advanced ergonomic features. *(Courtesy Haworth, Inc.)*

FIGURE 7.25
Haworth showing use of a premise integrated office system. (*Courtesy Haworth, Inc.*)

FIGURE 7.26
Haworth Series K conference table. (*Courtesy Haworth, Inc.*)

FIGURE 7.27
Haworth
Castelli 3D
System pro-
vides rapid
deployment,
assembly and
reconfigura-
tion. *(Courtesy
Haworth, Inc.)*

FIGURE 7.28
Haworth
Premise is an
integrated sys-
tem that
includes case-
goods, files
and storage
components.
*(Courtesy
Haworth, Inc.)*

Helikon

Helikon Furniture Company mainly manufactures casegoods and tables and was acquired by the ICF Group in 1996. Mark Logan, Helikon's Director of Design and Development, began to expand the product selection with collections by Gensler and Skidmore Owings and Merrill (SOM), and recently, he joined forces with Stephen Apking and Shashi Caan (SOM) to collaborate on the design of a new executive furniture collection, called Andante™ (initially called Epoch™, but was changed reportedly due to trademark issues). This Helikon system utilizes an integrated technology with classic architectural lines that is meant to address the needs of today's, non-hierarchical workplace (Figures 7.29 through 7.31).

FIGURE 7.29 Helikon's Andante™ system. The work surface opens like a briefcase and has outlets for electronic devices and easy connectivity, while the horizontal surface splits into individual sections so that laptops and other devices may be used to allow a meeting or discussion without obstructing conversation. Wires are hidden in grooves. The second element of the Andante™ system is the slender technology plane which contains interactive, group oriented technology such as flat-screen monitors, teleconferencing systems and white boards. The technology plane may be placed against the wall of an office or function as a spatial divider. The third element, which is the tower, provides professional and personal storage space. *(Courtesy Helikon Furniture Co.)*

The collection was developed to take into account private office, shared office, open plan and conferencing, and consists of three essential elements—a horizontal work surface, a storage tower, and a technology plane. The technology plane can accommodate personal electronic devices, flat plasma screen monitors, and Internet access, and is designed to anticipate current needs and future technological advances. (More information is available at www.helikon-furniture.com.)

Teknion

Teknion products address the large range of workplace criteria: supporting the complex integration of people and technology, facilitating productivity and creating an attractive workplace for millions of people working in Teknion office environments the world over. Teknion continuously introduces new products to support the evolving technology-driven office, and

FIGURE 7.30 Helikon's Taftville Executive 1, U-shape desk in crotch mahogany. (*Courtesy Helikon Furniture Co.*)

FIGURE 7.31 Helikon Presidio III Workstation with closet, workwall, organizing accessories, mobile pedestal, and tangent table. (*Courtesy Helikon Furniture Co.*)

that can be used to build complete, independent workstations and clusters, or to enhance the functionality of systems furniture already in place. With the addition of Ability® mobile furniture, for example, workspace components can be arranged to create different types of workstations and support changing work functions. In addition to office systems furniture and the Ability® line of mobile furniture, Teknion offers comprehensive storage and filing products, task and lounge seating, casegoods and executive furniture, as well as a full range of workplace accessories. (More information is available at www.teknion.com/home.asp.)

Technology intensive environments demand intelligent wire management solutions and effective distribution of power and data. To meet clients' specific requirements and enable businesses to cope with rapid technological change and evolving work processes, Teknion has developed and put in place an advanced electrical system solution (Figures 7.32 through 7.36).

FIGURE 7.32   Teknion Dharma Chair moves with the user to increase support and comfort. *(Courtesy Teknion Corporation)*

FIGURE 7.33
Teknion XM
Furniture
System in a
private office
context.
*(Courtesy
Teknion Cor-
poration)*

FIGURE 7.34
Teknion T/O/S
Panel System
used in a
teaming
area. *(Cour-
tesy Teknion
Corporation)*

FIGURE 7.35
Teknion Outpost
Column provides
lighting, as well as
power and data
connections.
*(Courtesy Teknion
Corporation)*

FIGURE 7.36
Teknion Transit
Off-Modular
System showing
a private office
configuration.
*(Courtesy
Teknion Corpo-
ration)*

Nucraft Furniture Company

Founded in 1944, Nucraft is a privately held manufacturer of high-quality wood office furniture. Based in Grand Rapids, Michigan, Nucraft manufactures and markets furniture specifically designed for conference and training rooms, reception areas, and private offices. They have an extensive line of products including conference tables, training tables, credenzas, media cabinets, visual boards, reception stations, occasional tables, modular shelving, bookcases, and benches. (More information is available at www.nucraft.com.) Nucraft emphasizes a comprehensive design oriented and technology driven philosophy relative to the niche markets it serves. For example, the company offers three distinctly different conference room furniture collections, each with its own particular design aesthetic. Nucraft's incorporation of some of the latest design elements, such as utilizing mixed materials of wood, glass and metal, set Nucraft products apart from other wood furniture manufacturers. The conference and training room furniture is designed to adapt to the changing technological needs of today's office environment and offers some of the most innovative technology integration available today. Innovative products include the Odyssey Table, an articulating conference table that opens to access power, voice and data connections down the center of table. This table, along with several other products in Nucraft's conference room collections, accommodates today's wide variety of conference and presentation formats including videoconferencing, dialogue conferencing, and electronic presentation formats (Figures 7.37 through 7.41).

FIGURE 7.37 Nucraft's Origin won the Gold Award for Furniture Systems at NeoCon World's Trade Fair 2002, and the Award for Best of Competition. *(Courtesy Nucraft Furniture Company)*

Technology Access

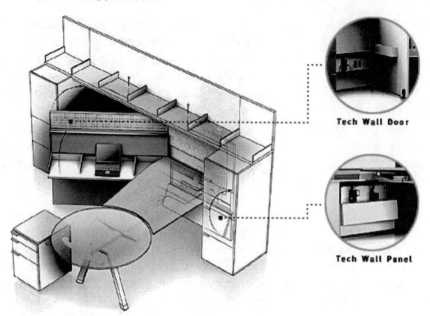

Tech Wall Door

Tech Wall Panel

FIGURE 7.38 Nucraft Origin Executive Furniture System showing technology integration. *(Courtesy Nucraft Furniture Company)*

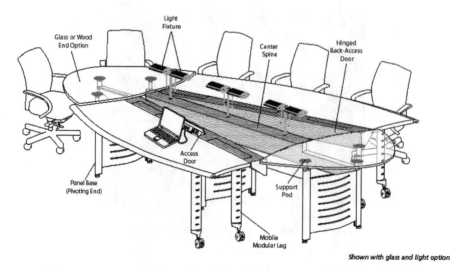

Light Fixture

Glass or Wood End Option

Center Spine

Hinged Back-Access Door

Access Door

Panel Base (Pivoting End)

Support Pod

Mobile Modular Leg

Shown with glass and light option

FIGURE 7.39 A perspective of Nucraft's Odyssey Table showing material options and construction. *(Courtesy Nucraft Furniture Company)*

Table Articulation is 25 degrees

Table Length	Closed Width	Open Width
149	70"	96"
198	79"	123"
259	87"	150"

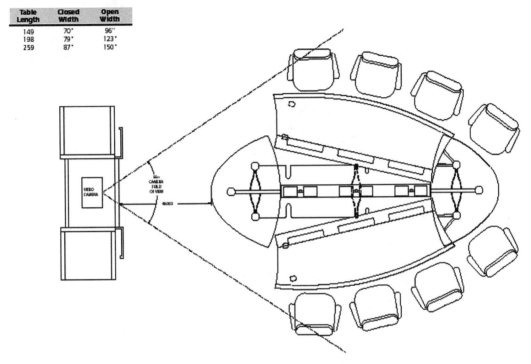

FIGURE 7.40 Plan drawing of Nucraft's Odyssey Table showing table articulation. *(Courtesy Nucraft Furniture Company)*

TYPES OF FURNITURE

Furniture is usually categorized according to the function it serves. These include seating, desks (workstations) and tables, office systems, storage, and beds.

Seating

From early Babylonian times through Roman times, the seat was reserved for royalty and nobility. The commoner used the floor. Throughout history, the chair has symbolized the throne, and it does so today. When a seated host or CEO rises, it is time for the others to depart.

High amongst the most talented seat designers of the last century are the husband-and-wife team of Charles and Ray Eames. Their own 1949 steel-frame house and studio in Pacific Palisades, California was also one of the century's most influential residential designs. From a

ELECTRICAL SECTION OF SPINE

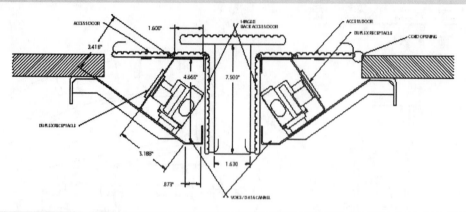

COMMUNICATION SECTION OF SPINE

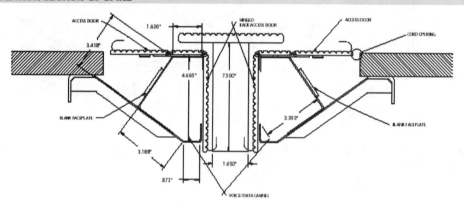

FIGURE 7.41 Nucraft Odyssey table detail showing electrical and communication set up. *(Courtesy Nucraft Furniture Company)*

technical stand point, Eames designs were highly innovative. They used plywood bent into compound curves and molded fiberglass-reinforced plastic for chair shells and rubber shock mounts for connections.

With the rapid advances in technology, more people find themselves seated for longer periods of time. This carries with it the inherent risk of increased back pain brought about by poor posture, cumulative strain and repetitive tasks. Chairs should provide good spinal and lateral support, incorporate adjustable features, and offer comfort to help users maintain correct posture. Manufacturers have become increasingly aware of these issues and have started introducing various ergonomic features to meet these challenges (Herman Miller is one of the pioneers), including adjustable height, pan tilt, depth, back height, back tilt, lumbar support, headrest (height and tilt), armrest (height, spacing, and tilt) and overall swivel and recline. Users should also have an adjustable footrest, if needed, to have feet resting flat. But no one type of seating can serve all functions, and seating must be appropriate for its use. A task chair that is used continuously throughout the day differs in its function from, say, a lounge chair or bar stool. Likewise, characteristics of a desk used by a child would differ from that used by an adult.

Desks and Tables

The workstation, or desk, is typically considered the most important element in the office, and where it is estimated that the majority of workers spend more than half of their waking hours. For some, the desk is a symbol of their importance and position in the corporate hierarchy, for others, it is a workbench where thoughts are crystallized and instructions are executed. When considering design criteria for a desk, one should obviously consider its size with respect to its function, but other factors also need to be considered, like its style, color, texture, and having a durable work surface, as well as its light reflectivity for the tasks performed.

Tables, like people, come in various shapes and forms. The conference table is one of the major status symbols of the corporation as can be seen from the examples illustrated in the previous sections. Some are very large and come in several segments, while others are smaller and less formal. You should plan enough space so that people do not feel cramped, which translates into about 24 inches to 30 inches per person. The coffee table is good for informal meetings, allowing people to gather at a closer social distance, while at the same time, is used to rest cups and paperwork. The utilitarian table serves other functions, whether it is collating reports or housing office equipment or for serving meals.

Modular and Office Systems

There is a growing database of information and available resources today, against which one can compare the adequacy, or otherwise, of existing or proposed workstation configurations. Open Ergonomics, Ltd, for example, offers a free 78 item online interactive workstation assessment tests. In addition, they maintain a comprehensive database of human dimensions, with a range of 280 dimensions for male and female adults (within eight distinct national populations—the United States, China, France, Germany, Holland, Italy, Japan and the U.K.).

It may be difficult today to imagine a time when open plan furniture systems did not exist, as we witness the profusion of designs currently flooding the market, making choosing a suitable system for a particular job no easy matter. System furniture is essentially a collection of modular components designed to fit together in a number of ways to create office workstations. Typically, they consist of panels that divide workstations and define areas, work surfaces, storage units, as well as lighting and wire management facilities. They are highly desirable because they save money by allowing space to be reconfigured economically, allow more people per square foot, and save the expense of enclosed offices for middle management.

David Ballast classifies systems furniture broadly into three types: The first he describes as using freestanding panels with conventional freestanding furniture. The second type, he says, "uses panels of various lengths and heights that link and provide support for work surfaces and storage units that are suspended from the panels," and the third is basically comprised of self-contained L-shaped or U-shaped workstations that include the work surface and other needed components. Systems furniture is used in open-office environments which necessitate a different office etiquette that takes into consideration the problems of visual and acoustical privacy. There has been considerable research in these fields in recent years.

Achieving an appropriate workplace environment in today's open plan offices, provides an enormous challenge to the space planner. To meet this challenge, several issues need to be satisfied, these include:

- Provision for privacy
- Promotion of communication
- Promotion of productivity
- Prevention of noise distraction, particularly conversational noise

Studies have shown that most common acoustical design problems in the open office can be resolved by integrated planning.

Storage

Storage is an important element in space planning and there never seems to be enough of it. In order to assess the amount of storage to be catered for, the space planner needs first of all to determine the types, sizes, and quantity of items to be stored, the desired location of the storage, and the frequency the items need to be accessed.

Beds

The majority of beds consist of one or two mattresses and some form of supporting framework, a footboard, and headboard. Other types of sleeping furniture are water beds, bunk beds, sofa beds and simple floor pads. In some European countries, they are sometimes part of a wall system with integrated lighting and storage units.

FURNITURE PROCUREMENT

Today, the majority of popular contract furnishers offer access to information and automated electronic order processing, along with features like online order tracking and online catalog.

This is particularly appealing to procurement personnel including facilities managers. In the forefront towards e-commerce expansion are manufacturers like Herman Miller and Steelcase.

Herman Miller's first foray into e-commerce was in 1998 via its SQA program that linked all sales and purchasing operations via the Internet. Then it formed *eZconnect*, which is a proprietary, Internet-based procurement program which is geared to medium to large companies and links customers, dealers, manufacturing operations, and suppliers.

Using eZconnect, end users can choose, design, order, build, ship, install, and move in, all online. This frees up much of the time of facility managers and other procurement staff. Herman Miller later introduced "Open Access," which expands and enhances its eZconnect B2B electronic ordering and delivery platform to include the support of non-Herman Miller manufactured products. Open Access is a direct response to their customers' feedback on how they could be served more effectively. Now, eZconnect enables customers to place and track orders, from desks and chairs to entire systems, any time of day.

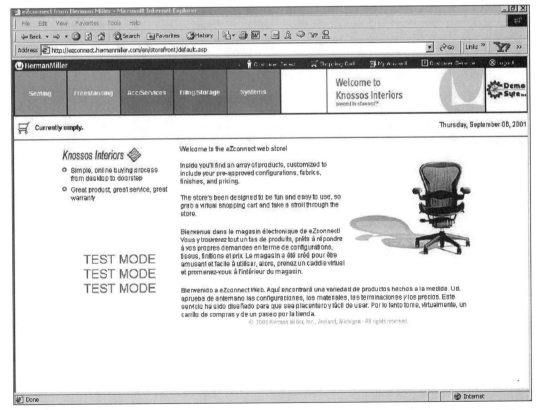

FIGURE 7.42 Knossos Interiors, using Herman Miller's eZconnect electronic ordering and delivery platform. *(Courtesy Herman Miller, Inc.)*

In 2000, Steelcase followed suit and launched its own online software procurement program, *Ensync*™, which enables customers to access a Web-based electronic catalog that greatly reduces the amount of time it takes to process an order. It is available exclusively through authorized Steelcase dealers. Delivery for many products can take place within seven to twelve days.

Like many of its competitors, Haworth introduced *World Resource*, an online ordering system that puts its customers' standards programs on the Web in a user friendly format, saving their customers time and money in travel. Haworth also introduced a new dealer e-tool called *Orderline*, which is a Web-based system that will help Haworth mistake-proof orders by giving dealers immediate feedback as they enter orders online.

Aside from saving the facilities department huge amounts of time during the ordering process, these new Web-based tools also eliminate the time needed when designing a furniture system. For example, eZconnect allows three dimensional design to take place in real time once a furniture system is chosen.

Nevertheless, some firms remain committed to the traditional format of ordering, particular firms that deal with residential furniture. Office furniture manufacturer Nucraft works through dealer supplied purchase orders, which, when approved, are entered into the scheduling system and the production process begins. Standard orders usually take five to six weeks lead time, and special orders generally require seven to eight weeks, depending on material availability and the complexity of the project. Many furniture manufacturers, including Nucraft, use CAP (Computer Aided Planning), a procurement product of the Sweets Group, a division of the McGraw-Hill Companies.

CAP Studio is an integrated software system developed specifically for interior designers and facility planners that enhances workplace performance. This modern suite of applications is interactive and works together seamlessly. It allows you to navigate manufacturers' catalogs, select products, specify furniture, design in plan view and 3D, assign options, create worksheets and build a project where and when you want. (More information at www.cap-online.com)

FABRICS

Fabric selection can have a profound impact on the atmosphere of an interior. In furniture applications, upholstered furniture also has a great influence on its appearance, durability, and safety. Because of the multitude of fabric types, colors, and prices that confront space planners or interior designers, they must have a fundamental understanding of the material to be able to select the right fabrics and padding for a specific use. This applies whether the designer is selecting from fabric offered by the furniture manufacturer or specifying the customer's own material. Also, today, many textiles consist of more than one type of fiber. For example, Knoll's *Analogy* fabric is made up of 48 percent PVC and 52 percent polyester, and can be used as a wall covering, panel, or upholstery material.

Types of Fabrics

Fabrics are either natural or synthetic, based on the type of fiber they're comprised of. Natural fibers can further be divided into two categories: cellulosic and protein. Cellulosic fibers, such as cotton and linen, originate from plants, while protein fibers, such as wool, are made from animal sources. Unlike natural fibers, manufactured fibers can be extruded in various thicknesses.

It is important to understand that each fiber has a unique composition and its own set of physical properties. The U. S. Federal Trade Commission has established generic names and definitions for manufactured fibers, such as acetate, acrylic, lyocell, modacrylic, nylon, polyester, polypropylene (olefin), rayon, and spandex. However, all fibers under a generic name are not exactly identical.

Fiber manufacturers have been able to modify the basic composition of each generic fiber, both chemically and physically, to produce variations which provide improved characteristics, a softer feel, greater comfort, brighter/longer lasting colors, better warmth/cooling, moisture transport/wicking, and better properties for blending with other fibers. These improved fibers are typically given a trademark name and are owned and promoted by the fiber producer. The most common fibers available on the market today include:

- *Wool* is generally obtained from the fleece of sheep, and is considered to be one of the best natural fibers for all types of fabrics. Wool is also dirt resistant, and, in many weaves, resists wear and tearing. It has excellent resilience and elasticity. Although wool will burn when exposed to flame, it is self-extinguishing when the flame is removed. It accepts dyes well and can be cleaned easily.

- *Cotton* is a cellulosic fiber that comes from the cotton plant's seed pod. Cotton breathes, is relatively inexpensive, and has moderately good abrasion resistance. However, cotton has poor resilience and recovery properties and degrades under prolonged sunlight exposure. It is also subject to mildew. Mercerized cotton is treated to permanently straighten the cotton fibers which then becomes a smooth, rod-like fiber that is uniform in appearance with a high luster. Cotton is often blended with other fibers such as polyester, linen, wool, to blend the best properties of each fiber.

- *Linen* is from flax, a bast fiber taken from the stalk of the plant. It is the strongest of the vegetable fibers and has 2 to 3 times the strength of cotton. However, it is seldom used for upholstery because it lacks resilience, flexibility, and is susceptible to abrasion. In addition, it does not take printed dyes very well.

- *Silk* is a natural protein fiber, taken from the cocoon of the silkworm. It is very strong and has good resilience and flexibility. The finish and luster of silk are generally highly valued, but it is very expensive and is weakened by sunlight and perspiration.

- *Acetate fiber* is a manufactured cellulosic fiber made from wood pulp—a natural, renewable resource—and acetic acid. It is a regenerated cellulosic fiber that is flammable and does not wear well. Like rayon, in its unmodified state it has poor sunlight resistance. Both light and flame resistance can be improved by treating the fiber. Improved formulations (for example, the incorporation of antimicrobial ingredient to inhibit the growth of bacteria, mold, mildew and fungi in products) include: Celanese®, Celebrate®, Microsafe®.

- *Nylon* is one of the most popular synthetic fibers. It has exceptional durability and tear strength, with high resiliency and elasticity. Nylon is lightweight, and resistant to many chemicals, water, and microorganisms. Some of the first nylons were not resistant to sunlight and had a shiny appearance, but these problems can now be compensated for by chemical formulations. Nylon works well solo or in combination with other popular synthetic or natural fibers to obtain the superior advantages of both. Prime nylon producers include: Allied Signal, BASF Corp., Cookson Fibers, DuPont, and Solutia.

- *Acrylic* is often used as a replacement for wool because of its appearance. It has moderately good strength and resilience and is very resistant to sunlight but can be flammable. Modacrylics have similar properties but have much greater resistance to heat and flame. Due to its lower specific gravity, acrylic fiber also produces fabrics having more bulk without extra weight. A recently introduced acrylic fiber is Weather Bloc™ which has many interesting properties; it is weather resistant, tough enough for fabrics which must perform out-of-doors, impervious to UV light degradation, excellent print base, withstands mold and mildew, remains brightly colorfast, and produces fabrics which sew easily, make up beautifully and possess excellent dimensional stability. Some of the better known trademarks are: MicroSupreme®, Cresloft™, Creslan® Plus, BioFresh™, WeatherBloc™, Dralon™, Acrilan®, Bounce-Back®, Duraspun®, Pil-Trol®, Sno-Brite™, The Smart Yarns®, Wear-Dated®.

- *Olefin* (polyolefin/polypropylene) is inexpensive and is highly resistant to chemicals, mildew, and microorganisms. It has good color retention and is highly resilient and nonabsorbent. Its desirable qualities make it useful for carpeting and carpet backing, but its low resistance to sunlight, heat, and flame makes it undesirable for most upholstery fabrics. Some of the better know trademarks include: Salus™, Telar®, Alpha Olefin™, Essera™, Kermel™, Innova®, Innova® AMP, Marvess™, Ryton™, Trace™.

- *Polyester* has many desirable qualities including good resilience and elasticity, high resistance to solvents and other chemicals, and good resistance to sunlight. Its lack-luster burning properties, can be remedied by treatment to make it more flame-resistance. It also tends to absorb and hold oily materials. Dupont is one of the prime manufacturers of polyester fiber; others include Cookson Fibers, Wellman, and KoSa.

- *Rayon* is the result of efforts to create a cheaper substitute for the precious and expensive silk fiber. Even though rayon is considered a manufactured fiber, it is made from tree cellulose. It has poor resistance to sunlight and poor resiliency. It is also flammable which is why it is not often used for upholstery. One common trade name for rayon is Modal®. Rayon is highly absorbent, soft and comfortable, easy to dye and drapes well. Rayon is commonly blended with other fibers to obtain the best characteristics from each fiber.

FABRIC SELECTION

To determine the best fabric for a particular piece of furniture or wallcovering, a balancing act takes place between the functional requirements and the aesthetic requirements, as well as other factors like cost and availability. The fabric for a restaurant would not be the same as that for child's room. Some of the determining factors for fabric selection are outlined below:

- *Appearance:* Often a well designed piece of furniture becomes totally inappropriate because the wrong color, texture, or pattern is chosen. The designer should ensure that the colors and patterns of the furniture blend in with the rest of the design.
- *Durability:* This includes resistance to abrasion, fading, and other abuses as well as its clean-ability and stain resistance. Fabrics like nylon and wool are more durable than say, rayon.
- *Flammability:* This is a very important consideration, particularly in public places like auditoriums, hospitals and restaurants. Certain fabrics are inherently more flame-resistant than others, but today, the majority of fabrics can be treated with various chemicals to enhance their resistance to ignition and smoldering. Many states and most federal agencies have flammability standards for furniture. These are discussed in the chapter on codes.
- Maintenance: Some fabrics require more maintenance than others. If the furniture is to be subjected to substantial wear, an appropriate fabric should be chosen.
- *Comfort:* David Ballast says, "People come in direct contact with furniture more than any other component of interior space, so comfort must be appropriate for the intended use and for ergonomic requirements. A waiting room chair does not need to be as comfortable as an office worker's chair." The designer should choose an appropriate fabric that is comfortable to the touch. A porous fabric breathes and is more comfortable for long periods of sitting, and where the temperature is high. Likewise, smooth fabrics are more comfortable than rough textured ones.

There are many other factors which the designer should consider in making a fabric selection such as fabric durability, its touch characteristics, the scale of its patterns or texture, and so on.

FLOORING

Flooring tends to set the tone of the interior whether in the home, the office, or the mall. Although aesthetics plays an important role in any design solution, flooring must be practical in today's environment. Today's designer has an enormous range of flooring types, colors and patterns from which to choose. Flooring can pull a design together or visually fragment it. The use of one continuous material increases the flow and homogeneity and suggests that areas share equal importance and are equally accessible, whereas the introduction of accent flooring suggests that special areas exist. An accent area can consist of a different material; or may only be a variation in color or pattern. The material itself often give a clue to the activity of the space, since it is the one material that is always in contact with the users. Thus, rubber flooring and vinyl tile suggests a high traffic area that is expected to take punishment and get dirty, and therefore should not require high maintenance.

Wood

Wood is a widely used floor material that has maintained its popularity over the centuries. It is practical, both functionally and aesthetically, and works in most environments. Its warm mellow tone, soft touch, and easy maintenance make it a favorite in residential applications. It lasts well, comes in a variety of formats, and makes an excellent base for decorative rugs.

Wood usually comes in hardwood strip, block, parquet, or board form. The most common species used are beech, maple, ash, birch, pine, or oak. Most types of strip flooring come tongue-and-groove so that the planks fit together without leaving any gaps. Parquet flooring is composed of small blocks of hardwood fitted together in certain patterns. In older homes, wood floorboards are typical, usually found laid horizontally across the room, resting on the joists that run from the front of the house to the back.

Carpet

Carpet denotes a more relaxed, contemplative, and higher status area because it is softer underfoot and therefore quieter. Moreover, designers can combine various colors, textures and patterns of carpet to create visual excitement, define specific work areas or to direct traffic in corridors and common areas. Corporations can also incorporate product colors and company logos in their flooring designs. Carpet also has low maintenance costs compared with other commercial floor coverings.

The inherent cushioning and non-slip characteristics of carpet contribute to a comfortable and safe work environment by reducing the likelihood of falls and minimizing potential injuries. These properties also may help lower insurance costs in commercial enterprises. Additionally, the insulating properties of carpet keep floors warm in winter and cool in summer, which helps reduce heating and cooling costs. Likewise, carpet provides acoustical benefits by absorbing airborne sound, reducing surface noise generation, and helps block sound transmission to floors below. The current trend in carpeting is for increasing specification of nylon fiber carpets for their superior long-term performance, including their improved resistance to staining, soiling, matting, crushing, texture loss, and abrasive wear compared to other fibers.

Vinyl and Linoleum

Vinyl comes in an infinite variety of colors and patterns, often with designs that simulate other more expensive types of flooring such as wood, tile, and marble. It is a wholly synthetic material and contains a varying percentage of PVC, which gives it a certain flexibility. Also, it is inexpensive, and comes in sheet or tile form.

Linoleum is also available in sheet or tile form and comes in a comprehensive range of colors and patterns. Its recent rediscovery is largely due to its improved performance and because it is made up of entirely natural ingredients

Hard Tiles and Mosaic

Hard tiles including ceramic, terracotta, and quarry tiles are generally machine-made, which gives them a precise size, and are particularly suited to areas where water is often present, like kitchens and bathrooms. Tiles of baked clay, such as the popular quarry tile, are similar to masonry materials and require a sturdy subfloor. The small scale of mosaic tiles gives them an almost soft appearance. They consist of small cubes of terracotta, marble, ceramic, or stone and are bedded in mortar. Mosaic is best restricted to small areas like bathrooms.

Marble, Granite, and Terrazzo

Marble and granite are more widely used in countries of the Middle East, Greece and Italy than in the United States. Both materials have prestigious connotations and are primarily used in banks and foyers of commercial buildings and some custom dwellings.

Terrazzo is a relative newcomer to the American domestic scene. It has been popular in Mediterranean countries from early times. Terrazzo is an aggregate of marble or granite chips mixed into a cement mortar and either laid in place or as slabs or tiles. The mix is then ground and polished to a smooth surface after it has set. Both formats are expensive in the United States and require professional installation.

Other Materials—Stone, Brick, Concrete, Rubber, Cork, Metal, Rugs

Stone is a traditional material which has been used for thousands of years in many countries around the world. It can bring an unmatched depth of richness and character to the interior or exterior. Natural stone comes in a variety of formats, colors, patterns, and textures. However, the thicker, larger flags or tiles are heavy and need a solid subfloor to bear their weight. Slate and limestone are the stones most frequently used by designers.

Several types of hard wearing brick are available for indoor use. These should be laid on concrete, and should be sealed for a stronger finish and to prevent dust, etc. Brick is also used for exterior paving and in restaurants and residential patios. Sometimes it is used as an accent or divider in conjunction with other materials.

Concrete is basically a structural material and can provoke strong reactions when used in commercial or domestic settings. It can be troweled to a smooth surface and treated in a number of ways to alter its texture and color. It should either be sealed and polished or painted with special floor paint. Although generally regarded as acceptable only in utility areas, the material has considerable machismo when properly used.

Studded rubber flooring was introduced to residential applications with the arrival of high tech, and enjoyed a brief spurt of popularity. It has now reemerged and is available in a variety of colors, and in sheet or tile, with either a smooth finish or in relief. Cork is a warm material and soft to the touch. It is produced in tile or sheet form and is sealed with polyurethane. It is used more in Europe than in the United States. Metal flooring is another material that has certain applications. It is used for raised floors and in some commercial applications.

The term *rug* is used for a movable unit of carpet, usually smaller than the room it is placed in. They come in a wide variety of sizes, colors and patterns. They are either handmade or machine made. Area rugs are used to group items of furniture within a larger space.

WALL TREATMENTS

Walls are important elements of any design scheme because they define spaces, segregate activities, and mark out personal domains within the home or office. Their importance is highlighted by the enormous variety of treatments available that draw attention to the walls themselves. In addition to the obvious paint, the market is saturated with all types of wallcovering material, including fabrics, leather and carpet, in addition to the paper and vinyl wallcoverings of the past. For high traffic areas, there are ceramic and clay tiles, metal panels, plastic laminate, and rubber, as well as rougher cinderblock, brick, and glass block.

Paint

Color is a key element in most contemporary interiors, and paint is one of the simplest and least expensive ways of providing an acceptable finish to our home, office or store, which is obviously why it is the most widely used. It wasn't long ago that the walls of corporations were plastered and painted white, because it was a neutral background for everything else. Unfortunately, white is highly reflective and hard on the eyes, which is why softer colors are now preferred in many applications. Special colors can be mixed on the job by skilled painters.

Wallpaper

Wallpaper offers a large variety of textures, patterns, and imagery, often making it a viable alternative to paint. Wallpapers are traditionally made of either paper, cloth, or paper-backed PVC. Vinyl papers are water and steam-proof, washable and tougher than normal paper, which makes them suitable for use in kitchens, bathrooms and utility areas. Wallpaper also remains popular because it is a practical way of hiding surface imperfections. The vinyl type is frequently used in commercial applications as well as in the home.

Marble, Stone and Brick

Marble is widely used in monumental spaces and prestige locations such as banks. Marbles are available in varied colors and veining patterns.

Cladding

Wall cladding makes practical sense in many situations, and allows the character of raw materials to be explored in the context of contemporary wall decoration. Wood is the classic cladding material, and often reflects a feeling of luxury. Plain pine cladding, readily available in tongue and groove boards, can be painted or left natural with a coat of matte varnish to seal the wood. Plywood and veneer panels when intelligently applied, also look impressive on walls.

Tiling is a tried and tested formula for areas of heavy wear or maximum exposure to water and heat, typically kitchens, bathrooms and areas around pools. The material comes in a vast variety of colors, shapes, textures, patterns, and sizes, from the tiny mosaic to the large squares and rectangles. Mirror is an ideal material for small areas where an illusion of increased space is desired.

Other Materials

Although fabric is traditionally popular as a material for wall covering, and is available in a variety of colors and textures, vinyl and other plastic sheet materials have increased in popularity and are now in wide use as wall covering. Many simulate other materials such as grass or cloth.

CHAPTER EIGHT

BUILDING CODES AND STANDARDS

*B*uilding codes are an essential part of the design process. They are the law of the land, enforced by local governments in the United States, whereas in Canada enforcement responsibility lies with the provincial and territorial governments. Codes have been put in place to regulate construction and thereby to protect the people's health, safety and welfare.

GENERAL OVERVIEW

There is no uniform building code in the United States, so building codes vary from one jurisdiction to another. Each municipality (county or district in sparsely populated areas) enforces a set of regulations. Most jurisdictions adopt all or part of one of the main Model Codes outlined later in the chapter. However, there is a general movement today that is gathering momentum and strength to unify the many local codes around the nation. In response to the building industry's repeated requests for the setting up of a single unified building regulatory system to be used throughout the nation, many states have already moved in that direction. With this in mind, the three main model code organizations came together and formed the International Code Council (ICC). Its mission is to unify the code system into a single set of codes and the creation of the first comprehensive set of building codes that can be used anywhere in the United States.

Construction can be a very complicated business, and the first step in any construction project is to get a building permit (Figure 8.1). This basically entails submission of plans and specifications with an application at the relevant department for checking and approval before a building permit is issued. By law, the code office must either approve or reject your application within a given time frame, typically 30 days. While most codes are neither easily understood nor user-friendly, positive attitudes, good communication, and technical expertise often control the outcome of most successful meetings with the inspector. During construction, inspections take place on a regular basis to verify that the building is being constructed according to approved drawings.

Computers are increasingly playing a pivotal role in code enforcement and information gathering. Various software packages and computerized versions of code publications are currently on the market and help explain the different applicable codes by providing search capabilities and other features. Today, computers are also increasingly being used in fire research and testing, using computer models and other means to develop the building codes still further.

HISTORICAL OVERVIEW OF BUILDING CODES AND STANDARDS

Antiquity

Building codes have been with us since the dawn of history, when people first learned to read and write. In Old Babylon we see the birth of building regulations, during the reign of King Hammurabi (1792-1750 B.C.). These codes meted harsh punishment to irresponsible builders, indicating that the building trade was already a specialized profession. According to the king's decree, if an architect built a house for a freeman and it collapsed and killed the occupant, then the architect could be put to death—the doctrine of "an eye for an eye, a tooth for a tooth." Biblical references of code-type requirements can also be found in the Old Testament with provisions like the one in Deuteronomy 22:8, which states, "When you build a new house you shall make a parapet for your roof that you may not bring the guilt of blood upon your house if anyone fall from it." This code has changed little over the years and now forms Section 1716 of the UBC, which reads, "All unenclosed floor and roof openings and roofs used for other than service for the building shall be protected by a guardrail."

Greek and Roman building regulations consisted of a series of detailed specifications governing contractual relationships rather than an actual code of law. Like today, buildings under construction were inspected regularly. Heinrick Lattermann, while restoring a document engraved in the stone of a Roman building built about 341 B.C., discovered that the engraving included detailed building procedures and regulations on how the stones were to be laid and the number of iron dowels to be used, all under the supervision of the architect.

Perhaps the most significant predecessor of the modern building code is Henry Fitz-Elwyne's *Assize of Buildings*, published in London in 1189. Scholars consider this document to be England's earliest building act and a representative example of municipal legislative power.

BUILDING PERMIT APPLICATION

FAIRFAX COUNTY OFFICE OF BUILDING CODE SERVICES
PERMIT APPLICATION CENTER
12055 Government Center Parkway, 2nd Floor   Telephone: 703-222-0801
Fairfax, Virginia 22035-5504   Web site: http://www.co.fairfax.va.us/dpwes

FILL IN ALL APPROPRIATE INFORMATION IN THIS COLUMN
(PLEASE PRINT OR TYPE)

JOB LOCATION
ADDRESS
LOT # _____ BUILDING _____
FLOOR _____ SUITE _____
SUBDIVISION
TENANT'S NAME

OWNER INFORMATION   OWNER ☐   TENANT ☐
NAME
ADDRESS
CITY _____ STATE _____ ZIP _____
TELEPHONE

CONTRACTOR INFORMATION   SAME AS OWNER ☐
CONTRACTORS MUST PROVIDE THE FOLLOWING:
COMPANY NAME
ADDRESS
CITY _____ STATE _____ ZIP _____
TELEPHONE
STATE CONTRACTORS LICENSE #
COUNTY BPOL #

APPLICANT

DESCRIPTION OF WORK
_____
_____
_____
_____
_____

HOUSE TYPE
ESTIMATED COST OF CONSTRUCTION
BLDG AREA (SQ FT OF FOOTPRINT)
USE GROUP OF BUILDING
TYPE OF CONSTRUCTION
SEWER SERVICE   PUBLIC ☐   SEPTIC ☐   OTHER ☐
WATER SERVICE   PUBLIC ☐   WELL ☐   OTHER ☐
OTHER PLEASE SPECIFY

DESIGNATED MECHANICS' LIEN AGENT
(Residential Construction Only)
NAME
ADDRESS

NONE DESIGNATED ☐   PHONE

CHARACTERISTICS FOR NEW SFD, TH, APT & CONDOS

# KITCHENS		EXTER. WALLS	
# BATHS		INTER. WALLS	
# HALF BATHS		ROOF MATERIAL	
# BEDROOMS		FLOOR MATERIAL	
# OF ROOMS		FIN. BASEMENT	%
# STORIES		HEATING FUEL	
BUILDING HEIGHT		HEATING SYSTEM	
BUILDING AREA		# FIREPLACES	
BASEMENT			

Any and all information and/or stamps on the reverse side of this form are a part of this application and must be complied with. I hereby certify that I have authority of the owner to make this application, that the information is complete and correct, and that the construction and/or use will conform to the building code, the zoning ordinance and other applicable laws and regulations which relate to the property.

_____
Signature of Owner or Agent   Date

_____
Printed Name and Title
(Notarization of signature is required if owner is listed as the contractor and is not present at time of application)

PERMIT # _____

FOR INSPECTIONS CALL   703-222-0455 (see back for more information)

DO NOT WRITE IN GRAY SPACES - COUNTY USE ONLY
PLAN #
TAX MAP #

ROUTING	DATE	APPROVED BY
LICENSING		
ZONING		
SITE PERMITS		
HEALTH DEPT.		
BUILDING REVIEW		
SANITATION		
FIRE MARSHAL		
ASBESTOS		
PROFFERS		

FEE $
FILING FEE $
AMOUNT DUE   = $

BUILDING PLAN REVIEW
REVIEWER _____ # OF HOURS
REVISION FEES $
FIRE MARSHAL FEES $
FIXTURE UNITS _____ PLAN LOC: J ☐   R ☐

APPROVED FOR ISSUANCE OF BUILDING PERMIT
(LOG OUT)
BY _____ DATE

ZONING REVIEW
USE
ZONING DISTRICT _____ HISTORICAL DISTRICT _____
ZONING CASE #
GROSS FLOOR AREA OF TENANT SPACE

YARDS:	GARAGE	1 ☐ 2 ☐ 3 ☐
FRONT	OPTIONS	YES ☐ NO ☐
FRONT	REMARKS	
L SIDE		
R SIDE		
REAR		

GRADING AND DRAINAGE REVIEW
SOILS   # _____ A ☐   B ☐   C ☐
AREA TO BE DISTURBED (TOTAL SQ FT THIS PERMIT)
IMPERVIOUS AREA (TOTAL SQ FT THIS PERMIT)
PLAN # _____ APPR. DATE

STAMPS

(See reverse side of application)

REMARKS _____
_____
_____
_____

NOTARIZATION (if required)
State (or territory or district) of _____
County (or city) of _____, to wit:
I, _____,
a Notary Public in the State and County aforesaid, do certify that

whose name is signed to this application, appeared before me in the State and County aforesaid and executed this affidavit.
Given under my hand this _____ day of _____, 20_____.
My commission expires the _____ day of _____, 20_____.

_____
(Notary Signature)

FIGURE 8.1   Sample application form for building permit.

Under this ordinance, individuals had the right to have construction halted until the Mayor could rule on the matter.

The earliest document on record that approaches the modern building code concept was the 1676 Act of Parliament for the rebuilding of London after the Great Fire of 1666. The Act was in many ways a reaction to the devastation and loss of life caused by the great Fire of London. Buildings were classified into various types and appropriate building materials were specified for use in new construction, while permit fees were espoused for inspection work. This building regulation was updated over the years until the Metropolitan Building Act of 1844 created a new building code that included its enforcement with regulations for types of buildings, heights, areas, and occupancies enforceable by official referees.

Recent History

In an attempt to address the problems of fire, disease, and natural disaster, the United States initially looked to English laws and slowly adopted them. The first American codes focused on fire prevention and the first building law on record dates to 1625 in New Amsterdam (now New York). The evolution of building codes in the United States was erratic. The 19th century witnessed the destruction of many important American cities by fire, and repeated outbreaks of yellow fever, typhus, and smallpox. This was partly due to the inadequate building regulations that prevailed at the time that led to overcrowding and the use of combustible construction void of firewalls. By the end of the century, many large cities had started to take building regulations seriously to safeguard the public, and to develop and enforce their own municipal building codes.

Among the pioneers in this respect was the Seattle Building Code and the Chicago Building Code of 1875. However, many of the efforts by municipal governments to create effective building laws were brought into question after the disastrous Baltimore fire of 1904. About this time, an attempt was made to bring some cohesion to the various city codes in existence. Under the visionary leadership of F.W. Fitzpatrick, an organization called "The International Society of State and Municipal Building Commissions and Inspectors" was formed. Even though the organization drafted Fitzpatrick's ideas for a national uniform building code, the concept never came to fruition. Instead, the National Board of Fire Underwriters, set up in the mid-1800's, founded the 1905 National Building Code. This first model code was written largely from the standpoint of the insurance industry to lessen fire risk. Concern over the evident bias of this code pushed municipal, county, and state building officials into establishing their own model codes on a regional basis. Under this system, the selection and enforcement of building regulations remain within the jurisdiction of state and local governments.

In 1915 in Hartford, Connecticut, the Building Officials Conference of America, or BOCA, was founded. BOCA was essentially an outgrowth of insurance interests, being incorporated since 1938. Today, this code is known as the BOCA National Building Code. In 1922, 13 building officials gathered in San Francisco and formed the Pacific Coast Building Officials Conference, also with the aim of developing a model building code. This group, which later became known as the International Conference of Building Officials or ICBO, was located primarily in the western regions of the United States and published their first edition of the Uniform Building Code in 1927. A similar group of building officials gathered in Alabama in 1940 and founded the Southern Building Code Congress International, or SBCCI. Their first Standard Building Code was published in 1945.

The Current Status

The active role of the federal government in state and local affairs after World War II led to a greater scrutiny of existing building codes and standards. One of the most confusing aspects of codes and standards in the United States is that, unlike Europe, Canada, and many other parts of the world, there is a complete absence of uniformity between federal agencies, states, counties, and municipalities. It should be said, however, that in recent years there have been major efforts to unify codes on the national level, and currently more than 85 percent of the states now have accepted model codes.

When dealing with counties and municipalities, we are confronted with other issues. For example, cities like Houston have large oil refineries that create certain hazards, and cities like Chicago and New York require special codes and standards that relate to high-rise buildings and population density. The state of California has also decided against using the IBC codes and elected to continue using the 1997 Uniform Building Code T as the basis for the 2001 edition of the California Standards Code.

On the other hand, a town that lies in the path of hurricanes may require special storm protection standards. It is no surprise therefore that some codes have evolved through modifications necessitated by particular geographic and population needs. Figure 8.2 shows the overlapping code structures and the authorities with jurisdiction that may be encountered at the local level.

While the terrorist attacks of September 11 and Oklahoma City are impacting code development, there is a general recognition that it is not feasible to mandate buildings capable of withstanding the devastating impacts and fires purposely caused by terrorists. New scientific evidence is being uncovered and detailed analyses of buildings' performance are being evaluated. These findings indicate that changes in building codes, fire codes, emergency planning, and emergency response procedures are warranted. Figure 8.3 is a general checklist to indicate whether the project is code compliant or not.

For decades, the building industry has been clamoring for a single, unified building regulatory system to be used throughout the United States. In 1994, The International Code Council (ICC) was established as a nonprofit organization dedicated to developing a single set of comprehensive and coordinated national model construction codes.

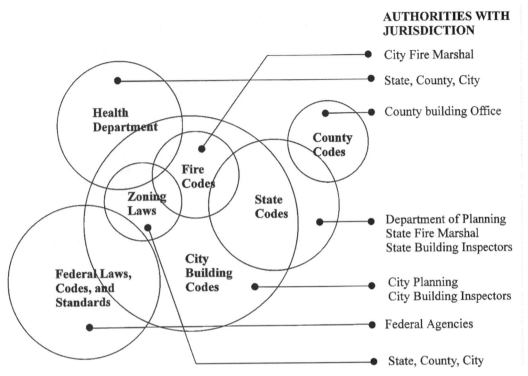

FIGURE 8.2 Overlapping code structure and complexity of current regulations. *(From Specifications for Commercial Interiors by S.C. Reznikoff)*

MODEL CODE ORGANIZATIONS

ICC (International Code Council)

According to ICC's mission statement, the organization was formed to "promulgate a comprehensive and compatible regulatory system for the built environment, through consistent performance-based regulations that are effective, efficient and meet government, industry and public needs." Among ICC's primary goals is to safeguard public health, safety, and welfare, while enhancing economic development through the use of state of the art technology in materials research, design and construction practices, and risks/hazards to the public in buildings and structures. ICC also seeks to simplify the existing building regulatory system by adopting a single family of codes that brings with it, consistency and compatibility while continuing to meet the many requirements at the international, federal, state, and local levels.

INTERIOR PROJECT CHECKLIST

1 DETERMINE WHICH CODES ARE REQUIRED
___ Building Code and Other Code Publications
___ Standards and Tests
___ Government Regulations
___ Local Codes and Ordinances

2 OCCUPANCY REQUIREMENTS
___ Determine Type of Occupancy Classification(s)
___ Calculate Occupancy Load(s)
___ Review Specific Occupancy Requirements
___ Compare Code and Accessibility Requirements

3 MINIMUM TYPE OF CONSTRUCTION
___ Determine Construction Type
___ Determine Ratings of Structural Elements
___ Calculate Maximum Floor Area (as required)
___ Calculate Building Height (as required)
___ Check All Enforced Standards

4 MEANS OF EGRESS REQUIREMENTS
___ Determine Quantity and Type of Each Means of Egress
___ Calculate Travel Distance
___ Calculate Minimum Widths
___ Determine Required Signage
___ Compare Code and Accessibility Requirements
___ Check All Enforce Standards

5 FIRE RESISTANT REQUIREMENTS
___ Determine Fire and Smoke Barriers
___ Determine Through Penetration Opening Protectives
___ Review Types of Fire Tests and Ratings Required
___ Compare Code and Accessibility Requirements
___ Check All Enforced Standards

6 FIRE PROTECTON REQUIREMENTS
___ Determine Fire and Smoke Detection Systems
___ Determine Fire Supression Systems
___ Review Possible Sprinkler Tradeoffs (as required)

7 REVIEW PLUMBING REQUIREMENTS
___ Determine Types of Fixtures Required
___ Calculate Number of Each Fixture Required
___ Compare Code and Accessibility Requirements
___ Coordinate with Engineer (as required)

8 REVIEW MECHANICAL REQUIREMENTS
___ Determine Access and Clearance Requirements
___ Figure Zoning and Thermostate Locations
___ Determine Type of Air Distribution System
___ Check for Accessibility Compliance
___ Coordinate with Engineer (as required)

9 REVIEW ELECTRICAL REQUIREMENTS
___ Determine Location of Outlets, Switches, and Fixtures
___ Determine Emergency Power and Lighting Requirements
___ Determine Types of Communication Requirments
___ Check for Accessibility Compliance
___ Coordinate with Engineer (as required)

10 FINISH AND FURNITURE REQUIREMENTS
___ Review Tests and Types of Ratings Required
___ Determine Special Finish Requirements
___ Determine Special Funiture Requirements
___ Compare Code and Accessibility Requirements
___ Check All Enforced Standards

NOTE: Consult the jurisdiction having authority at any step in question.

FIGURE 8.3 A general checklist used to determine general code compliance. *(From The Codes Guidebook for Interiors by S.K. Harmon and K.G. Kennon)*

There are many advantages to merging the efforts of existing code organizations into a single set of codes. Not only will it lead to safer, more efficient, and more durable buildings, but it will also allow code enforcement officials, architects, and other design professionals to work with a uniform and coherent set of standards and regulations throughout the United States. Moreover, it will allow manufacturers to focus their attention and energies on research, and development as well as allow them to be more competitive in marketing their products nationally and internationally. ICC made great strides in 2000 when it published their first codes, the International Building Code (IBC)—a single family of codes that is being adopted across the nation. It is hoped that as the IBC codes gain popularity, the existing regional and local model codes will be phased out.

The ICC was founded under the auspices of the three primary model code organizations. Which are as follows:

- The Building Officials and Code Administrators International, Inc. (BOCA).
- The International Conference of Building Officials (ICBO).
- The Southern Building Code Congress International, Inc. (SBCCI).

(The Council of American Building Officials (CABO) was also incorporated into the ICC in 1998.)

Since the early part of the last century, the three chief nonprofit model code organizations that founded the ICC have provided separate sets of model codes for use throughout the United States. Although these regional code developments have been effective and responsive to our country's needs, the time was seen to be ripe for a single set of codes. Today, an overwhelming majority (97 percent) of cities, counties and states that adopt building and safety codes are using documents published by the International Code Council and its members. The IBC, like its predecessors, will be updated every three years and will gradually replace the existing model codes. BOCA, ICBO and SBCCI have agreed to merge their respective organizations into one model code group. This will allow a single approach to the proper interpretation, training and other services for the International Codes. Below is a partial list of major national organizations that support the adoption of the International Building Code:

- U.S. Federal Emergency Management Agency (FEMA)
- U.S. Department of Housing and Urban Development (HUD)
- American Institute of Architects (AIA)
- American Institute of Building Design (AIBD)
- American Planning Association (APA)
- Building Owners and Managers Association (BOMA)
- Institute for Business & Home Safety (IBHS)
- National Apartment Association (NAA)
- National Association of Home Builders (NAHB)
- National Multi Housing Council (NMHC)

The appeal of ICC's International Codes continues to widen. Currently, the International Codes have been adopted in at least part of 37 states, as well as the District of Columbia, Puerto Rico and the United States Department of the Navy.

ICC has developed and made available numerous international code publications pertaining to building, energy conservation, fire, fuel gas, mechanical, plumbing, residential, property maintenance, private sewage disposal, zoning, as well as the ICC electrical code administrative provisions and the ICC Performance Code for Buildings and Facilities. All of the above codes are comprehensive and coordinated with each other.

BOCA (Building Officials and Code Administrators International, Inc.)

The Building Officials & Code Administrators (BOCA) model codes are adopted generally in the eastern parts of the United States. BOCA was incorporated in 1938, and is the oldest professional association of construction code officials in America. As previously stated, it is also a cofounder of the International Code Council, which created a single unified set of model regulatory codes for use in America and worldwide. BOCA was specifically set up as a forum for the interchange of information and expertise concerning building safety and construction regulation. BOCA now fully supports the ICC codes.

BOCA is one of the major publishers of model codes, and maintains international resources for a comprehensive collection of printed materials related to codes and code enforcement, including the ICC International Codes and the BOCA National Codes. BOCA states regulations in terms of measured performance rather than in rigid specifications of materials whenever possible and, in this way, encourages the introduction of new materials and methods of constructions that can be tested and evaluated by national standards. In determining the performance of materials or systems of construction, the code adopts nationally recognized standards as the criteria for evaluation of minimum safe practice.

ICBO (International Conference of Building Officials)

ICBO, which is headquartered in Whittier, California, was formed in 1922 and published its first edition of the UBC (Uniform Building Code) in 1927. ICBO's main purpose was the publication, maintenance, and promotion of the Uniform Building Code and its related documents. The Uniform Building Code is used mainly on the West Coast, but it has also been translated into many languages and serves as the bases for the national codes of numerous nations around the world. In addition, it has become the design basis for the Tri-services Manual of the Army, Navy, and Air Force of the United States.

SBCCI (Southern Building Code Congress International, Inc.)

The Southern Building Code Congress International (SBCCI), was founded by local government officials in 1940 as a nonprofit organization, with the purpose of developing and maintaining a set of model building codes for use by local jurisdictions. The Standard Building Code (SBC), formerly the Southern Standard Building Code, is performance based and was first published in 1945. The SBC is used in much of the southeastern United States.

The Southern Building Code Congress International (SBCCI), which has headquarters in Birmingham, Alabama, provides technical, educational, and administrative support to governmental departments and agencies engaged in building codes administration and enforcement. SBCCI also provides similar support to others in the building design and construction industry. SBCCI joined with BOCA and ICBO in 1994 to set up the International Code Council that publishes the International Codes.

CABO (Council of American Building Officials)

Following World War II, there emerged increased demands for reform and an outcry to replace the existing regulations with a more unified code system. This led to the establishment of the Council of American Building Officials (CABO). It was created in 1972 by the three nationally recognized model code organizations, BOCA, ICBO, and SBCCI. Its express purpose was to establish a communications channel in Washington, D.C., between building officials and congressional, federal, and industry organizations. CABO One and Two Family Dwelling Code is a compilation of BOCA, SBCCI and NFPA. The International One and Two Family Dwelling Code (IOTFDC), which is the principle code used for the construction of single and duplex family occupancy was originally developed by CABO, but was transferred to the ICC in 1996. The latest edition (2000) of the code has been renamed the International Residential Code (IRC).

National uniformity in code requirements has always been a major objective of CABO, and in 1998 it became part of the ICC. CABO established the BCMC (Board for the Coordination of the Model Codes) to provide a forum to identify and make recommendations for the elimination of conflicts between the three model codes and the National Fire Protection Association (NFPA) 101 Life Safety Code and other national standards. CABO later developed the National Evaluation Service (NES) as a national program for the evaluation of innovative building materials, products, and systems. CABO also established the Building Officials Certification Program to enhance professionalism in the field of building code enforcement.

INSTITUTES AND STANDARDS ORGANIZATIONS

General

There are hundreds of organizations writing and maintaining standards. Trade associations, government agencies, or standards writing organizations develop the vast majority. Unlike codes, standards have no legal standing unless stipulated by a particular code that is accepted by a jurisdiction. Building standards function as a valuable design guideline to architects while establishing a framework of acceptable practices from which many codes are later taken. When a standard is stipulated, the acronym of the standard organization and a standard number is called out. For example, NFPA 101 is the Life Safety Code, establishing minimum requirements for new and existing buildings to protect building occupants from fire, smoke, and toxic fumes. The most important and relevant of these organizations for space planners and designers are:

- American National Standards Institute (ANSI). Founded by five engineering societies and three government agencies in 1918 as the American Engineering Standards Committee to bring a halt to waste, duplication, and conflict in voluntary standards development activities and misunderstanding about the acceptability of standards. It is a private nonprofit, nongovernmental organizing center for U.S. standards. It administers and coordinates the efforts of organizations that establish standards and provides the means for evaluating the needs of standards development and ensures that capable organizations undertake the standards development work.

For interior designers and space planners, the most important national regulation is ANSI A 117.1 that is one of the first accessibility guidelines used throughout the United States. The latest edition was developed in conjunction with the ICC and the Access Board, and has been modified to be more consistent with ADAAG guidelines.

ANSI's mission is to enhance "U.S. global competitiveness and the American way of life by promoting, facilitating, and safeguarding the integrity of the voluntary standardization system." In addition ANSI approves standards as American National Standards, and provides information and access to the world's standards. It is also the official U.S. representative to the world's leading standards bodies, including the International Organization for Standardization (ISO). It provides and administers the only recognized system in the United States for establishing standards.

- American Society of Heating, Refrigerating and Air-Conditioning Engineers (ASHRAE). An international organization with chapters throughout the world, whose sole purpose is to advance the arts and sciences of heating, ventilation, air conditioning and refrigeration for the public's benefit. The society was formed in 1894 as the American Society of Heating and Ventilating Engineers, by a group of 75 professionals as a technical society. To cope with the emerging refrigeration technology, another group of technicians and industrialists gave birth to the American Society of Refrigerating Engineers in 1904. These two societies worked together and with the development of air conditioning, they merged under the name of ASHRAE in 1959.

ASHRAE's stated purpose is to write "standards and guidelines in its fields of expertise to guide industry in the delivery of goods and services to the public." ASHRAE standards and guidelines include standard methods of testing for rating purposes, outline and specify preferred procedures for designing and installing equipment, and provide other information to guide the industry. In addition, ASHRAE "sets design standards for occupant comfort, building commissioning, and specification of building automation control networks."

The U.S. federal government has mandated that the ASHRAE standard 90.1 be used by all states as the minimum standard for the building energy codes and all federal government buildings must comply with 90.1's energy requirements. This affects lighting, building mechanical systems, water heating, and the building envelope, including insulation, walls, and windows.

- ASTM International (previously known as American Society of Testing and Materials). One of the largest voluntary standards development organizations in the world, it is a not-for-profit organization founded in 1898 that today provides a global forum for the development and publication of voluntary consensus standards for materials, products, systems and services having internationally recognized quality and applicability. Building codes throughout the United States and Canada have adopted, by reference, a large number of ASTM International standards as a source of test procedures and as a basis for determining acceptable quality for materials and constructions.

- NSSN. Originally, NSSN was an acronym for the National Standards Systems Network. As it became global in character, the name was changed to NSSN. Its primary mission is promulgating standards information to a broad constituency, and serves as a one-stop information repository. As global commerce increasingly shapes the way organizations do business, technical solutions facilitating access to foreign markets becomes essential. Basically, NSSN—a National Resource for Global Standards is becoming the World Wide Web's most comprehensive data network on developing and approved national, foreign, regional and international standards and regulatory documents. Its chief goal is to become a leader in providing technical data and information regarding major developments in a world wide standardization arena.

- National Fire Protection Association (NFPA). A worldwide leader in providing fire, electrical, and life safety to the public since 1896, NFPA was incorporated in 1930 as an international nonprofit organization whose mission is to "reduce the worldwide burden of fire and other hazards on the quality of life by providing and advocating scientifically based consensus codes and standards, research, training and education." Their testing requirement coverage is comprehensive, from doors to fire fighting equipment and means of egress design. NFPA already publishes over 300 codes and standards through a full, open-consensus process, and the new NFPA 5000 set of codes which incidentally does not use the standard group designations, competes with the International Codes so each jurisdiction will have to choose the set of codes it wants to enforce.

- Underwriters Laboratory (UL). Founded in 1894, UL is essentially a testing agency that approves products. UL maintains and operates laboratories around the world for the testing and examination of devices, systems and materials to determine their properties and their relation to life, fire, casualty hazards, and crime prevention (Figure 8.4). UL's findings are recognized throughout the world.

REGULATIONS

General

Various federal agencies and departments collaborate with trade associations, private corporations and the general public to develop federal laws for building construction. Federal

Design No. U495
Nonbearing Wall Rating — 1 or 2 HR.
(See Items 5 and 7)

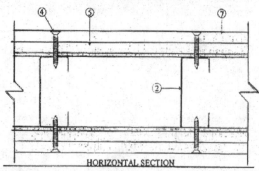

HORIZONTAL SECTION

1. **Floor and Ceiling Runners** — (Not Shown) — Channel-shaped runners, 3-5/8 in. wide (min), 1-1/4 in. legs, formed from No. 25 MSG (min) galv steel, attached to floor and ceiling with fasteners spaced 24 in. OC, max.
2. **Steel Studs** — Channel-shaped 3-5/8 in. wide (min), 1-1/4 in. legs, 3/8 in. folded back returns, formed from No. 25 MSG (min) galv steel, spaced 24 in. OC max.
3. **Batts and Blankets*** — (Optional, not shown) — Mineral wool or glass fiber batts partially or completely filling stud cavity.
   See Batts and Blankets (BZJZ) category for names of Classified companies.
4. **Screws** — Type S self-tapping screws, 1-1/4 or 2 in. long, (1 Hr) and 2-1/2 in. long (2 Hr).
5. **Building Units*** — For 1 Hr Rating — Nom 5/8 or 3/4 in. thick, 4 ft wide, faced gypsum wallboard panels with the faced side on the interior wall cavity. Panels attached to studs and floor and ceiling runners with screws spaced 8 in. OC along the edges of the panel and 12 in. OC in the field of the panel. Joints oriented vertically and staggered on opposite sides of the assembly.
   GENERAL ELECTRIC CO
   SILICONE PRODUCTS DIV —Type CoreGuard.
   NATIONAL GYPSUM CO —Type Gold Bond Fire-Shield Type X Hi-Impact Wallboard or Gold Bond Fire-Shield Type X Kal-Kore Hi-Impact Plaster Base.
6. **Joint Tape and Compound** — (not shown) — Vinyl, dry or premixed joint compound, applied in two coats to joints and screw heads; paper tape, 2 in. wide, embedded in first layer of compound over all joints.
7. **Wallboard, Gypsum*** — For 2 Hr Rating — any Classified 5/8 in. thick (minimum), 4 ft wide, wallboard applied over exterior face of Building Unit (Item 5). Wallboard to be applied vertically with joints staggered 24 in. from Building Unit (Item 5) and attached to studs and floor and ceiling runners with screws spaced 8 in. OC.
   See Wallboard, Gypsum (CKNX) Category for names of manufacturers.

*Bearing the UL Classification Marking

FIGURE 8.4 UL fire resistant assembly sample test.

agencies also use rules and regulations to implement laws passed by Congress. These regulations are often national laws that supersede or supplement local building codes. Each federal agency has its own set of rules and regulations that are published in the Code of Federal Regulations (CFR). Space planners and interior designers should be familiar with the following governmental agencies that produce building regulations that may impact your project:

- Access Board (previously named the Architectural and Transportation Barriers Compliance Board). Congress enacted the Architectural Barriers Act (ABA) in 1968, to make Federal facilities fully accessible to people with disabilities. Several years after the ABA became law, Congress decided a central agency was required to enforce the ABA and in 1973, created the Architectural and Transportation Barriers Compliance Board (ATBCB), later named the Access Board.

  The Board is an independent federal regulatory agency charged with ensuring that certain facilities designed, constructed, leased, or altered with federal funds since September 1969 are in compliance with standards developed under the ABA. Accessibility guidelines were developed by the Board to serve as the basis for standards used to enforce the ABA. The final guidelines, known as the "Minimum Guidelines and Requirements for Accessible Design," served as the basis for enforceable design standards issued in 1984. With the Rehabilitation Act Amendments of 1998, Federal agencies are required to purchase electronic and information technology that is accessible except where it would cause an "undue burden."

- The Department of Energy (DOE). The Department of Energy Act of 1977 consolidated the major federal energy functions into one Cabinet-level agency, the Department of Energy (DOE). Since its inception in 1977, the Department's emphasis and focus has shifted as the needs of the nation have changed. The DOE's primary goal is to provide a framework for a comprehensive and balanced national energy plan through the coordination and administration of the energy functions of the federal government.

- The U.S. Environmental Protection Agency (EPA). The EPA was created in 1970 by an act of Congress to protect human health and safeguard the natural environment, the nation's land, air, and water. It sets national standards for a variety of environmental programs and delegates to states and tribes responsibility for issuing permits, and monitoring and enforcing compliance. Its stated purpose is to "formulate and implement actions which lead to a compatible balance between human activities and the ability of natural systems to support and nurture life." It also seeks to minimize or eliminate pollution whether in the air or water, or in the areas of solid waste, noise, radiation, and toxic substances. This is to be accomplished through research, monitoring, standard setting, and enforcement activities.

- Federal Emergency Management Agency (FEMA). The Agency was formed by executive order in 1979 to help cope with the full spectrum of emergencies, from natural disasters to nuclear war. The agency coordinates its activities with the Office of Homeland Security.

- General Services Administration (GSA). The GSA was established by the Federal Property and Administrative Services Act in 1949. Its purpose is to "help federal agencies better serve the public by offering, at best value, superior workplaces, expert solutions, acquisition services and management policies."

- The U.S. Department of Housing and Urban Development (HUD). HUD was enacted by Congress in 1965 although its history extends back to the National Housing Act of 1934. HUD is the main federal agency responsible for programs concerned with housing and community development, fair housing opportunities, and improving and evolving the nation's communities. In 1998 Congress approved Public Housing reforms to reduce segregation by race and income, and to bring more working families into public housing.

- The National Institute of Standards and Technology (NIST). Originally founded in 1901 as the National Bureau of Standards (NBS) and later renamed NIST, the stated purpose of the NIST is to assist industry in the development of technology and procedures to enhance product quality, productivity, reliability, as well as to facilitate rapid commercialization of products based on new scientific discoveries. NIST maintains several facilities to implement its objectives.

- Occupational Safety and Health Administration (OSHA). In 1970, Congress passed the Occupational Safety and Health Act to protect the worker. The mission of OSHA is to ensure safe and healthful workplaces in America by regulating the design of buildings and interior projects where people are employed. The regulations deal with occupational health and safety and are used in conjunction with codes and other standards. OSHA is a branch of the Department of Labor.

NATIONAL ORGANIZATIONS

General

There are many national organizations that support organizations that produce codes and standards, and are essential to their development, while they are not themselves directly responsible for their production. Two such organizations are the National Conference of States on Building Codes and Standards (NCSBCS), and the National Institute of Building Sciences.

- The National Conference of States on Building Codes and Standards (NCSBCS). This is a nonprofit organization, founded in 1967 to promote the public safety and to serve the building codes' interests within the United States. The main objective of NCSBCS is the advancement of interstate cooperation and orchestration of intergovernmental reforms in building codes and standards. In addition, NCSBCS provides a wide range of technical, data, and other services to the states building regulatory agencies.

- National Institute of Building Sciences (NIBS). This is a non-governmental, nonprofit organization formed in 1974 by an act of Congress with the primary purpose of improving the building regulatory environment, disseminate nationally recognized technical and regulatory information, helping to bring in and absorb new and existing products and technology into the building process, and serve as an interface between government and the private sector.

OCCUPANCY REQUIREMENTS, CLASSIFICATIONS AND LOADS

The majority of code requirements for fire and smoke protection are based on occupancy classifications. Occupancy refers to the type of use of a building or interior space is put to, such as a residence, an office, a school, a restaurant. The occupant load is a term used to specify the number of people that a building code assumes will occupy a given building structure or portion of it. Occupant load calculations are based on the assumption that certain categories of occupancy have greater densities of people and that exiting provisions should adequately reflect this.

For example, theaters require more exits to allow safe evacuation than an office of the same area. Figure 8.5 is a chart from the Standard Building Code (SBC). Other building codes have similar charts; the NBC uses Table 1008.12 "Maximum Floor Area Allowances per Occupant," the UBC uses Table 33A, "Minimum Egress Requirements for Occupants." It should be noted that some of the load factors are depicted in gross square feet, and others in net square feet.

The formula used to determine the occupancy load is: Occupancy Load = Floor Area (sq. ft.) ÷ Occupant Factor. Thus, the square footage of the interior space assigned to a particular use is divided by the occupant load factor for the occupancy use as given in the code. In the UBC, occupant load factors are specified in Figure 8.6. This table delineates UBC egress requirements for providing two exits and barrier-free access.

Occupant load factors help determine the required occupant loads of a space or building, and range from a low of three square feet per person for a waiting space to a high of 500 square feet per person for storage areas. These numbers mean that, for the purposes of estimating exiting requirements, one person is occupying, on average, the number of square feet listed in the occupant load factor column of the table. In ascertaining the occupant load, it is presumed that all parts of the building will be occupied at the same time. Where a building or building area provides more than one use (i.e., has mixed occupancies), the occupant load is determined by the use that reflects the highest concentration of people.

TABLE 1003.1
MINIMUM OCCUPANT LOAD

USE	AREA PER OCCUPANT[2,3] (sq ft)
Assembly without fixed seats	
Concentrated (includes among others, auditoriums, churches, dance floors, lodge rooms, reviewing stands, stadiums)	7 net
Waiting Space	3 net
Unconcentrated (includes among others conference rooms, exhibit rooms, gymnasiums, lounges, skating rinks, stages, platforms)	15 net
Assembly with fixed seats	Note 1
Bowling alleys, allow 5 persons for each alley, including 15 ft of runway, and other spaces in accordance with the appropriate listing herein	7 net
Business areas	100 gross
Courtrooms without fixed seats	40 net
Courtrooms with fixed seats	Note 1
Educational (including Educational Uses Above the 12th Grade)	
Classroom areas	20 net
Shops and other vocational areas	50 net
Industrial areas	100 gross
Institutional	
Sleeping areas	120 gross
Inpatient treatment and ancillary areas	240 gross
Outpatient area	100 gross
Resident housing areas	120 gross
Library	
Reading rooms	50 net
Stack area	100 gross
Malls	Section 413
Mercantile	
Basement and grade floor areas open to public	30 gross
Areas on other floors open to public	60 gross
Storage, stock, shipping area not open to public	300 gross
Parking garage	200 gross
Residential	200 gross
Restaurants (without fixed seats)	15 net
Restaurants (with fixed seats)	Note 1
Storage area, mechanical	300 gross

For **SI:** 1 sq ft = 0.0929 m^2.

Notes:
1. The occupant load for an area having fixed seats installed shall be determined by the number of fixed seats. Capacity of seats without dividing arms shall equal one person per 18 inches (457 mm). For booths, one person per 24 inches (610 mm).
2. See 202 for definitions of gross and net floor areas.
3. The occupant load of floor areas of the building shall be computed on the basis of the specific occupancy classification of the building. Where mixed occupancies occur, the occupant load of each occupancy area shall be computed on the basis of that specific occupancy.

FIGURE 8.5 Standard Building Code (SBC) Table 1003.1 denoting minimum occupant load. Other building codes have similar charts. *(Reproduced from the 1999 SBC, with permission)*

TABLE 10-A—MINIMUM EGRESS REQUIREMENTS[1]

USE[2]	MINIMUM OF TWO EXITS OTHER THAN ELEVATORS ARE REQUIRED WHERE NUMBER OF OCCUPANTS IS AT LEAST	OCCUPANT LOAD FACTOR[3] (square feet) × 0.0929 for m²
1. Aircraft hangars (no repair)	10	500
2. Auction rooms	30	7
3. Assembly areas, concentrated use (without fixed seats)	50	
Auditoriums		
Churches and chapels		
Dance floors		
Lobby accessory to assembly occupancy		
Lodge rooms		
Reviewing stands		
Stadiums		
Waiting area	50	3
4. Assembly areas, less-concentrated use	50	15
Conference rooms		
Dining rooms		
Drinking establishments		
Exhibit rooms		
Gymnasiums		
Lounges		
Stages		
5. Bowling alley (assume no occupant load for bowling lanes)	50	4
6. Children's homes and homes for the aged	6	80
7. Classrooms	50	20
8. Congregate residences	10	200
9. Courtrooms	50	40
10. Dormitories	10	50
11. Dwellings	10	300
12. Exercising rooms	50	50
13. Garage, parking	30	200
14. Hospitals and sanitariums— Health-care center	10	80
Nursing homes		
Sleeping rooms	6	80
Treatment rooms	10	80
15. Hotels and apartments	10	200
16. Kitchen—commercial	30	200
17. Library reading room	50	50
18. Locker rooms	30	50

(Continued)

TABLE 10-A—MINIMUM EGRESS REQUIREMENTS[1]—(Continued)

USE[2]	MINIMUM OF TWO EXITS OTHER THAN ELEVATORS ARE REQUIRED WHERE NUMBER OF OCCUPANTS IS AT LEAST	OCCUPANT LOAD FACTOR[3] (square feet) × 0.0929 for m²
19. Malls (see Chapter 4)	—	—
20. Manufacturing areas	30	200
21. Mechanical equipment room	30	300
22. Nurseries for children (day care)	7	35
23. Offices	30	100
24. School shops and vocational rooms	50	50
25. Skating rinks	50	50 on the skating area; 15 on the deck
26. Storage and stock rooms	30	300
27. Stores—retail sales rooms		
Basements and ground floor	50	30
Upper floors	50	60
28. Swimming pools	50	50 for the pool area; 15 on the deck
29. Warehouses	30	500
30. All others	50	100

[1]Access to, and egress from, buildings for persons with disabilities shall be provided as specified in Chapter 11.
[2]For additional provisions on number of exits from Groups H and I Occupancies and from rooms containing fuel-fired equipment or cellulose nitrate, see Sections 1018, 1019 and 1020, respectively.
[3]This table shall not be used to determine working space requirements per person.
[4]Occupant load based on five persons for each alley, including 15 feet (4572 mm) of runway.

FIGURE 8.6 UBC Egress Requirements. *(Reproduced from the 1994 edition of the Uniform Building Code™, with the permission of the International Conference of Building Officials)*

Types of Occupancy

Occupancy refers to the type of use of the building or interior space, such as a residence, office, store or school. An occupancy classification must be assigned to any building or space, and determining the occupancy classification is an essential part of the code process. The concept behind occupancy classification is that certain building uses are more hazardous than others. For example, a large theatre with hundreds of people is more dangerous than a single-family residence.

Code publications divide their occupancies into different categories, based on the activities occurring in the space, the associated level of hazards present and the anticipated number of people occupying the space at any given time. A summary comparison of occupancy classification is given in Figure 8.7. Ten of the most common occupancy classifications used by model codes are:

1. Assembly
2. Business
3. Educational
4. Factory and Industrial
5. Hazardous
6. Institutional
7. Mercantile
8. Residential
9. Storage
10. Utility and Miscellaneous

Classification by Construction Type

Construction type indicates the fire resistance of elements such as: fire and party walls, stair and elevator enclosures, exterior and interior bearing and non bearing walls, columns, shaft enclosures, smoke barriers, floors, ceilings and roofs. Fire ratings are based on the number of hours a building element will resist fire before it is adversely affected by the flame, heat or hot gases.

All buildings are classified into one of five or six types of construction. Figure 8.8 compares the various categories according to the different codes. Type I buildings are the most fire resistive and typically contain structural members that are noncombustible. Type I buildings also have the highest fire rating, usually two to four hours. Type V buildings (Type VI in the SBCCI codes), have the lowest fire rating and are typically of wood frame construction.

For the interior designer and space planner, the most critical building element of a project is typically the interior walls, although other elements may also come into play. The four basic

COMPARISON OF OCCUPANCY CLASSIFICATIONS

I.C.C. INTERNATIONAL BUILDING CODE		B.O.C.A. NATIONAL BUILDING CODE		S.B.C.C. STANDARD BUILDING CODE		I.C.B.O. UNIFORM BUILDING CODE		N.F.P.A. LIFE SAFETY CODE	
A-1	Assembly, Theaters (Fixed Seats)	A-1	Assembly, Theaters, etc. with stage	A-1	Assembly, Large with working stage, O.L. ≥700	A-1	Assembly, with stage, O.L. ≥ 1000	A-A	Assembly, O.L. > 1000
A-2	Assembly, Food and/or Drink Consumption	A-2	Assembly, Public Assembly without stage	A-1	Assembly, Large without working stage, O.L. ≥1000	A-2	Assembly, with stage, O.L. < 1000	A-B	Assembly, O.L. > 300 ≤ 1000
A-3	Assembly, Worship, Recreation, Amusement	A-3	Assembly, Amusement, Entertainment, Recreation	A-2	Assembly, Small with working stage, O.L. ≥100 < 700	A-2.1	Assembly, without stage, O.L. ≥ 300	A-C	Assembly, O.L. ≥50 ≤ 300
A-4	Assembly, Indoor Sporting Events	A-4	Assembly, Place of Worship	A-2	Assembly, Small without working stage, O.L. ≥100 < 1000	A-3	Assembly, without stage, O.L. < 300		
A-5	Assembly, Outdoor Activities	A-5	Assembly, Outdoor			A-4	Assembly, Stadiums, Reviewing Stands, Amusement Parks		
B	Business	B	Business	B	Business	B	Business	B	Business
E	Educational (includes some Day Care)	E	Educational	E	Educational	E-1	Educational, O.L. ≥50	E	Educational
						E-2	Educational, O.L. < 50		
						E-3	Educational, Day Care		
F-1	Factory Industrial, Moderate Hazard	F-1	Factory and Industrial, Moderate Hazard	F	Factory-Industrial	F-1	Factory and Industrial, Moderate Hazard	I-A	Industrial, General
F-2	Factory Industrial, Low Hazard	F-2	Factory and Industrial, Low Hazard			F-2	Factory and Industrial, Low Hazard	I-B	Industrial, Special Purpose
								I-C	Industrial, High Hazard
H-1	Hazardous, Detonation Hazard	H-1	High Hazard, Detonation Hazard	H-1	Hazardous, Detonation Hazard	H-1	Hazardous, High Explosives		(included in Group I)
H-2	Hazardous, Deflagration Hazard or Accelerated Burning	H-2	High Hazard, Deflagration Hazard or Accelerated Burning	H-2	Hazardous, Deflagration Hazard or Accelerated Burning	H-2	Hazardous, Accelerated Burning or Moderate Explosives		
H-3	Hazardous, Physical or Combustible Hazard	H-3	High Hazard, Physical or Combustible Hazard	H-3	Hazardous, Physical or Combustible Hazard	H-3	Hazardous, High Fire or Physical Hazard		
H-4	Hazardous, Health Hazard	H-4	High Hazard, Health Hazard	H-4	Hazardous, Health Hazard	H-4	Hazardous, Repair Garages		
H-5	Hazardous, Hazardous Production Materials (HPM)					H-5	Hazardous, Aircraft Repair Hangers		
						H-6	Hazardous, Hazardous Production Materials (HPM)		
						H-7	Hazardous, Health Hazards		

FIGURE 8.7 A chart summarizing information in the International Building Code (IBC), the BOCA National Building Code (NBC), the Standard Building Code (SBC), the Uniform Building Code (UBC), and the Life Safety Code (LSC). The above organizations do not assume responsibility for the accuracy or completeness of this chart. *(From The Codes Guidebook for Interiors by S.K. Harmon and K.G. Kennon)*

I.C.C. INTERNATIONAL BUILDING CODE		B.O.C.A. NATIONAL BUILDING CODE		S.B.C.C. STANDARD BUILDING CODE		I.C.B.O. UNIFORM BUILDING CODE		N.F.P.A. LIFE SAFETY CODE	
I-1	Institutional, Supervised Personal Care, O.L. > 16	I-1	Institutional, Residential Care and Group Homes	I-U	Institutional, Unrestrained	I-1.1	Institutional, Health Care, Nonambulatory	D-I	Detentional/ Correctional Free Egress
I-2	Institutional, Health Care	I-2	Institutional, Health Care	I-R	Institutional, Restrained	I-1.2	Institutional, Health Care, Ambulatory	D-II	Detentional/ Correctional Zoned Egress
I-3	Institutional, Restrained	I-3	Institutional, Restrained			I-2	Institutional, Residential Care and Group Homes	D-III	Detentional/ Correctional Zoned Impeded Egress
I-4	Institutional, Day Care Facilities					I-3	Institutional, Restrained	D-IV	Detentional/ Correctional Impeded Egress
								D-V	Detentional/ Correctional Contained
								H	Health Care
								DC	Day Care
M	Mercantile	M	Mercantile	M	Mercantile	M	Mercantile	M-A	Mercantile, > 3 levels or > 30,000 sq.ft.
								M-B	Mercantile, floor above or below grade level, or > 3000 ≤ 30,000 sq.ft.
								M-C	Mercantile, one story and ≤ 3000
R-1	Residential, Transient	R-1	Residential, Hotels, Motels, Boarding Houses	R-1	Residential, Multiple Dwelling, Transient	R-1	Residential, Hotels Apartments, etc, O.L. > 10	R-A	Residential, Hotels, Motels, Dormitories
R-2	Residential, Multi-Dwelling Unit	R-2	Residential, Multi-Family Dwelling Units	R-2	Residential, Multiple Dwelling, Permanent	R-2	NOT USED	R-B	Residential, Apartments
R-3	Residential, One and Two Dwellings Units	R-3	Residential, Multiple One or Two Family Dwellings Units	R-3	Residential, Child Care Facilities, One and Two Family Dwellings	R-3	Residential, Dwellings, Lodging Houses, etc., O.L. ≤ 10	R-C	Residential, Lodging or Rooming Houses
R-4	Residential, Care and Assisted Living Facilities O.L. > 5 ≤ 16	R-4	Residential, Individual One and Two Family Dwellings	R-4	Residential, Care and Assisted Living Facilities			R-D	Residential, One and Two Family Dwellings
								R-E	Residential, Board and Care Facilities
S-1	Storage, Moderate Hazard	S-1	Storage, Moderate Hazard	S-1	Storage, Moderate Hazard	S-1	Storage, Moderate Hazard	S	Storage
S-2	Storage, Low Hazard	S-2	Storage, Low Hazard	S-2	Storage, Low Hazard	S-2	Storage, Low Hazard		
						S-3	Storage, Repair Garages		
U	Utility and Miscellaneous	U	Utility and Miscellaneous		Special Occupancies	U-1	Utility, Private Garages, Carports, Sheds, etc.		Special Structures and High Rise Buildings
						U-2	Utility, Fences over 6'-0", Tanks, Towers, etc.		

FIGURE 8.7 *(continued)* A chart summarizing information in the International Building Code (IBC), the BOCA National Building Code (NBC), the Standard Building Code (SBC), the Uniform Building Code (UBC), and the Life Safety Code (LSC). The above organizations do not assume responsibility for the accuracy or completeness of this chart. *(From The Codes Guidebook for Interiors by S.K. Harmon and K.G. Kennon)*

COMPARISON OF CONSTRUCTION TYPES

B.O.C.A. NATIONAL BUILDING CODE	S.B.C.C.I. STANDARD BUILDING CODE	I.C.B.O. UNIFORM BUILDING CODE	I.C.C. INTERNATIONAL BUILDING CODE	N.F.P.A. NFPA 220 STANDARD
TYPE 1A Protected	TYPE I	TYPE I Fire Resistive	TYPE IA Protected	I (443)
TYPE 1B	TYPE II		TYPE IB Unprotected	I (332)
TYPE 2A Protected	TYPE IV One-hour Protected	TYPE II Fire Resistive	TYPE IIA Protected	II (222)
TYPE 2B	TYPE IV Unprotected	TYPE II One-hour	TYPE IIB Unprotected	II (111)
TYPE 2C Unprotected		TYPE II No Resistance		II (000)
TYPE 3A Protected	TYPE V One-hour Protected	TYPE III One-hour	TYPE IIIA Protected	III (211)
TYPE 3B Unprotected	TYPE V Unprotected	TYPE III No Resistance	TYPE IIIB Unprotected	III (200)
TYPE 4 Heavy Timber	TYPE III Heavy Timber	TYPE IV Heavy Timber	TYPE IV Heavy Timber	IV (2HH) Heavy Timber
TYPE 5A Protected	TYPE VI One-hour Protected	TYPE V One-hour	TYPE VA Protected	V (111)
TYPE 5B Unprotected	TYPE VI Unprotected	TYPE V No Resistance	TYPE VB Unprotected	V (000)

FIGURE 8.8 Comparison of construction types as given by BOCA, SBCCI, ICBO, ICC and NFPA. *(From The Codes Guidebook for Interiors by S.K. Harmon and K.G. Kennon)*

materials that are generally considered to be noncombustible are iron, steel, concrete and masonry. On the other hand, combustible materials are those that will ignite and continue burning when the flame is removed. It is important when working with a new or existing space to know the construction type to ensure that the maximum allowable area is not exceeded.

ADJUNCTS TO BUILDING CODES

Building codes typically have additional companion codes and standards that govern other aspects of construction which, with the exception of the electrical code, are usually published by the same group that publishes the model building codes. For example, the International Code Council also publishes the International Mechanical Code (IMC) and the International Plumbing Code (IPC). The National Electrical Code (NBC) published by the National Fire Protection Association (NFPA) is the main electrical code used in the United States. The ICC published the ICC Electrical Code—Administrative Provisions (IEC) in 2000.

Model codes frequently use industry standards developed by trade associations, government agencies, and standards-writing agencies such as the American Society for Testing and Materials (ASTM), the American National Standards Institute (ANSI), and the National Fire Protection Association (NFPA). Building codes reference these standards by name, number and date of latest revision, and become law when a code is accepted by a jurisdiction.

In addition, there may be local jurisdictions that maintain energy conservation codes, health and hospital codes, fabric flammability regulations, and codes that regulate construction and finishes.

TEST RATINGS AND FIRE RESISTANT MATERIALS AND FINISHES

Roughly 75 percent of all codes deal with fire and life safety issues, and the primary aim of fire codes is to confine a fire to its area of origin, thus limiting its spread and preventing flashover. To facilitate this, all approved materials and construction assemblies referred to in building codes are assigned ratings based on standardized testing procedures. The rating of an assembly is ascertained by evaluating its performance during testing and by examining its fire resistive properties. There are hundreds of standardized tests for building materials and construction assemblies.

Any approved testing laboratory can undertake the testing of building materials, provided that standardized procedures are followed. The American Society for Testing and Materials (ASTM), the National Fire Protection Association (NFPA), and Underwriters Laboratories (UL), in collaboration with the American National Standards Institute (ANSI), are among the best known organizations, having developed a large variety of standardized tests and testing procedures.

Types of Tests: There are basically two categories of fire testing of materials for interior design components.

1. Tests that rate the ability of a construction assembly to prevent the passage of fire and smoke from one space to another.
2. Tests that rate the flammability of a finish material (Figure 8.9).

The most commonly used test of the first category is the *ASTM E119: Test Methods for Fire Tests of Building Construction and Materials.* Similar tests are ANSI/UL 263, NFPA 251, and UBC Standard 43-1. ASTM E 119 evaluates and monitors an assembly's ability to contain a fire and retain its structural integrity.

The *Steiner Tunnel Test* (ASTM E-84), remains the principal test used to determine the surface burning characteristics of building materials. The result is a material's flame spread rating compared to glass-reinforced cement board that is given an arbitrary rating of zero, and red oak flooring which is assigned an arbitrary rating of 100.

COMMON TEST NAMES	STANDARD NAME/NUMBER	TYPE OF RATING
CORNER TEST (applied finish)	NFPA 265 UBC 42-2 NBC "Room/Corner Fire Test" SBC "Standard Test Method for Evaluating Room Fire Growth Contribution of Textile Wallcoverings"	Pass or Fail
(upholstered materials)	NFPA 286	Ranked
MATTRESSES	NFPA 267 ASTM E1590 CAL 129	Ranked
	FF 4-72	Pass or Fail
PILL TEST	DOC FF1-70 DOC FF2-70	Pass or Fail
RADIANT PANEL TEST	ASTM E648 NFPA 253 NBS IR75-950	Class Rating
SMOLDER RESISTANCE TEST (applied finish)	NFPA 260 (was 260A) CAL 116 ASTM 1353	Pass or Fail
(mock-up)	NFPA 261 (was 260B) CAL 117 ASTM 1352	Class Rating
SMOKE DENSITY TEST	ASTM E662 NFPA 258	Class Rating
STEINER TUNNEL TEST	ASTM E-84 NFPA 255 UL 723 Chamber Test or UL 992	Class Rating
TOXICITY TEST	LC 50 PITTS TEST	Ranked
UPHOLSTERED SEATING TESTS (full scale)	NFPA 266 CAL 133 ASTM E1537 UL 1056	Pass or Fail
(small scale)	NFPA 272 (was 264A) ASTM 1474	Ranked
VERTICAL FLAME TEST	NFPA 701 ASTM D6413	Pass or Fail

NOTES:
1. Any number of the above tests may be required by a jurisdiction depending on the occupancy and its location within a building.
2. There may be other tests and/or test names not listed above that are more specific to a jurisdiction.

FIGURE 8.9 Summary chart of tests. (*From The Codes Guidebook for Interiors by S.K. Harmon and K.G. Kennon*)

The *Radiant Panel Test* (ASTM E-648, NFPA 253, NBS IR75-950) rates interior floor finishes and is measured in watts per square centimeter; the higher the number, the more resistant the material is to spread of flames.

Another test for carpet flammability that is required for all carpets produced for sale in the United States is the *Methenamine Pill Test*. The smoke developed from both flaming and non-flaming (smoldering) solid materials is measured.

The *Smoke Density Test* (NFPA 258, ASTM E-662) determines if a solid material will contain a flame or smolder and the amount of smoke it will emit. The test measures the optical density on a scale of 0 to 800, with many codes requiring a smoke developed rating of 450 or less for finish materials.

The *Vertical Flame Test* (NFPA 701, ASTM D6413) is typically used for vertical treatments such as curtains, draperies, window shades, tapestries, and wall hangings where the areas covered are not excessively large, in which case the Steiner tunnel test may also be required. Any vertical finish that is exposed to air on both sides is considered a vertical treatment. Vertical flame tests include NFPA 701 and ASTM D6413.

Where napped, tufted, or looped textiles or carpets are used on walls or ceilings, the *Corner Test* (the name may differ from one code to another) must be used. This test helps evaluate the degree that an interior finish material will increase fire growth (including heat and smoke), facilitate combustion products including gases, and cause fire spread beyond the fire's initial location.

Smolder Resistance Test, also known as *Cigarette Ignition Test*, analyzes the smoldering resistance of a finish. The test is used primarily to determine the flammability of upholstered furniture by testing the various textiles and finishes (NFPA 260, ASTM 1353, CAL 116) as well as furniture mockups (NFPA 261, ASTM 1352, CAL 117).

Ratings and Fire Resistive Standards of Materials and Finishes: Upon being subjected to one of the standard tests, a material is given a rating based on its performance during the test. With the ASTM E-84 test, materials are classified into one of three groups based on their tested flame spread characteristics. These groups and their flame spread indexes are listed below. Class I is the most fire resistant.

Class	Flame Spread Index
I (A)	0-25
II (B)	26-75
III (C)	76-100

Class A, B, and C designations for wall and ceiling finishes used by the Life Safety Code (LSC) and the Standard Building Code (SBC) correlate directly with the Class I, II, and III designations used by the National Building Code (NBC) and the Uniform Building Code (UBC). Sometimes, when an approved sprinkler system is used, the building code will allow you to reduce the required class of the finish materials by one. However, this may not apply to certain critical areas like enclosed vertical exitways or in certain occupancies. Certain cities and states (like Boston, California, Massachusetts, New Jersey, and New York City and State) have their own fire codes that are even stricter than those of the LSC.

For construction assemblies tested according to ASTM E-119, the rating given is according to time, that is, how long an assembly will contain a fire, retain its structural integrity or both. The test evaluates a construction assembly's performance regarding the temperature rise on the protected side of the assembly, the amount of smoke, gas or flame that penetrates the assembly, and the assembly's structural performance during exposure to fire. The ratings are one hour, two hour, three hour, and four hour; 20, 30, and 45 minute ratings are also used for doors and other opening assemblies. Assemblies that interior designers and space planners must be concerned with include firewalls, fire separation walls, shaft enclosures (like stairways exits, and elevators), and floor/ceiling constructions as well as doors and rated glazing.

Building codes typically have tables that stipulate the type of construction that meets the different hourly ratings. Thus, when a building code states that a one hour rated partition assembly is required between an exit corridor and an adjoining tenant space, the designer must select and detail a design that incorporate the requirements for one hour construction.

MEANS OF EGRESS

Exiting is one of the most critical requirements of a building code. It comprises essentially of three main categories: exit access, exit, and exit discharge (Figure 8.10).

Arrangement of Exits

Arrangement of exits is specified by code. They should be located as far apart from each other as possible so that if one is blocked in an emergency, the other(s) can still be reached (Figure 8.11). The code states, that when two or more exits are required, they must be placed a distance apart equal to not less than one-half the length of the longest diagonal dimension within the building or area to be served, as measured in a straight line between the exits. This is known as the half-diagonal rule and is shown diagrammatically in Figure 8.12.

Maximum Travel Distances

The codes limit the length of travel distance from within a single space to an exit access corridor. This is defined as the maximum distance and cannot exceed 200 feet (61m) in an unsprinklered building and 250 feet (76.25m) in a sprinklered building (Figure 8.13). There are exceptions to the rule such as when the last portion of the travel distance is entirely within a one hour-rated exit corridor. Basically, codes classify travel distances into two types: The first

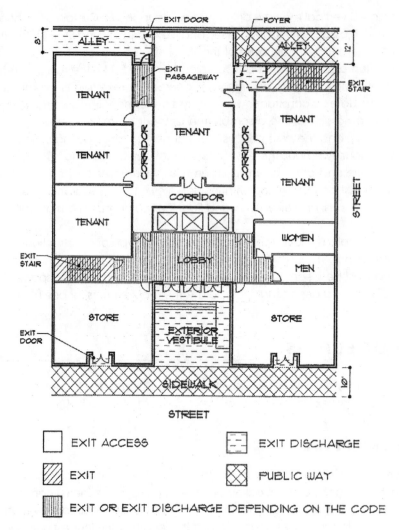

FIGURE 8.10 Typical building examples of means of egress. *(From The Codes Guidebook for Interiors by S.K. Harmon and K.G. Kennon)*

relates to the length of travel distance from within a single space to the exit access corridor (also known as the common path of travel), and the second regulates the length of travel distance from anywhere in a building to the floor or building's exit. Typically however, if the travel distance within a tenant space, exceeds 75 feet (22.9m), then an additional exit is required, even if the occupant load does not require it. Figure 8.14 outlines the IBC's requirements for buildings with one exit.

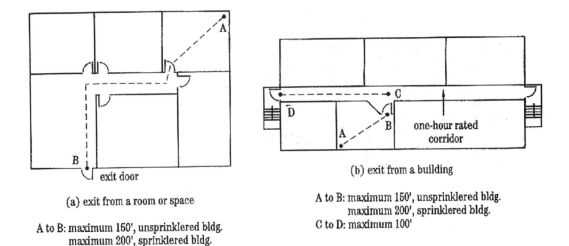

(a) exit from a room or space

A to B: maximum 150', unsprinklered bldg.
maximum 200', sprinklered bldg.

(b) exit from a building

A to B: maximum 150', unsprinklered bldg.
maximum 200', sprinklered bldg.
C to D: maximum 100'

FIGURE 8.11 Depicts maximum acceptable distances required to exits. *(From Interior Design Reference Manual by D.K. Ballast)*

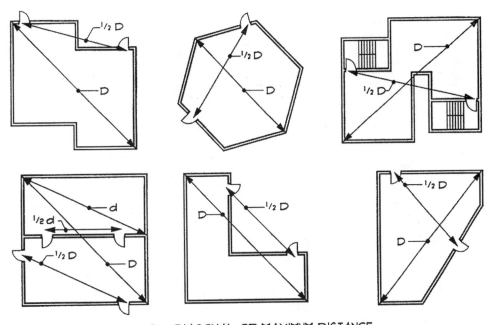

D = DIAGONAL OR MAXIMUM DISTANCE
½D = HALF OF DIAGONAL OR MINIMUM DISTANCE

FIGURE 8.12 Illustrates the Half Diagonal Rule. *(From The Codes Guidebook for Interiors by S.K. Harmon and K.G. Kennon)*

TRAVEL DISTANCE, DEAD-END LENGTH, EXIT AND MEANS OF EGRESS WIDTH

| OCCUPANCY CLASSIFICATION | MAXIMUM TRAVEL DIST. TO EXIT (FT) | | MAXIMUM DEAD END CORRIDOR LENGTH (FT) | EGRESS WIDTH PER PERSON SERVED (IN) | | MINIMUM CORRIDOR/ AISLE WIDTH (IN) | MINIMUM CLEAR OP'G OF EXIT DOORS (IN) | MINIMUM STAIR WIDTH[10] (IN) |
	UNSPRK.	SPRK.		LEVEL[12]	STAIRS			
Group A	200	250	20	0.2	0.37[14]	44[1,10]	32	44
Group B	200	250	20	0.2	0.37[14]	44[10]	32	44
Group E	200	250	20	0.2	0.37[14]	72[2]	32	44
Group F	200	250[7]	20	0.2	0.37[14]	44[10]	32	44
Group H	NP	100[13]	20	0.4	0.7	44[10]	32	44
Group I Restrained	Varies[11]	Varies[11]	20	0.2	0.37[14]	48	32	44
Group I Unrestrained	150	200	20	0.2	0.37[14]	44[3]	36[9]	44
Group M	200	250	20	0.2	0.37[14]	44[4,10]	32	44
Group R	200	250	20[8]	0.2	0.37[14]	44[5,10]	32	44
Group S	200[6]	250[6,7]	20	0.2	0.37[14]	44[10]	32	44

For SI: 1 in = 25.4 mm, 1 ft = 0.305 m.

Notes:
1. See 1019.10.2.
2. For occupant loads less than 100 persons, 44 inches may be used.
3. 96 inches shall be provided in areas requiring the movement of beds.
4. See 413 for covered mall buildings.
5. 36 inches shall be permitted within dwelling units.
6. Maximum travel distance shall be increased to 300 ft if unsprinklered and 400 ft if sprinklered for Group S2 occupancies and open parking structures constructed per 411.
7. See 1004.1.6 for exceptions.
8. See 1026.1.1 for exceptions.
9. 44 inches required in areas requiring movement of beds.
10. 36 inches acceptable if stair or corridor serves occupant load of less than 50.
11. See 1024.2.6.
12. Applies to ramps, doors and corridors.
13. For HPM facilities, as defined in 408, the maximum travel distance shall be 100 ft.
14. Use 0.3 for stairs having tread depths 11 inches or greater and riser heights between 4 inches minimum and 7 inches maximum.

FIGURE 8.13 Standard Building Code (SBC), Table 1004, Travel Distance, Dead-End Length, Exit and Means of Egress Width. *(Reproduced from the 1999 SBC by permission, Southern Building Code Congress International, Inc.)*

Exits Through Adjoining Rooms

Codes usually allow a room to have a single exit through an adjoining or intervening room providing it affords direct and unobstructed means of travel to an exit corridor or other exit, as long as the total stipulated maximum travel distances are not exceeded. Note that exiting is not permitted through kitchens, storerooms, rest rooms, closets, or spaces used for similar purposes. Foyers, lobbies, and reception rooms constructed with a one hour-rated wall as required for corridors are normally categorized by codes as intervening rooms, thereby allowing them to be used for exit purposes.

BUILDINGS WITH ONE EXIT

OCCUPANCY	MAXIMUM HEIGHT OF BUILDING ABOVE GRADE PLANE	MAXIMUM OCCUPANTS (OR DWELLING UNITS) PER FLOOR AND TRAVEL DISTANCE
A, B[d], E, F, M, U	1 Story	50 occupants and 75 feet travel distance
H-2, H-3	1 Story	3 occupants and 25 feet travel distance
H-4, H-5, I, R	1 Story	10 occupants and 75 feet travel distance
S[a]	1 Story	30 occupants and 100 feet travel distance
B[b], F, M, S[a]	2 Stories	30 occupants and 75 feet travel distance
R-2	2 Stories[c]	4 dwelling units and 50 feet travel distance

For SI: 1 foot = 304.8 mm.

a. For the required number of exits for open parking structures, see Section 1005.2.1.1.
b. For the required number of exits for air traffic control towers, see Section 412.1.
c. Buildings classified as Group R-2 equipped throughout with an automatic sprinkler system in accordance with Section 903.3.1.1 or 903.3.1.2 and provided with emergency escape and rescue openings in accordance with Section 1009 shall have a maximum height of three stories above grade.
d. Buildings equipped throughout with an automatic sprinkler system in accordance with Section 903.3.1.1 with an occupancy in Group B shall have a maximum travel distance of 100 feet.

FIGURE 8.14 International Building Code (IBC) Table 1005.2.2—Buildings with One Exit. *(By permission, International Code Council, Inc.)*

Widths of Exits

Upon determination of the occupant load for the floor or space, the resulting figure is multiplied by a specific width variable furnished by the codes. For exit stairs, a width variable of 0.3 is used and for level exits the occupant load is multiplied by 0.2 to determine the required width. According to most codes, the minimum total width of exits in inches is determined by taking the occupant load and multiplying it by 0.3 for stairways and by 0.2 for other exits. This total width must be divided approximately equally among the separate exits.

Corridors are intended to provide a safe means of egress from a room or space to a building exit or to another approved exitway, such as a stairway. Where two exits are required, corridors should be designed to allow travel in two directions simultaneously to an exit. Should one path be blocked, occupants can still exit by an alternate route. Lengths of dead-end corridors with only one means of exit are limited to a maximum of 20 feet in the model codes. Minimum corridor width (in feet) of a corridor is determined by taking the occupant load it serves and multiplying by 0.2. Where the corridor serves an occupant load of 50 or more, the minimum width must not be less than 44 inches (1.12m). For occupant loads less than 50, the minimum width is 36 inches (0.91m). The width of a corridor must be unobstructed, but handrails and fully opened doors can protrude a maximum of 7 inches (17.8cm) total. In certain occupancies, like educational and institutional construction types, codes may require wider corridors.

Typically, corridor construction must be of one hour fire-resistive construction (including walls and ceilings) when serving an occupant load of 10 or more in R-1 and I occupancies and when serving an occupant load of 30 or more in other occupancies. The one hour-rated corridors must extend through the ceiling to the rated floor or roof above unless the ceiling of the entire story is one hour rated. Where a duct penetrates a fire rated corridor, a fire damper must be provided that closes automatically upon detection of heat or smoke so as to restrict the passage of flame.

Doors and their components (door, frame, hardware and doorway or wall opening) are regulated by code and depend on the fire rating of the wall where they are to be located. Other door assemblies may comprise of more than the four main components listed above. Below are some of the more common types of door and window assemblies used:

Regulated Fire-Rated Doors	Regulated Fire-Rated Windows
• Access Doors	• Borrowed Lights
• Bi-Parting Doors	• Casement Windows
• Conveying System Doors	• Double-Hung Windows
• Chute Doors	• Fixed Windows
• Dutch Doors	• Glass Block
• Folding Doors	• Hinged windows
• Hoistway Doors	• Pivot Windows
• Horizontal Doors	• Side Lights
• Revolving Doors	• Sky Lights
• Rolling steel Doors	• Tilting Windows
• Service Counter Doors	• Transom Lights
• Swinging Doors	• Vision Panels
• Vertical Sliding Doors	

Egress doors should normally be side-hinged swinging doors. Exit doors should swing outward, i.e. towards the path of exit travel. Door assemblies placed in one hour corridors must also be rated, having a fire rating of at least 20 minutes; a door assembly must include approved smoke-and draft-control seals around the door, and be self-closing with a door closer or by automatic-closing using actuation of a smoke detector. The IBC requires fire-rated doors to be tested by a positive pressure test. Additionally, both the door and frame must bear the label of an approved testing agency, such as Underwriters Laboratories (UL). The table in Figure 8.15 shows various fire-rated door classifications.

Stairs are of various types including the straight run, curved, winder, spiral, scissor, etc. Most stair types are allowed by the codes on a limited basis, determined by certain safety considerations like occupancy classification, the number of occupants, stairs use, and tread dimensions. All stairs must meet specific code and accessibility requirements.

Exit stairs should be wide enough to allow for two people to descend side by side with no sudden decrease in width along the path of travel. Stairs must also adhere to specific code and accessibility requirements and constructed in a manner and using materials consistent with the construction type of the building. Model codes usually require that a run of stairs not rise in excess of twelve feet without an intermediate landing and must additionally have a landing at the top and bottom. Typically, new stairs are required to have a minimum width of 44 inches, an 11 inch tread depth, and a maximum riser height of 7 inches (Figures 8.16a, 8.16b). Handrails and guardrails are likewise regulated.

Elevators, whether passenger or freight, cannot typically be permitted to be considered for egress purposes, and are to be excluded in any egress exit requirements. However, in certain cases, an elevator may be considered for egress purposes in which case it must be provided with standby power and must comply with emergency operation and signaling device requirements.

Fire-Rated Door Classifications

Hour Rating	Class	Door Type	Frame Type	Use
20-minute	none	wood or hollow metal	wood or hollow metal	corridor doors in 1-hr partitions
$3/4$-hr	C	wood or hollow metal	hollow metal	1-hr corridor doors and exitway doors
1-hr	B	hollow metal	hollow metal	stairways in low-rise buildings and discharge corridors
$1^1/_2$-hr	B	hollow metal	hollow metal	2-hr vertical shafts for stairways
3-hr	A	hollow metal	hollow metal	3- or 4-hr walls

FIGURE 8.15 Fire-rated door classifications. *(From Interior Design Reference Manual by D.K. Ballast)*

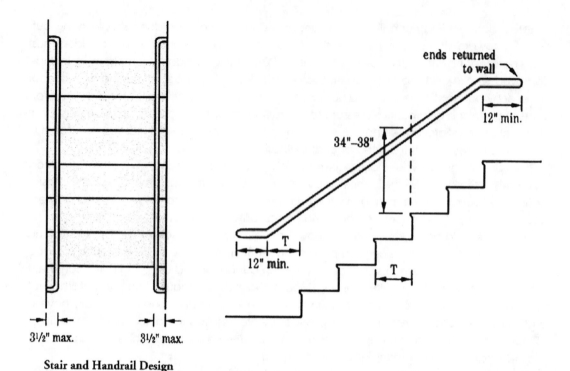

Stair and Handrail Design

FIGURE 8.16a   Code requirements for stair and handrails. *(From Interior Design Reference Manual by D.K. Ballast)*

Escalators and moving walks, like elevators, are not usually allowed as a means of egress and should not be taken into account as such in egress calculations, although there may be some exceptions.

Fire Protection Systems

Interior fire codes are designed to protect a building's occupants, allowing them time to evacuate during a fire, and afford access for fire fighters and equipment. Statistics show that smoke and toxic gases are the main cause of death in a building fire. Unhampered, fire and smoke travel quickly both horizontally and vertically, which is why action needs to be taken to prevent this from happening. Because the control of fire and smoke is such a life safety issue, the prevention of fire and smoke spread is addressed in the codes in several ways. The codes and standards place strict requirements on the materials that are used to construct a building. Depending on a building's classification, an hourly fire rating is typical of structural elements in a building, including walls and floor assemblies (Figure 8.17). Other parts of the codes place restrictions on the use of building materials internally for everything from windows and

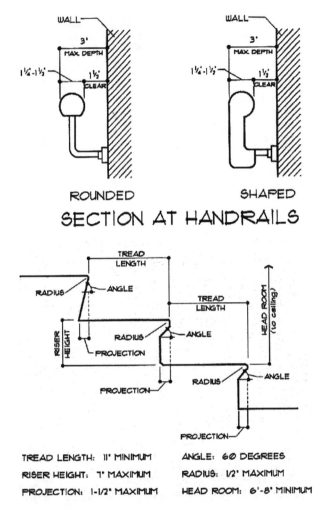

ROUNDED   SHAPED

SECTION AT HANDRAILS

TREAD LENGTH: 11" MINIMUM   ANGLE: 60 DEGREES

RISER HEIGHT: 7" MAXIMUM   RADIUS: 1/2" MAXIMUM

PROJECTION: 1-1/2" MAXIMUM   HEAD ROOM: 6'-8" MINIMUM

FIGURE 8.16b Code Requirements for Stairs and Handrail Design. *(From The Codes Guidebook for Interiors by S.K. Harmon and K.G. Kennon)*

doors to ductwork, wiring, and plumbing pipes. Codes and standards also regulate interior finishes and furniture.

The primary way that preventing systems are able to control the spread of fire and smoke within a building is by utilizing the concept of compartmentalization, or creating self-contained areas within a building. These areas are separated from each other by rated materials, such as walls, floors and doors. These rated materials in turn hamper the fire's rapid spread to other

OPENING PROTECTIVE FIRE PROTECTION RATING

TYPE OF ASSEMBLY	REQUIRED ASSEMBLY RATING (HOUR)	MINIMUM OPENING PROTECTION ASSEMBLY (HOUR)
Fire walls and fire barriers having a required fire resistance rating greater than 1 hour	4 3 2 1 ½	3 3[b] 1 ½ 1 ½
Fire barriers of 1 hour fire resistance rated construction :		
Shaft and exit enclosure walls	1	1
Other fire barriers	1	3/4
Fire partitions:		
Exit access corridor enclosure wall	1 ½	1/3[a] 1/3[a]
Other fire partitions	1	3/4

Note a. For testing requirements, see Section 714.2.2.
Note b. Two doors, each with a fire protection rating of 1 ½ hours, installed on opposite sides of the same opening in a building separation wall, shall be deemed equivalent in fire protection rating to one 3-hour fire door.

FIGURE 8.17 IBC Table 714.2—Opening protective fire protection rating. *(By permission, International Code Council, Inc.)*

parts of the building by providing resistance (depending on the materials used). In addition to regulating the materials that go into a building or space, the codes require various systems that are intended to aid in fire safety usually form an essential part of a building's overall life safety and fire protection strategy. There are four primary types of such systems.

Prevention Systems

Prevention systems are designed to prohibit and contain fires (e.g. fire and smoke barriers like walls, floors, and ceilings; open and through-penetration protectives like windows, doors, and firestops; and damper systems). Fire barriers are the principal means for containing a fire, and comprise of fire-rated building elements. There are three main types of fire barriers:

1. Fire walls (also called party walls) have the highest fire ratings and are usually built as part of the building shell.

2. Fire separation walls are used to "separate areas that are classified as different occupancy types within the same building," and usually have a one or two-hour fire rating. Corridor walls likewise usually need to be rated because they form part of the means of egress. Other fire barrier systems that often require rating include tenant separation walls, horizontal exits and vertical shaft enclosures.

3. Floor/ceiling assemblies are similar to walls and partitions. Fire ratings for floor/ceiling assemblies and for floor/roof assemblies are determined by the construction classification for the building and the walls that surround the assembly.

Detection Systems

Detection systems consist of devices to alert occupants and fire officials (e.g. smoke detectors and fire alarms). Most codes require smoke detectors to be tied into the fire alarm system. Smoke detectors are particularly effective in detecting smoldering fires that fail to produce sufficient heat to activate the sprinkler system. Fire alarm systems are activated either manually or automatically. They must be fully visible and located in the natural path of escape. Audio and accessible warning systems are also required in certain conditions. For example, some occupancies and building types necessitate an audio system to be tied into the fire alarm system. Likewise, the ADAAG requires that when an emergency warning system is required by the codes in public or commercial buildings, it should be both audible and visible.

Suppression Systems

Supression systems consist of methods to extinguish and control fires (such as fire extinguishers, fire hoses and sprinkler systems). Automatic sprinklers are the most common type of suppression system in the containment of a fire and are basically of four types:

1. Wet pipe system which is the most common system.

2. Dry pipe system which is used in unheated spaces to prevent freezing.

3. Deluge system which is a closed-head foam/water system that discharges foam to control severe fires.

4. Pre-action system, which is a combination of wet and dry systems and is used largely in areas where property is susceptible to water damage.

Automated Sprinkler system installations are usually tied into an alarm system and are now required in virtually all high-rise buildings. The NFPA 13: Standard for Installation of Sprinkler Systems is the source most referenced by the codes for sprinkler requirements.

Fire extinguishers are portable and do not require access to plumbing lines. They can be surface mounted or recessed within a wall using a custom cabinet. Standpipes and fire hoses are usually installed during the construction of a building.

Exiting Systems

Exiting systems facilitate means of evacuation (including signage and emergency lighting). Of note, the American with Disabilities Act Accessibility Guideline (ADAAG) and other accessibility standards do not play an essential role in fire prevention calculations, although many of the fire resistant elements (e.g. fire doors) are still required to meet the accessibility requirements.

MISCELLANEOUS ISSUES

Exit Lighting

Because each jurisdiction has slightly different requirements, one must review the local codes in force. In the event of a power failure, adequate lighting must be available for the evacuation of a building's occupants. This is usually given as one footcandle at the floor level. Where there are two or more exits, exit lighting (sometimes called emergency lighting) is required. Generally, artificial lighting is required in the path of exit discharge where a building is in use, with some exceptions for residential occupancies. Exit lighting and exit signs are required at all exits and corridors, aisles, ramps, passageways and lobbies leading to an exit. They must be located and illuminated so as to facilitate the exit of occupants safely out of a building. In fire-rated ceilings and wall assemblies, only certain types of light fixtures are permitted.

Glazing

The codes regulate the use of glass in hazardous locations such as doorways, vision panels, and places where people are likely to trip through a pane of glass accidentally. In such locations, the use of safety glazing (tempered, wired or laminated glass) is required. Common interior applications of approved rated glazing material are in corridor walls, room partitions and smoke barriers. When glass products are used in a rated wall, they must meet NFPA 257 requirements, providing the total area does not exceed 25 percent of the area of the wall of the room that it is separating (Figure 8.18). Fire rated glazing is essentially of three types:

1. Wired glass consists of wire mesh, sandwiched between two layers of glass. Wired glass is often used for vision panels and in smoke-stop barriers and in fire doors protecting stairway enclosures.

2. Glass block usually is a given a rating of 45 minutes although new products have 60 to 90 minute ratings.

3. Fire rated glazing including new or products like tempered glass, insulated glass, and multilayer laminate glass, which was developed as an alternative to wired glass. These new materials offer planners and office systems manufacturers new potential applications, allowing the use of larger sheets of glass.

When codes stipulate a rated window assembly, it should contain a permanent label etched into the glass, guaranteeing its fire rating (Figure 8.18).

Plumbing Systems

Plumbing and mechanical codes address issues relating to health and welfare concerns rather than life safety issues. Previously major code organizations published separate plumbing and mechanical codes. Then the International Code Council (ICC) published the first International Plumbing Code (IPC) in 1997 and the International Mechanical Codes in 1998, whichever code is used. Model codes specify in great detail how a plumbing or mechanical system should be designed. Plumbing codes specify the number of sanitary fixtures required based on the type of occupancy. Typically, in large interior projects, satisfying the requirements is the responsibility of the mechanical engineer and architect, although sometimes the space planner may be involved in the initial planning (Figure 8.19). These and other technical issues are discussed in greater detail in Chapter 11.

Sound Ratings

Model building codes sometimes require the use of insulation to control sound transmission in wall and floor assemblies separating dwelling units or guest rooms in residential occupancies from each other and from public spaces. Acoustics can dramatically influence the transmission

INTERIOR FIRE-RATED DOORS AND GLASS LITES

CLASS	FIRE RATING	LOCATION AND USE	GLASS LITE SIZE ALLOWED		
			AREA	HEIGHT	WIDTH
A	3 Hour	Fire walls separating buildings or various fire areas within a building. 3 to 4 hour walls	None Allowed	None Allowed	None Allowed
B	1½ Hours (H.M.) 1 Hour (other)	Vertical shafts and enclosures such as stairwells, elevators, and garbage chutes. 2 hour walls	100 inches	33 inches	10–12" inches
B	1 hour	Vertical shafts in low-rise buildings and discharge corridors. 1 to 1½ hour walls	100 inches	33 inches	10–12" inches
C	¾ hour	Exit access corridors and exitway enclosures. 1 hour walls	1296 inches	54 inches	54 inches
N/A	20-minute (⅓ hour)	Exit access corridors and room partitions. 1 hour walls	No Limit	No Limit	No Limit

* Final size depends on code publication used

FIGURE 8.18 Interior fire-rated doors and glass lites. *(From The Codes Guidebook for Interiors by S.K. Harmon and K.G. Kennon)*

TABLE 403.1
MINIMUM NUMBER OF PLUMBING FACILITIES[a]
(see Sections 403.2 and 403.3)

OCCUPANCY		WATER CLOSETS (Urinals, see Section 419.2) Male	WATER CLOSETS (Urinals, see Section 419.2) Female	LAVATORIES	BATHTUBS/ SHOWERS	DRINKING FOUNTAINS (see Section 410.1)	OTHERS
A S S E M B L Y	Nightclubs	1 per 40	1 per 40	1 per 75	—	1 per 500	1 service sink
	Restaurants	1 per 75	1 per 75	1 per 200	—	1 per 500	1 service sink
	Theaters, halls, museums, etc.	1 per 125	1 per 65	1 per 200	—	1 per 500	1 service sink
	Coliseums, arenas (less than 3,000 seats)	1 per 75	1 per 40	1 per 150	—	1 per 1,000	1 service sink
	Coliseums, arenas (3,000 seats or greater)	1 per 120	1 per 60	Male 1 per 200 Female 1 per 150	—	1 per 1,000	1 service sink
	Churches[b]	1 per 150	1 per 75	1 per 200	—	1 per 1,000	1 service sink
	Stadiums (less than 3,000 seats), pools, etc.	1 per 100	1 per 50	1 per 150	—	1 per 1,000	1 service sink
	Stadiums (3,000 seats or greater)	1 per 150	1 per 75	Male 1 per 200 Female 1 per 150	—	1 per 1,000	1 service sink
	Business (see Sections 403.2, 403.4 and 403.5)	1 per 50		1 per 80	—	1 per 100	1 service sink
	Educational	1 per 50		1 per 50	—	1 per 100	1 service sink
	Factory and industrial	1 per 100		1 per 100	(see Section 411)	1 per 400	1 service sink
	Passenger terminals and transportation facilities	1 per 500		1 per 750	—	1 per 1,000	1 service sink
I N S T I T U T I O N A L	Residential care	1 per 10		1 per 10	1 per 8	1 per 100	1 service sink
	Hospitals, ambulatory nursing home patients[c]	1 per room[d]		1 per room[d]	1 per 15	1 per 100	1 service sink per floor
	Day nurseries, sanitariums, nonambulatory nursing home patients, etc.[c]	1 per 15		1 per 15	1 per 15[e]	1 per 100	1 service sink
	Employees, other than residential care[c]	1 per 25		1 per 35	—	1 per 100	—
	Visitors, other than residential care	1 per 75		1 per 100	—	1 per 500	—
	Prisons[c]	1 per cell		1 per cell	1 per 15	1 per 100	1 service sink
	Asylums, reformatories, etc.[c]	1 per 15		1 per 15	1 per 15	1 per 100	1 service sink
	Mercantile (see Sections 403.2, 403.4 and 403.5)	1 per 500		1 per 750	—	1 per 1,000	1 service sink
R E S I D E N T I A L	Hotels, motels	1 per guestroom		1 per guestroom	1 per guestroom	—	1 service sink
	Lodges	1 per 10		1 per 10	1 per 8	1 per 100	1 service sink
	Multiple family	1 per dwelling unit		1 per dwelling unit	1 per dwelling unit	—	1 kitchen sink per dwelling unit; 1 automatic clothes washer connection per 20 dwelling units
	Dormitories	1 per 10		1 per 10	1 per 8	1 per 100	1 service sink
	One- and two-family dwellings	1 per dwelling unit		1 per dwelling unit	1 per dwelling unit	—	1 kitchen sink per dwelling unit; 1 automatic clothes washer connection per dwelling unit[f]
	Storage (see Sections 403.2 and 403.4)	1 per 100		1 per 100	(see Section 411)	1 per 1,000	1 service sink

a. The fixtures shown are based on one fixture being the minimum required for the number of persons indicated or any fraction of the number of persons indicated. The number of occupants shall be determined by the *International Building Code*.

b. Fixtures located in adjacent buildings under the ownership or control of the church shall be made available during periods the church is occupied.

c. Toilet facilities for employees shall be separate from facilities for inmates or patients.

d. A single-occupant toilet room with one water closet and one lavatory serving not more than two adjacent patient rooms shall be permitted where such room is provided with direct access from each patient room and with provisions for privacy.

e. For day nurseries, a maximum of one bathtub shall be required.

f. For attached one- and two-family dwellings, one automatic clothes washer connection shall be required per 20 dwelling units.

FIGURE 8.19 International Plumbing Code (IPC), Table 403.1—Minimum number of plumbing facilities. *(By permission, International Code Council, Inc.)*

of sound and noise. Preventing or minimizing the transmission of sound between spaces is affected by the materials used, their mass, and, to a lesser degree, their stiffness. Codes usually specify the minimum sound transmission class (STC) for walls or impact insulation class (IIC) for floors. Construction details can then be designed to satisfy these requirements. Acoustics are discussed in greater detail in Chapter 11.

Residential Exiting

Requirements for residential exiting (individual dwelling units and single-family houses) are not as strict as for commercial occupancies. Codes typically have a sub-classification specifically for dwelling units, although the one best covered is the International Residential Code (IRC), which is specifically designed for one and two family houses. The designer must verify which code is applicable to a particular project.

The IRC requires at least one regulated exterior door per residence with minimum dimensions of 3 foot 6 inches by 6 foot 8 inches. Bedrooms located on upper floors typically require an emergency means of egress for these areas, which can be an operable window as long as it is not more than 44 inches from the floor. Stair and ramp dimensions are also regulated, but are not as strict as those for commercial use. One handrail is normally required in residential stairs and ramps.

CHAPTER
NINE

BARRIER FREE
DESIGN—ADA
REQUIREMENTS

*T*he United States is without question a world leader when it comes to providing built environments that are accessible to people with disabilities.

The two most recent pieces of legislation dealing with accessible design are the Americans with Disabilities Act (ADA) and the Fair Housing Amendments Act of 1988. The latter extends the nondiscrimination protections of the Fair Housing Act to persons with disabilities as well as persons with families.

GENERAL OVERVIEW

The ADA is a federal civil law signed into legislation on July 26, 1990 by President George Bush that prohibits discrimination against people with disabilities. Britain has the Disability Discrimination Act (DDA) which is modeled on the ADA and which came into law in November of 1995. The Dutch have the *Geboden Toegang* (Access Demanded!), and the European Union has issued the *European Manual for Accessibility*.

The ADA is a wide-ranging legislation designed to make American society more accessible to persons with disabilities. Currently, all buildings, existing as well as new construction, must comply with the Americans with Disabilities Act (with certain exceptions that will be discussed later). Moreover, ADA requirements are liable to change as regulations are modified to improve access or to make it easier for entities to comply with ADA guidelines.

When new requirements are proposed, a formal procedure is used which calls for public comment followed by an agency review before the proposal is finalized. Modifications to existing requirements or to new requirements are initially issued as a proposed rule and published in the Federal Register. The ADA is comprised of the following five titles:

(Title I) Employment

Business must provide reasonable accommodations to protect the rights of individuals with disabilities in all aspects of employment. Possible changes may include restructuring jobs, altering the layout of workstations, or modifying equipment. Employment aspects may include the application process, hiring, wages, benefits, and all other aspects of employment. Medical examinations are highly regulated.

(Title II) Public Services

The regulations of Title II apply to public services provided by state and local governments, and include public school districts, the National Railroad Passenger Corporation, port authorities and other government units, whether or not they receive federal funds. In order to make the services offered accessible to people with disabilities, new construction and alterations are required to incorporate barrier-free design. Additionally, program accessibility in existing buildings may necessitate alterations in order to enhance the present degree of accessibility.

(Title III) Public Accommodations

This segment of the law applies mainly to commercial facilities, and prohibits privately owned and operated businesses from denying goods, programs or services to persons with disabilities. All new and altered commercial facilities are subject to the accessibility requirements of Title III Moreover, it has been incorporated into the Americans with Disabilities Act Accessibility Guidelines (ADAAG) as developed by the Architectural and Transportation Barriers Compliance Board (ATBCB or Access Board). Certain entities however, such as facilities that are owned and operated by religious entities, one and two-family dwellings, private clubs, and certain government facilities, may not be required to conform to ADA guidelines.

The United States Constitution states that Americans have the freedom to worship as they please, without interference from the state. This implies that if a church operates a daycare center or private school, the building used would not be bound to comply with ADA guidelines. On the other hand, a private residence can legally be covered as a place of public accommodation to the extent that it is used as a facility falling within one of 12 categories specified by the ADA. An example of this is where a professional office is located in a private residence. The section of the residence that houses the office and is dedicated to its use would, under the ADA, be considered a place of public accommodation and must typically comply to ADA guidelines.

A place of public accommodation, as defined by the ADA, is any facility that is owned and operated by a private entity whose operation affects commerce and falls within at least one of 12 specified categories:

- Places of lodging: e.g. hotels, motels, inns (does not include establishments in which the owner resides and rents out no more than five rooms)
- Establishments serving food or drink: e.g. restaurants, cafeterias and bars
- Places of exhibition or entertainment: e.g. theaters, stadiums, and concert halls
- Places of public gathering: e.g. auditoriums, convention centers, and lecture halls
- Sales or rental establishments: e.g. stores, bakeries, and shopping centers
- Service establishments: e.g. banks, dry-cleaners, travel agents, gas stations, attorney premises, hospitals, clinics
- Stations used for specified public transportation: e.g. private company bus terminals and depots
- Places of public display or collection: e.g. museums, libraries, and galleries
- Places of recreation: e.g. parks, zoos, and amusement parks
- Places of education: e.g. private sector educational establishments
- Social service center establishments: e.g. daycare centers, facilities for the elderly, and homeless shelters
- Places of exercise or recreation: e.g. health spas, gymnasiums, and golf courses

New construction as well as modifications to existing buildings must typically be accessible to individuals with disabilities. Where full accessibility is not technically feasible, due to structural, physical or site constraints, accessibility is to be provided to the maximum extent possible. For existing facilities, barriers to services must be removed if readily achievable. When an existing place of public accommodation is structurally altered, the ADA stipulates that the place must then comply with its guidelines.

(Title IV) Telecommunications

This section is aimed at federally regulated telecommunications companies and federally funded public service television offering services to the general public. Telephone companies offering general service to the public must offer telephone relay service to individuals who use telecommunication devices for the deaf (TTYs) or their equivalent. Additionally, close-captioned messages for hearing impaired viewers must be available for public service messages.

(Title V) Miscellaneous

Includes a provision prohibiting coercion, threatening or retaliating against the disabled or those attempting to aid people with disabilities in the assertion of their rights under the ADA.

Of particular importance to space planners and designers are Titles III and IV of the ADA. The Department of Justice (DOJ) and the Department of Transportation (DOT) enforce Titles III and IV of the Act throughout the United States, to jumpstart American society to being more accessible to people with disabilities.

ACCESSIBILITY GUIDELINES

Accessibility is achieved by addressing the requirements of the ADA and other applicable codes as well as state and local regulations. There are essentially three accessibility documents that space planners and interior designers most frequently use and should be familiar with. These are:

- ANSI A117.1 was developed by the American National Standard Institute (ANSI), and is one of the first accessibility guidelines to be used in the United States. The latest edition of the ANSI A117.1/ICC is the 1998 edition, which was developed jointly with the International Code Council and the Access Board. This edition has been modified to be more in step with the ADAAG.

- The Americans with Disabilities Act Accessibility Guidelines (ADAAG) was developed by the Architectural and Transportation Barriers Compliance Board (ATBCB or Access Board) as guidelines for ADA legislation. It was based on the 1986 ANSI A117.1, but after the incorporation of additional requirements it became stricter than ANSI. The Access Board is responsible for making revisions to the ADAAG and is currently working with the DOJ on updating the ADAAG.

- The Uniform Federal Accessibility Standards (UFAS) is based on the 1980 ANSI standard and applies mostly to government buildings and organizations that accept federal funding. These buildings are not currently required to conform to ADA regulations.

Although there is not a great deal of difference between them, it is nevertheless, important to know which document applies to the project in hand. It is outside the scope of this book to elaborate on all the requirements of the above accessibility documents. However, relevant issues are discussed, backed by clear illustrations to give the reader a broad understanding and overview of accessibility requirements.

The ADA stipulates that new construction and alterations to existing facilities must comply with the ADAAG. Of note, a new tenant space within an existing building is considered by the ADA to be new construction and must comply with the ADAAG. Rules of compliance for alterations and renovations to existing buildings are sometimes complex, and under Title III of the ADA, altered buildings must be made accessible if that is readily achievable. The commentary to the Title III rule is backed by a list of 21 examples of barrier removals that it considers readily achievable. However, when prevailing conditions prevent barrier removal, a public accommodation has to make its services available through alternative means, such as relocating activities to accessible locations.

At present, state and local governments maintain the option whether to choose the ADA Accessibility Guidelines (ADAAG) or the 1984 Uniform Federal Accessibility Standard (UFAS). However, the ADAAG does not address all building types; for example, residential construction, jails and correctional facilities are not covered. These are covered by the UFAS guidelines. The problem is that the UFAS is gradually being phased out as a design criteria option and some federal agencies have already commenced revising their regulations to comply with ADAAG but without the elevator exception.

ACCESSIBLE ROUTES

The ADAAG defines an accessible route as "a continuous, unobstructed path connecting all accessible elements and spaces in a building or facility." This includes pathways, corridors, doorways, floors, ramps, elevators, and clear floor space at fixtures. Safe and barrier-free accessible routes are essential for people with disabilities, and enhancing their movement is critical to their well being. The standards for accessible routes are designed primarily to accommodate persons using wheelchairs, but they should also accommodate people with other disabilities. Well designed and well placed signage is important in giving direction to people with these limitations, including vision, hearing and mobility. Travel distances should also be taken into consideration, particularly when designing for persons with low stamina capabilities or who use mobility devices.

Adequate corridor width is essential to passage for someone with mobility or vision impairment. The ADAAG puts great emphasis as the provisions for access and egress and clearly delineates the requirements for length, space, lighting signage, and safety measures. Corridors for example, should ideally, be a minimum of 42 inches (1065 mm) wide and not more than 75 feet (22.9m) long. They should be well lit with indirect lighting to prevent glare. Wall finishes should incorporate blends of contrasted colors to increase visual acuity. Figure 9.1a shows minimum width and length requirements for straight hallways.

Openings that form part of an accessible route should not be less than 32 inches (815 mm) wide. The minimum passage width for two wheelchairs is 60 inches (1525 mm) as shown in (Figure 9.1b). If an accessible route is less than 60 inches (1525 mm) wide, then passing spaces at least 60 inches by 60 inches must be provided at intervals not to exceed 200 feet (61 m). Figure 9.2 shows width requirements for corridors, in the context of turns around obstructions.

The ADAAG stipulates that the minimum clear floor space required to accommodate one stationary wheelchair is 30 inches (762 mm) by 48 inches (1220 mm). For maneuverability, a minimum 60 inch (1525 mm) diameter circle is required for a wheelchair to make one 180 degree turn. In place of this, a T-shaped space may be provided as shown in Figure 9.3.

DOORS AND DOORWAYS

Doors should have a clear opening width of between 32 (815 mm) and 36 inches (915 mm) when the door is opened at 90 degrees. The maximum depth of a 32 inches wide (815 mm) doorway is 24 inches (610 mm) as shown in Figure 9.4. If the depth exceeds this, then the width must be increased to 36 inches (915 mm). Threshold heights should not exceed ½ inch (12.7 mm),

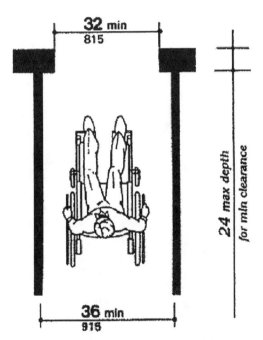

Minimum Clear Width for Single Wheelchair

FIGURE 9.1a Openings in straight hallways should not be less than 32 inches (815 mm) wide. *(From 28 Code of Federal Regulations (CFR) Ch.1, Pt. 36, App. A, Fig.1, 7-1-94 Edition)*

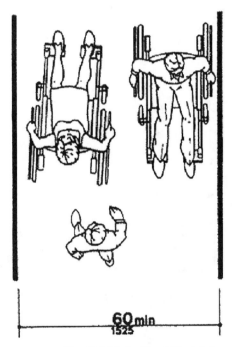

Minimum Clear Width for Two Wheelchairs

FIGURE 9.1b When an accessible route is less than 60 inches (1525 mm) wide, passing spaces not less than 60 inches x 60 inches must be provided at intervals not exceeding 200 feet or 61 meters. *(From 28 CFR Ch.1, Pt. 36, App. A, Fig. 2, 7-1-94 Edition)*

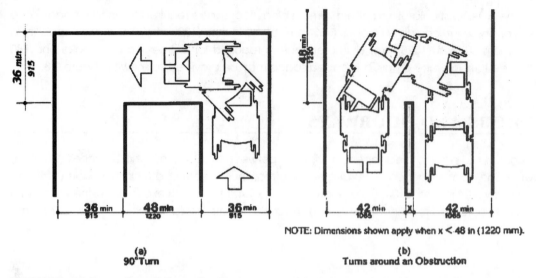

NOTE: Dimensions shown apply when x < 48 in (1220 mm).

(a)
90° Turn

(b)
Turns around an Obstruction

FIGURE 9.2   Minimum clear width required for access corridor in the context of turns around obstructions. *(From 28 CFR Ch.1, Pt. 36, App. A, Fig.7a and 7b, 7-1-94 Edition)*

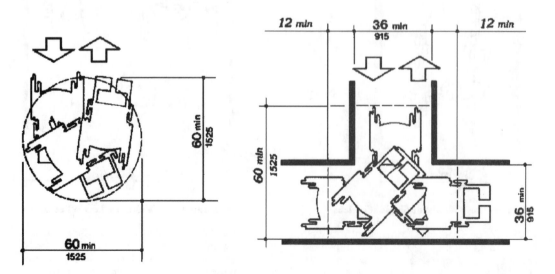

FIGURE 9.3   Wheelchair turning space. *(From 28 CFR Ch.1, Pt. 36, App. A, Fig.3, 7-1-94 Edition)*

and should not contain any sharp slopes or abrupt changes but should be beveled so no slope of the threshold is greater than 1:2. Door closers should not hamper a door's use by the handicapped.

No part of an accessible route may have a slope more than 1:20 (1 inch rise for every 20 inches/508 mm distance). Slopes any greater than this are classified as a ramp and must meet different requirements including the provision of handrails (Figure 9.5).

Minimum maneuvering clearances are required for wheelchairs at standard swinging doors (that are not automatic or power assisted) to allow easy operation of the latch and provide for a clear swing (Figure 9.6). The floor or ground area within the required clearances shall be level and clear for a minimum distance of five feet in the direction of the door swing. When inadequate maneuvering clearance at doors is provided, impaired persons and persons using wheelchairs find opening the door very awkward (Figure 9.7). Ideally, the opening of an inward opening single door can be facilitated by the provision of a clear wall space to the

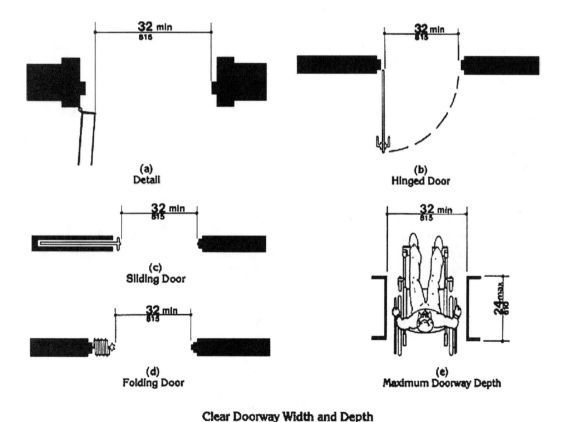

Clear Doorway Width and Depth

FIGURE 9.4 Clear doorway width and depth. *(From 28 CFR Ch.1, Pt. 36, App. A, Fig.24, 7-1-94 Edition)*

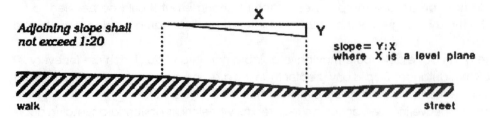

FIGURE 9.5   Maximum slope of any part of an accessible route, is 1:20. Otherwise it is classified as a ramp. *(From 28 CFR Ch.1, Pt. 36, App. A, Fig.11, 7-1-94 Edition)*

side of the door handle of about 30 inches (762 mm) as shown in Figure 9.7d. For two hinged or pivoted doors in a series the minimum space is 48 inches (1220 mm) plus the width of any door swinging into the space (Figure 9.8). Doors in series shall swing either in the same direction or away from the space between the doors.

Door closers where provided, should be adjusted to slow the closing time. The pressure or opening force required to push or pull open interior doors should not exceed five pounds (2.27 kg). Pocket doors with push plates are preferable because their swing is not in the direction of a wheelchair user. Automatic openers are useful for making doors accessible when the door opening pressure is excessive or there is insufficient maneuvering clearance on one or both sides of the door. Such automatic or power-assisted doors when used, should comply with relevant codes (Figure 9.9).

Barrier-free codes also require that door hardware meets certain specifications. Lever handles on doors for disabled people is usually cost effective. All hardware on doors, cabinets and windows should be easy to grasp and operate with one hand, and should not need a tight grip for turning. This includes lever operated and push type mechanisms, and U-shaped handles (Figure 9.10). Standard door knobs are not allowed.

Controls should be clearly visible and accessible. Switches and controls for lights, heat, fire alarms, windows, etc. which are often of essential use, should be located no higher than 48 inches (1220 mm) above the floor nor lower than 15 inches (381 mm), as shown in Figure 9.11.

PLUMBING FIXTURES AND PUBLIC LAVATORIES

Toilet Stalls

Figure 9.12 shows the requirements for toilet stall doors. If toilet stall approach is from the latch side of the stall door, clearance between the door side of the stall and any obstruction may be reduced to a minimum of 42 in (1065 mm). Many toilet stalls are positioned at the end of

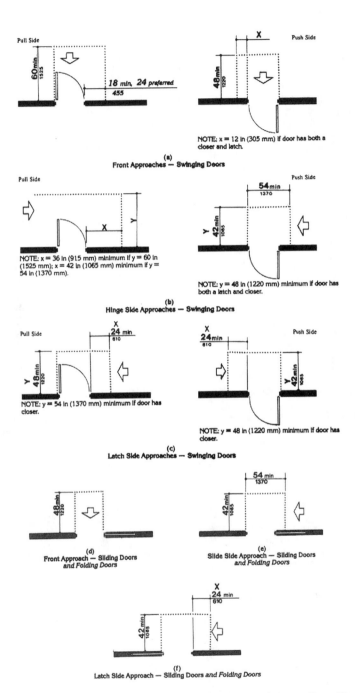

FIGURE 9.6 Minimum maneuvering clearances at doors. *(From 28 CFR Ch.1, Pt. 36, App. A, Fig.25, 7-1-94 Edition)*

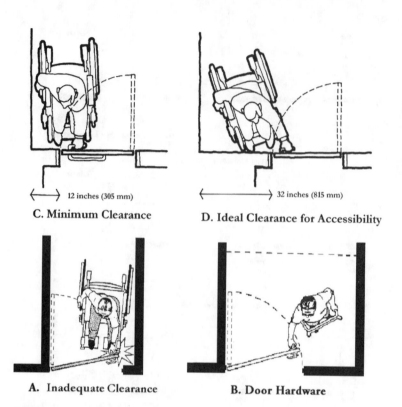

C. Minimum Clearance

←——→ 12 inches (305 mm)

D. Ideal Clearance for Accessibility

←————————→ 32 inches (815 mm)

A. Inadequate Clearance

B. Door Hardware

FIGURE 9.7   Inadequate clearances can hamper accessibility. *(Figure 9.7C and D, courtesy Selwyn Goldsmith, Designing for the Disabled: The New Paradigm, Architectural Press)*

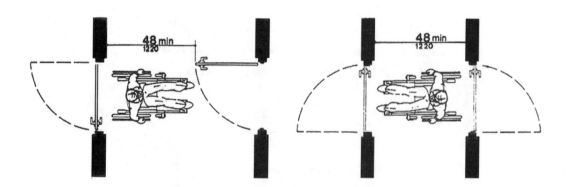

48 min
1220

48 min
1220

Two Hinged Doors in Series

FIGURE 9.8   Two hinged doors in series. *(From 28 CFR Ch. 1, Pt. 36, App. A, Fig. 26, 7-1-94 Edition)*

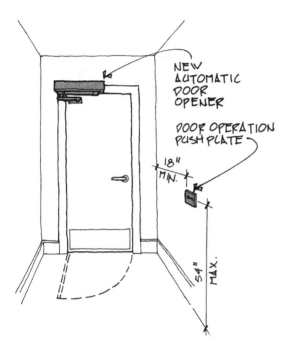

FIGURE 9.9 Automatic doors. *(Courtesy of Means ADA Compliance Pricing Guide, R.S. Means Company, Inc.)*

FIGURE 9.10 Example of lever-type handle. Door hardware must also comply with ADA codes. *(Courtesy Deborah, S. Kearney, The ADA in Practice, R.S. Means Company Inc.)*

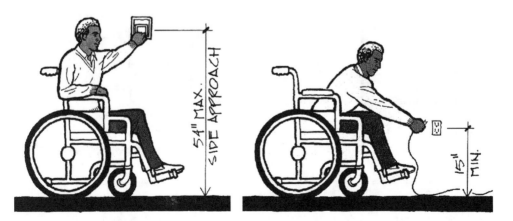

FIGURE 9.11 Positioning controls to be accessible. *(Courtesy of Means ADA Compliance Pricing Guide, R.S. Means Company, Inc.)*

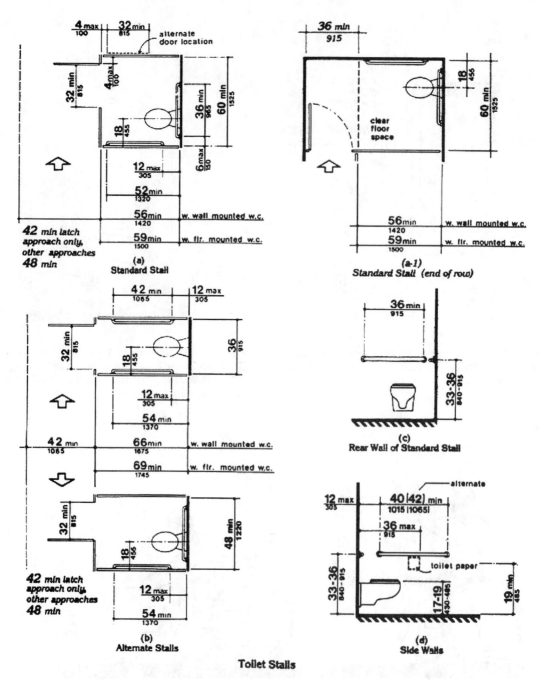

FIGURE 9.12 Various toilet stall layouts. *(From 28 CFR Ch.1, Pt. 36, App. A, Fig. 30, 7-1-94 Edition)*

a path of travel between the row of stalls and the wall (Figure 9.13). The advantage of using an end toilet for the accessible stall is that the grab bars can be fixed to the wall rather than to a partition, which allows sturdier anchoring to meet minimum strength requirements. Where the stall has compliant maneuvering space, it is sometimes possible to form an accessible stall by extending the stall across the path of travel to the opposite wall and entering straight on. In existing buildings that have a multiple-stall toilet room with typical inaccessible stalls, it is usually possible to create an accessible stall by removing one toilet and combining the space of two stalls, providing it continues to meet the local plumbing codes requiring a certain number of fixtures for a given building density (Figure 9.14).

There are several toilet stall layouts that meet ADA requirements. Minimum clearances for standard stall layouts are shown in Figures 9.15a and 9.15b. Toilet rooms as well as toilet stalls must have a minimum 60 inch (1525 mm) clear internal turning space. However, the clear floor space at fixtures and controls may extend up to 19 inches (483 mm) under a wall-mounted sink. The clearance depth varies depending on whether a wall-hung or floor-mounted water closet (60 inch by 56 inch minimum clear inside dimensions) is used. In most cases, the door must provide a minimum clear opening of 32 inches (815 mm) and must swing out, away from the stall enclosure. If a stall is less than 60 inches (1525 mm) deep, a 9 inch (225 mm) toe clearance is required under partitions. In planning toilet rooms, a five foot diameter (1525 mm) clear space should be allowed for.

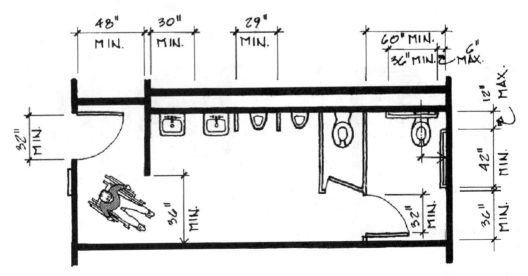

FIGURE 9.13 An example of a typical end toilet stall. *(Courtesy of Means ADA Compliance Pricing Guide, R.S. Means Company, Inc.)*

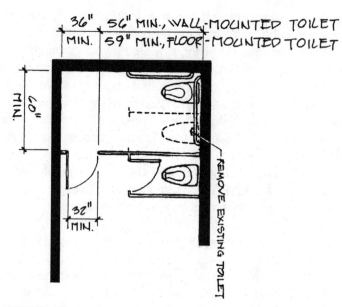

FIGURE 9.14 An accessible stall can often be create by removing one toilet and combining the space. *(Courtesy of Means ADA Compliance Pricing Guide, R.S. Means Company, Inc.)*

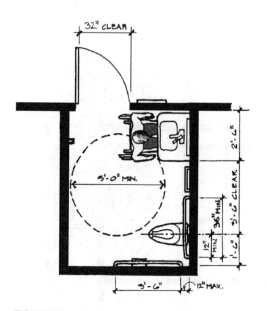

FIGURES 9.15a Minimum ADA toilet and stall configurations. *(Courtesy of Means ADA Compliance Pricing Guide, R.S. Means Company, Inc.)*

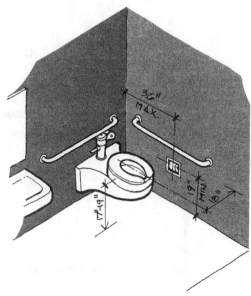

FIGURES 9.15b Minimum ADA toilet and stall configurations. *(Courtesy of Means ADA Compliance Pricing Guide, R.S. Means Company, Inc.)*

Grab bars must also be provided as shown in Figure 9.16, mounted from 33 inches (838 mm) to 36 inches (915 mm) above the finished floor. Grab bars should be a minimum of 42 inches (1065 mm) long at a side wall and 36 inches (915 mm) long minimum at a rear wall. It should have a diameter of 1½ inches (38 mm), and be not more than 1½ inches (38 mm) from the wall. Research shows that in special toilets for the disabled, three rails are important: the side horizontal fixed rail, the drop-down rail and the vertical rail on the side wall. In many toilets, there is a lateral space to the side of the water closet which only allows provision of a side horizontal rail. Toilet paper dispensers are to be located below the grab bar, a minimum of 19 inches (483) above finished floor.

In the absence of toilet stalls, the centerline of the toilet must still be 18 inches (455 mm) from a wall with back and side grab bars. A clear space should be provided in front of and to the side of open water closets. If an existing toilet is categorized by an accessible location but is not ADA compliant, and expense or other difficulties prevent full ADA compliance, several elements can still be modified to improve accessibility. These include reversing the flush valve, adding a seat height extender, or relocating the toilet paper holder and grab bars.

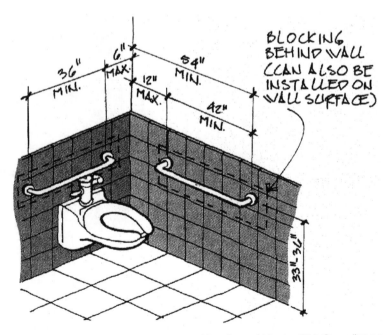

FIGURE 9.16 Positioning of grab bars. *(Courtesy of Means ADA Compliance Pricing Guide, R.S. Means Company, Inc.)*

Urinals

Where urinals are installed, the stall type or wall-mounted urinals must be used with an elongated rim no more than 17 inches (430 mm) above the floor. A clear floor space of 30 inches (762 mm) by 48 inches (1220 mm) must be provided in front of the urinal (Figure 9.17). This space may adjoin or overlap an accessible route.

Lavatories

Public lavatories must allow wheelchair users to move under the sink and easily use the basin and water controls (Figures 9.18 and 9.19). Notice that because of these clearances wall-mounted lavatories are the best type to use when accessibility is a concern. Any exposed piping below the lavatory must be insulated or otherwise protected. ADAAG makes a distinction between lavatories, which are basins for hand washing, and sinks, which are other types of basins. Faucets must be easy to operate with one hand without tight grasping, or twisting of the wrist. Lever-operated, push-type, and automatically controlled mechanisms are acceptable. In Figure 9.20, we see how a lavatory basin is treated to make it accessible.

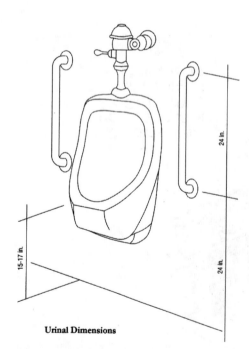

FIGURE 9.17 Typical urinal dimensions. *(Courtesy Deborah, S. Kearney, The ADA in Practice, R.S. Means Company Inc.)*

FIGURE 9.18 Typical accessible wall-hung lavatory dimensions. *(Courtesy of Means ADA Compliance Pricing Guide, R.S. Means Company, Inc.)*

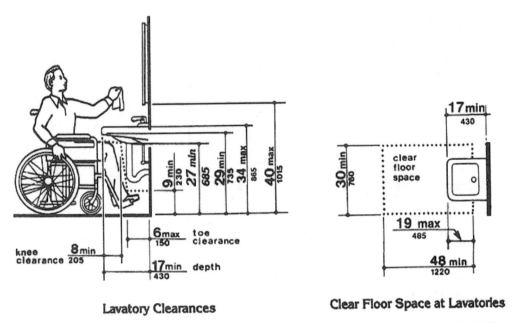

Lavatory Clearances

Clear Floor Space at Lavatories

FIGURE 9.19 *Typical accessible lavatory dimensions. (From 28 CFR Ch.1, Pt. 36, App. A, Fig. 31/Fig. 32, 7-1-94 Edition)*

At least one mirror must be accessible with the bottom edge of the reflecting surface mounted no higher than 40 inches (1015 mm) above the floor, and should preferably be tilted for reflectance.

Residential Bathrooms

Although private residences are not typically subject to Title III of the ADA requirements, space planners and interior designers should familiarize themselves with such requirements to be able to serve their clients better, particularly elderly or disabled clients with special needs. The Bureau of the Census estimates that by 2050 more than 25 percent of Americans will be over 65 years old. The potential ramification of this on design criteria is substantial. In Figure 9.21, we see a prefabricated shower unit with strong grab bars in the shower, installed at different heights, along with a hand-held showerhead. These are some of the essentials of the accessible bathroom in the home. In Figure 9.22, see various accessible bathroom options offered by Universal Home Series which are designed to allow a variety of bathing features: a standard tub with a fold-up seat, a tub with a transfer surface, a whirlpool tub, a three foot square transfer shower and a five foot square roll-in shower. Offset controls make it easy to turn on bath water and regulate temperature from outside the tub or shower.

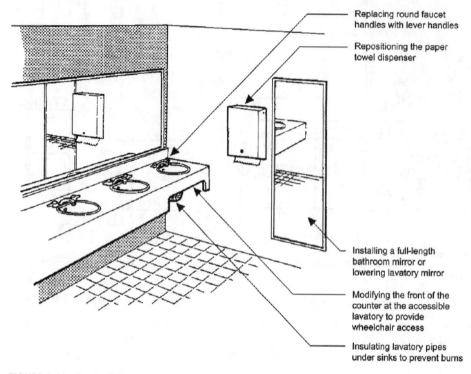

Replacing round faucet
handles with lever handles

Repositioning the paper
towel dispenser

Installing a full-length
bathroom mirror or
lowering lavatory mirror

Modifying the front of the
counter at the accessible
lavatory to provide
wheelchair access

Insulating lavatory pipes
under sinks to prevent burns

FIGURE 9.20 Barrier-free lavatory design.

Water Fountains and Coolers

Drinking water should be accessible with up-front spouts and controls that can be either hand or floor-operated as shown in Figure 9.23. Accessible height should not exceed 36 inches (915 mm), and an alcove recess should not be less than 30 inches (762 mm) wide. Drinking fountains that are freestanding or built in without a clear space below, must maintain a clear floor space in front not less than 30 inches (762 mm) by 48 inches (1220 mm), to allow a parallel approach the unit by a person in a wheelchair.

Where only one drinking fountain is provided per floor, it should be accessible to people using wheelchairs, as well as persons who have difficulty bending or stooping. This can be resolved by the use of a hi-lo type fountain, whereby one fountain is at a low level and accessible to those using wheelchairs, and another is at the standard height for those that have difficulty bending.

FIGURE 9.21 Prefabricated shower unit with strong grab bars. (*Courtesy Charles A. Riley II, High-Access Home, Rizzoli International Publications, Inc.*)

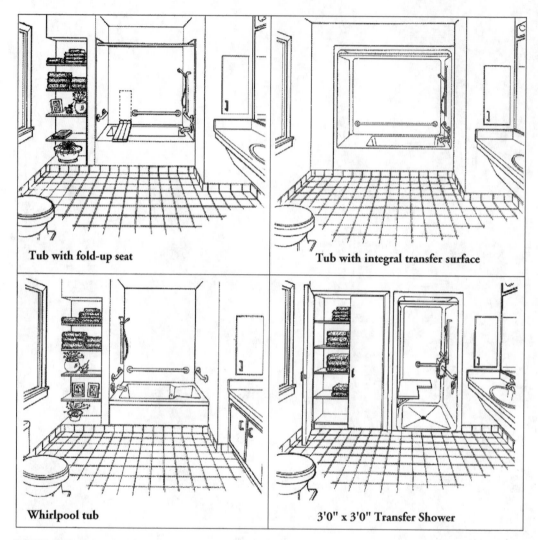

Tub with fold-up seat

Tub with integral transfer surface

Whirlpool tub

3'0" x 3'0" Transfer Shower

FIGURE 9.22 Accessible bathroom options offered by Universal Home. *(Courtesy Steven Winter Associates, Accessible Housing by Design, McGraw-Hill)*

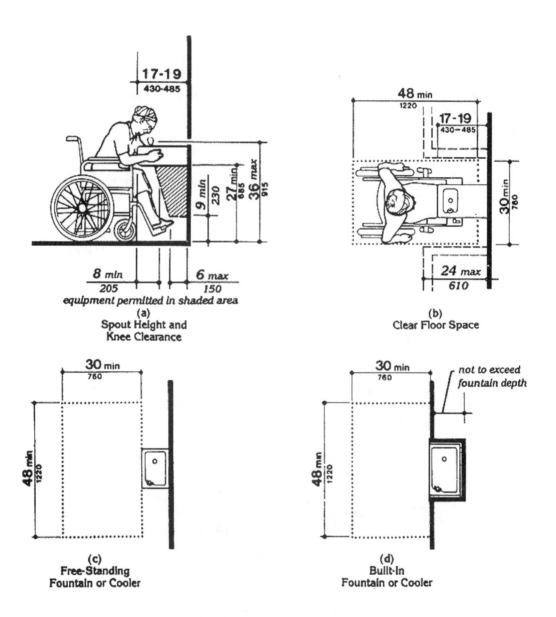

Drinking Fountains and Water Coolers

FIGURE 9.23 Drinking fountains and water coolers. *(From 28 CFR Ch.1, Pt. 36, App. A, Fig. 27, 7-1-94 Edition)*

STAIRS AND RAMPS

Ramps are required to provide a smooth transition between changes in elevation for both wheelchair-bound persons as well as those whose mobility is otherwise restricted. In general, space planners should use the lease possible slope, but in no case can a ramp have a slope greater than 1:12 (1 inch in rise for every 12 inches in run). The maximum rise for any ramp is limited to 30 inches (762 mm) after which a level landing is required. Where local exiting conditions do not allow for a 1:12 slope, a 1:10 slope is permitted providing the maximum rise does not exceed 6 inches (152 mm). A steeper slope of 1:8 is permitted if the maximum rise does not exceed 3 inches (76 mm).

A ramp's clear width must not be less than 36 inches, with landings that are at least as wide as the widest segment of the ramp leading to them. Landing lengths must not be less than 60 inches (1525 mm), and if ramps change direction at a landing, the landing must be at least 60 inches square (Figure 9.24).

Ramps that have a rise greater than 6 inches (152 mm) or lengths exceeding 72 inches (1825 mm) must have handrails on both sides with the top of the handrail from 34 (864 mm) to 38 inches (965 mm) above the ramp surface. They must extend at least 12 inches (305 mm) beyond the top and bottom of the ramp segment and have a diameter or width of gripping surface from 1¼ inches (32 mm) to 1½ inches (38 mm) is required for both ramps and stairs (Figure 9.25).

The ANSI code states that stairs that are required as a means of egress and stairs between floors not connected by an elevator must be designed according to certain standards specifying the configuration of treads, risers, nosings, and handrails. The maximum riser height

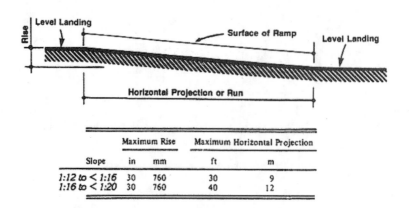

Slope	Maximum Rise		Maximum Horizontal Projection	
	in	mm	ft	m
1:12 to < 1:16	30	760	30	9
1:16 to < 1:20	30	760	40	12

Components of a Single Ramp Run and Sample Ramp Dimensions

FIGURE 9.24   Ramp dimensions. *(From 28 CFR Ch.1, Pt. 36, App. A, Fig.16, 7-1-94 Edition)*

is 7 inches (178 mm) and the treads must be a minimum of 11 inches (280 mm) as measured from riser to riser. Open risers are not permitted. The undersides of the nosings must not be abrupt and must conform to one of the styles shown in Figure 9.26. Stairway users are more likely to stumble or fall while going down stairs than when going up. Tread depth is pivotal in stair design. Typically when climbing a stairs, users place only part of their foot on the tread, whereas when descending, the whole foot or most of the foot is placed on the tread.

Stairway handrails must be continuous on both sides of the stairs. The inside handrail on switchback or dogleg stairs must always be continuous as it changes direction. Other handrails must extend beyond the top and bottom riser as shown in Figures 9.27 and 9.28. A handrail's top gripping surface must be between 34 (864 mm) and 38 inches (965 mm) above stair nosings.

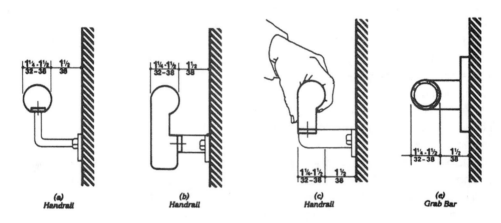

Size and Spacing of Handrails and Grab Bars

FIGURE 9.25 Handrail requirements for ramps and stairs. *(From 28 CFR Ch. 1, Pt. 36, App. A, Fig. 39, 7-1-94 Edition)*

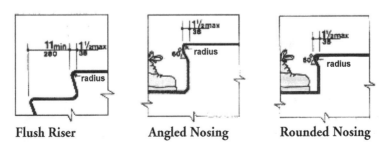

Flush Riser   **Angled Nosing**   **Rounded Nosing**

FIGURE 9.26 Tread and nosing requirements. *(From 28 CFR Ch. 1, Pt. 36, App. A, Fig. 18, 7-1-94 Edition)*

In addition, handrails must have a diameter or width of gripping surface of between 1¼ inches (32 mm) and 1½ inches (38 mm). There must also be a clear space between the handrail and the wall of at least 1½ inches (38 mm) as shown in Figure 9.25. When an exit stairway is part of an accessible route in a building not incorporating a sprinkler system (excluding residences), there a clear width of 48 inches between the handrails must be maintained.

FLOOR SURFACES AND TACTILE PAVINGS (DETECTABLE WARNINGS)

Floor surfaces must be firm, and slip-resistant. If there is a change in level, the transition must meet the following requirements. If the change is less than ¼ inch (6.4 mm), it may be vertical and without edge treatment. If the change is between ¼ inch (6.4 mm) and ½ inch (12.7 mm), it must be beveled and its slope no greater than 1:2 (Figure 9.29). Changes greater than ½ inch changes the classification to a ramp which must then meet the requirements outlined in the previous section. Bathroom floors should have a non-slip finish.

Carpet must have a firm cushion or backing or no cushion and have a level loop, textured loop, level-cut pile, or level-cut/uncut pile texture and its pile must not exceed ½ inch (12.7 mm) in height. Carpet must be securely attached to the floor and all exposed edges concealed with a trim along its length.

Detectable warning surfaces are required for areas in front of stairs, hazardous vehicular areas, and other places where a hazard may exist in the absence of a guardrail or other method of warning someone. The surfaces must be comprised of textured surfaces that contrast with their surrounds, like exposed aggregate concrete, cushioned surfaces of rubber or plastic, raised strips, or grooves. A British study noted that a prerequisite for the successful use of tactile paving is that the visually impaired person understood the meanings assigned to the different paving surfaces (Figure 9.30).

Door handles are also required to have a textured surface if they are part of a door that leads to an area that might prove dangerous to a blind person, including doors to loading platforms, boiler rooms, and stages.

PUBLIC TELEPHONES

Telephones are one of the easiest building elements to make accessible. They should be positioned so that they can be reached by person(s) in a wheelchair. Accessible telephones may be designed for either front or side access. The dimensions required for both of these types are shown in Figures 9.31a and 9.31b. In either case a clear floor space of not less than 30 inches (762 mm) by 48 inches (1220 mm) is to be provided. Telephones should have pushbutton controls and telephone directories that are accessible by a person in a wheelchair.

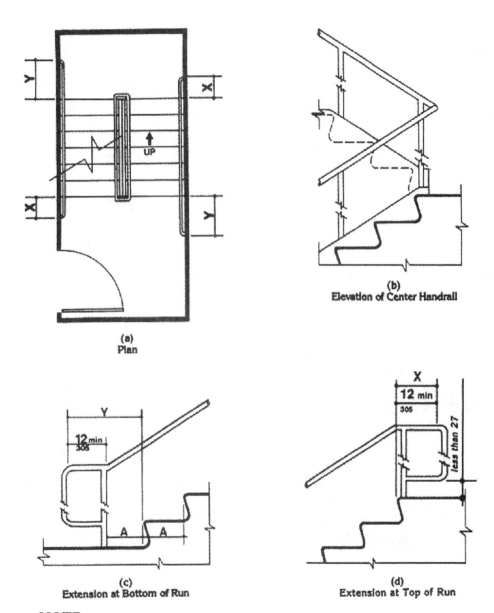

(a)
Plan

(b)
Elevation of Center Handrail

(c)
Extension at Bottom of Run

(d)
Extension at Top of Run

NOTE:
X is the 12 in. minimum handrail extension required at each top riser.
Y is the minimum handrail extension of 12 in. plus the wall width of
one tread that is required at each bottom riser.

FIGURE 9.27 Stair and handrail design. *(From 28 CFR Ch. 1, Pt. 36, App. A, Fig. 19, 7-1-94 Edition)*

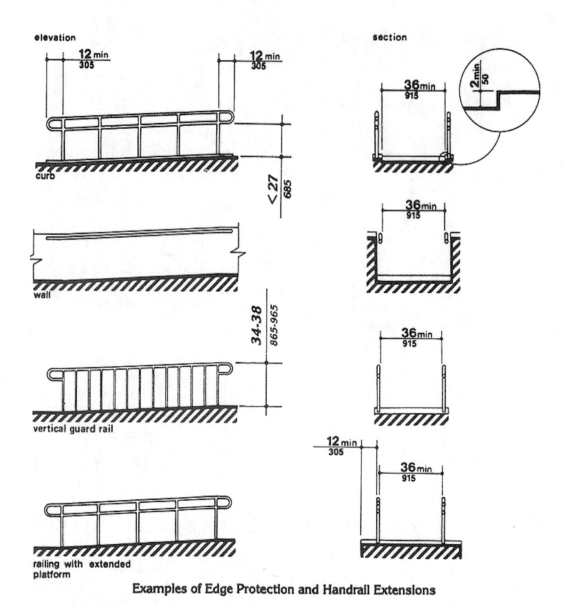

elevation

section

12 min
305

12 min
305

2 min
50

36 min
915

curb

< 27
685

wall

34-38
865-965

36 min
915

vertical guard rail

36 min
915

12 min
305

36 min
915

railing with extended
platform

Examples of Edge Protection and Handrail Extensions

FIGURE 9.28   Examples of edge protection and handrail extensions. *(From 28 CFR Ch.1, Pt. 36, App. A, Fig.17, 7-1-94 Edition)*

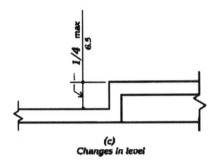

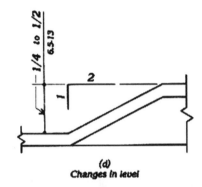

FIGURE 9.29 Changes in levels. *(From 28 CFR Ch.1, Pt. 36, App. A, Fig.7 (c), (d), 7-1-94 Edition)*

FIGURE 9.30 Example of tactile paving. *(Courtesy of Means ADA Compliance Pricing Guide, R.S. Means Company, Inc.)*

Title III stipulates that in new construction, at least one TTY is to be provided inside any building that has four or more public pay telephones (counting both interior and exterior phones). A TTY must also be provided whenever there is an interior public pay phone in a stadium, convention center, hotel with a convention center, covered shopping mall or hospital emergency, recovery, or waiting room. Title III also stipulates that one accessible public phone must be provided for each floor of new construction, unless the floor has two or more banks of phones, in which case one accessible phone should be provided for each bank.

PROTRUDING OBJECTS

There are restrictions on objects and building elements that project into corridors and other walkways because protruding objects present a hazard for visually impaired people. These restrictions are shown in Figure 9.32, and are based on the needs of people with severe vision

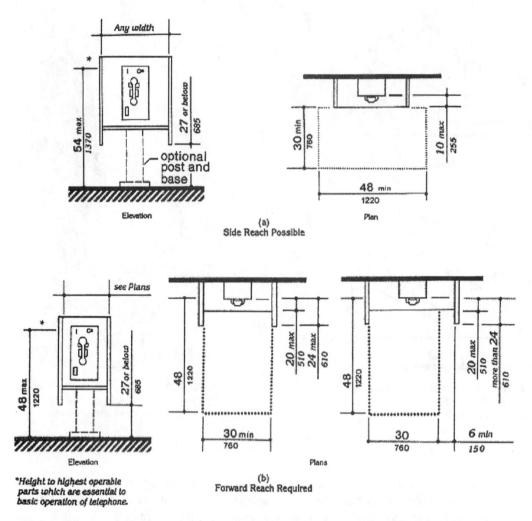

FIGURE 9.31a Dimensional requirements for accessible telephones. *(From 28 CFR Ch.1, Pt. 36, App. A, Fig. 44, 7-1-94 Edition)*

impairments walking with a cane. There are no restrictions on protruding objects where their lower edge is less than 27 inches (686 mm) above the floor because these can be detected by a person using a cane. However, protruding objects cannot reduce the clear width required for an accessible route or maneuvering space, and a guardrail or other barrier must be provided areas adjacent to accessible routes where the vertical clearance is reduced to less than 80 inches (2 m).

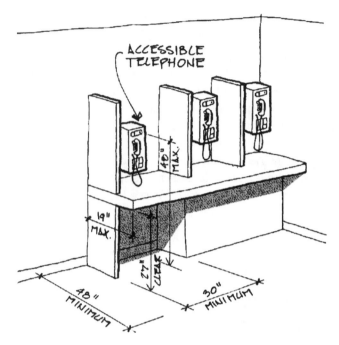

FIGURE 9.31b Three-dimensional depiction of accessible public telephone requirements. *(Courtesy of Means ADA Compliance Pricing Guide, R.S. Means Company, Inc.)*

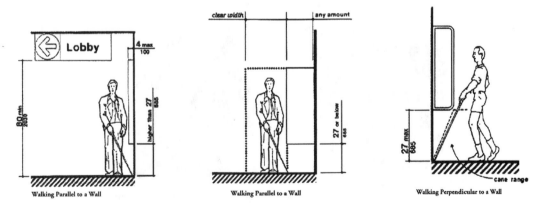

FIGURE 9.32 Objects should not protrude more than four inches (100 mm) into walks, corridors or passageways. *(From 28 CFR Ch.1, Pt. 36, App. A, Fig. 8, 7-1-94 Edition)*

SIGNAGE AND ALARMS

Signage should be give clear guidance for visually impaired people with emergency information and general circulation directions. Of importance in evaluating signage criteria is the ability to be viewed by people with low vision (i.e. 20 percent of normal) from a distance of 30 feet (9.14 m). Signage is also required for elevators. For optimum clarity, adequate luminescence should be provided. Contrasted colors can also enhance legibility (70 percent or more contrast between letters and background is recommended).

The ANSI standards specify the width-to-height ratio of letters and how thick the individual letter strokes must be. They also require that characters, symbols, or pictographs on tactile signs be raised ½₂ inch (0.79 mm). If accessible facilities are identified, the international symbol of accessibility must be used (Figure 9.33). Braille characters must be Grade 2.

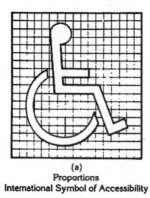

(a)
Proportions
International Symbol of Accessibility

International Symbols

(b)
Display Conditions
International Symbol of Accessibility

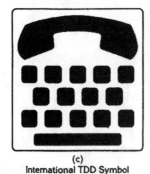

(c)
International TDD Symbol

(d)
International Symbol of Access for Hearing Loss

FIGURE 9.33 International symbols for accessibility. *(From 28 CFR Ch. 1, Pt. 36, App. A, Fig. 43, 7-1-94 Edition)*

The ADA Accessibility Guidelines 4.1.3(14) states that, "If emergency warning systems are provided, then they shall include both audible alarms and visual alarms complying with 4.28. Audible alarms must produce a sound that exceeds the prevailing sound level in the room or space by at least 15 decibels. Visual alarms must be flashing lights that have a flashing frequency of about one cycle per second. Sleeping accommodations required to comply with 9.3 shall have an alarm system complying with 4.28. Emergency warning systems in medical care facilities may be modified to suit standard health care alarm design practice."

MISCELLANEOUS ISSUES

Elevators and Elevator Cars

Accessible elevators shall be located on an accessible route and shall comply with 4.10 and with the ASME A17.1-1990, Safety Code for Elevators and Escalators. Elevators must be provided with handrails fixed 32 inches above the floor, on all three sides of the cab. Minimum cab size should be 67 inches (1.7 m) to allow a wheelchair to maneuver (Figure 9.34). Both visual and audible hall signals are important to inform elevator users where an elevator is and in which direction it is proceeding. This is particularly important at elevator banks comprising of more than one car. Elevator controls should comply with ANSI A117.1 standards, regarding visual, tactile and audible controls (Figure 9.35).

Theater Seating

Theater design takes into account many factors including sight lines, acoustics, maximizing seating, and existing during a fire. Traditionally, however, accessibility has not been a major element in the design process, and integrating accessible seating into existing theaters has often been overlooked. Yet, it is of paramount importance to make these public facilities accessible and compliant (Figure 9.36).

Dining and Seating

In new construction, dining areas, loggias, and outdoor seating areas are required to be accessible. Dining areas are often designed to maximize seating capacity, and access may not be a prime consideration. Where dining areas are on an accessible route, it is usually possible to create accessible seating and accessible services without major alterations to the space. This can typically be implemented by removing some seating, and widening aisles. A clear 36 inch (915 mm) path of travel is required with slip-resistant floor surfaces.

Fixed or built-in seating or tables are required to comply with 4.32.2 through 4.32.4 of ADAAG (Figure 9.37). Tops of accessible tables and counters shall be from 28 inches to 34

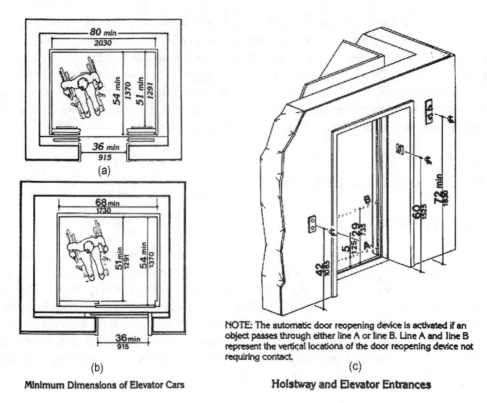

NOTE: The automatic door reopening device is activated if an object passes through either line A or line B. Line A and line B represent the vertical locations of the door reopening device not requiring contact.

Minimum Dimensions of Elevator Cars

Holstway and Elevator Entrances

FIGURE 9.34 Minimum dimensions for elevator cabs. *(From 28 CFR Ch.1, Pt. 36, App. A, Fig.22, 20, 7-1-94 Edition)*

inches (710 mm to 865 mm) above the finish floor level. Adequate clear floor space below the tables is also required (30 inches x 48 inches (762 mm x 1220 mm)), with 19 inches (485 mm) under-table space. Figure 9.38 shows accessible food counters and salad bars requirements.

Space Allowances and Reach Ranges

The ADA mandates rights for people with disabilities, and a very significant portion of the provisions prescribed in its accessibility guidelines (ADAAG) are geared to facilitate accessibility by wheelchair users. This is why it is imperative to understand and familiarize oneself with the dimensions and characteristics of a typical adult wheelchair (Figure 9.39).

According to the ADA Standards for Accessible Design, "Fixed storage facilities such as cabinets, shelves, closets, and drawers required to be accessible" as shown in Figure 9.40. It is further stipulated that storage facilities provide a clear floor space of not less than 30 inches x 48 inches (762 mm by 1200 mm), to permit either a forward or parallel approach by a person using a wheelchair.

FIGURE 9.35 Elevator hall signals. *(Courtesy of Means ADA Compliance Pricing Guide, R.S. Means Company, Inc.)*

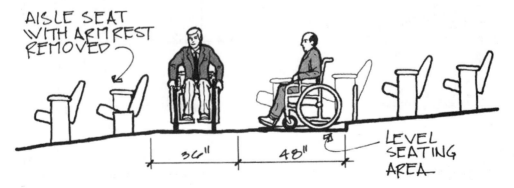

FIGURE 9.36 Accessible theater seating dimensions. *(Courtesy of Means ADA Compliance Pricing Guide, R.S. Means Company, Inc.)*

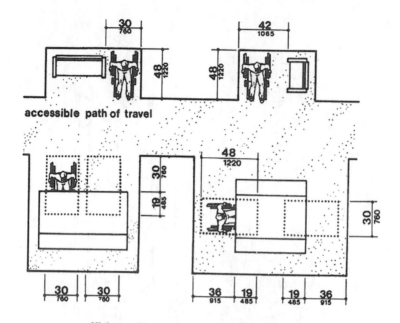

Minimum Clearances for Seating and Tables

FIGURE 9.37 Accessible seating in dining areas and restaurants. *(From 28 CFR Ch.1, Pt. 36, App. A, Fig. 45, 7-1-94 Edition)*

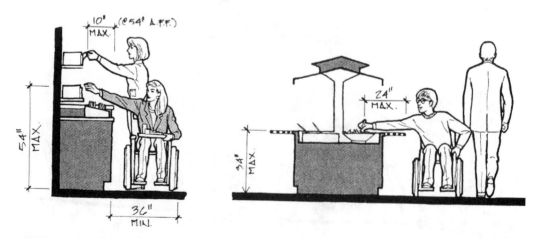

FIGURE 9.38 Accessible food counters and salad bars. *(Courtesy of Means ADA Compliance Pricing Guide, R.S. Means Company, Inc.)*

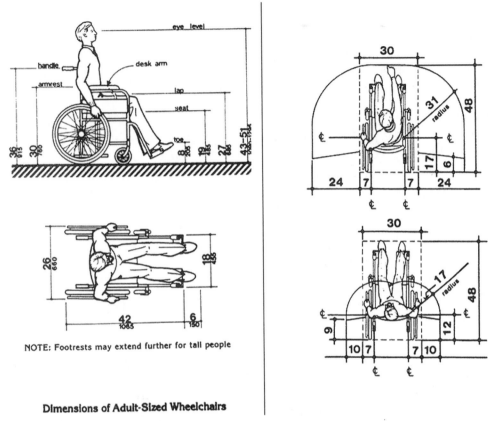

Dimensions of Adult-Sized Wheelchairs

NOTE: Footrests may extend further for tall people

FIGURE 9.39 Typical adult wheelchair dimensions are given to assist in the design of passageways and ADA compliant spaces. *(From 28 CFR Ch.1, Pt. 36, App. A, Fig. A3, A3 (a), 7-1-94 Edition)*

The maximum height for fixtures and fittings is generally put at 54 inches (1370 mm) prior to 1996 for unobstructed situations and 46 inches (1170 mm) for side reach over an obstruction. In 1996 the 54 inches was reduced to 48 inches (1200 mm) in response to representations from national organizations of people of short stature (Figures 9.41, 9.42). Goldsmith, in his book, *Designing for the Disabled, The New Paradigm,* states that for height criteria, the important anthropometric measure is upward oblique reach, and compares the ADAAG maximum height reaches with the levels to which the notional paraplegic woman and an average-height man can reach obliquely (Figure 9.43). The eye level of disabled persons (including chair-bound persons) is another factor that must be taken into consideration, particularly when designing or positioning signage, displaying goods, positioning lift controls, etc. (Figure 9.44).

Transient Lodging Facilities

The ADA Guidelines stipulate that transient lodging facilities must comply with applicable requirements, and such facilities are to provide accessible sleeping rooms in the ratios stipulated in ADAAG; this depends on the size and nature of the facility. Factors to keep in mind when designing such a facility include the following:

- The entrance into the facility should be clearly demarcated by appearance, signage, and access and be located on an accessible route.
- Adequate lighting should illuminate the entrance into the facility.
- Flush transitions from driveways to pavements are essential to facilitate transfer from the street to the pavement and to assist in unloading of luggage.
- Outdoor walkways should consist of smooth but non-slip surfaces.
- Elevators should have a 20 second time delay on door closing to facilitate access.
- Provide a variety of seating options in public places.
- Provide flexibility to allow the reconfiguration of space to add or remove furnishings or equipment.

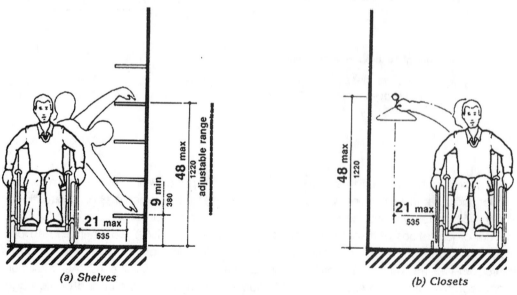

(a) Shelves   (b) Closets

Storage Shelves and Closets

FIGURE 9.40 Storage shelves and closets. *(From 28 CFR Ch.1, Pt. 36, App. A, Fig. 38, 7-1-94 Edition)*

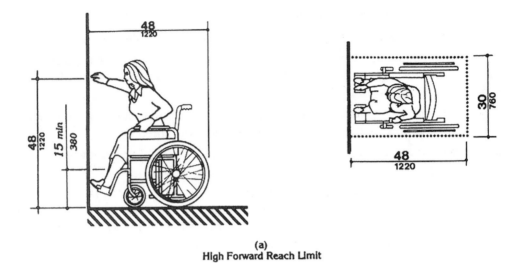

(a)
High Forward Reach Limit

NOTE: x shall be ≤ 25 in (635 mm); z shall be ≥ x. When x < 20 in (510 mm), then y shall be 48 in (1220 mm) maximum. When x is 20 to 25 in (510 to 635 mm), then y shall be 44 in (1120 mm) maximum.

(b)
Maximum Forward Reach over an Obstruction

FIGURE 9.41 High forward reach limit and maximum forward reach over an obstruction. *(From 28 CFR Ch.1, Pt. 36, App. A, Fig. 5, 7-1-94 Edition)*

- Ensure that controls are easy to operate with limited hand function.
- Circulation routes should be well organized with clear signage to exits and functions.
- Guestrooms and guest bathrooms should have adequate widths for maneuverability (Figure 9.45). Critical to guest bathrooms is the ability to maneuver between the toilet, lavatory, and bathing areas.
- Emergency signal systems (visual and auditory) with visual alarms that flash in conjunction with other building emergency systems must meet ADA requirements.
- At least one of each type of storage (i.e. shelves, drawers, closets) to be accessible to ADA standards).

Finally, space planners and designers are advised to keep abreast of the new ADAAG requirements as they are issued. Compliance requirements with ADAAG are usually clearly stated. However, when additional information or clarification is needed, help can be received from the Access Board's web site at www.access-board.gov.

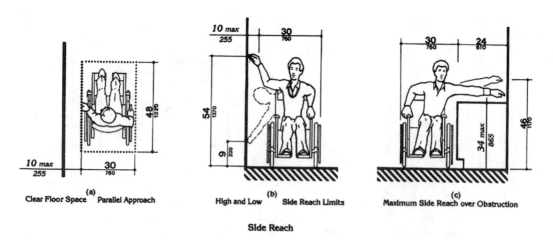

FIGURE 9.42 Side reach limits and maximum side reach over an obstruction. *(From 28 CFR Ch. 1, Pt. 36, App. A, Fig. 6, 7-1-94 Edition)*

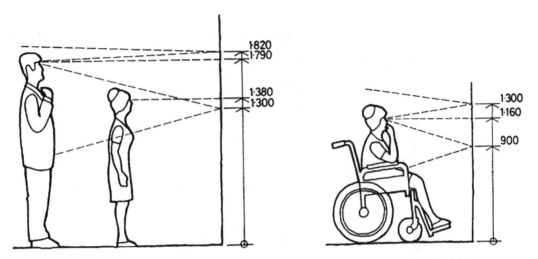

FIGURE 9.43 The oblique upward reach of a paraplegic woman and an average height man compared with the maximum height reach prescribed for the purposes of the ADA. *(Courtesy Selwyn Goldsmith, Designing for the Disabled, The New Paradigm, Architectural Press)*

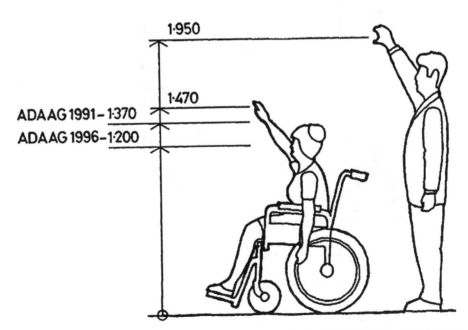

FIGURE 9.44 Height considerations when designing for the disabled. *(Courtesy Selwyn Goldsmith, Designing for the Disabled, The New Paradigm, Architectural Press)*

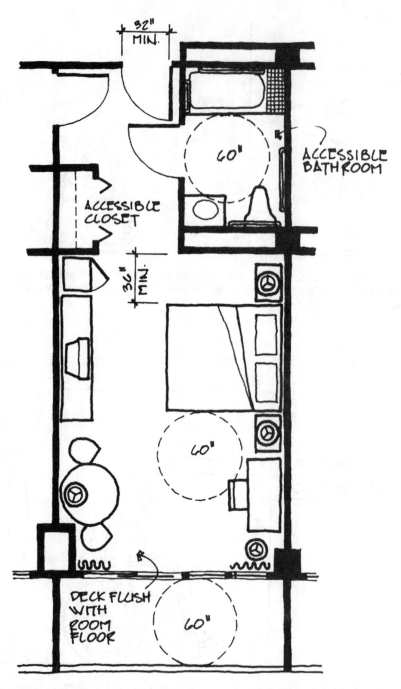

FIGURE 9.45 Requirements for an accessible sleeping room. *(Courtesy of Means ADA Compliance Pricing Guide, R.S. Means Company, Inc.)*

CHAPTER TEN

COMPUTER DRAFTING AND SOFTWARE SYSTEMS

*T*oday's younger generation of designers may not remember the good old days, when all phases of architectural design were done manually. Gradually, computer aided design began to take hold, particularly as computer technology advanced by leaps and bounds, while computer hardware became increasingly accessible and software programs increasingly user-friendly. But even today, technology has some way to go before it becomes fully integrated into architectural practice.

GENERAL OVERVIEW: COMPUTER DRAFTING DEVELOPMENTS

Since computers were first introduced in construction in the 1960s and early 1970s, there have been enormous innovations in digital practice, ranging from simple single line drawings, depicting plans and elevations, to current programs that offer 3D modeling, real-time visualization to Internet-enabled project delivery and intranet-based practice management. With more powerful hardware, multidiscipline design software has its genesis.

Design drawings in progress often require daily revisions and modifications, and it is a constant challenge to remain productive while performing tedious drafting tasks. The situation is further compounded by the need to disseminate the most up-to-date information to all members of the design team. Not having immediate access to current design data could spell disaster for a remote team working on the site of a project. It is cases similar to this that call for a solution to address the need for easier, more immediate access to current data.

From the very beginning of CAD development, vendors and users sought a software system that integrated the design data for all design disciplines. Until recently, slow processor speeds and memory limitations of computer hardware curbed software's capabilities to provide such applications. Architects, space planners and engineers initially had to settle for 2D drafting software that provided them with digital equivalents of paper drawings, but failed to help in the coordination of these drawings across disciplines. Recently, however, a number of leading software developers have released multidiscipline design tools that address this long-standing challenge to the A/E industry.

Jerry Laiserin, in an article, "Using Digital Tools to Expand and Enhance Services," says "Easy translation of digital information among participants in building projects has opened the way for management consultants, space planners, value engineers, and a dozen other disciplines to offer computerized services to building owners on matters that were once the exclusive domain of architectural services." Designers are now using digital technology extensively to market, enhance, and expand their services to clients. Digital technology can enlarge the scope of conventional design services. In one project for the Greater London Authority (GLA), Arup Acoustics teamed up with Foster and Partners to create digital visualizations using software developed by Arup to predict speakers' intelligibility in a proposed design for GLA's new council chamber.

Integrated and object-oriented 3D CAD is gradually becoming the mainstream design and documentation tool for architectural practices, and traditional 2D drafting-based systems appear to be in the process of being phased out in favor of 3D model-based solutions that allow architects and designers to create rather than draw, build rather than draft.

The focus on 3D modeling has helped push CAD firms to develop rendering software that allows designers to produce schematic drawings that can be transformed into three dimensional renderings or animations and that can walk you through the interior of a space. This has given designers an important tool by which to produce 3D architectural models that can help a client understand and visualize a scheme.

GOING ONLINE: INTERNET-ENABLED DESIGN

Reflecting the need for modern CAD systems to move towards Internet-enabled design, most systems have incorporated important features to facilitate Web publishing. Today, sharing design information among the entire project team has never been easier. With new and improved Internet collaboration features, designers can now post drawings to the Web, connect to design resources, drag architectural content directly into drawings, and conduct online meetings—all in real time. AutoCAD 2002 for example has adopted new features and enhancements relating to data conferencing and online publishing.

USE OF COLOR IN COMPUTER AIDED DESIGN

Many of the CAD systems currently on the market and in the development stage support millions of colors. This may confuse some designers, particularly since colors were rarely used in manual drafting. The use of color in CAD programs have two primary objectives: First to provide operator cues (e.g. using the color green to depict plants makes reading a drawing easier), and second, for controlling the plotter. Traditional CAD drafting software matches color numbers with pens of various line thickness (e.g. color numbers 1, 2, and 3 are matched with the plotter's 000 pen, color number 4 with the 00 pen, and so forth). Thus, everything drawn with colors 1, 2, and 3 is drawn with a thin line; anything drawn with color number 4, will be drawn with a thicker line, and so on. If the output is required to be in color, the CAD operator matches the color number to the plotter's pen number. Thus, color 1 is matched to the blue pen. Everything drawn with the number 1 pen will be plotted in blue. CAD software therefore, matches color numbers with color names.

Color Numbering Systems—How They Work

Each CAD software system has its own preferred method of matching numbers with colors. AutoCAD for example, matches a number to each of 255 colors. The first eight colors are listed using their ACI system. MicroStation, on the other hand, has developed a similar system but uses a different set of numbers, as listed under DGN. MicroStation also allows you to change the color associated with each number. TurboCAD uses the RGB and HSL systems to specify color. Many of today's CAD systems go well beyond simple matching of CAD colors to pen colors, and provide an overwhelming variety of options.

Ralph Grabowski, author and editor of *AutoCAD User* magazine, outlines the more relevant coloring systems below:

- RGB: Red-green-blue is the system used primarily for display (e.g. Microsoft Windows) and scanners. Each of the three primary colors ranges in intensity from 0 (black) to 255 (full color).

- HSL: Hue-saturation-luminance was developed to specify a numerical hue saturation and brightness, and is an alternative form of color specification system. Hue starts with red (0) and goes through yellow (43), green (85), blue (170), and back to red (255). Saturation ranges from 0 (gray) to 255 (full color). Luminance, or brightness, ranges from black (0) to white (255). With HSL, you cannot perform arithmetic mixtures of colors expressed in polar coordinates.

- EGA: Named after IBM's enhanced graphics adapter, is used by many CAD systems.

- HTML: Hypertext markup language includes a color specification system used by Web sites. Identical to RGB but hexadecimal (base 16) in notation.

- DGN: This is a color numbering system (and file format) that is used by Bentley Systems' MicroStation.
- ACI: Autodesk's AutoCAD color index, also used by AutoSketch.
- CYMK: A color system using cyan, yellow, magenta as the primary colors, and also uses black. The system is used mainly by color printers.

According to Grabowski, there are various methods of matching the number with the color displayed on the screen. The following table from *CAD Manager's Guidebook* shows the color names for the first eight color numbers for several color systems:

Name	RGB	HSL	EGA	HTML	DGN	ACI
Black	0,0,0	0,0,0	0	#000000	255	0
Blue	0,0,255	170,255,128	1	#0000FF	1	5
Green	0,255,0	85,255,128	2	#00FF00	2	3
Cyan	0,255,255	128,255,128	3	#00FFFF	7	4
Red	255,0,0	0,255,128	4	#FF0000	3	1
Magenta (pink)	255,0,255	213,255,128	5	#FF00FF	5	6
Yellow	255,255,0	43,255,128	6	#FFFF00	4	2
White	255,255,255	0,0,255	7	#FFFFFF	0	7
Gray	128,128,128	0,0,128	8	#808080	9	8

It should be noted that with the advent of low cost PostScript printers, the need for obsolete pen plotters and plotter drivers has diminished, and today's CAD market has been continuously moving to the ink jet printer with PostScript for many years.

CAD SOFTWARE SYSTEMS

There is now a wide variety of drafting software programs available for space planners, architects, engineers and other professions in the industry. These programs meet the needs of different budgets, different disciplines, and different specifications. The most popular of these CAD programs that were developed for architects, space planners and designers are outlined below:

- AutoCAD, Architectural Desktop, and AutoCAD LT (by Autodesk; www.autodesk.com).
- ArchiCAD (by Graphisoft; www.graphisoft.com).
- VersaCAD (by Archway Systems, Inc.; www.versacad.com).

- TurboCAD (by International Microcomputer Software Inc.; www.turbocad.com).
- MicroStation, Project Architect, Project Architect-Plus, MiscroStation TriForma, and Architecture for MicroStation TriForma (by Bentley Systems, Inc.; www.bentley.com).
- PowerCADD (by Engineered Software; www.engsw.com).
- VectorWorks and VectorWorks ARCHITECT (by Nemetschek N.A.; www.nemetschek.net).
- Architect Studio (by Arris; www.arriscad.com).

AutoCAD®, Architectural Desktop, VIZ, and AutoCAD LT

AutoCAD

AutoCAD 2002 is a sophisticated and powerful, general-purpose 2D CAD program that retains its traditional command-line driven features. It has added capabilities for 3D modeling and rendering.

AutoCAD's fundamental problem, however, has always been its complexity. There are too many commands, features, and options for the average user. Moreover, each new release seems to add more complexity, rather than reducing it to make the software more intuitive and user-friendly. Many of today's CAD software programs no longer use type-in commands. For novice users, in particular, this aspect of AutoCAD can be very challenging. Unlike the expert operator who finds everything easy to comprehend, the novice quickly discovers that learning such a complex program as AutoCAD is beset with difficulties. Whether it is setting up a new drawing or making a scaled print out, the novice will find that AutoCAD can be a daunting program to master, and not particularly user-friendly.

In AutoCAD's 2002 version, a serious attempt is made at resolving some of the thorny problems that dogged its earlier releases. These problems include difficulty creating blocks with attributes and extracting attribute data, determining when to use external references, setting up dimensions to the right scale for printing, and all aspects of 3D modeling and rendering. Yet even though in the latest versions these problems have been largely overcome, and various enhancements have been introduced along the way to the online publishing front, which are certainly welcome, the program continues to lag behind in its user-friendly appeal (Figure 10.1).

One way the dimensioning capabilities of AutoCAD 2002 has improved is by making them associative. Essentially, this means that they are actually connected to the objects they dimension rather than to definition points, or defpoints. If any modifications are made to the shape, size, or orientation of the object by rotating, scaling, or editing it using grips, the corresponding dimensions get updated automatically. You no longer have to move and reposition the defpoints to ensure the accuracy and consistency of the dimensions.

Some aspects of AutoCAD such as the 3D-modeling capabilities are still far from intuitive, having been largely untouched in the latest upgrades and thus still require improvement. For example, there is poor rubberbanding, which makes it difficult to see exactly what you are modeling until you finish the operation. Modifying 3D objects after creating them is far from

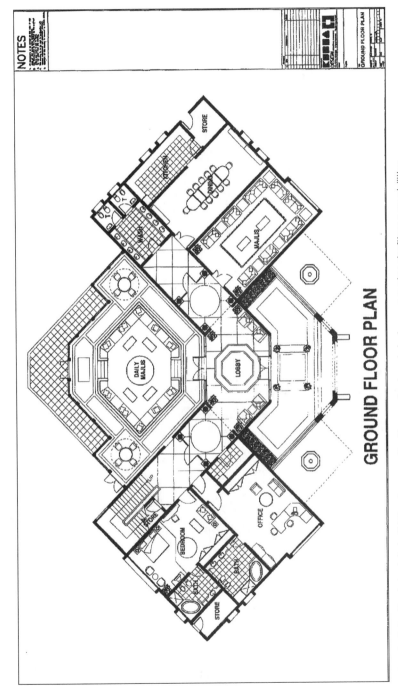

FIGURE 10.1 The latest AutoCAD releases offer the professional designer greater drafting capabilities.

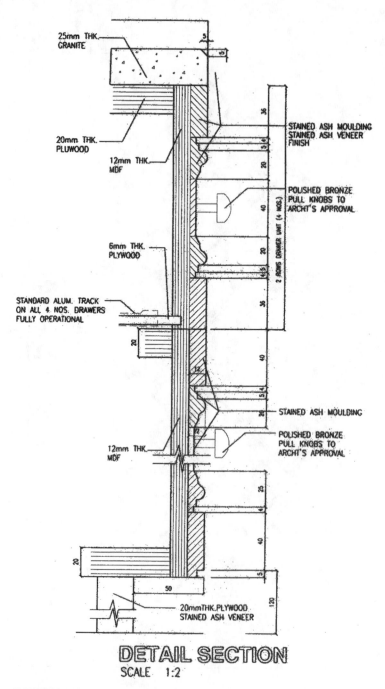

25mm THK.
GRANITE

20mm THK.
PLUWOOD

12mm THK.
MDF

6mm THK.
PLYWOOD

STANDARD ALUM. TRACK
ON ALL 4 NOS. DRAWERS
FULLY OPERATIONAL

12mm THK.
MDF

STAINED ASH MOULDING
STAINED ASH VENEER
FINISH

POLISHED BRONZE
PULL KNOBS TO
ARCHT'S APPROVAL

2 ROWS DRAWER UNIT (4 NOS.)

STAINED ASH MOULDING

POLISHED BRONZE
PULL KNOBS TO
ARCHT'S APPROVAL

20mmTHK.PLYWOOD
STAINED ASH VENEER

DETAIL SECTION
SCALE 1:2

FIGURE 10.1 (continued) The latest AutoCAD releases offer the professional designer greater drafting capabilities.

straightforward. Texture mapping remains needlessly complex, and placing lights exactly where you want them requires considerable skill.

Publish to Web II

Publish to Web was introduced as a feature to provide a way for users to easily create a web page that contained images of drawing files created using AutoCAD. Publish to Web handled all details of generating the HTML code and outputting the images, allowing users with little or no prior web development knowledge to use the feature easily. The upgraded version, Publish to Web II, offers several key enhancements, including additional templates and the introduction of themes that offer users greater control over the formatting of their generated web pages. The DWF format, the lightweight file format for posting DWG files online, has been upgraded to support raster image formats and can be reviewed online, marked up, and printed using Autodesk's Volo View. Other enhancements include the ability to select different publishing sizes for each of the three file types (DWF, JPG, and PNG), giving added control over the size of the images posted to the website.

AutoCAD's recently developed i-drop™ technology, which facilitates the publication of design data, and i-drop–enabled websites, which allow members of the project team to drag content directly from a web page into their Autodesk design file. For example, you might publish block libraries on your corporate intranet. Dr. Lachmi Khemlani, author and CAD specialist, says, "The most exciting new feature for online design is the ability to activate i-drop capability while publishing drawing files as Web pages. This would enable someone visiting such a Web page to drag the published drawing and drop it into their current AutoCAD session for viewing or editing. The drawing is placed as a block, and it can be in 3D as well."

Figure 10.2 illustrates an example of the 3D model of a chair, which was dragged and dropped from an online manufacturer's catalog created using the i-drop technology. An increasing number of manufacturers are now creating online catalogs, and at some point we may find contractors building from drawings that are basically assemblies of components and furniture blocks procured online, similar to the way our real-life buildings are assembled from components and furniture supplied by different vendors.

I-drop is XML (extensible markup language) based technology, the data it can carry is potentially limitless, and can be used to obtain geometric data and photometric data online, as well as related non-graphical data such as material, cost information, and so on. Autodesk's own XML initiative, DesignXML, is now supported in AutoCAD 2002. Following the same procedure for creating a block, some or all of the objects in a drawing can be saved as a DesignXML file. This format enables geometric information about the selected objects to be easily extracted and processed over the Web, possibly for other applications such as cost estimating or energy analysis. Because DesignXML is not a standard agreed upon by major AEC software vendors, but rather a proprietary to Autodesk, it is too early to tell whether the building industry's overall goal to exchange data easily between CAD and non-CAD applications in building design can be achieved.

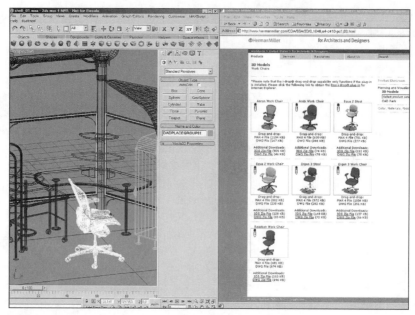

FIGURE 10.2   An example of a 3D model of an Aeron chair which was dragged-and-dropped from the Herman Miller, Inc. online catalog using the i-drop technology. (*Courtesy Karen Witzel, Herman Miller, Inc.*)

Autodesk's Architectural Desktop

Autodesk Architectural Desktop is a comprehensive suite of architectural tools that gives you greater freedom and flexibility in design—whether your design preference is 2D, 3D, or both, and whether you prefer model-based design using intelligent architectural objects that behave according to real world properties, or traditional drawing methods. Architectural Desktop also includes all the traditional AutoCAD software drawing tools, with a library containing well over 1,000 materials. The library allows you to represent detail components in plan, elevation, and section views, as well as store, retrieve, and automatically scale detail drawings.

Although 2D design with lines, arcs, and circles will eventually get you to your destination, architectural objects can get you there faster. Autodesk maintains that, "Architectural Desktop software's intelligent architectural objects—such as stairs, curtain walls, and roofs—behave according to real-world properties, so they automatically update whenever you make a design change. Use these objects in 2D or 3D to create a single building model. This building model is your single data set from which you generate all project documents: scheduling information, elevations, plans, and sections. All information throughout the building model is dynamically linked, so you're creating the data only once—which cuts cycle time and reduces the potential for costly errors."

In addition, Lonnie Cumpton of Avatech Solutions states that, "Autodesk's Architectural Desktop provides an all-in-one integrated environment for architectural firms to accomplish conceptual design, design development and design documentation" (Figure 10.3).

Architectural Desktop 3.0 (ADT3) is Autodesk's response to the emerging vendors that are threatening its dominance in today's market, by providing a product with a good blend of 2D and 3D capabilities. ADT3 is equipped with intelligent object technology, and can dynamically reconfigure and update interrelated building components—such as walls, windows, doors, and curtains—whenever something is resized, intersected, or modified. Autodesk states that, "ADT3 can link all of its drawings dynamically" and "changes update in the building model in a synchronized, coordinated fashion." Architectural Desktop has AutoCAD 2000i at its foundation, and also offers compatibility with many of the Web-based features such as Meet Now, e Transmit, and Publish to the Web.

FIGURE 10.3 An example of Autodesk Architectural Desktop, giving the designer improved conceptual design, design development and design documentation capabilities.

Autodesk Inventor is a feature-based parametric solid modeler that Autodesk says gives users "major new enhancements in assembly modeling, surfacing, 2D to 3D tools, family of parts, and sheet metal as well as new plastics part design tools". A new 'iParts' command allows users to create a family of parts (configurations), that can be accessed through a spreadsheet-style dialog box that permits you to set up different parameters based on the features in the part. Any of the parameters based on the features in the part can then be suppressed. Other non-graphical information, such as part number and cost, can be added to the spreadsheet.

Autodesk's AutoCAD LT

This is a fairly simple 2D CAD drafting tool targeting active professionals who only have occasional need for the use of CAD programs. It is completely DWG file compatible with AutoCAD. It also boasts intuitive e-mail, web, and multimedia tools.

In addition to the above well-known products, the Autodesk family of products also includes programs like Architectural Studio which is re-creating the traditional design studio with intuitive, pen-based design tools that can bring your conceptual ideas to life. Likewise, there is 3D Studio VIZ (Figure 10.4), which according to Autodesk, "is a revolutionary 3D visualization solution that introduces advanced global illumination rendering technology, allowing all aspects of your project to be greatly enhanced, from design exploration to communication to validation. With Autodesk VIZ, you can integrate design visualization capabilities into an Autodesk Architectural Desktop-based design workflow, resulting in truly rich, accurate design animations."

ArchiCAD

For nearly two decades, Graphisoft has been developing and evolving design solutions around its Virtual Building concept for architects, incorporating a leading-edge intelligent object that offers automatic documentation, instant visualization and maximum interoperability. The Virtual Building is a 3D digital database that tracks all components that make up a building and is at the core of all Graphisoft products. The Virtual Building model makes it possible to administer and manage a building throughout its entire life cycle. It is not surprising therefore, that the developers of the ArchiCAD program consider it to be the easiest way for architects and designers to embrace the new CAD standards.

Graphisoft states that, "Unlike a simple 3D model on a computer, the Virtual Building contains significantly more information about the building's materials and properties. The data can include surface area and volume; thermal properties; room descriptions; price; specific product information; window, door and finish schedules; and more."

Graphisoft also considers the Virtual Building model useful for all professionals connected to the building industry—architects and residential designers, interior designers, real estate agents, facility managers and marketing staff. By working from the same Virtual Building as the

FIGURE 10.4 An example of Studio VIZ 3D rendering.

architect, the real estate agent or space planner can easily obtain exact room dimensions and area calculations, present perspective views from any vantage and even invite prospects on a virtual tour of the building. Graphisoft says that, "Interior designers can begin working during the planning phase on the same Virtual Building model. After construction is complete, building managers are able to use the comprehensive materials list and integrated 3D partition plan to track building assets and modify spaces." (Figure 10.5)

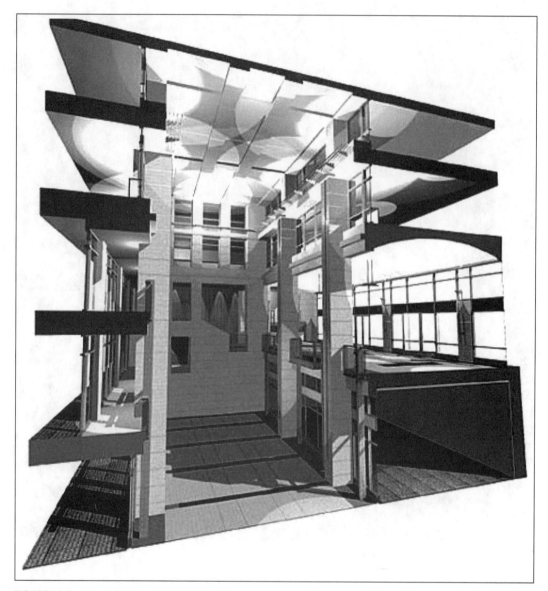

FIGURE 10.5 An example of ArchiCAD's 3D computer modeling capabilities. *(Courtesy Studios Architecture, Washington D.C.)*

When Graphisoft first began developing ArchiCAD, its primary objective was not to simply replace the drafting board. Rather, it sought to transform CAD from an electronic drafting board to a full fledged architectural tool, by introducing the power of the integrated 3D model and object technology to the architectural design process.

In its software package, ArchiCAD is able to comprehensively address the various aspects of the architectural process, from design and documentation, to communication and collaboration. And because you are working from an intelligent 3D computer model (that is a simulation of the project in hand), the process becomes streamlined.

When designing in ArchiCAD, the brochure states, "One automatically creates a simulation of the real building: the Virtual Building. Instead of drawing lines, ellipses and arcs, you raise walls, add windows and doors, lay down floors, build stairs and construct roofs. While you build elements on your floor plan, ArchiCAD creates a central database that can simultaneously handle 3D model data with plan and section views, dimensions, material finishes, component lists and more. Which means you can extract all the information needed to completely describe your design from the Virtual Building, and make changes at any time without having to manually recreate working drawings or schedules." Since all the building's information is stored in a single project file, the building model remains integrated and up-to-date as you work, and any changes made in one view are automatically updated in the others, including plans, sections, elevations, 3D models, and bills of materials.

This permits you to access and extrapolate your precise needs for each phase of the design. This also applies to all other participants involved in the project. Furthermore, a client is able to see not only the functional arrangement and the site plan, but also how it feels to walk through the space, or how sunlight affects a particular room at different times of the day. Because the file is in an electronic format, it can be transmitted to other consultants, regardless of which CAD platform they are on, and they can make changes and return the file for further work with no loss of Virtual Building data in the process. ArchiCAD provides comprehensive schedules and bills of materials for builders and sub-contractors, as well as detailed drawings of scale-sensitive jambs. Builders can plan tasks, create time-based animations and document any phase of a project's construction or demolition, and developers can use the photo-realistic renderings to produce sales brochures.

ArchiCAD Highlights

Graphisoft highlights of ArchiCAD's prominent features include:

- The Virtual Building: ArchiCAD stores all the information about the building in a central database; changes made in one view are updated in all others, including floor plans, sections/elevations, 3D models and bills of material.

- Intelligent Objects: ArchiCAD's intelligent building elements like doors, windows and columns understand and react to their environment. This accelerates work, makes the management of the project easier and allows you to design instead of draft. Even working from drafted lines, arcs, and splines, the Magic Wand can create intelligent building elements. The ability to think and work "live" in 3D: Architects can design and edit the model in 3D view, navigate in real time to check the design, and hold interactive design sessions with clients.

- Instant visualization: ArchiCAD's rendering tools are simple to use and help you visualize your design, and prepare compelling client presentations, with no special knowledge required. Virtual Reality (VR) presentations can be generated directly in ArchiCAD, allowing clients to take a virtual tour of their project, and freely navigating among spaces by simply moving the mouse. No doubt, clients will better understand a designer's vision if a project is presented as animation, a virtual reality scene, or a photo-realistic rendering. With ArchiCAD, views can be taken from any point, looking anywhere—even using fully rendered 3D cutaway sections. Additional realism can be achieved by placing site photos and other backgrounds in the renderings to create accurate animated sun studies, and to cast shadows for any date, time and position on earth.

- Internet communication tools: Architects can distribute documents to colleagues, clients and consultants via the Internet for review and mark-up, then merge change requests back into the project. The Virtual Building environment supports open communication, modifications and enhancements to the design, regardless of physical distances.

- Documentation: Construction documents and files can be derived automatically from the Virtual Building model. The door/window schedules and bills of material can be quickly generated and always reflect the current state of the building model. The Zone tool identifies and labels rooms, and tracks area and volume, while the components' list shows price, number of pieces and labor costs. In recent releases, the interactive door/window schedule automatically updates the building model, and vice versa. Dimensions are both automatic and associative. The Label tool can attach text or symbols to identify parts of your design.

In addition to its adherence to IFC standards, ArchiCAD has improved much of its object technology, including wall features; the introduction of trusses; and through its ability to interact with analysis and estimating software such as Lawrence Berkeley Laboratories Energy Plus and Timberlines Precision Estimating. Its enhanced Internet capabilities allow users to drag and drop GDL objects from a manufacturer's Web site into a design.

VersaCAD

Although VersaCad was one of the earliest CAD programs initially developed for Apple Macintosh computers, it has recently been reintroduced as a Windows only product (however, it will still work on Macs). The latest VersaCAD release included a comprehensive overhaul of the underpinnings to make it more Windows friendly and present a faster, more stable platform. In addition, the developers incorporated new built-in functions into the software enabling powerful new zoom and pan functions such as zoom-window while performing another operation such as drawing or dimensioning . For those interested in using 3D solid modeling, either 3Djoy or Rhino 3D may be a good 3D surface modeling software to start with. Archway Systems lists VersaCAD's main features as:

- Productivity. It may be that the industry is so caught up in extraneous issues that we forget that the original and continuing purpose of CAD is to produce design work with fewer man-hours or more results per man-hour. For production design drafting or mechanical drafting, VersaCAD is at least competitive, and perhaps even more productive than the other major CAD.

- Easy to learn: It reportedly takes new employees less time to learn the software. A new employee can be productive in VersaCAD after one day of training. It takes a minimum of two days for AutoCAD. VersaCAD is more popular in educational institutions to introduce future designers and engineers to CAD. Students who learn VersaCAD can always transfer to other CAD systems. It also offers a friendly, intuitive way to generate 2-D drawings.

  New or improved features have been incorporated into the program, including improved viewing functions, zoom and pan functions, such as zoom-window while performing another operation such as a drawing or dimensioning. Other features include: auto-dimensions, create drawing objects with user-definable properties, ability to change properties individually or globally, single keystroke commands, dynamic "no-hands" coordinate entry, powerful grouping functions, and automatic functions such as joining of walls.

- Has good libraries of drawing elements.

On the downside, VersaCAD has some bugs to iron out in its latest releases, and it can't handle GIF or JPEG images, although it includes translators for DXF and IGES import and export. It also lacks the power of competitors like PowerCADD and VectorWorks.

TurboCAD

IMSI's latest TurboCAD Professional offers designers and CAD users, great flexibility and performance through a wide array of powerful 2D and 3D drawing tools. It also fully supports AutoCAD DWG/DXF file formats, MicroStation and Microsoft Office file compatibility. It should satisfy the expectations of most CAD users, boasting features that are only found in its more expensive counterparts, and some that even they lack. TurboCAD previously had a "hobbyist software" tag; this perception should be dispelled with the latest professional versions of the software.

TurboCAD Professional has built-in intelligent object support, featuring the latest in ACIS 3D solid modeling technology, and allows multiple view windows for LightWorks and Hidden Line rendering. Its Materials Editor lets you select from common construction materials like brick, metals, plastics, glass, wood; it also lets you import BMP images as new textures. All materials are fully editable. By introducing materials and lighting properties, TurboCAD Professional gives you the ability to develop interactive photo-realistic architectural renderings and 3D models (Figure 10.6a, 10.6b). It also has a full set of Web access and publishing tools. In addition to TurboCAD Professional's user-friendly interface and ease-of-use features, it boasts other distinctive qualities including:

- Extensive Drafting and Design 2D tools (such as geometric alignment aids, automatic dimensioning, lines, arcs, polygons, polylines and multilines, mirror and offset copy, layering capability), 2D Boolean Operations for surfaces. The wall tool for example, communicates with associative blocks intelligently, and window and door symbols automatically orient themselves when you drop them onto a wall. Likewise, if you move a window or join two walls, the wall would 'heal' automatically.

- A complete set of 3D Design and Modeling tools including 3D surface and solids modeling capability, user definable work planes, one-step 3D shapes, 3D polylines, 3D Boolean operations and more. Surface-to-solid conversion.

FIGURE 10.6a   A bedroom interior rendering by Richard Brehm using TurboCad software.

- Rendering, visualization, and presentation tools include advanced LightWorks Rendering and Radiosity, open GL/Acceleration support, dynamic rotations and walk-throughs that are fully programmable.
- Supports AutoCad and Microstation file formats and over 20 other industry standard file formats including 3DS and EPS export format.
- Web publishing tools and Internet compatibility allows you to embed hyperlinks and get access to Web content. Easily saves files in JPG and publish to HTML.
- Over 16,000 CAD symbols and clip art in ISO and ANSI formats, including 1000+ editable HomeStyles house plans, ANSI and ISO Templates and FloorPlan 3D software.

MicroStation

MicroStation is the keystone of Bentley's solutions for building, civil engineering, transportation, process plants, discrete manufacturing facilities, utilities and telecommunication networks. Microstation PowerDraft provides industry-recognized tools for 2D and simple 3D production drafting. Bentley View is a powerful viewing and printing application that extends the programs accessibility of engineering data, and Bentley Redline combines easy-to-use markup tools with the viewing and printing capabilities of Bentley View.

FIGURE 10.6b A digital rendering by Tony Primerano using TurboCad software.

The program gives users the ability to create 3D models of permanent assets; the models and all of their components are electronic simulations of real world objects. Whether it is design and engineering, or construction and operation, created models hold all information about the asset and its configuration, simplifying project management and making the operation of the facility more efficient and cost-effective.

MicroStation architectural design applications are delivered with libraries of parametric building parts and support i-links to vendor and manufacturer product catalogs. All aspects of the design are integrated into a 3D model, and a powerful set of visualization and simulation tools provides dynamic and photo-realistic reviews. Traditional drawings, bills of materials and other reports can also be extracted from the model, acting as a geometrically indexed database of AEC content.

MicroStation TriForma and Architecture for MicroStation TriForma

MicroStation TriForma is 3D solids modeling software for architectural and engineering design (Figure 10.7). In particular, it provides a common technology platform for the building and plant industry, and consistent user interface for architectural and engineering design. It also provides a robust set of tools designed to address object management, modeling and drafting, visualization, drawing and report extraction and interference review; resulting in faster, better, more cost effective projects. MicroStation TriForma improves communication and coordination by laying the foundation for a set of discipline-specific applications that address the needs of the other disciplines involved in the building process; including solutions for architectural, structural, mechanical, piping, equipment, and electrical raceway design.

The recently released V8 Generation of Architecture for MicroStation TriForma, essentially provides a parametric modeling product that offers architects unprecedented topological modeling capabilities, automated extraction of production drawings and reports, and tight integration with related Bentley applications. Architecture for MicroStation TriForma automates the architectural design and production process, from conceptual design to construction documentation by integrating 3D modeling and 2D drawing production, reporting, visualization and animation for producing vivid presentations.

Architecture for MicroStation TriForma provides a large array of drawing aids such as associativity between elements, space planning tools, parametric components, an AIA/NCS compliant dataset and the ability to create shapes of any kind. Likewise, it will provide a unified and flexible design environment for any project, and is no longer explicitly tied to the DGN file format, as it will natively reference and edit AutoCAD® DWG files directly, making it the universal engineering design platform for the world's two most popular Computer-Aided Design formats.

Tom Anderson, AIA, Vice President of Product Marketing at Bentley, commented that, "Architecture for MicroStation TriForma adds discipline-specific functionality to MicroStation TriForma, Bentley's parametric Building and Plant Engineering Configuration." Nigel Davies, CAD Development Manager of Whitby Bird says, "The developments in Architecture for MicroStation for TriForma over the recent months have improved the product incomparably," adding "Building on top of the advances V8 has allowed, the product is now the premier integrated project modeling tool, not just for engineers, but the complete AEC community."

The program was developed in consultation with leading architectural firms and built on the sturdy MicroStation TriForma foundation, Architecture for MicroStation TriForma enables architects to design with greater efficiency and better productivity. In addition to the Architecture for MicroStation TriForma architectural application, there is HVAC for MicroStation TriForma (for mechanical engineers), and Structural for MicroStation TriForma (primarily optimizes MicroStation TriForma for structural design and construction documentation and performs structural analysis and design of steel and reinforced concrete structures).

FIGURE 10.7 An interior rendering using MicroStation software. *(Cooper Carry, Inc. Architects, Atlanta, GA)*

Project Architect and Project Architect Plus

Project Architect, is a comprehensive, plan-based architectural design and production drawing software built to work on the MicroStation CAD engine, and extends the MicroStation commands with over 300 features that are specific to the architectural workflow, and greatly simplifying the process of putting architectural designs into CAD (Figure 10.8). Many of the complex generic drawing commands are combined and are easy to understand, using colorized design tools (that are customizable and dockable) to create floor plans with intelligent building components (such as columns, walls, doors, windows, stairs, and furniture) and three-

FIGURE 10.8 An interior rendering using MicroStation software.

dimensional models. In addition, data created during pre-construction phases can be used later for essential building management tasks. Furthermore, they integrate seamlessly with the underlying MicroStation CAD platform. Revisions are also fast and simple.

The program supports and automates the workflow from project management though schematic design and automatic 3D model creation to construction documentation. It also automatically extracts schedules, quantity reports, sections, elevations, and models from the building database, ensuring total coordination with floor plans. This dramatically increases an operator's productivity over generic CAD or manual drafting design, and is ideally suited for architectural environments of all sizes, from single-seat design studios to large multi-discipline architecture and engineering firms.

Intergraph's Project Architect Plus includes intelligent 3-D models, clash envelopes and familiar PDS project integration commands to share models, part information, and interference information among the PDS design environments.

Project Architect Plus is a plan-based architectural design and modeling tool for MicroStation users, which includes all of the functionality of Project Architect with enhancements that further improve the level of integration with the Intergraph PDS family of products. The program allows you to design sophisticated buildings, generate intelligent 3D models for inspection and presentation, extract envelope files for PDS clash detection, review clashes with objects from the PDS family tools (PDS, PE-HVAC, FrameWorks Plus, RaceWay and EQP) and call up and locate objects created in any other PDS design environment.

Project and file management capabilities allow for creation, tracking, sharing and protection of designs across a network and for the tracking and initialization of files from any application on the desktop, and is ideal for handling complex assortment of data created in today's busy architectural office. MicroStation Converter is another useful application that is a two-way translator designed for AutoCAD users that need compatibility with Intergraph Microstation Files.

Herman Miller is one of many manufacturers of furniture and architectural elements that provide software packages for Cad systems like MicroStation and AutoCAD. These software packages include 2D plan and elevation cells and tag data, and are discussed in greater detail in Chapter 7.

PowerCADD

Power CADD is essentially a 2-D technical drafting package, designed for architects and engineers using the Macintosh operating system. It provides competent professional drafting capabilities within a user-friendly Macintosh interface that doesn't hamper your design capabilities (Figure 10.9). It also has enhanced color management capabilities, and added support for popular file formats as well as built-in direct translation for DesignWorkshop making for a powerful 2D/3D CAD combination for Macintosh design professionals.

PowerCADD tends to give the impression of a simple draw program, because it lets you use any font you want in your drawing. Photographs or scanned images for tracing maps are easily imported. Likewise, a drawing can have many layers which is like drawing on multiple sheets of clear acetate. Formatted tables from Microsoft Word or Excel can be imported with publish and subscribe. Recent PowerCADD releases have reference files to allow multiple designers to work on a single project. It also contains some interface refinements, and supports a 64-bit, double-precision internal calculations for increased accuracy and performance.

PowerCADD also differs from other CAD programs in the way it works and in the way that you interact with your drawing, by letting you work with your drawing and become completely connected with the drawing process. Unlike programs such as AutoCAD, PowerCADD's easy to learn, user-friendly features, together with the seamless, intuitive way that you work with the drawing, has made it popular among its users. With many other CAD programs, the process of drawing is linear, and each operation requires a series of steps that must be taken, and a determination made in advance of what the objective is. With PowerCADD, designers are able to make up their mind as they draw, by assisting, without getting in the way. An operator can draw with one hand on the mouse, and the other on the lower left corner of the keyboard, using the Shift key to constrain to snap angles or fixed offsets and dimensions.

Designers have an option to choose between PowerCADD's two main tool palettes, a combination of WildTools and PowerCADD that sets you free to draw with substantial power. WildTools basically takes the fundamental concepts of PowerCADD and adds many enhancements and refinements. Additionally, you can add plug-in tools and commands called Externals. These include the PowerDWG converter for direct translation to and from AutoCAD DWG format, Autodesk's DXF, JPEG, Encapsulated PostScript, ClarisCAD, and others.

PowerCADD is your drawing board, your drafting paper, and your drawing tools. How you arrange your world and how it works is your decision, your business. You have direct control over how command keys work for tools and commands, and you have complete flexibility to assign the command keys of your choice. Setting up is simple, allowing you to work with great rapidity. Drawing tools are used to create the lines, rectangles, circles and curves that make up the drawing. These are considered objects, and they behave like things that you can pick up and move around. You can select the objects, move them, duplicate and rotate them or put objects along a path. There are also tools for trimming, chamfers, and fillets, tools for text, with a built-in spell checker (Figures 10.10a, 10.10b).

Naturally, one can set pen weights and dash patterns with ease, and create hatch patterns with the ability to fill patterns, so that you can have colored textures for brick, stone, water, concrete, marble and many other materials. Even designing custom tool palettes is a simple task. Likewise, new colors can be created which can be added to the menu color palette, and which can later be modified if desired. These colors can be identified with numbers or text, according to popular color-matching systems. Indeed, an entire custom color palette can be created and saved for use on other drawings.

PowerCADD give you the ability to cover up portions of the drawing with white-filled objects, without having to cut and trim all of the objects in the drawing, and allows the use of non-printing guidelines and reference points in the drawing. You can do area and perimeter

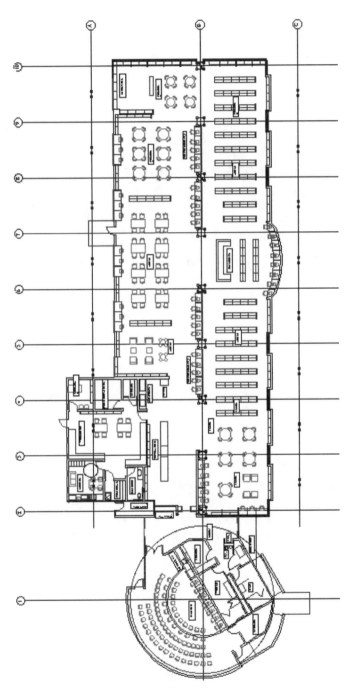

FIGURE 10.9 A design by Erik Mar of the Canoga Park branch library produced in PowerCADD.

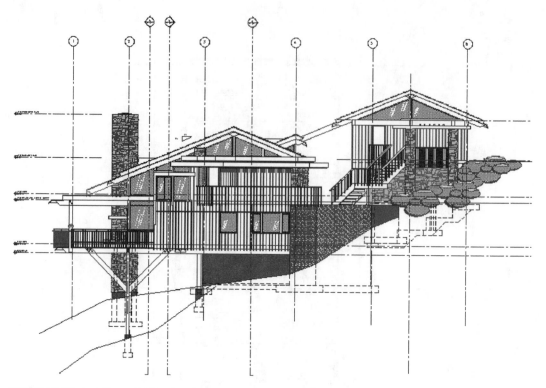

FIGURE 10.10a   A PowerCADD drawing of a waterfall residence by Adam Wisler.

calculations as you design, and you have advanced dimensioning tools, as well as the Dimension window to edit dimensions already placed in the drawing.

While in the drawing mode, the designer has a number of ways to view the drawing while allowing easy in and out movement, including the Overview window for a bird's-eye view of the drawing. The WildTools zooming feature (called Zoomer) also allows easy in and out movement, even while in the process of drawing.

Although PowerCADD is primarily a 2D program, it does offers some distinctive capabilities for three-dimensional depictions. Included with the PowerCADD package is a copy of Design-Workshop Lite, a very useful solid modeling program, which also gives you the ability to save your PowerCADD drawing in DesignWorkshop format.

Symbol libraries are not difficult to create. Symbols can be placed in the drawing using the Symbol tool or the Symbol Palette. The package comes with a number of symbol available libraries, including the Landscape Library, Machinery Designer's Library, Color Portfolio, Architectural Images Library, Residential Construction Library, and the Architectural Delight Library. PowerCADD contains many other drawing tools and drafting aids, such as the Parallel Offset

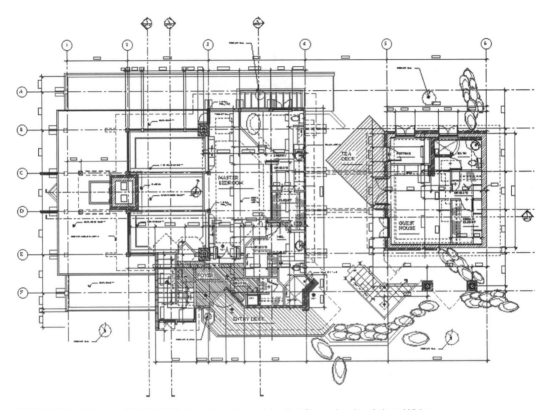

FIGURE 10b   A PowerCADD 2000 drawing of a residential floor plan by Adam Wisler.

tool, Door and Window placement tools, an Eyedropper tool, a Paint Bucket tool for filling areas of the drawing, S-Breaks and Long breaks. Selection discrimination allows you to select only the types of objects that you choose, be it rectangles or circles.

The Defaults window lets you set the attributes of tools or selected objects, offering you the choice of working on all layers or on the current layer only. The Status window can be used to adjust the nudge distance, change the drawing scale, or to change to the layer of a selected object. When finished, the drawing can be plotted on a pen plotter or printed it on a laser printer or large-format ink-jet plotter. The drawing can also be transmitted to a client or colleague in Adobe Acrobat PDF format.

To maximize the power of PowerCADD's capabilities, you need WildTools external PowerDWG translator for direct translations to and from AutoCAD DWG files, and Professional Layer Manager to let you activate and make visible any layer—one at a time—while hiding the rest. Other options provided by Advanced Engineering Tools include S-blends, moments of inertia, and outlines of selected object. While everyone aspires to having beautiful drawings, at the end of the day it is productivity that really counts—how quickly you can get up to speed and how quickly you can draw. This is where the PowerCADD/WildTools combination reportedly comes into its own. It has the capability to do a simple sketch yet powerful enough to do the largest project. There are also a number of third party products that enhance, add to, or work with PowerCADD, including Color PRUF/3, RenderPAK, Detail Manager, Toborét, ADD Professional CAD Symbol Library, Design Workshop, and others.

VectorWorks, and VectorWorks ARCHITECT

VectorWorks (formally MiniCAD), is a product of Nemetschek N.A., a recognized leader in CAD technology. The firm marked the new millennium with the release of VectorWorks ARCHITECT, its first architecturally specific add-on module and claims it is the CAD industry's first definitive integration of CAD and project management for architecture professionals. ARCHITECT is an add-on module, powered by VectorWorks, a general purpose, object-based CAD software engine. Together, the two maximize VectorWorks' general purpose functionality in four areas specific to architecture professionals: drawing organization, project management, drawing notes management and design tools. This integration allows the architecture professional to be more productive, his/her process workflow more efficient and his/her designs more accurate (Figure 10.11).

VectorWorks, is perennially the best-selling CAD program for the Macintosh. Since 1996, MiniCAD has been marketed as a cross-platform product, thereby bringing its drafting and design power to Windows users. Nemetschek N.A. recently released a new advanced modeling extension, VectorWorks 3D Power Pack. 3D Power Pack seamlessly plugs into all VectorWorks 9.5.1 products and offers designers advanced solid and surface modeling technology. Users can now easily visualize and conceptualize 3D forms that were previously impossible to create in VectorWorks. In addition, with breakthrough non-manifold modeling technology from an independent modeling kernel, users get advanced 3D capabilities that can't be found in modeling programs like Form Z.

Vector Works has increased its competitiveness through its versatility, with precision 2D drafting, sophisticated tools for dimensioning and notation, high-end presentation capabilities, and the introduction of advanced 3D modeling technology. Designers no longer have to waste time continuously moving files between programs to get the capabilities they're looking for.

VectorWorks enjoys greater popularity in many parts of Europe than in the United States. In Switzerland for example, the BauNetz Ranking shows it being used by 50 percent of the top ten Swiss offices listed. Vector Works's key features include:

- Integrated design environment that integrates all of a project's information (2D plans, 3D models, data) into a single file, making it easy to coordinate and manage. Changes made in one view, will be updated in all other views.

- Space planning module offers new ways to visualize and evaluate a project's program. Allows you to create bubble, stacking, and adjacency matrix diagrams without

FIGURES 10.11 Examples of VectorWorks/MiniCAD drafting produced on the Macintosh. *(Courtesy Herring and Trowbridge, Architects)*

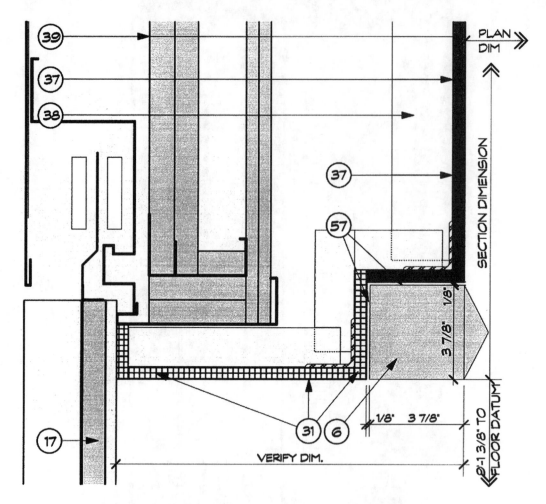

A6 ELEVATOR HEAD SECTION
SCALE: 3" = 1'-0"   2nd - 4th FLOORS

FIGURES 10.11 (continued) Examples of VectorWorks/MiniCAD drafting produced on the Macintosh. (Courtesy Herring and Trowbridge, Architects) heartache. Interactive bubble diagramming tools also make it easy to analyze a space plan and optimize a project's programs.

- Sophisticated 2D drafting capabilities allows you to create precise 2D designs.

- Powerful free form 3D modeling makes it easier to explore concepts, create massing models and present final designs in 3D.

- Built-in database and spreadsheet functions allow you to track your project's costs and materials, and can also be used to generate reports.

- Solar Animation is an interesting feature that by entering the date, latitude, longitude, you can see how shadows will be cast across your design as the sun's position changes throughout the day.

- Notes Manager helps you to accurately and quickly annotate drawings.

- The MEP module integrates designing, documenting, and analyzing HVAC, piping, plumbing, and electrical building systems, plus a host of other valuable features.

- Seating Layout command can automatically array seating, either linearly or concentrically, as well as report seat counts, by merely inputting relevant information.

- Site Modeler allows you to create 2D topographies and 3D models of a site.

- Offers high-quality rendering capabilities for client presentations.

In addition it has a wizard-like Setup Assistant that helps organize the drawings, and comes with over 60 free architectural objects and symbol libraries and other tools.

Architect Studio and ARRIS CAD

Architect Studio

ARRIS Architect is a CAD program that is both powerful and flexible and provides the tools needed to create complete contract drawings. It extends the capabilities of ARRIS to automate the entire drawing process (Figures 10.12a, 10.12b). The program is easily customized, and the system lets you work with minimum constraints. Arris points out that some of its more prominent features include:

- Smart structural elements eliminate tedious work. Many CAD systems continue to construct drawings line by line. ARRIS design automation routines have built-in intelligence to generate architectural elements including stairs, lavatories, elevators and column grids in response to a few simple prompts. Smart walls place window and door openings automatically, clean up intersections and heal changes. Designed stairs creates and stores 250 different solutions. This resident intelligence lets you modify drawings as if you created them one line at a time.

- Design refinement tools enhance productivity. Make changes and design refinements quickly, completely and accurately. Change an object and all facts associated with it dimensions, colors, costs, etc. are automatically updated and made available for reports. Changes made on one drawing are reflected on all associated drawings for consistency throughout your project.

- Standard architectural symbol libraries. ARRIS Architect contains many standard architectural symbols libraries for details, section bubbles and markers, as well as plumbing and electrical fixtures. Repeat and scale them to any size. Create and store custom symbols.

- 3D extrusion helps visualize your project. ARRIS Architect lets you immediately visualize your project in 3D. Smart walls, doors and windows can be automatically extruded to create sophisticated 3D architectural models.

- Intelligence makes reporting easy. With ARRIS Architect, design elements contain both graphic and non-graphic information: materials, fire ratings, costs, U values, colors, manufacturer part numbers, etc. can be included. Select a specific area or the entire drawing and ARRIS Architect estimates the job automatically.

- Furniture, Fixtures and Equipment. Choose from a selection of over 250 generic 2D and 3D furniture, fixture and equipment items or select them from a manufacturer's library. Create your own items and add them to the library.

ARRIS Architect claims to be the first software written specifically for architects and building management professionals. It consists of ARRIS CAD plus several highly focused architectural plug-ins that together offer a comprehensive architectural software solution.

ARRIS CAD

ARRIS CAD provides most of the drafting and management tools needed to handle an architectural project. Furthermore, its seamless integration with other ARRIS plug-ins, helps create a

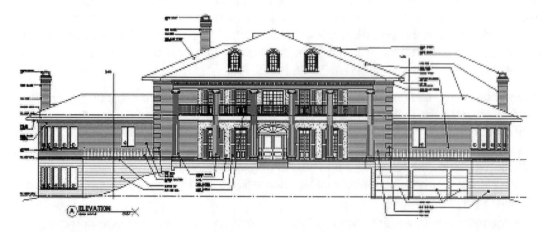

FIGURE 10.12a Examples of ARRIS CAD drafting and rendering capabilities.

FIGURE 10.12b   Examples of ARRIS CAD drafting and rendering capabilities.

comprehensive AEC software environment in the industry. Moreover, ARRIS CAD is an easily customizable, network-compatible solution that supports a wide variety of Windows and UNIX-based platforms. ARRIS CAD's key features are:

- Ease of use by incorporating an intuitive, icon-based menu system that makes learning faster and easier. Moreover, learning ARRIS CAD's point-and-click interface further facilitates understanding the entire family of ARRIS applications.
- The user can quickly activate commands with simple gestures of the mouse.

- The drag-and-drop icon feature allows you to personalize the Toolbar for faster access. Icons are customizable to create shortcut menus.

- Dynamic Viewports: Cut viewport windows into your drawings at any scale or rotation to provide a fast and flexible sheet composition tool. Use viewports to quickly load drawings, or as a productivity tool to automatically update design modifications.

- The program has powerful 3D tools that use geometric primitives and construction planes to easily generate both simple and complex structures. Cut holes in slabs. Extrude any shape along a user-defined path to quickly create highly-detailed models.

- Its shared drawing access facility allows you to simultaneously share drawings with other project team members over a network while using different hardware platforms. Multiple design changes are automatically saved to a single, project database. ARRIS CAD provides true workgroup computing.

- The data compatibility function lets the user export and import ARRIS drawings to DXF and DWG file formats.

ARRIS 3D

Modeling and Rendering, and Vantage Point

ARRIS Modeling and Rendering is a versatile, yet powerful system that even lets a novice operator be productive. Models can rapidly be constructed and viewed from any vantage point with a click of the mouse. The program has intuitive tools to help you build models by building wireframe skeletons and automatically stretching surfaces over the frame.

Vantage Point also adds useful tools for designers and animators, that allow free movement within ARRIS computer models. The icon-based menu interface lets you visualize alternatives and explore new ideas without going through complex routines.

The combined power of ARRIS Modeling and Rendering, and Vantage Point visualization products can significantly increase a designer's ability to communicate design concepts (Figure 12.b). ARRIS 3D includes the tools needed to create both simple and complex wireframe geometry, and when used in conjunction with ARRIS Architect, ARRIS models are linked directly to construction documents.

ARRIS Details

The ARRIS Details application greatly enhances the ability of ARRIS to produce detail drawings and to compose sheets of details without restriction. ARRIS Details simplifies one of the most labor-intensive aspects of the drafting process and enables users to work with several differently scaled drawings on the same sheet.

The ability to create and assemble detail sheets of varying scales is essential to producing contract documents. ARRIS Details lets you compose sheet layouts and assign the desired scale to each of the work areas. Users are not limited in the number of drawings or scales that can be included on a sheet. The Details Library can be utilized to effortlessly create, manage, and categorize libraries of standard details (Figure 10.13).

SYSTEM REQUIREMENTS

Minimum recommended system requirements vary depending on the program used. Obviously the faster the processor and greater the storage capacity, the greater the efficiency and production. The following are minimum and/or recommended requirements for running the CAD systems outlined below:

- For Autodesk Architectural Desktop and AutoCAD, recommended requirements are: Intel Pentium III or AMD K6-III PC, 450MHz minimum, 256MB RAM, Windows 98 SE, Windows NT 4.0 (Service Pack 5 or later), Windows 2000 Professional, Windows XP Professional or Windows ME operating systems, 1024x768 VGA video display, Windows video display driver, 550MB

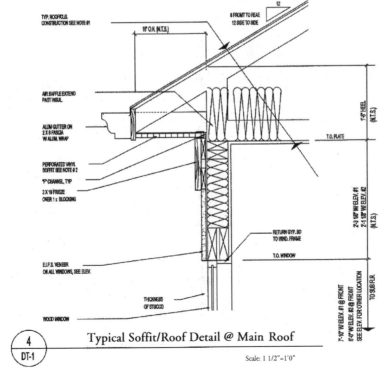

FIGURE 10.13   A drawing of a roof detail using Arris CAD software.

free hard disk space and 75MB swap space, Pointing device (mouse or digitizer with Wintab driver), 4X CD-ROM drive, Serial port (for digitizers and some plotters), Modem (connection to Internet), Sound card for multimedia learning, TCP/IP or IPX support (required only for multiuser, or floating license configurations).

- ArchiCAD requirements include: Microsoft Windows 95/98/2000/NT 4.0. Macintosh OS 8.6 or later. Intel Pentium, Pentium Pro, Pentium II or III, Celeron or compatible (such as AMD K7 Athlon/Duron), Power PC, 64Mb minimum, but 128Mb or more recommended, 220Mb minimum free hard drive space required for full installation. More than 200Mb free hard disk space after installation is recommended for optimal performance on Windows, free hard disk space dependent on model complexity on Macintosh; 100Mb suggested, but in excess of 200 Mb recommended for complex 3D visualization. The Video Card should also have a 256 color, minimum resolution of 1024x768; 24-bit TrueColor with a resolution of 1280x1024 or higher recommended.

- VersaCAD software runs on the Macintosh Performa or later, with at least two megabytes of RAM. VersaCAD also runs on PowerMac, G3, G4, and iMac. Single or multiple screens may be used, including high-resolution color. Hard disk requires a minimum of 10MB. Installation is with CD-ROM.

- Running TurboCAD requires a Pentium processor, Windows 95/98/NT, 32MB RAM, a VGA display, 2X CD-ROM, a mouse or other pointing device, and 30MB free disk space.

- Microstation Architect's minimum requirements are, an Intel Pentium processor (or better), Windows 95/98/NT, 64 MB Ram, 80 MB of disk space, a mouse or other pointing device, and access to a CD-ROM drive.

- PowerCADD requires a PowerPC processor, System 8.5 or later, 13MB hard disk, minimum memory allocation 6 MB, recommended memory allocation 16 MB.

- VectorWorks and VectorWorks ARCHITECT for Windows requires a minimum of Pentium processor or greater, 96 MB RAM, 200 MB of hard-disk space for full installation (150 MB for typical installation), Windows 95 or later or Windows NT or later, SVGA Monitor with 250 colors, CD-ROM drive. For Macintosh, minimum requirements are: Power Macintosh or greater, Mac OS 8.6 or greater, 96 MB RAM, 200 MB of hard-disk space for full installation (150 MB for typical installation), and CD-ROM Drive.

CHAPTER ELEVEN

TECHNICAL ISSUES

Prior to the 20th century, heating and ventilation was little understood and most installations were usually based on data from manufacturers' catalogues and rule of thumb calculations. Indeed, contractors were typically more interested in the commercial aspects of the business than the scientific aspects. In 1895, The American Society of Heating and Ventilating Engineers was incorporated in the state of New York, and in 1922 the Society's newly established Research Bureau issued its first major benchmarking resource publication, The Guide.

GENERAL HISTORIC OVERVIEW

It is rather surprising that it wasn't until the 1920s that the public first became aware of the benefits of air conditioning, and only then because it started being used in public places like theaters and department stores.

Mechanical and electrical systems have made tremendous strides during the last century. Changes have been even more evident during the past two decades due to the use of computer-based design aids, which have radically transformed the design and operation of the comfort systems for buildings. Moreover, there have been major advances in intelligent management systems for buildings and energy conservation imperatives have also had a major impact. Also, the principles of life-cycle economics are regularly used in design selections and trade offs. Added to this, the terrorist attacks that have hit the homeland in recent years have also impacted design perceptions and strategies. While the standard of care for the mechanical/electrical engineering profession has changed to a lesser degree than one might have expected as a result of these attacks, the change is particularly noticeable with respect to federal buildings and GSA tenants. In addition, issues of indoor air quality, environment considerations, water quality, and energy efficiency have taken on global implications.

Although it is typically outside the scope of space planners and interior designers to design or produce construction drawings for mechanical or electrical systems, it is nevertheless essential to have a fundamental understanding of these systems in order to be able to coordinate and integrate the location of plumbing fixtures, air diffusers, sprinklers, and other mechanical elements and equipment within the general design concept. This chapter concentrates the discussions on the following five basic issues:

- Heating, Ventilating, and Air Conditioning (HVAC) Systems
- Electrical Services
- Plumbing Services
- Fire Protection
- Conveyance Systems

HEATING, VENTILATING, AND AIR CONDITIONING SYSTEMS (HVAC)

The facets of comfort—temperature, humidity, air quality, and sound—vary in importance based on the type of occupancy and business priorities. Budgets, social commitments, and code requirements collectively influence the design of the building comfort system. Professor Jan Kreider, editor of *Handbook of Heating, Ventilation, and Air Conditioning*, says, "One of the major expenditures in the life cycle of a building is the operation of its space conditioning systems—heating, ventilation, and air conditioning (HVAC)—dwarfing the initial cost of these systems or of even the entire building itself." It is imperative, therefore, to try and design the most efficient systems possible to minimize operational and maintenance costs throughout the building life cycle. Particularly in larger buildings, this means it is important to bring a service engineer on board the design team from the very outset of the design process to allow the servicing proposals to interact with the building's organization, structure and costing.

Types of HVAC Systems

HVAC systems are often classified by the carrying mediums used to heat or cool the building. The two main transfer mediums for this purpose are air and water. On smaller projects, electricity is often used for heating. Steve Millnick, of Gerard Engineering, adds that areas having milder climates also utilize electricity for most of their heating systems. He states that this is due to power rate structures and the fact that most buildings in milder climates are in a cooling mode for most of the year. Likewise, some systems now use a combination of transfer media.

Air conditioning is the term typically applied to the cooling effect of a system. For a system to operate in the cooling mode, several processes take place: air circulation, air cleaning, cooling and dehumidifying the air. The heating mode, on the other hand, involves: heating, circulation, cleaning, and humidifying the air. In both modes, air circulation is critical to the system's success.

All-air systems cool or heat spaces through the utilization of conditioned air. Heat is ducted to the space with supply and return air ducts. With rectangular ducting, for optimum efficiency, the section should be as close to a square as is possible. Constrictions and sharp changes of direction should be avoided. A typical example of an all-air system is a residential forced hot-air furnace. Furnaces powered by oil or gas heat the air that is then delivered to room emitters throughout the house via ducts. Plenum return (plenum rated materials must be used) or return air ducts in each room collect the cooled air and allow it to permeate freely back to the furnace for reheating. Some of the advantages associated with the use of central, all-air systems include:

- Piping is not within the conditioned space. This reduces the risk of potential damage in occupied spaces.
- It is possible to use outdoor air to cool buildings.
- Provides flexibility in zoning and comfort control.
- Having the equipment centrally located, facilitates maintenance.

There are also negative aspects associated with all-air systems, including:

- Additional space is required for ducting.
- Correct air-balancing is necessary to achieve zone comfort and proper operation of the system.
- Servicing of zones with diverse loads may require extensive cooling and reheating of supply air.
- The central distribution fan may have to operate frequently during unoccupied hours in cold weather.

Larger buildings in the United States generally incorporate one of several variations of primary system types, including: central chilled water plant with floor by floor air handling units and variable air volume distribution, central condenser water with floor by floor self contained air units, variable air volume distribution systems, and central condenser water systems with console heat pumps and constant volume on the interior zones. High-velocity dual duct (parallel hot and cold ducts allowing blended supply locally; high performance), and multizone systems are also used for small buildings and outside the U.S.

Constant air volume systems utilize single duct, single zone systems (air ducts from plant to single large space), whereas single duct, multiple zone systems, dual duct systems, and multizone systems can be either constant air volume or variable air volume systems. A multizone system is typically used in large multistory buildings where it is not practical or efficient to use many AHUs, each serving a single zone. Instead, several zones are served, each with its own thermostat control. The challenge for designers here is to accommodate diverse loads while maintaining system efficiency (Figures 11.1a, b, c).

The various system types all require supply air ductwork, supply air diffusers or registers, and return air grilles in all spaces. Registers are grills that cover the opening of a duct in a heating or cooling system, and some are designed to open or close to regulate the flow and volume of air coming through them. Sometimes, particularly in small buildings, separate ductwork is not used for return air, but extract grilles are simply placed in the suspended ceiling (*plenum*) to collect return air. Their location is influenced by the need to find the least obtrusive and most economic routes so that the mechanical system can efficiently draw the return air and direct it to a central collecting point where it is then redirected through associated ducts to the building's heating plant.

A *plenum void* is the space between the suspended ceiling and the structural floor above. In a plenum system, a duct delivers air into the ceiling void, where the resulting surplus pressure causes the air to permeate into the space below, either through perforations in the ceiling tiles, or through slots in the supporting metal channels. However, plenum overhead supply systems are rarely used today except perhaps in very small buildings, due to inefficiency and potential indoor air quality issues. Where fire-rated partitions extend above the suspended ceiling, then building regulations usually require supply air ducts and openings for return air to be provided. Fire dampers are required where ducts penetrate a fire wall. Modern fire dampers are dynamically rated to operate when the system is flowing full air at normal operating pressures. Fire dampers contain a fusible link that melts and separates when a particular temperature is reached, causing it to slam shut in the event of a fire.

Supply air registers are essentially grilles equipped with double deflection adjustable vanes at the face and a damper behind the face for balance and to control the direction of flow and/or flow rate. They are usually connected to the main ductwork with flexible ducting to allow some adjustability in its placement, which can be extremely useful when its location is in conflict with another ceiling-mounted element. Return air grilles are not usually connected to ducts in commercial construction, and so they too may be relocated if overall circulation is maintained. In any case, the mechanical engineer should be consulted when a register is to be moved.

In hot water systems, a central boiler converts fuel to heat and the heat is delivered to the rooms in the form of hot water, using some type of coil unit called a *convector*. In the rooms, the emitters give out the heat from their surfaces by radiation and convection. The cooled water is then returned to the boiler. There are also combination systems that use ducts for supplying air from the central air handling unit, and water to heat the air before it is transferred into the conditioned space. These are called terminal reheat systems. Because these systems often function in a mode

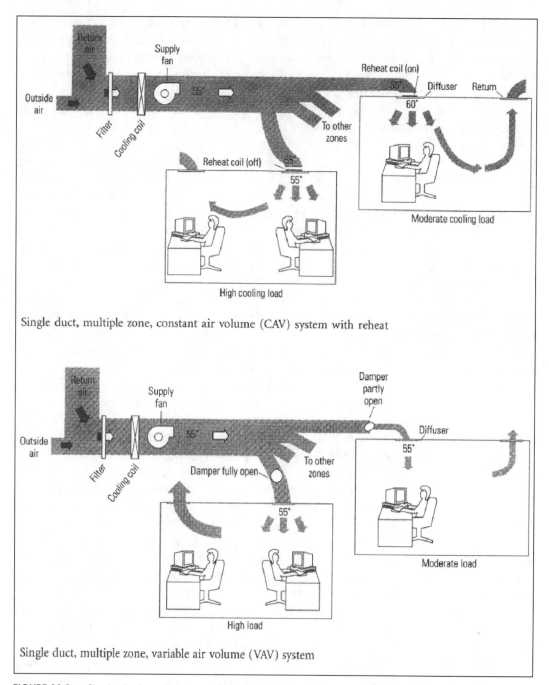

Single duct, multiple zone, constant air volume (CAV) system with reheat

Single duct, multiple zone, variable air volume (VAV) system

FIGURE 11.1a   Single duct, multiple zone systems. *(Courtesy E-Source, Boulder, Colorado)*

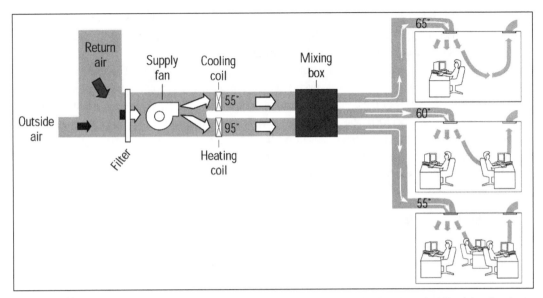

FIGURE 11.1b A multizone system is functionally the same as a dual-duct system, but the blending happens upstream, with a single duct going to each zone. The downstream end of the multizone air handler in the photograph (right) has four damper actuators that blend hot and cold air for four different air-conditioning zones. *(Courtesy Platts)*

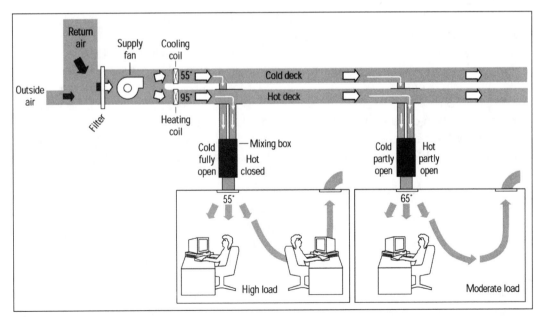

FIGURE 11.1c Dual duct systems provide simultaneous heating and cooling. Mixing boxes at the zones blend air as necessary to meet cooling loads. *(Courtesy Platts)*

where the air is cooled by a vapor compression cycle, and then reheated at the terminal units, they tend to use a significantly greater amount of energy than other comparable systems. In addition, there are various residential systems that use an all water system for heating and a separate duct system for ventilation and cooling. Although the cost of using electric heat in large spaces can be prohibitive, nevertheless, there are occasions where its use is justified, such as over an external door to create an air-curtain draught barrier, or in lobbies where one wants to avoid visually intrusive pipes and radiators. Here, Steve Millnick points out that, "Lobbies typically require a low heat source due to potential drafts from large expanses of glass and the higher than normal ceiling heights—for this baseboard heaters or recirculation heaters are required with low discharge." Occasionally, electric panels are used where it is necessary to avoid drafts.

HVAC System Requirements

There are a number of important HVAC considerations that space planners and interior designers need be aware of when designing a particular space. One of these is incorporating adequate space for ducts and pipes. Small ducts and sanitary pipes are typically designed to run within the walls and floor joists in residential construction. Sometimes, circumstances necessitate that a horizontal duct run below the floor joists of a house and a suspended ceiling built to conceal it.

Commercial construction usually takes advantage of ceiling plenums to run horizontal ducts while vertical ducts are contained within their own chases. Depending on the type of structure and depth of the plenum (distance between the suspended ceiling and the underside of the structure above), large ducts may occupy much of this depth leaving little or no space for recessed light fixtures. One must therefore determine the amount of dedicated space for ducts, as well as the size and location of ductwork prior to placement of the light fixtures. Sprinkler may be located with sleeves through the beams to reduce the depth of the overall floor to floor height. Occasionally, commercial construction uses access flooring (typically in computer room applications), which consists of a false floor of individual panels raised by pedestals above the structural floor. This is designed to provide sufficient space to run electrical and communication wiring as well as HVAC ductwork. Also, in commercial construction, small pipes can be designed typically to run within a wall system, whereas larger pipes may need deeper walls or even chase walls to accommodate the pipes.

Where the plenum is used as a return air space, the use of combustible materials such as wood or exposed wire are prohibited by most local and national building codes from being used within the space in commercial construction. Of note, some special types of telephone and communication wiring are plenum rated for use in such locations in place of running the wires in steel conduit.

Building codes stipulate that access be provided to certain components of mechanical and electrical systems. This is usually for maintenance and repair, and includes such elements as valves, fire dampers, heating coils, mechanical equipment, and electrical junction boxes.

Where these components are located above a suspended acoustical ceiling, access is achieved by simply removing a ceiling tile. In other locations such as gypsum wallboard ceilings and partitions, access doors should be incorporated to avoid the need for potential repairs. It is usually part of the mechanical engineer's scope to determine the location of thermostats so as to render optimum performance. They are typically placed 48 to 60 inches above the floor and away from exterior walls and heat sources. The space planner should coordinate their location with light switches, dimmers and other visible control devices.

At the same time, the location of supply air diffusers and return air grills should be integrated with other ceiling elements such as lights, sprinkler heads, smoke detectors, and speakers, so that the ceiling aesthetically pleasing and well planned. Linear diffusers are located approximately two feet from windows and utilize the coanda effect to distribute the air evenly around the exterior office while maintaining an even temperature gradient. Here too, the mechanical engineer must be consulted to verify that the desired locations do not adversely affect the operation of the HVAC and other systems.

Window drapes, curtains, blinds, and other coverings, as well as glass performance must be coordinated with the engineer at the beginning of the project to verify that adequate capacity is provided at exterior zones. These factors can have a significant affect on the heating and air conditioning load in a space and may interfere with supply air diffusers or other heating units near the window. Horizontal miniblinds are typically down and set at 45 degrees to offset direct solar heat.

Although HVAC systems are often designed to work independently of furniture placement, there are times when the designer/planner may want to consider a precise location for a floor registers, fin-tube baseboard radiators, or other equipment which may affect the placement of furniture and built-in woodwork.

Reading HVAC Drawings

Space planners should have a fundamental understanding of HVAC systems and know the basics of reading HVAC plans to enable them to verify existing conditions and to coordinate the planning of the work with the mechanical engineer. HVAC drawings are often drawn with single lines representing piping and ductwork, although drawing in double line is preferable, when representing proper graphic coordination. Figure 11.2 shows a portion of a typical commercial mechanical plan. Duct sizes are indicated with a line and a number such as 18 x 12. These numbers depict the width and height respectively of the duct in inches.

ELECTRICAL SERVICES

Electricity is a vital primary energy source for operating not only much of the HVAC equipment in buildings, such as fans, chillers, pumps, and electrical auxiliaries, but also for lighting, convenience outlets, communications, and machinery. It is surprising, therefore, given the importance of electricity in daily life and the current rapid evolution of the electrical industry, that it should be so little understood. It is important for the space planner to have a basic understanding of what transformers and substations are and the difference between a single and three-phase supply system, as well as both present and future options for electricity generation.

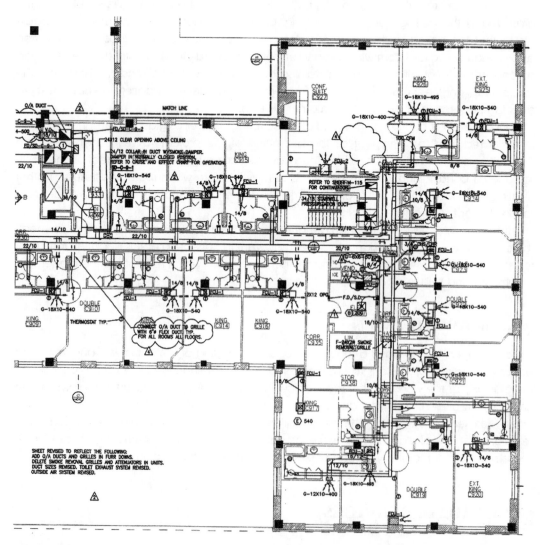

FIGURE 11.2 An example of a section of a mechanical plan for a commercial building.

Power System Requirements

Electrical systems provide power for lighting, convenience outlets, and fixed equipment, and their installation requires considerable expertise. It is no surprise therefore that, except for very small projects, the space planner rightly turns to the electrical engineer or electrical contractor to design, specify and determine the exact type of circuiting, wire sizes, cable routing, and other technical related issues of these systems. However, interior designers and space planners are often required to show schematically the designated location of outlets and switches, where power is required for specific built-in equipment. They often also determine or input on the appearance of cover plates and other visible electrical devices. Space planners should also have a fundamental understanding of power supply.

There are various types of conductors (such as circuit breaker boxes to the individual switches, lights, and outlets) that supply power throughout a building. Non-metallic sheathed cable (NM), also known by the trade name *Romex*, consists of two or more plastic insulated conductors and ground wire surrounded by a moisture-resistant plastic jacket. This type of cable can be used in one and two-family dwellings, many multifamily and commercial buildings that do not exceed three floors or where it would be used as service entrance cable. However, unprotected Romex cable must not be installed within six feet of an attic access, nor within seven feet of a permanently installed attic stairway. There are also other restrictions that are outlined in the National Electrical Code (NEC), which the planner should be aware of. It is particularly important to review these restrictions and guidelines as there are a number of significant changes in the 2002 NEC regarding metal-clad (MC) cable.

Flexible armor-clad cable (AC) is an armored building wire, also known by the trade name *BX* (or sometimes called *flex*), which consists of individual plastic-insulated conductors encased in a continuous spiral-wound layer of metal or tough paper. It is used in commercial work (more than three stories high) and renovation work because it can be pulled through existing spaces within a building. It is also used to connect commercial light fixtures so they can be relocated in a suspended acoustical ceiling.

NM cable protection (e.g. enclosed in sleeves, tubes, trough, or other approved carrier) may be required for commercial construction (more than three stories high) and large multifamily residential construction. NM cable protection is also necessary where the cable must exist the interior of the building structure to provide power for fixtures or devices (e.g. floodlights) on the exterior of the building. Conduit is required in certain construction because it not only supports and protects the wiring, but it serves as a system ground, and protects surrounding construction from fire should the wire short or overheat.

Recent developments in cabling technology include the use of under-carpet wiring, which is basically a cable distribution system that uses thin, flat cables placed beneath carpet squares (which allows for access to cables) to provide voice, data, video and power services capability to open office workstations, where there is no access to horizontal cable tray areas. Such cables are crush-resistant, flexible and only 0.105 inches thin (Figure 11.3).

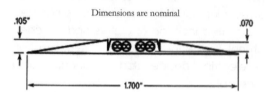

Dimensions are nominal

.105"   .070

1.700"

FIGURE 11.3 Flexible under-carpet wiring.

FIGURE 11.3 (continued) Flexible under-carpet wiring.

Grounded junction boxes must be used to house outlets and other types of connections to the power supply. They are also used to house jacks, volume controls, switches and receptacles and can be purchased pre-wired. These boxes may be made of cast iron, polypropylene, aluminum, or some other material to which the conduit or other cable system is attached. They vary in size and shape, depending on their use, but generally for single switches and duplex outlets, they measure about 2 inches wide by 4 inches high. Larger boxes are 4 inches square, and several can be connected if there are more than two switches or two duplex outlets. The NEC also requires that junction boxes be provided where light fixtures are connected to the electrical system.

Building codes stipulate requirements for all aspects of electrical systems, including the location of outlets. In residential construction for example, spacing of outlets must not exceed 12 feet. Additionally, there must be a duplex outlet on each wall surface (greater than 2 feet in length), where furniture might be placed so lamp and radio cords and the like do not have to be cross the path of door openings.

Often in commercial projects, special power outlets must be placed on their own circuit. This is particularly important where there is a secure, mission-critical high capacity communications requirement between two or more locations. In such cases, point-to-point circuits are provided with capabilities to carry voice, data, and video traffic in many types of different configurations. These are termed *dedicated* circuits and are designed to achieve increased security, and to prevent unwanted electrical interference from disturbing sensitive electrical equipment, such as computers, that are connected to them. These circuits should also be clearly depicted on the plan and the exact electrical requirements of the equipment given to the electrical engineer. Circuits that require voltages greater than 120 volts (including outlets for electric ranges, large copy machines, and other special equipment) should also be depicted on the drawings.

Insulation and grounding (the act or process of making an electrical connection with the earth) are two recognized means of preventing injury in electrical wiring, in addition to the protection provided by circuit breakers in the panel boxes that trip off if the circuit is over-loaded. Conductor insulation may be provided by placing a nonconductive material (such as plastic) around the conductor. Grounding, which is a separate wire in addition to the two that provide power, may be achieved through the use of a direct connection to a known ground such as a metal cold water pipe. Thus, if a hot wire contacts a grounded enclosure, a ground fault results which would typically trip a circuit breaker or blow a fuse. The ground provides a path for the fault.

However, ground fault protection is not always complete using the above methods, as when there is a break in the grounding system that may occur without the user's knowledge. This necessitated the use of another method to overcome grounding and insulation deficiencies. It is the ground fault circuit interrupter (GFCI), a safety device that monitors the amount of incoming and outgoing current; whenever the entering current does not equal the leaving current, indicating current leakage, the GFCI instantly shuts off the flow of electricity. It is a faster overcurrent protection device than either a fuse or circuit breaker. GFCIs are designed therefore, to detect small current leaks and can be a part of a circuit breaker or installed as an outlet. Their use is obligatory for outdoor outlets, bathrooms, kitchens and other locations specified in the National Electrical Code.

Telecommunication System Requirements

A structured cable system is the infrastructure of any communication, computer and information network. Copper and/or fiber cables are linked together to carry all of the voice, data, video and Internet traffic throughout a building. Usually hidden within building walls and ceilings, the cable infrastructure should be designed, or *structured*, to maximize data rates and optimize network efficiency. It is the foundation on which all the other technologies will run. Telecommunication systems include telephones, intercommunication systems, alarm systems, computer terminals, radio and TV rediffusion, and other specialist equipment. These systems are usually drawn on the same plan as the power outlets and are usually the responsibility of the space planners/designer. As with power outlets, the design of circuiting, wire sizing, and connections to central equipment is typically executed by the electrical engineer or the contractor responsible for installing the equipment.

Telephone and communication systems are low-voltage systems (main telephone systems work at around 50 volts), which makes the requirements for conduit and other protection not quite as stringent as for high-voltage power. But as with all telecommunications wiring, good insulation and separation from the mains electrical wiring is necessary. Often, an outlet box is provided at the connection in the wall, and the wire is run within the walls and ceiling spaces without conduit. However, in some commercial construction all cable is required to be protected in conduit to avoid having it catch fire or release toxic fumes in case of a fire. Special assembled and unassembled plenum-related cable is now available which is used above drop ceilings, air plenum areas, in-wall cabling applications and other areas dictated by local fire codes since plenum rated cables do not emit toxic gases in case of a fire. Also, while this type does not require conduit, it is more expensive than standard cable.

Electrical System Plans

Electrical, telephone and communication outlets can be shown on one of several plans. With residential construction, they can be drawn on the construction floor plan because installation is fairly simple. On commercial projects on the other hand, the floor plan may be crowded with other unrelated information, and so a separate power plan is usually needed. In addition to showing the outlets themselves, exact dimensions are given when their location is critical. Outlets can also be shown on furniture plans as the outlets most often directly relate to the placement of desks, seating groups, and other furniture.

   Power plans developed by the space planner are then given to the electrical engineer to prepare the electrical plans. These plans will contain all the detailed information concerning circuiting, wire size, conduit size, panel boxes, and other data required by the electrical contractor. Figures 11.4 and 11.5 illustrate typical electrical plans as drawn by a space planner or interior designer and an electrical engineer. As with mechanical plans, standard symbols are used to indicate common electrical items. Some of the more common ones are shown in Figure 11.6.

PLUMBING SERVICES

Space planners and designers are often required to locate plumbing fixtures in both new construction and renovation work. They should also be familiar with the relevant sections of the International Plumbing Code or other local plumbing codes that have jurisdiction where the project is located, as these requirements must be complied with.

Plumbing System Criteria

Plumbing generally includes water supply and sewerage piping for potable water, drains, waste piping, and vent piping. It also includes plumbing fixtures, pipe supports, and other accessories that may be needed to provide a complete plumbing system. Water supply consists essentially of cold and hot water, and in all plumbing installation and design, residential or commercial, certain design criteria need to be taken into account. These include: assessment of demand (since generally not all appliances are used simultaneously), estimate demand in loading units (refer to local plumbing codes), direct or indirect supply system to be used, storage (capacity, tanks, location), and pipe sizing (material, velocity, flow rate, pressure head).

SUITE 503   SUITE 504

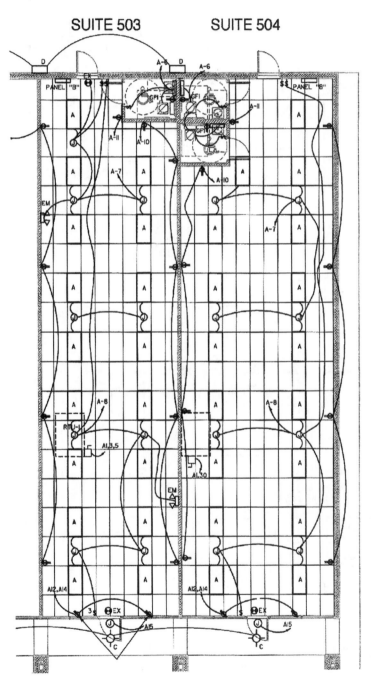

FIGURE 11.4 Typical electrical plan drawn by an interior designer.

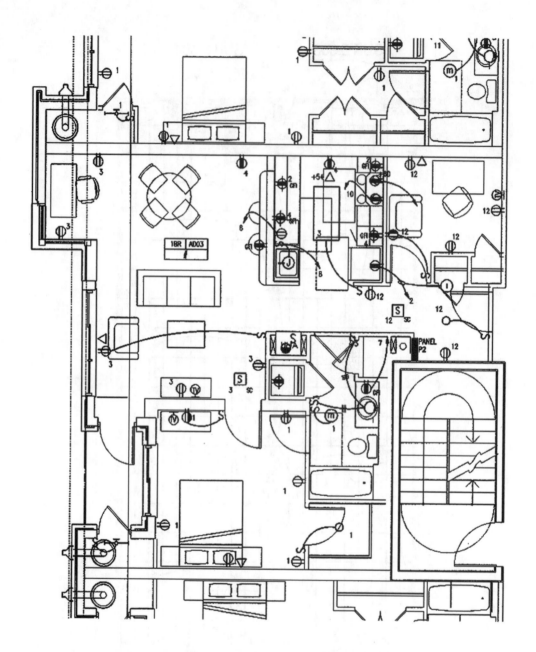

DRAWING NOTES:

1. SEE DRAWING E-1 FOR NOTES, SYMBOLS, AND LIGHT FIXTURE SCHEDULE.

KEY NOTES:

① HOMERUN FOR CIRCUIT 2 SHALL COME FROM REFRIGERATOR RECEPTACLE.

FIGURE 11.5   Typical electrical plan drawn by an electrical engineer.

ELECTRICAL SYMBOLS

FIGURE 11.6   Some of the more common standard electrical symbols used in the industry.

In all plumbing installation, water is supplied under pressure to individual plumbing fixtures. Water supply should be capable of satisfying the peak requirements of a proposed building or project, including fire protection and air conditioning requirements. The delivery pressure from a pipe is proportional to the *head* or height of filled pipe above it. Because of this and because the pipes are generally small, it is relatively easy to locate them within wall cavities, ceiling structure, and other areas to supply a fixture, even if it is some distance from the main source of water (Figure 11.7).

Domestic potable water supplies within a building must be protected from contamination by mechanical and irrigation system equipment by the use of a backflow prevention on each system connection (governed by the International Plumbing Code). In addition, the domestic hot water systems must be designed to provide hot water in a timely fashion, often requiring recirculating the hot water piping back to the water heating source to provide a loop of hot water with branches to fixtures.

Drainage systems require different considerations because they work by gravity—drain pipes must be sloped downward to carry away wastes. They should be independent of any other piping system, and drains that are too low for gravity flow must be drained into a sump, from which the effluent will be pumped. In addition, the systems should be vented to prevent the traps from being subject to overpressures and vacuum. The basic design philosophy of sanitary drainage system pipe sizing and gravity flow, relies on maintaining a flow of at least two feet per second within sanitary piping to allow solids to be carried through the system. In addition, the flow within sanitary piping must be managed (by sizing criteria and pipe/fitting installation) to prevent excessive pressure build-up or clogging.

Figure 11.8 shows a simplified diagram of a typical drainage and vent system. Storm drainage, falls into two categories: the first being the piping system used to convey rain from roofs, areaways, other exposed areas, and the second being the sub-soil drainage system provided to prevent water seepage through walls and floors that are located below grade.

An essential component attached to sanitary fixtures is the trap. Traps work by giving the pipe a dip in its run, so that a water seal is in place after the discharge has passed, and which prevents gases from the sewage system from entering the building. All sanitary appliances are trapped unless they are part of a bank, e.g. urinals, that discharge into a common branch that would have a common trap. Local code considerations may require individual traps on each sanitary fixture.

The traps are connected to the drainage system, as well as the vents. Waste or soil vents are pipes that are connected to the drainage system. *Vent stacks* typically extend through the roof of a building to the open air, or *stack vents* are connected above the highest horizontal drain emptying into the stacks. Vents have two main objectives. First, they help prevent odors and back smells by permitting built-up sewage gases to escape instead of bubbling through the water in the traps. They also permit pressure in the system to equalize so discharging waste does not create a siphon that breaks the seal by draining the water out of the traps.

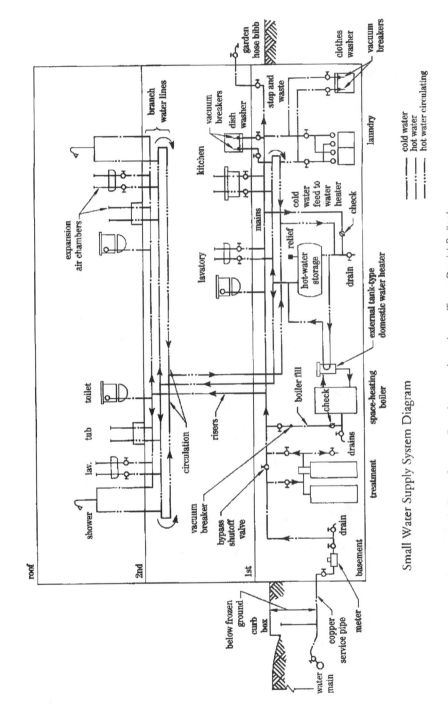

Small Water Supply System Diagram

cold water
hot water
hot water circulating

FIGURE 11.7 Schematic representation of a small water supply system. *(From David Ballast,*
Interior Design Reference Manual, Professional Publications, Inc., 1998)

433

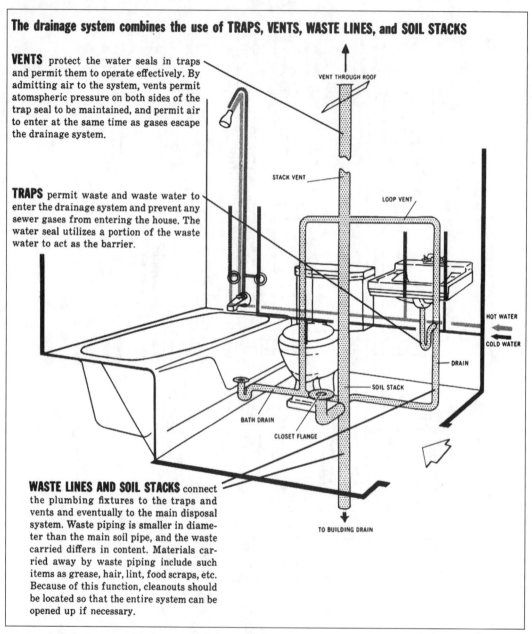

The drainage system combines the use of TRAPS, VENTS, WASTE LINES, and SOIL STACKS

VENTS protect the water seals in traps and permit them to operate effectively. By admitting air to the system, vents permit atomspheric pressure on both sides of the trap seal to be maintained, and permit air to enter at the same time as gases escape the drainage system.

TRAPS permit waste and waste water to enter the drainage system and prevent any sewer gases from entering the house. The water seal utilizes a portion of the waste water to act as the barrier.

WASTE LINES AND SOIL STACKS connect the plumbing fixtures to the traps and vents and eventually to the main disposal system. Waste piping is smaller in diameter than the main soil pipe, and the waste carried differs in content. Materials carried away by waste piping include such items as grease, hair, lint, food scraps, etc. Because of this function, cleanouts should be located so that the entire system can be opened up if necessary.

FIGURE 11.8 Illustrates plumbing and drainage systems in a typical residential bathroom, showing use of vents, traps, waste lines, and soil stacks. *(From Muller, Edward, J. et al, Architectural Drawing and Light Construction, Fifth Edition, Prentiss Hall, New Jersey, 1999)*

The sewage travels from the traps in fixture branch lines to vertical stacks (soil stacks or waste stacks). *Soil stacks* are vertical drainage systems that carry discharge from water closets (toilets), whereas *waste stacks* are vertical drainage systems that discharge all of the plumbing fixtures except that of the water closets. Every building in which plumbing is installed is required to have at least one three-inch stack vent (or vent stack) carried full size through the roof. A stack vent either connects to a soil or waste stack that is above the highest horizontal fixture or drain emptying into the stack, or is a soil or waste stack that extends through the roof (Figure 11.9). A stack vent or main vent shall be installed with a soil or waste stack whenever individual vents, relief vents, or branch vents are required for stacks of three or more branch intervals, and should be a vertical extension of the drainage stack.

Plumbing Fixture Placement

Cost and the need to slope the drainage pipes makes it necessary for plumbing fixtures to be located as close as possible to existing plumbing lines. These include horizontal lines or vertical risers that run continuously through a multistory building. Minimum slopes for drains are ¼ inch per foot (or ⅛ inch per foot for pipes larger than 3 inches). The size and slope of pipes concealed within a floor space, is limited by the distance from the fixture to a connection with a riser.

In commercial structures, designers try to concentrate most plumbing in a single area near the core where it serves the toilet rooms, drinking fountains, and similar facilities. To provide service to sinks, private toilets, and the like, wet columns are sometimes included in the building. These are usually positioned at structural columns, where hot and cold supply and drainage and vent risers are located. They are designed to allow individual tenants to easily tap into them, without having to connect to more remote plumbing at the core of the building.

Where a project contains extensive plumbing work, the necessary pipes may not fit within the space provided by standard partitions. Soil stacks from toilets, for example, require 4 inch (10 cm.) diameter pipes that have an actual outside diameter somewhat larger than 4 inches. In this case, plumbing chases need to be incorporated. They can be constructed of two sets of studs with a space between large enough for the pipes. Where vents pass through insulated assemblies, an insulation shield shall be installed to provide clearance between the vent and the insulation material. Where vents pass through attic space, the shield shall terminate not less than 2 inches (51 mm) above the insulation materials and shall be secured in place to prevent displacement.

Plumbing Plans

Except for small projects like residences, plumbing plans are normally executed by the mechanical engineer. Planners and designers should be familiar with standard plumbing plan symbols, examples of which are shown in Figure 11.10.

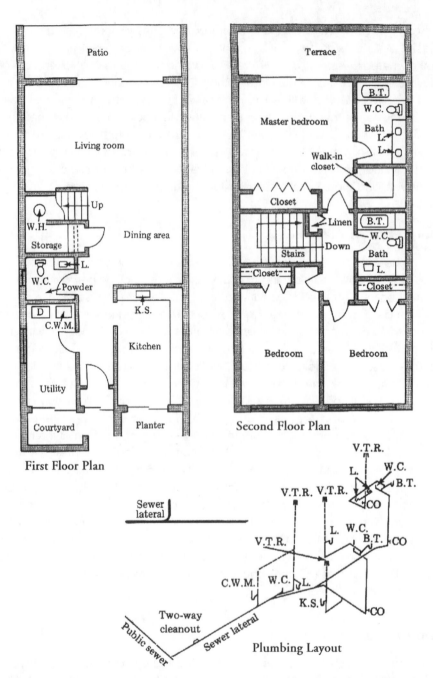

FIGURE 11.9 Illustrates plumbing and drainage layout for a single family residence. *(From Massey, Howard, C., Estimating Plumbing Costs, Craftsman Book Company, Carlsbad, CA)*

PLUMBING SYMBOLS AND ABBREVIATIONS

Symbol	Abbreviation	Description
———————	S. P. OR W. P.	SOIL OR WASTE PIPE
- - - - - - - - -	V. P.	VENT PIPE
——— — ———	C. W.	COLD WATER
——— — — ———	H. W.	HOT WATER - 120°
— — ——— —	ST. D.	STORM DRAIN
———————	GD	GARAGE DRAIN PIPE
———G-C———	G(CUSTOMER)	NATURAL GAS PIPING, PROVIDED/INSTALED BY OWNER
———G———	G(EMSL)	NATURAL GAS PIPING-EXTENDED METER SUPPLY LINE, PROVIDED/INSTALLED BY WASH. GAS
⊠	FLD	FLOOR DRAIN
⊠	RD	ROOF DRAIN
⊠	GD	GARAGE DRAIN
⊠	PLD	PLAZA DRAIN
○	OSD	OPEN SITE DRAIN
□⊢	WH	WALL HYDRANT, BOX TYPE-FREEZE PROOF
———○		PIPING RISER OR STACK UP
———⊃	DN.	PIPING DOWN
——☩——		SHUT-OFF VALVE ON DOMESTIC WATER
——→		DIRECTION OF FLOW IN PIPE
INV EL =57.00'		INVERT ELEVATION OF PIPE
(S)		DENOTES SANITARY STACK/RISER
(W)		DENOTES WATER RISER
(G)		DENOTES NATURAL GAS RISER
(RL)		DENOTES RAINLEADER - ROOF STORM DRAINAGE GRAVITY DRAIN TO STORMWATER TANK
———F———		FIRE PROTECTION WATER - WET STANDPIPE SYSTEM
——☩——	O S. &Y	OPEN STEM & YOKE VALVE
⋈	FHV	FIRE HOSE VALVE
—SP—☩—		SPRINKLER SYSTEM SUPPLY PIPING - WET SYSTEM IN BUILDING WITH ZONE CONTROL VALVE TAMPER SWITCH, AND TEST/DRAIN ASSEMBLY
(F)		DENOTES FIRE PROTECTION STANDPIPE - WET STANDPIPE SYSTEM IN BUILDING

FIGURE 11.10 Standard plumbing symbols.

FIRE PROTECTION

Sprinkler systems were first developed in the United States in the 1870s to protect high-hazard industrial buildings, and today, represent the most common type of fire protection in use, and are especially common in new construction. The reason is that automatic sprinklers have provided an outstanding safety record in various applications, industrial, commercial and institutional, for well over a century.

Much like plumbing systems, sprinkler system piping is installed on inside walls adjacent to the ceiling framing and then insulated to entrap the available heat lost from the area below. There are essentially two types of sprinkler systems: 1. The *wet system* basically consists of a water system that is filled with water at design pressure and connected to sprinkler pipes on each floor that distribute the water to the individual sprinkler heads. Pressure gauges are located in the sprinkler risers, above and below each check valve (Figure 11.11). The water is released upon activation. 2. The *dry system* (or *dry-pipe system*), on the other hand, is a fire extinguishing sprinkler system whose pipes remain empty of water, using the pressure of compressed air or nitrogen to keep the pipes free of water until the system is activated. It is typically used in areas liable to freezing temperatures.

Halogenated extinguishing agents or *halons* may be used (instead of water) where water would damage the contents of a space such as in a computer facility. In this type of dry system, the halon gas is released when the system is triggered, smothering the fire while allowing people in the space to breathe. Halons can be extremely useful because they leave no residue to clean up after a fire and they do not cause thermal shock to delicate equipment. Dry chemical extinguishing agents are used mainly to combat fires involving flammable liquids (Class B) and electrical equipment (Class C). Local jurisdictions may additionally require the provision of back-up water based sprinkler systems (wet or dry) in areas of dry chemical use to provide supplemental basic building structure protection, as dry chemical systems may be considered incapable of providing adequate building/structural protection in a prolonged fire.

Modern sprinklers are inconspicuous, and typically, only the sprinkler heads are visible (except in parking garages and some warehouses). Moreover, sprinklers, cover plates, and escutcheons can be custom painted by the manufacturer to match any décor, and several styles are available, including recessed, upright, pendent, and sidewall. Recessed head types have a smooth cover that is set flush with the ceiling. When a fire occurs, the cover falls away and the sprinkler head lowers and activation is triggered. The activation temperature and density of discharge are determined by the risk factor and the ceiling height. Where aesthetic considerations are not critical, upright heads are used, for example, with exposed plumbing and high, unfinished ceilings. Pendent sprinklers are the traditional types for finished ceilings, but the head extends a few inches below the ceiling. Dry-pendent type are sometimes used in areas that are subject to freezing. Sidewall heads are used for corridors and small rooms when one row of sprinklers will provide adequate coverage for narrow spaces. Horizontal side-

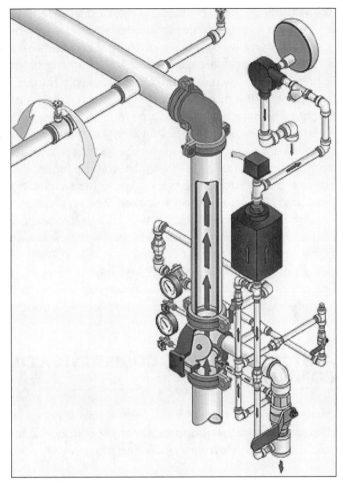

FIGURE 11.11 Typical sprinkler system diagram.

wall sprinklers also can be plumbed from the walls instead of from the ceiling, which makes them ideal for renovation work.

Local building codes govern the design and installation of sprinkler systems, although often, the National Fire Protection Association, NFPA-13, *Standard for the Installation of Sprinkler Systems*, is used as the standard reference. The NFPA has completely revised NFPA 13 to address all aspects of automatic sprinkler system design. It should be noted that statistics show that flame is not the main killer; it is the smoke that is the most lethal. Smoke spreads faster than a raging fire and contains lethal carbon monoxide. The NFPA-13 classifies the relative fire hazard of buildings into three main divisions: light hazard, ordinary hazard, and extra hazard.

Hazard classification and other requirements are the main requisites to determine the required spacing of sprinklers and the required water flow to sprinklers. The light hazard classification includes occupancies were combustibility is low, quantity of combustibles is low and fires with relatively low rates of heat release are expected. Office, educational residences, hospitals, restaurants, schools and Religious use groups are classified as light hazard.

In light hazard occupancies, the maximum protection area per sprinkler is 200 square feet, i.e., there must be one sprinkler for each 200 square feet, or 225 square feet if the system is designed to meet certain requirements. For open wood joist ceilings, the area decreases to 130 square feet. The maximum allowable distance between sprinkler heads, either on branch lines or between branch lines, shall be 15 feet for light hazard occupancies, for the 225-square foot coverage requirement. The distance from sprinklers to walls should not exceed one-half of the allowable distance (15 feet) between sprinklers. Maximum distance from sprinkler to wall is 7 feet 6 inches, except within small rooms, where sprinklers may usually be permitted to be located up to 9 feet from any single wall. The distance from sprinklers to walls shall not exceed one-half of the allowable distance (15 feet) between sprinklers.

Sprinkler head locations must be coordinated with other ceiling mounted items. When installing sprinkler pipes above the ceiling, the designer must ensure that there is sufficient space so as not to interfere with recessed lighting and other ceiling construction.

VERTICAL AND HORIZONTAL COMMUNICATIONS SYSTEMS (CONVEYANCE)

This section is concerned mainly with elevators, escalators and walks. Installing new elevators or refurbishing existing ones means the space planner may be required to become involved with the interior finishes of the cab, elevator lobbies, and the signal system of call buttons and up/down lanterns.

Elevators

In the 19th century, new iron and steel production processes revolutionized the construction industry as well as the way we lived. Architects and engineers now had the technology to build skyscrapers hundreds of feet in the air. But this would have meant little if not for another technological innovation that was introduced about the same time, the modern elevator (originally called hoists).

Most early elevators were powered by steam engines, and the world's first power elevator was a freight hoist installed in New York in 1850 by the inventor and manufacturer, Elisha Otis, and in 1857 he installed the first passenger elevator (also in New York). The great advances in electronic systems over the years resulted in many changes in elevator design and installation. Computing equipment was developed for compiling automatically information that greatly improved the operational efficiency of elevators in large buildings. The use of automatic programming equipment eventually eliminated the need for starters at the ground level of larger commercial buildings, and therefore the operation of elevators became completely automatic. This ushered in their use in buildings like New York's Empire State Building, the World Trade Center, Chicago's John Hancock Center, and Toronto's CN Tower. Factors that affect the number of cars needed, and hence, floor space to allocate, are based on:

- Building size and type
- A car's capacity
- Car speed
- Maximum acceptable waiting time (e.g. offices about 30 seconds, apartments about 90 seconds)
- Mode of control/operations. Modern systems are user-operated, with call buttons on each lobby, and floor-selector buttons in the cars.

There are essentially two main categories of elevator designs in common use today: *Roped elevators* and *Hydraulic elevators*. The most popular of these is the roped elevator (or cable system), in which the car is raised and lowered by traction steel ropes rather than pushed from below. The cable system is used in high-rise elevator installations that typically use gearless traction systems, as well as in mid-rise installations that generally use geared traction systems. The elevator has a counterweight that balances the weight of the car, and at the same time ensuring that the hoist-rope's friction grips the driving sheaves (pulleys) so that when you rotate the sheave, the ropes move too. The sheave is connected to an electric motor, and when the motor turns in one direction, the sheave raises the elevator, and when it turns in the opposite direction, the elevator is lowered.

The machinery to drive the elevator is housed in a machine room usually directly above the elevator hoistway. To feed electricity to the car and receive electrical signals from it, a multi-wire electrical cable connects the machine room to the car. The end is attached to the car and moves with it (Figure 11.12). Most modern traction elevators now have microprocessor controls that require air conditioning.

Hydraulic elevators are primarily used in low-rise installations, where moderate car speed is acceptable. The car is connected to the top of a long fluid-driven piston that moves up and down inside a cylinder. The hydraulic system is very simple and has three main elements:

1. A tank (the fluid reservoir)
2. A pump, powered by an electric motor
3. A valve located between the cylinder and the reservoir

Hydraulic elevators are not as versatile or efficient as roped elevators, nor do they have as many built-in safety systems.

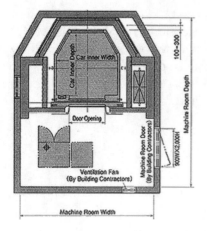

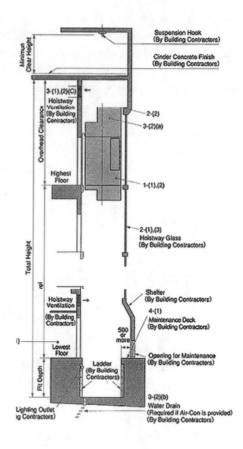

FIGURE 11.12 How a typical elevator works.

Escalators and Walks

In 1900, Charles D. Seeberger (inventor of the forerunner of the modern escalator) with Otis installed the first step-type escalator made for public use in the Paris Exhibition, where it won first prize. Escalators are suited to moving large numbers of people through a limited number of floors, particularly in department stores, airline terminals and public concourses (Figures 11.13, 11.14). Moving walks are increasingly being used at airports, train stations and major department stores to provide people with controlled and rapid horizontal and inclined transportation from one location to another, and are ideal for use wherever the elimination of long walks is desired (Figure 11.15). Capacity for both escalators and walks is governed mainly by an escalator's width. The planner should be aware of the weight of escalators and take it into consideration when using them in new or existing buildings.

The core of an escalator and walk, is a pair of chains that is looped around two pairs of gears that are driven by an electric motor (the motor also moves the handrails). The steps are designed to always stay level, at both top and bottom of the escalator, collapsing on each other to create a flat platform to allow persons to get on and off.

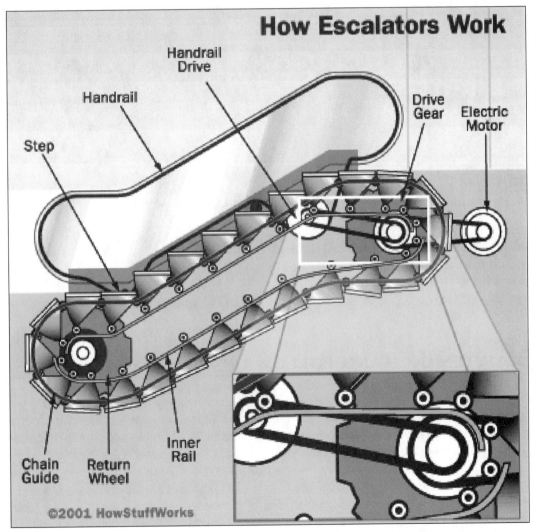

FIGURE 11.13 How escalators work. (*From How Escalators Work, http://www.howstuffworks.com, by Tom Harris, HowStuffWorks, Inc, 2002*)

FIGURE 11.14 A spiral escalator effectively used in the Yamako Department Store in Kofu, Japan. *(Courtesy Mitsubishi Electric Corporation)*

MAINTENANCE AND FOLLOW-UP

In commercial, institutional and other facilities, various hardware systems such as HVAC, emergency alarms, fire extinguishers, public address systems, emergency lighting, exit and evacuation route signs, emergency power generators, smoke and fire doors, fire department and hose systems, and fire pumps typically aid or play a direct role in controlling and mitigating the effects of disasters. Good maintenance of these systems is critical to the security and well being of the workplace and its occupants. In addition, periodical inspection and testing is often required by local, state or federal codes for compliance. Also, there are today numerous maintenance management software packages that offer various modules that can be of considerable assistance, particularly to larger facilities for tracking such as recording data on inspections, service and maintenance of key equipment.

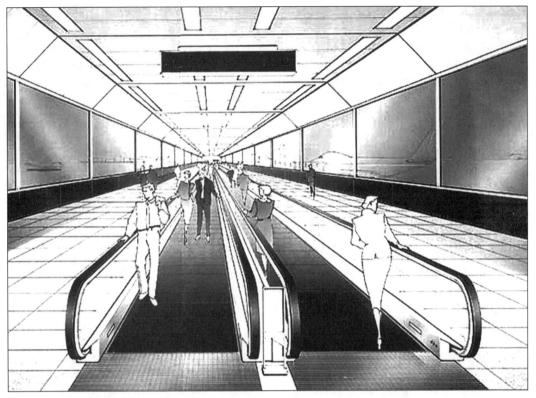

FIGURE 11.15 Example of a moving walk system often used in airports and train stations. *(Courtesy Mitsubishi Electric Corporation)*

THE FUTURE—WHAT LIES AHEAD?

In recent years, there has been a significant increase in the desire to develop innovative technologies with the aim of reducing emissions through improved combustion and environmental controls. This is apparent in HVAC systems in particular, and there is a real need for the development of a thermal strategy in design. In fact, we already have sufficient product technology to achieve the principal thermal goals. The question is, how can we achieve its optimum application at the design stage to meet the specific needs of particular buildings? There are a wide spectrum of factors that influence a building's thermal performance, including climate, building size, shape and orientation, site characteristics, fenestration type, size, shape and location, exterior and interior wall design and thermal characteristics and other factors including interior operating processes. It is one thing for a designer to be aware of these different factors, and it is another to be able to evaluate each element's relative importance in a particular situation.

Electrical service has a limited impact on the shape or form of a building, yet it has tremendous impact on its functionality. Not only does it impact the comfort systems, but it also plays a pivotal role in other building performance related functions like service control systems, telecommunications and security.

With respect to utility services, MEP designers often find themselves struggling to overcome the negative impact of human obstacles including resistance to innovation. However, there is increased evidence of a rising concern being voiced by many environmentalists and water authorities with both ecological and economic implications; it is the need to reduce water waste. Likewise, in drainage systems, one finds that hydraulic theory and potential systems innovation is well ahead of practice. There appears to be a lingering resistance to incorporating new materials and new ideas. Nevertheless, Green Building Council programs are becoming very popular and are resulting in great creativity to reduce energy and fostering reuse of existing and recycled materials.

With regard to fire safety, a reassessment of fire safety principles and their enforcement is overdue, and increased efforts need to be exerted—particularly with regard to improving basic escape provisions and related constructional compartmentation in areas where provisions are deficient or absent.

Advancement in conveyance system technology, on the other hand, is motivated largely by continuous economic incentives and increasing efficiency, even though it is already quite sophisticated in terms of speed and computerized control. Recent decades have been a witness to dramatic improvements in elevator controls, optimum response time, and improved ride quality.

CHAPTER
TWELVE

SECURITY
ISSUES

*I*n today's built environment, security has taken on a new meaning. Terrorism as well as natural disasters usually strike with little or no warning. Terrorism in particular is now a recognized international phenomenon against which governments need to institute protective measures. It is hardly surprising that in the wake of the gruesome 1995 Oklahoma City bombing and the September 11, 2001 terrorist attacks on the World Trade Center and the Pentagon, the issue of security in office buildings took on a new imperative.

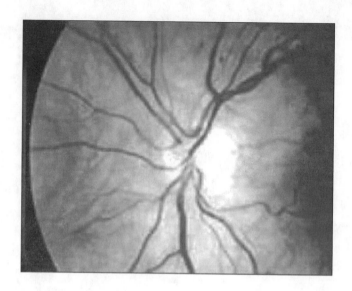

THE SECURITY EQUATION

The Oklahoma City bombing and World Trade Center disasters highlighted the lack of adequate security in public facilities as well as in the workplace. But today's disasters come in different shapes and forms, from inside or outside the building. Even disgruntled employees can become potential time bombs. Planners must, therefore, study all aspects of security including the new challenges they face today, whether it concerns employees, the building's structure, or the business.

Following the terrorist attacks of the last decade, designers and planners were suddenly faced with new questions about balancing security, freedom of movement and market realities. In the nine-story Alfred P. Murrah Federal Building in Oklahoma City, 168 people were killed, and in the World Trade Center attacks of 9/11, nearly 3,000 people were killed.

So, does this mean the end of the skyscraper as we know it? How does one design a more secure environment without turning the building into a fortress? Prince Charles of Britain, an outspoken adversary of tall buildings, was quite emphatic when he recently stated at a

London conference, "The destruction of the World Trade Center is unlikely to mark the end of tall buildings."

Society's need for security must be balanced against our traditional values as well as our psychological and spiritual needs, including those of openness and accessibility and all their ramifications in a free society. But even with revised design and engineering measures the threat of terrorism against property will not completely resolved. No building can be made 100 percent terrorist-proof. We must accept new realities in which there will always be a small risk involved with everything we do and wherever we live. Most building codes have developed over many decades, if not centuries, and this development reflects societal consensus. And while terrorism is a real threat, it is improbable that the September 11, 2001 attacks will, in the long term, force major changes. Changes will occur but only through innovation and only those that we as a society are willing to pay for. Employers should approach disaster preparedness in a pragmatic manner and develop a plan to minimize disaster exposure. Some local authorities and agencies mandate disaster preparedness programs, and require specific plan elements.

FIGURE 12.1 The September 11, 2001 terrorist attacks on the World Trade Center created a new imperative on the issues of building security.

TYPES OF SECURITY THREATS

There are many types of threats to an organization that can impact the safety and welfare of its employees, its profitability, and its very existence. The most important include:

Loss from Natural Disasters (Fire, Floods and Earthquakes)

Space planners and facilities professionals must ensure that disaster preparedness programs are put in place to combat the potential toll of natural forces such as floods, fires and earthquakes. Security expert Larry Chase says, "Flood waters often carry debris that can ram and rupture flammable liquid tanks or piping. These liquids, generally lighter than water, can float into areas where they might come into contact with an ignition source." Electric short circuits and broken gas lines are common occurrences after a flood and are a potential source of ignition.

Another potential security threat is that posed by earthquakes, and here, Chase correctly points out that much of the damage is the result of fires that follow the earthquake. Chase goes on to suggest that the threat of such post-tremor fires can be reduced by providing gas lines with shock-activated automatic shut-off valves that are activated by moderate ground motions. Chase also recommends the use of sway bracing on sprinkler systems to minimize movement, and also to avoid using automatic starting process equipment to prevent electrical service being restored without warning.

While direct fire exposure can cause enormous and costly damage to a facility, the emission of smoke and corrosive substances can be even more costly and can be extremely damaging to switches, computers and other electronic equipment. Planners should consider ways of minimizing these harmful effects, like installing low-smoke non-halogenated cables that resist fire propagation and generate minimum amounts of smoke and corrosive compounds, like.

Intellectual Property Loss

The American Society for Industrial Security indicates that intellectual property losses could surpass a quarter of a trillion dollars annually in the United States alone. Although a recent survey showed that 56 percent of respondents have had one or more incidents of attempted or suspected information misappropriation, 62 percent of the companies surveyed had no procedures in place for reporting information loss. No organization can afford continuous theft and loss of productivity that occurs daily due to inadequate security in many of today's businesses. Ira Winkler, an information security expert, says, "Information can make the difference between success and failure in business. Lose a trade secret to a competitor, and you lose the edge your product had. Lose a client list, and you lose the account. Lose too much, and you're out of business." In this electronic world we live in, one needs to apply simple common sense rules to protect your vital corporate information.

Techno-Terrorists and Hackers

During recent years, there have been many serious virus attacks on corporate systems. A single virus can bring down a company's computer network and cost thousands, if not millions, of dollars in terms of lost profits, productivity, and intellectual property.

Workplace Violence

There has been a recent increase in the public's awareness of the magnitude of workplace violence. The Bureau of Justice statistics shows that nearly one million individuals are victims of workplace violence and about 500,000 of those victims lose an estimated 1.8 million workdays and $55 million in lost wages. Furthermore, according to the National Institute of Occupational Safety and Health, 800 people are murdered at work annually. In many cases, it is disgruntled employees or employees recently fired from their jobs. The seriousness of the problem has prompted the Occupational Safety and Health Administration (OSHA) to commence citing employers who fail to protect workers from assault.

The first step in addressing this problem is through employee training. According to Laura Merisalo, a writer on workplace violence issues, "Facility managers need to examine issues such as building access control, design and layout of lobbies, reception and service areas; making sure there are no gaps in physical security." Surveys show that one of the weaknesses in building security is the loading dock or back door. Disgruntled or ill intentioned personnel who seek to do harm will seek out such vulnerable points. Access through rear or side doors should therefore be controlled, either through an electronic code or card system, or by some other means like a buzzer system. Likewise, isolated work spaces should be eliminated and high-visibility work areas created, because openness has been shown to be a strong deterrent. Once the vulnerable points are identified, steps can be taken to eliminate them.

Terrorism—Bombs and Explosives

In 1995, the National Research Council (NRC) published a report entitled *Protecting Buildings From Bomb Damage: Transfer of Blast-Effects Mitigation Technologies from Military to Civilian Applications.* This report showed that much of the knowledge acquired from structural research and testing carried out during the Cold War was generally applicable to civilian design practice today. The report also recommended continued research to find ways to reduce the damage and casualties caused by such attacks on large buildings as the Oklahoma City bombing and the 1993 World Trade Center attack. The design of blast-resistant structures and their subsystems is a long-established discipline practiced mostly by the military; however, these structures are usually located below grade. It is impractical to design conventional, above grade structures to be blast-resist because the potential risk cannot often be defined because we do not know which building is to be attacked and when. Furthermore, the potential threat cannot be quantified, because we are unaware of the type of weapon to be used, its capacity, or the proposed mode of delivery. In addition, as the general impact of blast pressures is far greater than that of gravity or wind loads; the resultant impact on cost, function, and appearance can be enormous and, therefore, unacceptable. Nevertheless, major improvements in susceptibility to a car bomb attack can be achieved by simply incorporating common sense, good structural systems, effective countermeasures and a well developed contingency or security plan.

Anatol Longinow, an expert on behavior of structures, states, "Over the past several decades a great deal of work has been performed to develop methods for mitigating the effects of a blast. Some of these methods were produced during the height of the cold war; others were developed as a result of the 1983 bombing of the U.S. Embassy in Beirut." Other devices, mitigation techniques, and materials are currently being developed to protect buildings against car bombs as well. At this point in time, to protect a building against bomb blasts would add additional design and construction costs which would be prohibitive.

Biochemical Terrorism

The potential for a bioterrorism attack on a building's air-handling system is daunting. Increased attention is now being paid to mechanical systems in terms of security and access, as well as filtering and detection.

DEFINING SECURITY NEEDS AND THE ROLE OF THE SPACE PLANNER

Security in the built environment is for the protection of people, information, and property. Security determinations are therefore essential in defining security needs prior to designing new facilities or retrofitting existing facilities. Attempting to overlay security strategies and measures after a design concept is in place can be very counter productive, causing delays and cost overruns. Moreover, while the scope and level of assessments within each facility will vary, the ultimate goal will remain the same—to decide upon an acceptable minimum level of security protection. There is an acute need for designers to develop strategies and methods for planning, designing, and constructing buildings that mitigate or minimize security threats, while simultaneously meeting other client needs for functional, comfortable, and aesthetically pleasing buildings.

The space planner must recognize the nature of security threats to the company and the built environment and the relative risks associated with those threats. To improve safety and security, steps need to be taken which should include:

1. *Asset Analysis:* The space planner/designer must identify and prioritize the assets that require protection. These include people, operations, vital data and property. People are essentially the chief asset of any organization as they have the operational and technical

know-how. Prioritizing assets can be achieved by examining the importance of various organizational functions to the survival of the organization. An AIA publication, *Building Security Through Design*, states that an asset analysis should address the following points:

- The nature of the asset needing protection (e.g., employees, proprietary information, trade secrets, personnel records)
- The value of the asset, including current and replacement value
- Where the asset is located
- How, when, and by whom an asset is accessed and used

2. *Threat Analysis—Identify and Fortify Security Weaknesses:* This includes understanding the real role of security in your organization and increasing security's importance in the day-to-day running of the business, and the understanding that security is a continuous process and not an end state. An evaluation should be conducted on the impact of inadequate security on the company's bottom line. An action plan should be in place with countermeasures for security breach prevention where possible incendiary situations exist, and after the fact when not. Contingency plans should be developed to counter various forms of security threats in the organization, including the following:

- Measures to counter threats at schools, medical facilities and other public places
- Conducting realistic drills to measure users' level of preparedness
- Determining what needs to go into your security plan, and putting your plan into action with a minimum of headaches
- Measuring the effectiveness of your plan and measures to be taken if the plan is not working to meet your needs
- Defining which areas of your property comprise the greatest safety and security risks. The owner must decide whether to contract out the company's security or use in-house security staff. If in-house security staff are used, strict standards need be set and met

3. *Vulnerability Assessments and Appropriate Response:* Vulnerability means any weakness that allows the implementation of a threat. Once vulnerable points are identified, corrective countermeasures can be put in place. Your vulnerability assessment and a cost-benefits analysis determine what kind of response is appropriate, passive or active. Active systems include electronic entry controls, closed circuit TV, intrusion detection and many other technology solutions. Scanners, turnstiles and cameras are expensive but manpower costs even more. Effective passive systems like landscaping, bollards, lighting, physical barriers and evacuation and response plans can be incorporated in place of or in addition to active systems. Many designers are also now considering the use of explosion-resistant glass in important structures. There would be a premium of possibly 20

percent or more for features like two inch (5 cm.) thick glass, Kevlar panels, and special fireproof fabrics. It is unlikely that typical new construction will incorporate these changes without further drastic events. Nevertheless, "We can make effective changes through common sense threat assessment, responding appropriately, and using good design to ensure that solutions are effective and lasting," says Kate Kirkpatrick of Gensler.

4. *Risk Analysis and Threat Assessment:* Risk potential can be determined from the findings of asset, threat, and vulnerability analyses. These results can help determine the security measures that need to be put in place to effectively counteract a potential threat. The most realistic threat to the majority of us is day-to-day is workplace violence. Threats must be gauged in the context of the existing facilities. For example, are the facilities a likely target for workplace violence or a car bomb or somewhere in between? We need to examine the vulnerability of our infrastructure systems. Ira Winkler, author of *Corporate Espionage* uses the Risk Equation shown below to define an organization's specific level of risk.

$$\text{RISK} = \frac{\text{Threat} \times \text{Vulnerability}}{\text{Countermeasures}} \times \text{Value}$$

METHODS FOR IMPROVING SAFETY AND SECURITY

The most common methods and approaches that are practiced today to improve safety and security of building environments are outlined below:

Access Control

According to security expert Jeffrey Dingle, the basic concept of access control is simple: "Decide who can come in, and keep everyone else out." Dingle defines access control as "the use of barriers and recognition devices to restrict access into a controlled area." Access control systems can provide an enhanced level of security. But as with all security systems, any increase in the level of security brings with it a potential increase in the level of inconvenience.

Although access control can be overt and obvious, in most applications it makes better sense to be low key and unobtrusive. Building occupants and visitors often experience a certain level of discomfort when physical barriers are present, particularly if they appear obtrusive. Safety and security measures should be balanced and integrated into the design so as to give the appearance of art, or blend into its surrounds so as to become inconspicuous. Better control of entrances can be achieved through integrated bollards and standards that act as barriers to protect entrances from vehicles.

Access control systems typically consist of two main parts: The first is Equipment and Hardware, and the second, Policies and Procedures. A successful access control system must achieve two principle objectives: First, the building or area must be secured to prevent all unauthorized persons from gaining access except by going through a control point; second, there must be a specific list of persons that have authorized access. Once the decision is made on who is allowed access, systems can be designed and put into place to keep everyone else out.

In multi-tenant facilities, there are many forms of additional controls that can be established to prevent unauthorized access. A very common form is the use of card-controlled elevators, in which an access card is needed to stop the elevator on the desired floor. In new high-rise construction, garage and basement level elevators are typically located in a different area from those serving tenant floors. This is a conscious design decision and necessitates a person first exiting the garage or basement elevator in order to re-enter a tenant floor elevator, passing through the lobby area on the way.

Some facilities are spread out and have multiple entrances which makes them more difficult to control and sustain. In such circumstances, a single access control system can be spread out over several buildings, or a single access point, such as a gate in a fence, can be established for the entire facility. In many applications it is pertinent to install a single-door access system, even if the cost is high. When retrofitting existing facilities, high costs can be mitigated by the use of a single-door system or an off-line reader—a single-door system that operates independently and is not tied into the control system.

Types of Access Control Systems

Access control systems basically rely on one or a combination of four basic operating concepts: personal recognition, unique knowledge, unique possession, and biometric devices.

Personal Recognition

This depends on the ability of an individual to recognize employees and authorize access. A facility with small employee base along with a low turnover rate can make personal recognition very secure. The main disadvantages are that security staff turnover wipes out the access control database, and turnover of employees can make it difficult for the security staff to keep track of who is and is not allowed in.

Unique Knowledge

This requires a person to have special information or knowledge to gain access, for example, a push-button combination lock. The advantage is that there is nothing to lose. The disadvantage is that it is possible for an authorized user to give a code or combination to an unauthorized user. Another common mistake is that individuals predictably write codes or combinations down. During security surveys, security specialists routinely look in Rolodexes under safe, combination or door, and very often find combinations or access codes. Codes also are often written under desk calendars. Keypad access systems also require a person to have knowledge of the correct numerical access code to gain access. The combination or code is entered into a four-, six- or ten-digit keypad. Keypad systems can be electronic and tied into a system, or mechanical and stand-alone like a single-door, push-button door access system.

Unique Possession

Systems based on unique possession require a person to possess something that allows access. The most common unique possession system is a key and lock. A weakness in a unique possession system is that it will allow access to anyone who is in possession of the item, whether or not they are allowed access.

One increasingly common way to control access is through card readers. Each person who will require access receives a card. Each access card leaves an audit trail—a record of who enters and when. Most systems allow access time windows to be created, so that the time when each person has access can be limited. Remember, the system records what card opened the door, not who opened the door. Employees must be discouraged from loaning their cards to others, and it is very important for the user to protect his or her card. To overcome this problem, smart cards have been developed with embedded microchips that contain an encoded biometric description of the cardholder, so that when the card passed through a reader, the machine would verify that the card belonged to the person who presented it.

Biochemical Terrorism

The potential for a bioterrorism attack on a building's air-handling system is daunting. Increased attention is now being paid to mechanical systems in terms of security and access, as well as filtering and detection. While no building can be completely immune from a determined individual who is intent on releasing a chemical, biological, or radiological (CBR) agent, the threat from such an attack, can be minimized by taking certain precautions. One of the most important steps in protecting a building's indoor environment is the security of the outdoor air intakes (Figure 12.2a), Physically inaccessible outdoor air intakes are the preferred protection strategy. Where this is not possible, perimeter barriers that prevent public access to outdoor air intake areas may form an effective alternative. The use of iron fencing or similar see-through barriers that will not obscure visual detection of terrorist activities are recommended (Figure 12.2b).

Biometric Devices

Biometric systems are generally considered the most secure single method, and the biometrics industry alone is expected to grow to about $2 billion by 2004. These systems grant or deny access to buildings, information and benefits by automatically verifying the identity of people through their unique physical characteristics, such as thumbprints, palm scans, voiceprints or iris checks. The information received is translated algorithmically into a complex string of numbers and is compared with a stored template of that person in a central database. Many biometric

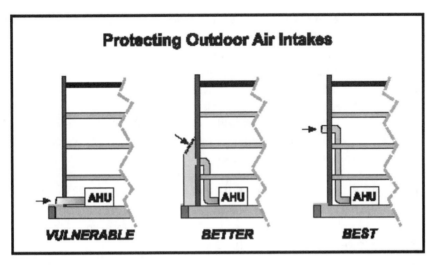

FIGURE 12.2a Securing the outdoor air intakes is a critical line of defense in limiting an external CBR attack on a building.

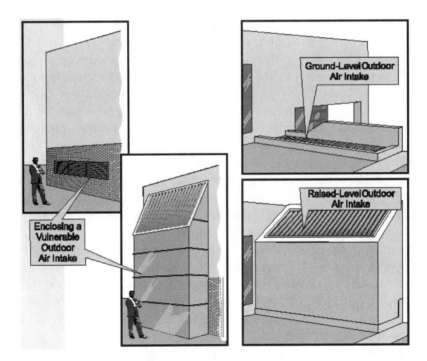

FIGURE 12.2b Where the establishment of a security zone around an outdoor air intake is not a viable option, the erection of iron fencing or similar see-through barriers may be an acceptable alternative.

experiments are underway throughout the world, particularly following the September 11, 2001 terrorist attacks. Such systems are based on digital analysis using cameras or scanners of biological characteristics such as facial or palm structures, fingerprints (Figure 12.3) and retinal and iris patterns that are matched with profiles in available databases of people such as suspected terrorists (Figures 12.4, 12.5).

The main disadvantage of biometric devices is that some systems can be extremely expensive. Nevertheless, some of the newer biometric technology such as face recognition (Figure 12.6), is being adopted at several international airports, but while potentially very promising, it still has some way to go before it can be used with confidence.

Typically, a combination of more than one of these methods offers the soundest security solution. One method is the use of a card access system with a PIN number: Access is achieved by both having the card as well as knowing the PIN number. Modern photo ID cards can contain a combination of unique possession (the card), unique knowledge (PIN) and personal identification (a person's photo on the card).

Choosing the Right System

Before making a determination on what system is right for a particular facility, many issues need to be considered, including access time, imposter resistance, reliability and error rate, ease of use, user acceptance, input time and effort, storage, and cost.

Access time and imposter resistance are critical factors when selecting access control systems. Access is the time taken by someone to use the system and for the system to respond positively. Access can take from a few seconds to a few minutes. Access time (sometimes called throughput) becomes critical in situations where large numbers of people require simultaneous passage, for example, during a shift change. Imposter resistance is the ability of unauthorized persons to gain access by convincing the system that they are authorized. Thus, a simple key and lock has no imposter resistance, whereas biometric systems have a high level of imposter resistance. The level for imposter resistance relates directly to the level of security required.

Other critical aspects of access control systems are their error rate and effectiveness. An access control system can respond in one of four ways to a request for access: 1. positive (the rate at which persons who are allowed access are granted access), 2. false/positive (the rate at which persons who should be denied access are granted access; access is allowed through deception or error), 3. negative (the rate at which persons who should be denied access are denied access) and 4. false/negative (the rate at which persons who should be allowed access are denied due to error). It is obviously better from a failure rate and security standpoint to keep out people who should get in than let people in who should be kept out.

Ease of use and user acceptance are unique to each site. Ease of use simply means that the intended users are capable of using the system. User acceptance is often a function of good public relations. People often associate additional security measures with additional

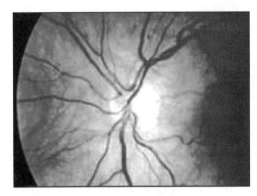

FIGURE 12.4 Retinal scanning.

FIGURE 12.3 Plug-and-play fingerprint reader can confirm if people are who they claim to be, by matching fingerprint templates stored in a central database.

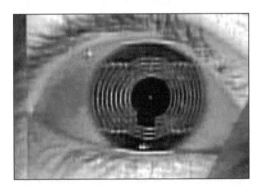

FIGURE 12.5 Iris scanning is one of the promising biometric devices being developed.

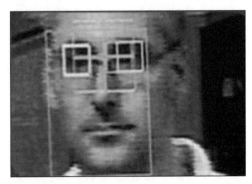

FIGURE 12.6 Face recognition shows promise but is still not totally reliable.

inconvenience; it is essential therefore, to keep access systems simple and whenever possible, to minimize the inconvenience.

The initial amount of time and effort to input everyone into the system is called the input or enrollment time. Biometric systems compare the biological characteristics of a person to those on file in a central database. These biometric features need at some point to be entered into the system. So, if it takes five minutes to input data for an employee into the system, and the organization has a thousand employees, it would take more than ten days to input (i.e. create employee files) all employees into the system, and that's based on the premise that one is working a continuous eight hour day. One must also not forget the importance of reliability and cost of any system considered.

Security technology is evolving at a rapid pace and recent developments include intelligent software such as Loronix's BehaviorTrack, that generates real-time alert alarming, thus allowing for the appropriate proactive action to be taken immediately. Such proactive action may be related to addressing a security breach or a customer service need.

EGRESS PLANNING AND EMERGENCY MANAGEMENT

Confusion often contributes to the loss of life at times of emergency, partly due to the issuing of conflicting instructions on where to go, unclear exit signs, etc. A survey conducted by the Society for Human Resource Management after the September 2001 attacks found that 35 percent of American companies had no emergency plans in place.

The education of owners and tenants about emergency systems of buildings should go hand in hand with engineering and design. Corporate clients are now showing a heightened awareness concerning the security of their buildings and sites. Enlightened clients are more frequently asking architects and space planners to explore increasing the width of exit stairs over code minimums to allow firefighters to travel up while still permitting the building occupants to exit. During an emergency, good communication is vital. An evacuation response to a bomb threat will differ significantly from a fire. One calls for a controlled exit while the other necessitates a speedy exit.

THE PARKING PROBLEM

The 1993 World Trade Center experience clearly highlighted the fact that a public parking garage located within a building is a likely target to place a car bomb. To eliminate this potential threat, one can implement one of two strategies: restrict the garage to building occupants and inspect every car that enters, or eliminate parking in the building altogether. These choices obviously raise serious practical issues, particularly in urban areas, and the inconvenience may not be acceptable.

Kate Kirkpatrick of Gensler states, "While garages that serve government tenants require employee badges for parking or restrict truck access to patrolled areas, most of us just pay and drive in. And now we're all wondering what kind of threats are pulling into the basement. Potential solutions include requiring employee badges for garage entry, limiting self-parking to badge holders, and restricting large vehicles to controlled areas." Some local parking companies are assessing the situation and making changes as needed, but the majority feel that they have the situation under control.

The installation of a strong perimeter fence around a building offers better protection against a car bomb attack than one where a car may be parked directly next to the building. Furthermore, a strong perimeter fence located some distance from the building is likely to marginalize the effect of a car bomb, unless the bomb is massive in size. Security areas and lobby functions are interdependent. Security screening should occur at entry and lead directly to the lobby and other areas. A lobby's internal circulation, should not impede security processing. Further, the lobby should function freely and logically, and not compromised the circulation pattern.

NEW GSA (GENERAL SERVICES ADMINISTRATION) STANDARDS

Planners can find federal government standards for security requirements for their buildings on line, providing a good resource on the subject. In the United States, several design firms like Gensler have taken the initiative in convening a series of regional dialogues regarding strategic planning and ways to balance security with openness. These seminars covered a number of topics including topics such as facility audits, circulation diagrams, and strategies for integrating security procedures and equipment in a "Class A" environment. In the United Kingdom, firms like Foster and Partners assembled a multidisciplinary team to investigate rapid evacuation concepts and the emergency response of buildings. Also, as mentioned earlier, in the wake of the September 11, 2001 terrorist attacks, the American Institute of Architects (AIA) published an excellent booklet, *Building Security by Design: A Primer for Architects, Design Professionals, and their Client*, which summarizes security issues and ways to deal with them. Design professionals understanding that it will take both government and private sector organizations working in close liaison to rise to the new challenges facing our nation and the free world. A steering committee was formed by the Infrastructure Security Partnership (TISP) to guide the collaborative efforts of several federal agencies and leading design and construction industry groups on issues relating to the security of the nation's structures and other types of man-made infrastructure.

Many studies are underway in the search for ways and means to improve safety and security in tall buildings. These include examining the impact resistance of structural fire protection materials, additional protection to escape routes as well as hardening escape stairs and corridors to provide impact resistance and protection against extreme fire events, a more detailed analysis of the risk of severe damage to structural elements in the event of fire, increasing the number or capacity of stairs, upgrading lifts with emergency power, and employing or training fire evacuation marshals.

The consulting firm Arup Ltd., of London, proved that properly protected elevators can assist rapid evacuation. Their study on a 50-story building in London showed that the use of elevators nearly halved the escape time compared to using stairs only. Arup believes that building owners and tenants should be informed of relative risks from difference sources. Reconfiguring the core can provide cost-effective refuge areas with a dedicated elevator and stairwell for emergency egress without increasing core square footage. The system bundles a service elevator for use by firefighters, a lobby, and a stairwell in a pressurized shaft. Arup is looking at evacuation procedures from offshore oil rigs, and aviation and other industries. The National Fire Protection Association has begun the development of a security code that will mandate minimum levels of protection.

LEGAL AND LIABILITY ISSUES

Due to the complexity of the matters involved, this chapter cannot possibly address the many concerns and legal issues that may arise with regard to liability issues, and designers are strongly advised to consult their attorneys and professional liability insurance carriers for advice on these matters. The number of liability lawsuits filed against American companies have increased over 260 percent in the last decade. Statistics show that the average negotiated settlement in a liability lawsuit is more than $545,000 and the average jury award is $3.35 million.

Planners need to understand the measures that can be taken to reduce an organization's legal liability within the building, the parking lot and further. Planners must also comprehend and address scope of work, disclaimers, and other essential elements of premises liability lawsuits with respect to how far the law defines an owner's responsibility to protect facility users. In addition, planners should identify the interaction between OSHA and organizational security and check whether the client is compliant under OSHA's General Duty Clause. The client should be made aware of the safety and security requirements relating to ADA. Unusual behavior of disgruntled employees should be tracked, and protective measurements should be put in place when management terminates a troubled employee.

Finally, while people may be tolerant of inconvenience while the image of terror is still fresh in their minds, they will soon resist security that is inconvenient once the image of terror fades. Innovative solutions are needed when retrofitting traditional office buildings and, in particular, federal government and institutional lobbies, which were not designed to accommodate current security equipment and needs. Since it seems that increased security is going to be with us for the foreseeable future, designers need to take advantage of advances in technology to make security stations less imposing and more acceptable. The psychological and functional requirements for increased security and defensible space should be achieved through the use of integrated security solutions that are balanced, pleasing and do not disrupt a building's efficiency.

CHAPTER THIRTEEN

SPECIFICATION WRITING

*D*rawings alone cannot define the qualitative issues of a scheme, which is why specifications are necessary. Specifications are the written portion of the contract documents that are used to execute the project, and should complement the drawings, not overlap or duplicate information on the drawings. Design decisions are continuously made as drawings proceed from schematic sketches to construction documents.

GENERAL OVERVIEW

Drawings depict the general configuration and layout of the interior design, including its size, shape, and dimensions. It tells the contractor the quantities of materials needed, their placement, and their general relationship to each other. Technical specifications, on the other hand, are a form of materials list that requires similar decision making that reflects the design intent and describes in detail the quality and character of materials, the standards to which the materials and their installation shall conform, and other issues that are more appropriately described in written, rather than graphic form.

Specifications are legal documents, and should therefore be complete, accurate, and unambiguous. Specification writing has two main roles: defining the scope of work, and acting as a set of instructions. At the core of specification writing is defining the scope of work. Ensuring that the required level of quality of the product and services is clearly communicated to bidders and that the completed project conforms to this specified quality is extremely important, yet often misunderstood. Construction specifications, on the other hand, differ from furniture specifications in their content, scope, and form. Most projects now incorporate the specifications within a project manual (a concept first developed by the AIA in 1964) and are issued along with the drawings, bidding requirements, and other contract conditions as part of the contract documents package.

New technologies are changing the way we do business, and spec writing is not immune. Specification production and reproduction have advanced by leaps and bounds in just a short time period, due to these new technologies. Master systems are now commercially available in electronic form using a number of word processors. The specifier simply loads the master system into the computer and gets instant access to the master system, complete with drawing checklist and explanation sheets. Upon editing the relevant sections, a print out can be made with an audit trail that informs what has been deleted and what decisions must be made. Most offices in the United States use an 8½ x 11 inch format while in Europe an A4 (8¼ x 11¾ inches) format is typically used.

SPECIFICATION MATERIAL SOURCES

Because of time and cost restraints, few individuals (or small firms) would today venture to write a completely new set of specifications for each job. Specifiers would normally rely on the many sources and reference material that is currently available and from which they could compile a set for each new project. Moreover, because of liability issues, specifiers often feel more comfortable relying on specifications that have repeatedly proved satisfactory in the past. When specs have to be modified to fit the conditions of a given job, or new specs incorporated, text is generally taken from one of the master spec systems. These contain guide specifications for many materials, allowing the specifier to edit out unnecessary text rather than generate new information each time.

Another advantage of using master systems is that they use correct specification language and format for ease of specification preparation. Listed below are some of the major sources from which specification material is available, much of which can be retrieved via the Internet:

- Master specifications (Masterspec®, SPECSystem™, MasterFormat™, SpecText®, BSD Speclink®, ezSPECS On-Line™, CAP Studio—for the furniture industry, and many others)
- City and national codes and ordinances
- Manufacturers' industry associations (Architectural Woodworking Institute, American Plywood Association, Door and Hardware Institute, Title Council of America)
- Manufacturers' catalogs (Sweet's Catalog File, Man-U-Spec, Spec-data)
- Manufacturers' online catalogs via the Internet (Figure 13.1)

- National standards organizations such as the American National Standards Institute, National Institute of Building Sciences, The National Fire Protection Association, The National Institute of Standards and Technology, and the Association for Contract Textiles (Figure 13.2)
- Testing societies (American Society for Testing and Materials, Underwriters Laboratories)
- Federal specifications (Specs-In-Tact, G.S.A., N.A.S.A., N.A.F.V.A.C.)
- Magazines and publications (Construction Specifier, Architecture, Architectural Record)
- Books on specifications (see bibliography)
- Individual files of previously written specifications

During recent years, numerous firms that provide online specification writing services have emerged. These services are discussed later in the chapter.

TYPES OF SPECIFICATIONS

One of the first things that a specifier has to decide upon when preparing a specification document is the format or method to be used to communicate the desired intent to the contractor. There are essentially two broad categories of specifications, *Closed* or *Open*, and most items can be specified by either method. Within these two broad categories, there are basically four generic types of specifications: 1. Propriety Specifications 2. Description Specifications, 3. Performance Specifications, and 4. Reference Standards Specifications. The type chosen depends on several factors (Figure 13.3). These are discussed below.

Closed Specification

Closed (also called Prescriptive or Restrictive) specification is one that limits acceptable products to one or a few brand-identified types or models and prohibits substitutions. This type of specification is sometimes used where specifiers feel more comfortable resorting to a specific propriety product with which they are familiar, and which will meet the specific criteria of the project. However, it should be noted that this procedure (particularly when only one product is named) is not competitive, and rarely attracts the most favorable price for the owner. Although closed specifications is common in private construction work, most public projects are required by law to be bid under open specifications.

The *closed proprietary specification* method is the easiest form to write but is the most restrictive, in that it names a specific manufacturer's product. It generally establishes a narrower definition of acceptable quality than do performance or reference standard methods, and gives the designer/space planner complete control over what is installed. The specification can also be written as an open proprietary section, in which multiple manufacturers or

FIGURE 13.1 Knoll Upholstery Textiles downloaded from the Internet. Specifications for the desired material can be downloaded and/or printed directly from the manufacturer's website.

products are named or alternatives solicited. This would increase the potential competition and encourage a lower installation price from vendors. In some cases, a multiple choice may not be appropriate, as for example where a specific brick is required for repairs to an existing brick facade. When the specification does not allow for any substitution of materials, it is known as a *base bid* proprietary specification.

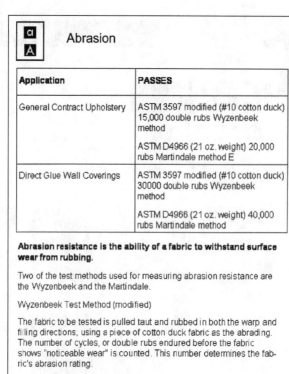

FIGURE 13.2 The Association for Contract Textiles (ACT) Requirements for Abrasion Resistance of Upholstery and Direct Glue Wall Covering Fabrics.

Open Specifications

Also called Performance or Nonrestrictive, this type of specification gives the contractor some choice in how to achieve the desired results. *Proprietary specifications* may also be used as open specifications but with the addition of the "or equal" clause, which allows the contractor to consider other products for bid if they are shown to be equal in performance and specifications. Due to the ambiguity surrounding this clause, and the disagreements it often perpetuates, specifiers generally shy away from incorporating it into the proprietary specifications.

Performance Attribute / Open Planned Office Components	Health-Safety						Durability					Maintenance				Function				
	Flammability	Cause falls	Sharp projections	Anthropomorphic fit	Reflectance: glare	Handicapped use	Structurally sound	Positive attachment	Color stability	Lightfastness	Abrasion resistance	Cleanability	Component repair	Component storage	Relocation	Flexibility	Privacy	Color homogeneity	Acoustic control	Energy control
Vertical Panels	•	•	•		•	•	•	•	•	•	•	•	•	•	•	•	•	•	•	
Worksurfaces		•	•	•	•		•	•	•	•	•	•	•	•	•	•		•		
Filing	•	•	•	•		•	•	•	•			•	•	•	•	•		•		
Shelves and Storage		•	•	•	•	•	•	•	•			•	•	•	•	•		•		
Lighting				•	•		•	•	•			•	•	•	•	•				•
Seating	•	•	•	•	•	•	•	•	•	•	•	•	•	•	•	•		•		
Tables		•	•	•	•	•	•	•	•	•	•	•	•	•	•	•		•		
Other																				

Performance Attributes of Open Plan Office Furniture.

FIGURE 13.3 Illustrates the various types of specifications. *(From S.C. Razni-coss, Specifications for Commercial Interiors, Whitney Library of Design)*

A second method of open specifications that is gaining popularity is the *descriptive specification.* This type of specification describes in detail the requirements for the material or product and the workmanship required for its fabrication and installation without providing a trade name. This type of specifications is often stipulated by some government agencies to allow the maximum competition among product manufacturers. Descriptive specifications are also more difficult to write than proprietary ones because the specifier must include all the product's relevant characteristics in the specification.

A third type of specification that is often used is the *reference standard.* This standard simply describes a material, product, or process referencing a recognized industry standard or test method as the basis for the specification and is often used to specify generic materials such as portland cement and clear glass. Thus, in specifying gypsum wallboard for example, you can state that all gypsum wallboard products shall meet the requirements of ASTM C36. As this document describes in detail the requirements for this product, the specifier is relieved of having to repeat the requirements and can instead refer to the recognized industry standard. In using a reference standard, the specifier should not only have a copy of that standard, but should also know what is required by the standard, including choices that may be contained therein, and which should be enforced by all suppliers. This type of specification is fairly easy to write and is generally short. In addition, the use of reference standard specifications reduces your liability and the possibility for errors.

The fourth major type of specifications used is the *performance specifications*. This type of specification establishes the performance requirements without dictating the methods by which the end results are to be achieved. This gives the greatest leeway to contractors because it allows them to use any material or system that meets the performance criteria specified, provided the results can be verified by measurement, tests, or other types of evaluation.

Performance specifications are not often used by space planners or interior designers because they are the most difficult to write. The specifier must know all the criteria for a product or system, state the appropriate methods for testing compliance, and write an unambiguous document. In addition, sufficient data must be provided to ensure that the product can be demonstrated. Performance specifications are mostly used in specifying complex systems, and where a specifier wants to encourage new ways of achieving a particular result. Figure 13.4 compares the different types of specifications.

Product specifications often use a combination of methods to convey the designer's intent. For example, a specification for a ceramic tile would use a proprietary specification to name the product or products selected by the specifier, a descriptive specification to specify the size and design, and a reference standard to specify the ASTM standard, grade, and type required.

ORGANIZING THE PROJECT MANUAL

Traditionally, the organization of the project manual has been a matter of individual preference by the design firm producing them, resulting in a wide diversity of method around the country that became confusing. As design firms and contractors became increasingly nationwide in their operations, a pressing need grew for a consistent arrangement of building construction specifications. To meet this challenge, the American Institute of Architects (AIA) in 1964 developed the concept of the Project Manual, which has now gained wide acceptance. Essentially, it contains the technical specifications, as well as several other types of documents, which together with the drawings, constitute the contract documents. A typical table of contents for the Project Manual might show the following major divisions:

- Bidding Requirements. This applies where contracts are awarded through the bidding process. These would include:
  - Invitation to bid (or Advertisement)
  - Prequalification forms

Prescriptive—Restrictive				Performance—Nonrestrictive	
Proprietary Base Bid	**Proprietary or Equal**	**Descriptive**	**Reference Standards**	**Performance**	**Performance plus Descriptive**
Part 2: Materials	**Part 2: Materials**	**Part 2: Materials**	**Part 1: General**	**Subsystem: Carpet**	**Part 2: Materials**
Manufacturer: Corporation A: Brand Name Style: #245 Cascade Color: 17849	*Manufacturers:* Corporation A: Brand name Corporation B: Brand name Corporation C: Brand name *or*	*Carpet:* (no brand name)	*Quality Assurance References:* ANSI A17.1-1986, "Specifications for Making	*Attribute:* Fire Safety	*Carpet Performance and Design Requirements:* Design carpet for the following conditions:
Base Bid: When brand names are used no substitute products will be considered.	*Approved Equal* Proposed substitutions must be given complete consideration, statement of procedure for determining what is "equal" must be included.	*Construction Type:* Tufted or other *Pile Yarn:* Generic *Gauge or Pitch* *Stitches per Inch or Wires* *Pile Height or Wire Height* *Dyeing Method* *Yarn Size and Ply* *Width*	Buildings and Facilities Accessible to, and Usable by, the Physically Handicapped." American National Standards Institute, 1430 Broadway, New York, NY 10018 (A-210,	*Requirement:* Provide flame-spread resistance. *Criteria:* This subsystem shall provide a maximum flame-spread rating of 25.	1. Maximum static electricity . . .2.5 Kv 2. Tuft bind to resist . . .12 lbs/in.
	or Modified or Approved Equal. (1) Required definite prebid deadline for submittal of request. (2) Federal, state or city projects require specifier to include salient characteristics of the item to provide a basis for judging equality.	*Pile Yarn Weight and Total Weight* *Primary and Secondary Backing* *Detailed Installation Information*	A-5-2.2.4a., A-8-4.5, A-10-1.1.2). NFPA 255-1984, "Standard Method of Test for Critical Radiant Heat Energy Source." National Fire Protection Association, Batterymarch Park, Quincy, MA 02269 (A-12-3.3.2)	*Test:* Type—Calculation method ASTM-E 84, "Surface Burning Characteristics of Building Materials." American Society for Testing and Materials.	*Carpet Construction* Materials to conform to AATCC 134-1979. Electrostatic Propensity of Carpets. 2.5 Kv at 20% RH and 70° F.

These types of "closed" or restrictive specifications require exact products by brand name, model number, and all important characteristics. Quoted test data is supplied by the manufacturer. Drawings also show dimensions and engineering aspects of the particular product. Examples on pages 105, 107, and 139.

Descriptive: (1) Avoid conflicts with drawings. (2) Research all products. (3) Compare costs vs. performance. (4) State required submittals, including tests and standards.
Reference: (1) Know the standard. Have a copy in designers' office files. (2) Avoid use of only minimum standards. (3) Use full names and dates of the referenced standards. (4) Enforce the requirements. Examples on pages 127 and 130.

Performance specifications: (1) Use no manufacturers or trade names. (2) Desired results are stated. (3) Method to achieve end result not included in document.
Performance combination: Descriptive and reference standard specifications can produce nonrestrictive specifications. Only essential criteria that will meet intended use are stated. Specifier must ensure that criteria can be met by several manufacturers. See example on page 257.

FIGURE 13.4 Diagram illustrating performance attributes of open plan office furniture. *(From S.C. Raznicoss, Specifications for Commercial Interiors, Whitney Library of Design)*

- Instructions to bidders
- Bid form
- Information available to bidders

- Contract forms, may include:
  - Agreement (the contract between owner and contractor)
  - Performance bond
  - Labor and materials payment bond
  - Certificates of insurance

- Contract Conditions (general and supplementary). General conditions of the contract such as AIA Form 201 or similar preprinted forms. Supplementary conditions include anything that is not covered in the general conditions, such as addenda (changes made before contract signing), and change orders (changes made after contract signing).

- Technical specifications: These provide technical information concerning the building materials, components, systems and equipment shown on the Drawings with regard to quality, performance characteristics, and stipulated results to be achieved by application of construction methods (Figure 13.5).

WRITING AND COORDINATION GUIDELINES

As mentioned earlier, specifications are legal documents and their language must be precise, and if the written text is ambiguous or inadequate, the specification will not communicate. Moreover, a convention has developed over the years as to the information that should be shown on the drawings and that which should be indicated in the specifications. This is essentially based on a number of broad general principles which include:

- Drawings should convey information that can be most readily and effectively expressed graphically by means of drawings and diagrams. This would include data such as dimensions, sizes, gauges, proportions, arrangements, locations and interrelationships.

- Specifications should convey information that is easier to convey through the written word, such as descriptions, standards, procedures, guarantees, and names

- Drawings are used to express quantity, whereas specifications should describe quality

- Drawings should denote type (for example, wood) while specifications will clarify the species (for example, oak)

Some exceptions to these understandings sometimes create confusion. For example, building departments of the majority of municipalities will only accept drawings with applications

MASTERSPEC®

TABLE OF CONTENTS   SMALL PROJECT™ Specifications

©2001 American Institute of Architects

Issue Date	Sect. No.	SECTION TITLE	Issue Date	Sect. No.	SECTION TITLE
DIVISION 1 - GENERAL REQUIREMENTS			**DIVISION 6 - WOODS AND PLASTICS**		
5/1/01	00000	SECTION TEMPLATE	5/1/01	06100	ROUGH CARPENTRY
5/1/01	01100	SUMMARY	5/1/01	06105	MISCELLANEOUS CARPENTRY
5/1/01	01200	PRICE AND PAYMENT PROCEDURES	5/1/01	06176	METAL-PLATE-CONNECTED WOOD TRUSSES
5/1/01	01300	ADMINISTRATIVE REQUIREMENTS	5/1/01	06185	STRUCTURAL GLUED-LAMINATED TIMBER
5/1/01	01400	QUALITY REQUIREMENTS	5/1/01	06200	FINISH CARPENTRY
5/1/01	01420	REFERENCES	5/1/01	06401	EXTERIOR ARCHITECTURAL WOODWORK
5/1/01	01500	TEMPORARY FACILITIES AND CONTROLS	5/1/01	06402	INTERIOR ARCHITECTURAL WOODWORK
5/1/01	01600	PRODUCT REQUIREMENTS			
5/1/01	01701	EXECUTION AND CLOSEOUT REQUIREMENTS	**DIVISION 7 - THERMAL AND MOISTURE PROTECTION**		
5/1/01	01732	SELECTIVE DEMOLITION	5/1/01	07115	BITUMINOUS DAMPPROOFING
			5/1/01	07131	SELF-ADHERING SHEET WATERPROOFING
DIVISION 2 - SITE CONSTRUCTION			5/1/01	07210	BUILDING INSULATION
5/1/01	02230	SITE CLEARING	5/1/01	07241	EXTERIOR INSULATION AND FINISH SYSTEMS - CLASS PB
5/1/01	02300	EARTHWORK	5/1/01	07311	ASPHALT SHINGLES
5/1/01	02361	TERMITE CONTROL	5/1/01	07317	WOOD SHINGLES AND SHAKES
5/1/01	02510	WATER DISTRIBUTION	5/1/01	07320	ROOF TILES
5/1/01	02525	WATER SUPPLY WELLS	5/1/01	07411	METAL ROOF PANELS
5/1/01	02530	SANITARY SEWERAGE	5/1/01	07412	METAL WALL PANELS
5/1/01	02540	SEPTIC TANK SYSTEMS	5/1/01	07460	SIDING
5/1/01	02553	NATURAL GAS DISTRIBUTION	5/1/01	07511	BUILT-UP ASPHALT ROOFING
5/1/01	02554	FUEL OIL DISTRIBUTION	5/1/01	07631	EPDM MEMBRANE ROOFING
5/1/01	02620	SUBDRAINAGE	5/1/01	07552	SBS-MODIFIED BITUMINOUS MEMBRANE ROOFING
5/1/01	02630	STORM DRAINAGE	5/1/01	07610	SHEET METAL ROOFING
5/1/01	02741	HOT-MIX ASPHALT PAVING	5/1/01	07620	SHEET METAL FLASHING AND TRIM
5/1/01	02751	CEMENT CONCRETE PAVEMENT	5/1/01	07710	MANUFACTURED ROOF SPECIALTIES
5/1/01	02780	UNIT PAVERS	5/1/01	07720	ROOF ACCESSORIES
5/1/01	02810	IRRIGATION SYSTEMS	5/1/01	07811	SPRAYED FIRE-RESISTIVE MATERIALS
5/1/01	02821	CHAIN-LINK FENCES AND GATES	5/1/01	07841	THROUGH-PENETRATION FIRESTOP SYSTEMS
5/1/01	02832	SEGMENTAL RETAINING WALLS	5/1/01	07920	JOINT SEALANTS
5/1/01	02920	LAWNS AND GRASSES			
5/1/01	02930	EXTERIOR PLANTS	**DIVISION 8 - DOORS AND WINDOWS**		
			5/1/01	08110	STEEL DOORS AND FRAMES
DIVISION 3 - CONCRETE			5/1/01	08153	SLIDING ALUMINUM-FRAMED GLASS DOORS
5/1/01	03300	CAST-IN-PLACE CONCRETE	5/1/01	08211	FLUSH WOOD DOORS
5/1/01	03371	SHOTCRETE	5/1/01	08212	STILE AND RAIL WOOD DOORS
5/1/01	03410	PLANT-PRECAST STRUCTURAL CONCRETE	5/1/01	08263	SLIDING WOOD-FRAMED GLASS DOORS
5/1/01	03450	PLANT-PRECAST ARCHITECTURAL CONCRETE	5/1/01	08311	ACCESS DOORS AND FRAMES
5/1/01	03470	TILT-UP PRECAST CONCRETE	5/1/01	08331	OVERHEAD COILING DOORS
			5/1/01	08351	FOLDING DOORS
DIVISION 4 - MASONRY			5/1/01	08361	SECTIONAL OVERHEAD DOORS
5/1/01	04810	UNIT MASONRY ASSEMBLIES	5/1/01	08410	ALUMINUM ENTRANCES AND STOREFRONTS
5/1/01	04815	GLASS UNIT MASONRY ASSEMBLIES	5/1/01	08520	ALUMINUM WINDOWS
5/1/01	04860	STONE VENEER ASSEMBLIES	5/1/01	08550	WOOD WINDOWS
			5/1/01	08561	VINYL WINDOWS
DIVISION 5 - METALS			5/1/01	08610	ROOF WINDOWS
5/1/01	05120	STRUCTURAL STEEL	5/1/01	08620	UNIT SKYLIGHTS
5/1/01	05210	STEEL JOISTS	5/1/01	08710	DOOR HARDWARE
5/1/01	05310	STEEL DECK	5/1/01	08716	POWER DOOR OPERATORS
5/1/01	05400	COLD-FORMED METAL FRAMING	5/1/01	08800	GLAZING
5/1/01	05500	METAL FABRICATIONS	5/1/01	08960	SLOPED GLAZING SYSTEMS
5/1/01	05520	HANDRAILS AND RAILINGS			

FIGURE 13.5 The Masterspec Table of Contents for a small project.

Issue Date	Sect. No.	SECTION TITLE	Issue Date	Sect. No.	SECTION TITLE
		DIVISION 9 - FINISHES			**DIVISION 15 - MECHANICAL**
5/1/01	09210	GYPSUM PLASTER	5/1/01	15050	BASIC MECHANICAL MATERIALS AND METHODS
5/1/01	09215	GYPSUM VENEER PLASTER	5/1/01	15080	MECHANICAL INSULATION
5/1/01	09220	PORTLAND CEMENT PLASTER	5/1/01	15110	VALVES
5/1/01	09260	GYPSUM BOARD ASSEMBLIES	5/1/01	15130	PUMPS
5/1/01	09271	GLASS-REINFORCED GYPSUM FABRICATIONS	5/1/01	15140	DOMESTIC WATER PIPING
			5/1/01	15150	SANITARY WASTE AND VENT PIPING
5/1/01	09310	CERAMIC TILE	5/1/01	15160	STORM DRAINAGE
5/1/01	09385	DIMENSION STONE TILE	5/1/01	15181	HYDRONIC PIPING
5/1/01	09511	ACOUSTICAL PANEL CEILINGS	5/1/01	15183	REFRIGERANT PIPING
5/1/01	09512	ACOUSTICAL TILE CEILINGS	5/1/01	15194	FUEL GAS PIPING
5/1/01	09638	STONE PAVING AND FLOORING	5/1/01	15410	PLUMBING FIXTURES
5/1/01	09640	WOOD FLOORING	5/1/01	15430	PLUMBING SPECIALTIES
5/1/01	09651	RESILIENT FLOOR TILE	5/1/01	15480	DOMESTIC WATER HEATERS
5/1/01	09652	SHEET VINYL FLOOR COVERINGS	5/1/01	15512	CAST-IRON BOILERS
5/1/01	09653	RESILIENT WALL BASE AND ACCESSORIES	5/1/01	15513	CONDENSING BOILERS
5/1/01	09680	CARPET	5/1/01	15519	ELECTRIC BOILERS
5/1/01	09681	CARPET TILE	5/1/01	15530	FURNACES
5/1/01	09720	WALL COVERINGS	5/1/01	15554	FLUES AND VENTS
5/1/01	09751	INTERIOR STONE FACING	5/1/01	15628	RECIPROCATING/SCROLL WATER CHILLERS
5/1/01	09771	FABRIC-WRAPPED PANELS			
5/1/01	09910	PAINTING	5/1/01	15671	CONDENSING UNITS
			5/1/01	15731	PACKAGED TERMINAL AIR CONDITIONERS
		DIVISION 10 - SPECIALTIES	5/1/01	15732	ROOFTOP AIR CONDITIONERS
5/1/01	10155	TOILET COMPARTMENTS	5/1/01	15745	WATER-SOURCE HEAT PUMPS
5/1/01	10200	LOUVERS AND VENTS	5/1/01	15763	FAN-COIL UNITS
5/1/01	10265	IMPACT-RESISTANT WALL PROTECTION	5/1/01	15764	RADIATORS
5/1/01	10431	SIGNS	5/1/01	15766	UNIT HEATERS
5/1/01	10520	FIRE- PROTECTION SPECIALTIES	5/1/01	15772	RADIANT HEATING PIPING
5/1/01	10651	OPERABLE PANEL PARTITIONS	5/1/01	15810	DUCTS AND ACCESSORIES
5/1/01	10750	TELEPHONE SPECIALTIES	5/1/01	15838	POWER VENTILATIORS
5/1/01	10801	TOILET AND BATH ACCESSORIES	5/1/01	15855	DIFFUSERS, REGISTERS, AND GRILLES
			5/1/01	15900	HVAC INSTRUMENTATION AND CONTROLS
		DIVISION 11 - EQUIPMENT			
5/1/01	11132	PROJECTION SCREENS			**DIVISION 16 - ELECTRICAL**
5/1/01	11451	RESIDENTIAL APPLIANCES	5/1/01	16060	BASIC ELECTRICAL MATERIALS AND METHODS
5/1/01	11460	UNIT KITCHENS	5/1/01	16122	UNDERCARPET CABLES
			5/1/01	16140	WIRING DEVICES
		DIVISION 12 - FURNISHINGS	5/1/01	16410	ENCLOSED SWITCHES AND CIRCUIT BREAKERS
5/1/01	12356	KITCHEN CASEWORK			
5/1/01	12484	FLOOR MATS AND FRAMES	5/1/01	16420	ENCLOSED CONTROLLERS
5/1/01	12491	HORIZONTAL LOUVER BLINDS	5/1/01	16442	PANELBOARDS
5/1/01	12492	VERTICAL LOUVER BLINDS	5/1/01	16461	DRY-TYPE TRANSFORMERS (600 V AND LESS)
5/1/01	12496	WINDOW TREATMENT HARDWARE			
			5/1/01	16500	LIGHTING
		DIVISION 13 - SPECIAL CONSTRUCTION	5/1/01	16750	VOICE AND DATA COMMUNICATION CABLING
5/1/01	13038	SAUNAS			
5/1/01	13100	LIGHTNING PROTECTION			
5/1/01	13125	METAL BUILDING SYSTEMS			
5/1/01	13851	FIRE ALARM			
5/1/01	13930	WET-PIPE FIRE SUPPRESSION SPRINKLERS			
		DIVISION 14 - CONVEYING SYSTEMS			
5/1/01	14240	HYDRAULIC ELEVATORS			
5/1/01	14420	WHEELCHAIR LIFTS			

FIGURE 13.5 *(continued)* The Masterspec Table of Contents for a small project.

for building permits, and will not accept a project manual with specifications. Furthermore, all data demonstrating compliance with the building code must be indicated on the drawings. This stipulated repetition of identical data on both the specifications and the drawings exposes the documents to errors and inconsistency. Nevertheless, this aside, to achieve better communication, the specifier should:

- Have a good understanding of the most current standards and test methods referred to and the sections that are applicable to your project. Use accepted standards to specify quality of materials or workmanship required, such as "Lightweight concrete masonry units: ASTM C-90-85; Grade N. Type 1."

- Avoid specifications that are impossible for the contractor to carry out. Also refrain from specifying the results and the methods proposed to achieve those results as the two may conflict. For example, if you specify that a fabric should meet certain ASTM standards and then specify a specific fabric that fails to meet the stated requirements, the specification will be impossible to comply with.

- Do not specify standards that cannot be measured. Using phrases like *a workmanlike job*, for example, should be avoided as they are subject to wide interpretation.

- The clarity of specifications depends on the use of simple, direct statements, concise use of terms, and attention to grammar and punctuation. Avoid the use of words or phrases like etc., *and/or, any,* and *either,* which are ambiguous and imply a choice that may not be intended.

- Avoid exculpatory clauses such as, "the General Contractor shall be totally responsible for all....," which try to shift responsibility. Be fair in designating responsibility.

- Keep specifications as short as possible, omitting words like *all, the, an,* and *a.* Describing only one major idea per paragraph makes reading easier while improving comprehension. It also facilitates editing and modifying the specifications at a later date.

- Capitalize the following: major parties to the contract, such as Contractor, Client, Owner, Space Planner, Architect; the contract documents, such as Specifications, Working Drawings, Contract, Clause, Section, Supplementary Conditions; specific rooms within the building, such as Living Room, Kitchen, Office; grade of materials, such as No.1 Douglas Fir, FAS White Oak; and, of course, all proper names. The specifier should never underline anything in a specification, as this implies that the remaining material can be ignored.

- Use Shall and Will correctly. *Shall* is used to designate a command: "The Contractor shall...." *Will* implies a choice: "The Owner or Space Planner will....."

The coordination of the specifications with the construction drawings is essential, as they complement each other (Figure 13.6). They should not contain conflicting requirements, omissions, duplications, or errors. To minimize the possibility of errors, the specifier should:

- Ensure that the specifications contain requirements for all the materials and construction depicted on the drawings.

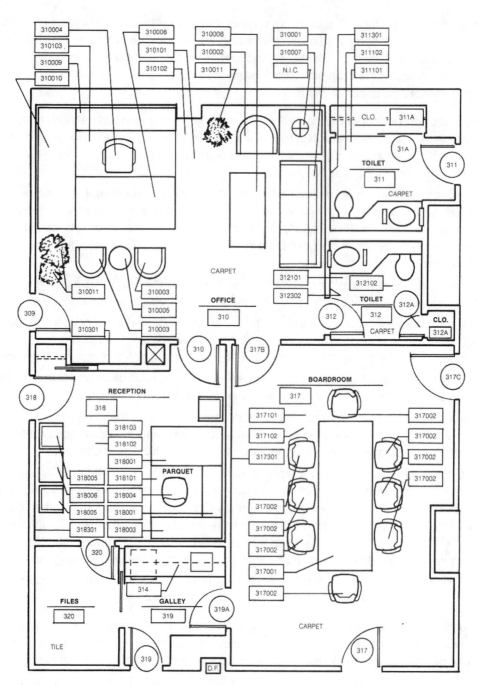

FIGURE 13.6 Coordination guidelines. Dimensions and thickness should be indicated only on one document, preferably the drawings.

- Use the same terminology in both documents (i.e. drawings and specifications). If metal studs are used in the specifications, the same term should be indicated on the drawings.

- Check that dimensions and thicknesses are shown only on one document and not duplicated. Typically, sizes are indicated on the drawings, and the standards for the materials and components that those sizes reference are written into the specifications (unless the project is a very small one without a project manual).

- Make sure that notes on drawings should not describe installation methods or material qualities as these normally belong in the specifications.

SPECIFICATION FORMAT AND ORGANIZATION

The 16-division MasterFormat™ was created in 1963, and is a product of The Construction Specifications Institute and Construction Specifications Canada. It is a widely used format both in the United States and Canada for specifications concerning nonresidential building projects. MasterFormat is the standard for titling and arranging construction project manuals containing bidding requirements, contracting requirements, and specifications. The Construction Specification Institute (CSI), has been working since its inception in 1948 on trying to standardize the specification numbering system and the format of the Sections, which was last modified MasterFormat in 1995. The CSI is actively seeking to add new divisions to address the rapidly evolving and growing computer and communications technology. The proposed modified MasterFormat would increase its division numbers from 16 to 40, of which 20 divisions would be left blank to provide room for future revisions as construction products and technology evolve. The consensus at CSI is that adding divisions is better than trying to fit everything into the existing format of 16 divisions.

This move to modify and enhance the MasterFormat is driven in part by changes in the construction marketplace. Construction technology has advanced rapidly since 1995. For example, there have been major developments in the scope and complexity of computer and communications systems for buildings and also security systems.

The Construction Specification Institute says, "MasterFormat is a master list of numbers and titles for organizing information about construction requirements, products, and activities into a standard sequence. Construction projects use many different delivery methods, products and installation. Successful completion of projects requires effective communication among the people involved on a project. Information retrieval is nearly impossible without a standard filing system familiar to each user. MasterFormat facilitates standard filing and retrieval schemes throughout the construction industry. MasterFormat is a uniform system for organizing information in project manuals, for organizing cost data, for filing product information and other technical data, for identifying drawing objects and for presenting construction market data."

MasterFormat arranges related construction products and activities into 16 level one titles, called *divisions*. Each Division is further defined in MasterFormat by level two and three numbers and titles and suggested level four titles. Level two numbers and titles identify clusters of products and activities having an identifying characteristic in common. An explanation of the titles used in MasterFormat is provided giving a general description of the coverage for each title. A keyword index of requirements, products, and activities is also provided to help users find appropriate numbers and titles for construction subjects.

The current MasterFormat consists essentially of dividing the Specs into 16 Divisions plus a Division for Owner/Contractor Agreements, etc. Each Division has many sections as outlined below:

- Division 0 is the Division for Owner/Contractor Agreements, Bid Form, General Conditions, etc.
- Division 1 is the Division for the General Requirements of the project and Summary of Work, i.e., the contractor's responsibilities
- Division 2 through 16 are the trade Divisions, grouped by generic work such as Wood and Plastics and Finishes

These Divisions provide a general grouping for similar sections, such as Concrete, Masonry, Doors and Windows, Finishes, etc. Each Division has many sections. Figure 13.7 is an index of the MasterFormat system, showing the various Divisions.

SPECIFICATION SECTION FORMAT

Each Specification Section covers a particular trade or sub trade (e.g. drywall, carpet, ceiling tiles). Furthermore, each Section is divided into 3 basic parts, each of which contains the specifications about a particular aspect of each trade or sub trade (Figure 13.8).

Part 1: General

This part of the specification outlines the general requirements for the section and describes the scope of work of the project as well as providing the bidder or contractor with the administrative requirements for the Section. In general, it sets the quality control, requirements for delivery and job conditions, notes the related trades with which this section needs to be coordinated, and specifies the submittals required for review prior to ordering, fabricating, or installing material for that Section. It consists generally of the following:

- *Description and Scope:* This Article should include the scope of the work and the interrelationships between work in this Section and the other sections. In addition, it should include definitions and options.
- *Quality Assurances:* To include requirements for qualification of Consultants, Contractors, Subcontractors. Also included here are the standards and test requirements, and any full size "mock-up" models of items for testing.

MasterFormat™ Index

Introductory Information
Bidding Requirements
Contracting Requirements
Facilities and Spaces
Systems and Assemblies

SPECIFICATIONS

Construction Products and Activities
Division 1 — General Requirements
Division 2 — Site Construction
Division 3 — Concrete
Division 4 — Masonry
Division 5 — Metals
Division 6 — Wood and Plastics
Division 7 —Thermal and Moisture Protection
Division 8 — Doors and Windows
Division 9 — Finishes
Division 10 — Specialties
Division 11 — Equipment
Division 12 — Furnishing
Division 13 — Special Construction
Division 14 — Conveying Systems
Division 15 — Mechanical
Division 16 — Electrical

Introductory Information
00001 Project Title Page
00005 Certifications Page
00007 Seals Page
00010 Table of Contents
00015 List of Drawings
00020 List of Schedules

Bidding Requirements
00100 Bid Solicitation
00200 Instructions to Bidders
00300 Information Available to Bidders
00400 Bid Forms and Supplements
00490 Bidding Addenda

Contracting Requirements
00500 Agreement
00600 Bonds and Certificates
00700 General Conditions
00800 Supplementary Conditions
00900 Modifications

Facilities and Spaces
Note: **MasterFormat** currently does not include a list of
facilities and spaces.

Systems and Assemblies
Note: **MasterFormat** currently does not include a list of
Systems and Assemblies. Use **UniFormat** for element
numbers, titles, and descriptions, associated with systems
and assemblies.

Construction Products and Activities
Division 1 — General Requirements
01100 Summary
01200 Price and Payment Procedures
01300 Administrative Requirements
01400 Quality Requirements
01500 Temporary Facilities and Controls
01600 Product Requirements
01700 Execution Requirements
01800 Facility Operation
01900 Facility Decommissioning

Division 2 — Site Construction
02050 Basic Site Materials and Methods
02100 Site Remediation
02200 Site Preparation
02300 Earthwork
02400 Tunneling, Boring, and Jacking
02450 Foundation and Load-bearing Elements
02500 Utility Services
02600 Drainage and Containment
02700 Bases, Ballasts, Pavements, and Appurtenances
02800 Site Improvements and Amenities
02900 Planting
02950 Site Restoration and Rehabilitation

Division 3 — Concrete
03050 Basic Concrete Materials and Methods
03100 Concrete Forms and Accessories
03200 Concrete Reinforcement
03300 Cast-in-Place Concrete
03400 Precast Concrete
03500 Cementitious Decks and Underlayment
03600 Grouts
03700 Mass Concrete
03900 Concrete Restoration and Cleaning

Division 4 — Masonry
04050 Basic Masonry Materials and Methods
04200 Masonry Units
04400 Stone
04500 Refractories
04600 Corrosion-Resistant Masonry
04700 Simulated Masonry
04800 Masonry Assemblies
04900 Masonry Restoration and Cleaning

Division 5 — Metals
05050 Basic Metal Materials and Methods
05100 Structural Metal Framing
05200 Metal Joists
05300 Metal Deck
05400 Cold-Formed Metal Framing
05500 Metal Fabrications
05600 Hydraulic Fabrications
05650 Railroad Track and Accessories
05700 Ornamental Metal

FIGURES 13.7   An index of the MasterFormat System. *(Copyright Construction Specification Institute, Inc., and Construction Specification Canada)*

05800 Expansion Control
05900 Metal Restoration and Cleaning

Division 6 — Wood and Plastics
06050 Basic Wood and Plastic Materials and Methods
06100 Rough Carpentry
06200 Finish Carpentry
06400 Architectural Woodwork
06500 Structural Plastics
06600 Plastic Fabrications
06900 Wood and Plastic Restoration and Cleaning

Division 7 — Thermal and Moisture Protection
07050 Basic Thermal and Moisture Protection Materials and Methods
07100 Dampproofing and Waterproofing
07200 Thermal Protection
07300 Shingles, Roof Tiles, and Roof Coverings
07400 Roofing and Siding Panels
07500 Membrane Roofing
07600 Flashing and Sheet Metal
07700 Roof Specialties and Accessories
07800 Fire and Smoke Protection
07900 Joint Sealers

Division 8 — Doors and Windows
08050 Basic Door and Window Materials and Methods
08100 Metal Doors and Frames
08200 Wood and Plastic Doors
08300 Specialty Doors
08400 Entrances and Storefronts
08500 Windows
08600 Skylights
08700 Hardware
08800 Glazing
08900 Glazed Curtain Wall

Division 9 — Finishes
09050 Basic Finish Materials and Methods
09100 Metal Support Assemblies
09200 Plaster and Gypsum Board
09300 Tile
09400 Terrazzo
09500 Ceilings
09600 Flooring
09700 Wall Finishes
09800 Acoustical Treatment
09900 Paints and Coatings

Back to Top

Division 10 — Specialties
10100 Visual Display Boards
10150 Compartments and Cubicles
10200 Louvers and Vents
10240 Grilles and Screens
10250 Service Walls
10260 Wall and Corner Guards
10270 Access Flooring
10290 Pest Control
10300 Fireplaces and Stoves

10340 Manufactured Exterior Specialties
10350 Flagpoles
10400 Identification Devices
10450 Pedestrian Control Devices
10500 Lockers
10520 Fire Protection Specialties
10530 Protective Covers
10550 Postal Specialties
10600 Partitions
10670 Storage Shelving
10700 Exterior Protection
10750 Telephone Specialties
10800 Toilet, Bath, and Laundry Accessories
10880 Scales
10900 Wardrobe and Closet Specialties

Division 11 — Equipment
11010 Maintenance Equipment
11020 Security and Vault Equipment
11030 Teller and Service Equipment
11040 Ecclesiastical Equipment
11050 Library Equipment
11060 Theater and Stage Equipment
11070 Instrumental Equipment
11080 Registration Equipment
11090 Checkroom Equipment
11100 Mercantile Equipment
11110 Commercial Laundry and Dry Cleaning Equipment
11120 Vending Equipment
11130 Audio-Visual Equipment
11140 Vehicle Service Equipment
11150 Parking Control Equipment
11160 Loading Dock Equipment
11170 Solid Waste Handling Equipment
11190 Detention Equipment
11200 Water Supply and Treatment Equipment
11280 Hydraulic Gates and Valves
11300 Fluid Waste Treatment and Disposal Equipment
11400 Food Service Equipment
11450 Residential Equipment
11460 Unit Kitchens
11470 Darkroom Equipment
11480 Athletic, Recreational, and Therapeutic Equipment
11500 Industrial and Process Equipment
11600 Laboratory Equipment
11650 Planetarium Equipment
11660 Observatory Equipment
11680 Office Equipment
11700 Medical Equipment
11780 Mortuary Equipment
11850 Navigation Equipment
11870 Agricultural Equipment
11900 Exhibit Equipment

Division 12 — Furnishings
12050 Fabrics
12100 Art
12300 Manufactured Casework
12400 Furnishings and Accessories
12500 Furniture
12600 Multiple Seating
12700 Systems Furniture

FIGURES 13.7 (continued)   An index of the MasterFormat System. (Copyright Construction Specification Institute, Inc., and Construction Specification Canada)

12800 Interior Plants and Planters
12900 Furnishings Repair and Restoration

Division 13 — Special Construction
13010 Air-Supported Structures
13020 Building Modules
13030 Special Purpose Rooms
13080 Sound, Vibration, and Seismic Control
13090 Radiation Protection
13100 Lightning Protection
13110 Cathodic Protection
13120 Pre-Engineered Structures
13150 Swimming Pools
13160 Aquariums
13165 Aquatic Park Facilities
13170 Tubs and Pools
13175 Ice Rinks
13185 Kennels and Animal Shelters
13190 Site-Constructed Incinerators
13200 Storage Tanks
13220 Filter Underdrains and Media
13230 Digester Covers and Appurtenances
13240 Oxygenation Systems
13260 Sludge Conditioning Systems
13280 Hazardous Material Remediation
13400 Measurement and Control Instrumentation
13500 Recording Instrumentation
13550 Transportation Control Instrumentation
13600 Solar and Wind Energy Equipment
13700 Security Access and Surveillance
13800 Building Automation and Control
13850 Detection and Alarm
13900 Fire Suppression

Division 14 — Conveying Systems
14100 Dumbwaiters
14200 Elevators
14300 Escalators and Moving Walks
14400 Lifts
14500 Material Handling
14600 Hoists and Cranes
14700 Turntables
14800 Scaffolding
14900 Transportation

Division 15 — Mechanical
15050 Basic Mechanical Materials and Methods
15100 Building Services Piping
15200 Process Piping
15300 Fire Protection Piping
15400 Plumbing Fixtures and Equipment
15500 Heat-Generation Equipment
15600 Refrigeration Equipment
15700 Heating, Ventilating, and Air Conditioning Equipment
15800 Air Distribution
15900 HVAC Instrumentation and Controls
15950 Testing, Adjusting, and Balancing

Division 16 — Electrical
16050 Basic Electrical Materials and Methods
16100 Wiring Methods
16200 Electrical Power
16300 Transmission and Distribution
16400 Low-Voltage Distribution
16500 Lighting
16700 Communications
16800 Sound and Video

FIGURES 13.7 (continued) An index of the MasterFormat System. (Copyright Construction Specification Institute, Inc., and Construction Specification Canada)

- *Submittals:* Instructions for submittal of product samples and other relevant information, including warranties, certificates, product data and installation instructions.

- *Product Handling, Delivery, and Storage:* To include instructions for things like packing, location for delivery, temperature control and protection for the product after delivery.

- *Project and Site Conditions:* Stipulate the requirements and conditions that must be in place prior to installation, such as temperature control and the use of necessary utilities. For example, all wall tiling should be completed prior to cabinet installation.

- *Alternatives:* Whether alternatives are acceptable is detailed in the General Requirements.

- *Sequencing and Scheduling:* This is used where timing is critical and where tasks and/or scheduling need to follow a specific sequence

- *Warranties:* This Section typically includes warranties that exceed one year. Terms and conditions of the warranty should be spelled out and the Owner should be provided with copies.

Part 2: Products

This Section defines and details the materials and products being specified, including fabrication or manufacturing of the product, what standards and the standards to which the materials or products must conform to so as to fulfill the specifications, and similar concerns (Figure 13.9). The itemized sub-sections would therefore include:

- *Manufacturers:* This Section is used when writing a proprietary specification, and will list approved manufacturers. The Section should be coordinated with the Product Options and Substitutions Section.
- *Materials, Furnishings and Equipment:* A list should be provided of materials to be used. If writing descriptive or performance specifications, detail the performance criteria for materials, furnishings and equipment.
- *Mixes:* This Section specifies the proportions of materials to be used when mixing a particular product.
- *Fabrication:* In this Section, fabrication and construction details should be given.

Part 3: Execution

This part of the Specification describes the quality of work—the standards and requirements specified in the installation of the products and materials. It also describes the conditions under which the products are to be installed, the protection required, and the closeout and clean-up procedures. The sub-headings in this Section include:

- *Inspection:* Outline what the Contractor is required to do, for example to the subsurface, prior to installation. Wording may include, "the moisture content of the concrete should meet manufacturer's specifications, prior to installation of the flooring material."
- *Preparation:* Stipulates the improvements to be made prior to installation.
- *Installation and Performance:* The specific requirements for each finish should be specified, as well as the quality of work to be achieved.
- *Field Quality Control:* Specify the tests and inspection procedures to be used to determine the quality of the finished work.
- *Protection:* Where special protection is necessary for a particular installation, such as marble flooring, this Section must be included.
- *Adjust and Clean:* Outline in detail the cleaning and adjustments requirements.
- Schedules: To be used only if deemed necessary.

SECTION 09751 - INTERIOR STONE FACING

Copyright 1998, The American Institute of Architects (AIA). This is an Interior Design Library Section.

PART 1 - GENERAL

1.1   SECTION REQUIREMENTS

   A.   Submittals: [Shop Drawings] [stone Samples at least 12 inches (300 mm) square] [and grout samples showing the full range of colors available].

   B.   Verify dimensions of stone countertops by field measurements before fabrication and indicate on Shop Drawings.

PART 2 - PRODUCTS

2.1   STONE

   A.   Granite: As follows:

      1.   ASTM C 615, <Insert descriptive requirements, such as color, grain size, etc.>.

Select subparagraph above for nonproprietary Specification or subparagraph below if varieties are preselected.
      2.   <Insert names of acceptable varieties.>
      3.   Finish: [Polished] [Honed] [Thermal].

   B.   Limestone: As follows:

      1.   ASTM C 568, Classification [I Low-Density] [II Medium-Density] [III High-Density], <Insert descriptive requirements, such as color, etc.>.

Select subparagraph above for nonproprietary Specification or subparagraph below if varieties are preselected. If retaining above, select one density classification. First generally applies to shell limestone; second to oolitic limestone and some varieties of dolomitic limestone; third to some varieties of dolomitic limestone.
      2.   <Insert names of acceptable varieties.>
      3.   Finish: [Polished] [Honed].

   C.   Marble: As follows:

      1.   ASTM C 503, Classification [I Calcite] [II Dolomite] [III Serpentine] [IV Travertine], <Insert descriptive requirements, such as color, etc.>.

Select subparagraph above for nonproprietary Specification or subparagraph below if varieties are preselected.
      2.   <Insert names of acceptable varieties.>
      3.   Finish: [Polished] [Honed].

   D.   Quartz-Based Dimension Stone: As follows:

      1.   ASTM C 616, Classification [I Sandstone] [II Quartzitic Sandstone] [III Quartzite], <Insert descriptive requirements, such as color, etc.>.

INTERIOR STONE FACING   09751 - 1

FIGURE 13.8 Section 09751—Interior Stone Facing Specification, from MasterSpec—Interior Design.

MASTERSPEC - INTERIOR DESIGN

Select subparagraph above for nonproprietary Specification or subparagraph below if varieties are preselected.
  2.   **<Insert names of acceptable varieties.>**
  3.   Finish: [**Natural cleft**] [**Honed**].

  E.   Slate: As follows:

  1.   ASTM C 629, Classification [**I Exterior**] [**II Interior**], **<Insert descriptive requirements, such as color, etc.>**.

Select subparagraph above for nonproprietary Specification or subparagraph below if varieties are preselected.
  2.   **<Insert names of acceptable varieties.>**
  3.   Finish: [**Natural cleft**] [**Honed**].

2.2   SETTING MATERIALS

  A.   Molding Plaster: ASTM C 59.

  B.   Water-Cleanable Epoxy Adhesive: ANSI A118.3.

  C.   Sealant for Countertops: Clear silicone sealant.

  1.   **<Insert manufacturers and products.>**

  D.   Dry-Set Grout (Unsanded): ANSI A118.6, for joints 1/8 inch (3 mm) and narrower.

  1.   **<Insert manufacturers and products.>**

  E.   Latex-Portland Cement Grout: ANSI A118.6.

  1.   **<Insert manufacturers and products.>**
  2.   Use unsanded grout for joints 1/8 inch (3 mm) and narrower.
  3.   Use sanded grout for joints 1/8 inch (3 mm) and wider.

  F.   Wire Tiebacks: [**No. 9 AWG copper-, bronze-, or brass-alloy**] [**0.120-inch- (3.0-mm-) diameter, stainless-steel**] wire.

2.3   STONE FABRICATION

  A.   Cut stone to produce pieces of thickness, size, and shape indicated.

  1.   For granite, comply with recommendations of National Building Granite Quarries Association's "Specifications for Architectural Granite."
  2.   For marble, comply with recommendations of Marble Institute of America's "Dimensional Stone— Design Manual IV."
  3.   For limestone, comply with recommendations of Indiana Limestone Institute of America's "Indiana Limestone Handbook."
  4.   Quirk-miter corners, unless otherwise indicated. Install anchorage in top and bottom bed joints of corner units.
  5.   Cut stone to produce uniform joints [**1/16 inch (1.5 mm)**] [**1/8 inch (3 mm)**] [**1/4 inch (6 mm)**] [**3/8 inch (10 mm)**] wide. Cut stone to produce joints of uniform width and in locations indicated.
  6.   Produce moldings with machines having abrasive shaping wheels made to reverse contour of molding shape; do not sculpt moldings.

FIGURE 13.8 *(continued)*   Section 09751—Interior Stone Facing Specification, from MasterSpec—Interior Design.

MASTERSPEC - INTERIOR DESIGN

7. Miter moldings at corners, unless otherwise indicated, with edges of miters slightly eased at outside corners.

B. Pattern Arrangement: Fabricate and arrange panels with veining and other natural markings [horizontal] [vertical] [in a random pattern].

2.4 STONE COUNTERTOP FABRICATION

A. Fabricate stone countertops to comply with recommendations of Marble Institute of America's "Dimensional Stone--Design Manual IV."

1. Thickness: [3/4 inch (20 mm)] [7/8 inch (22 mm)] [1-1/4 inches (32 mm)].
2. Edge Detail: [Straight, slightly eased at top] [3/4-inch (20-mm) bullnose] [Radius edge with apron, 2 inches (50 mm) high with 3/8-inch (10-mm) radius] [1-1/2-inch (40-mm) laminated bullnose].

B. Splashes: 3/4-inch20-mm nominal thickness backsplashes and end splashes, 4 inches (100 mm) high, with top edges [straight, slightly eased at corner] [beveled] [rounded to 3/8-inch (10-mm) radius].

C. Seams: Fabricate countertops [without seams] [in sections indicated for joining in field, with sealant-filled seams 1/16 inch (1.5 mm) in width].

PART 3 - EXECUTION

3.1 INSTALLATION

A. Execute stonework by skilled mechanics experienced with the kind and form of stone and installation method indicated.

B. Erect interior stone facing plumb and true with uniform joint widths. Use temporary shims to maintain joint width.

C. Set interior stone facing units firmly against setting spots located at anchors and spaced a maximum of 18 inches (450 mm) apart over back of unit, but no less than 1 spot per 2 sq. ft. (0.18 sq. m).

D. Provide a minimum of 4 anchors per stone up to 12 sq. ft. (1.1 sq. m) in face area, plus a minimum of 2 additional anchors for each additional 8 sq. ft. (0.7 sq. m).

E. Provide a minimum of 2 anchors per piece for stone trim up to 48 inches (1200 mm) in length, plus 1 additional anchor for each additional 24 inches (600 mm) of length.

F. Set stone base by adhering with water-cleanable epoxy adhesive. Hold adhesive back from exposed edge of joint to allow for grouting.

G. Set stone window stools in a full bed of water-cleanable epoxy adhesive.

H. Grout joints after setting. Tool joints uniformly and smoothly with plastic tool.

3.2 INSTALLING COUNTERTOPS

FIGURE 13.8 *(continued)*   Section 09751—Interior Stone Facing Specification, from MasterSpec—Interior Design.

```
┌─────────────────────────────────────────────────────────────────────────────┐
│                                                                               │
│                          MASTERSPEC - INTERIOR DESIGN                         │
│                                                                               │
│    A.    Install countertops [over plywood subtops with a full spread of]     │
│          [by adhering to supports with] water-cleanable epoxy adhesive.       │
│                                                                               │
│    B.    Space seams with 1/16-inch (1.5-mm) gap for filling with sealant.    │
│          Use temporary shims to ensure uniform spacing and use clamps to      │
│          eliminate lipping.                                                   │
│                                                                               │
│    C.    Complete cutouts not finished in shop. Mask areas of countertops     │
│          adjacent to cutouts while cutting.                                   │
│                                                                               │
│    D.    Install backsplash and end splashes by adhering to wall with water-  │
│          cleanable epoxy adhesive. Leave 1/16-inch (1.5-mm) gap between       │
│          countertop and splash for filling with sealant. Use temporary        │
│          shims to ensure uniform spacing.                                     │
│                                                                               │
│    E.    Apply sealant to seams and to gap between countertops and splashes.  │
│                                                                               │
│  3.3     CLEANING                                                             │
│                                                                               │
│    A.    Clean interior stone facing as work progresses. Remove grout smears  │
│          before tooling joints.                                               │
│                                                                               │
│    B.    Clean interior stone facing at least six days after completion of    │
│          grouting, using clean water and soft rags or stiff-fiber brushes.    │
│                                                                               │
│                                                                               │
│  END OF SECTION 09751                                                         │
│                                                                               │
│                                                                               │
│  INTERIOR STONE FACING                                               09751 - 4│
│                                                                               │
└─────────────────────────────────────────────────────────────────────────────┘
```

FIGURE 13.8 *(continued)*   Section 09751—Interior Stone Facing Specification, from MasterSpec—Interior Design.

FURNITURE SPECIFICATIONS

The MasterFormat and Masterspec systems provide a place to specify furnishings in Division 12, but this has proven to be totally inadequate to meet the requirements of most space planners and interior designers. Furthermore, most interior projects prefer separate specifications for construction and for furniture and accessories. This is because the procedure for specifying, contracting for, and building construction items is different from specifying, purchasing, delivering, and installing furniture. To meet the needs of interior designers and space planners, Masterspec came out with an interior design package. This software package, simply called *Interior Design,* includes over 75 short-form specifications that cover interior construction, finish, and equipment topics in Divisions 1-16 as well as flammability and performance criteria (Figure 13.10). A second package, *Furnishings,* is expected to be released shortly, and consists of data-sheet format, master specifications easily edited for specific projects and informative

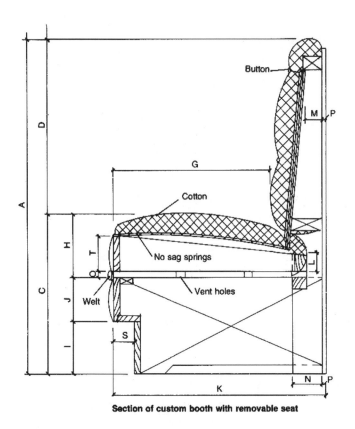

Dimensions (not to scale):

	in.	cm
A	= 54	137.16
B	= 39	99.06
C	= 18	45.72
D	= 22	55.88
E	= 40	101.60
F	= 21	53.34
G	= 19	48.26
H	= 7	17.78
I	= 6	15.24
J	= 5	12.70
K	= 25½	64.77
L	= 2¼	5.72
M	= 2	5.08
N	= 3½	8.89
O	= ¾	1.91
P	= ½	1.27
Q	= 12	30.48
R	= 1	2.54
S	= 2½	6.35
T	= 4	10.16

Section of custom booth with removable seat

FIGURE 13.9 Section of a custom upholstered restaurant banquette seating detail by Selje, Bond, Steward & Romberger.

background information that eases design decision making. The package covers furniture, fixtures, and miscellaneous furnishings typically contracted for and installed separately through furnishings dealers after initial construction is complete.

As a late entrant, the release of Masterspec's *Furnishings* software is unlikely to have a substantial impact on the furniture industry. CAP Studio, a software package developed by the McGraw-Hill Companies remains the industry standard for furniture specifying and design software (www.cap-online.com). The CAP Studio software suite is an integrated package of applications that automates the processes of space planning, design and specifications, and facilities management (Figure 3.11). Studio can link AutoCAD-based graphics and planning functions with up-to-date electronic catalogs from leading furniture manufacturers. CAP software simplifies the time-consuming, error-prone tasks of specifying, pricing, ordering, and managing complex systems furniture.

MASTERSPEC® OUTLINE™
TABLE OF CONTENTS
© 2002 The American Institute of Architects

INTERIORS LIBRARY
Construction Version

Issue Date	Sect. No.	SECTION TITLE	SECTION DESCRIPTION
DIVISION 1 - GENERAL REQUIREMENTS			
9/98	01100	SUMMARY	Summary of the Work and miscellaneous provisions.
9/98	01125	SUMMARY OF MULTIPLE CONTRACTS	Responsibilities of each contract for the Work, coordination, and temporary facilities and controls.
9/98	01140	WORK RESTRICTIONS	Limitations on use of premises.
9/98	01210	ALLOWANCES	Provisions for allowances.
9/98	01230	ALTERNATES	Provisions for alternates.
9/98	01250	CONTRACT MODIFICATION PROCEDURES	Procedural requirements for changing the Contract.
9/98	01270	UNIT PRICES	Provisions for unit prices.
9/98	01290	PAYMENT PROCEDURES	Administrative requirements for payment.
9/98	01310	PROJECT MANAGEMENT AND COORDINATION	Administrative requirements for coordination and project meetings.
9/98	01320	CONSTRUCTION PROGRESS DOCUMENTATION	Administrative and procedural requirements for Contractor's Construction Schedule, Submittals Schedule, and reports.
9/98	01322	PHOTOGRAPHIC DOCUMENTATION	Construction photographs and videotapes.
9/98	01330	SUBMITTAL PROCEDURES	Procedures for submitting Action and Information Submittals.
5/02	01351	SPECIAL PROCEDURES FOR HISTORIC TREATMENT	Storage, temporary protection, and procedures.
9/98	01400	QUALITY REQUIREMENTS	Quality-assurance and quality-control requirements.
11/01	01420	REFERENCES	Common definitions and terms; and acronyms, trade names, and addresses of associations, government agencies, and other entities referenced in MASTERSPEC.
9/98	01500	TEMPORARY FACILITIES AND CONTROLS	Temporary utilities and facilities for support, security, and protection.
9/98	01600	PRODUCT REQUIREMENTS	Administrative and procedural requirements for product selection and handling, warranties, and product substitutions.
9/98	01700	EXECUTION REQUIREMENTS	Field engineering, progress cleaning, and general requirements for product installation.
9/98	01731	CUTTING AND PATCHING	Special procedures.
2/99	01732	SELECTIVE DEMOLITION	Demolition and removal of selected portions of buildings and site elements.
9/98	01770	CLOSEOUT PROCEDURES	Administrative and procedural requirements for contract closeout.
9/98	01781	PROJECT RECORD DOCUMENTS	Record Drawings, Specifications, and Product Data.
2/99	01782	OPERATION AND MAINTENANCE DATA	Emergency, operation, and maintenance manuals for products and equipment.
2/99	01820	DEMONSTRATION AND TRAINING	Administrative and procedural requirements for instructing Owner's personnel.
DIVISION 3 - CONCRETE			
8/97	03542	CEMENT-BASED UNDERLAYMENT	Self-leveling, hydraulic-cement underlayment.
DIVISION 4 - MASONRY			
U 8/02	04810	UNIT MASONRY ASSEMBLIES	General applications, walls, partitions.
8/98	04815	GLASS UNIT MASONRY ASSEMBLIES	Glass block.

N = NEW   U = UPDATE

MASTERSPEC OUTLINE INTERIORS TABLE OF CONTENTS - AUGUST 2002 - Page 1 of 5

FIGURE 13.10 Table of contents for Masterspec Outline Interiors: Construction Version.

MASTERSPEC® OUTLINE™

TABLE OF CONTENTS

© 2002 The American Institute of Architects

INTERIORS LIBRARY
Construction Version

	Issue Date	Sect. No.	SECTION TITLE	SECTION DESCRIPTION
			DIVISION 5 - METALS	
	2/02	05500	METAL FABRICATIONS	Iron and steel items (not sheet metal).
	2/02	05511	METAL STAIRS	Steel; with pan, plate, and grating treads.
	2/02	05521	PIPE AND TUBE RAILINGS	Railings fabricated from aluminum, stainless-steel, and steel pipe and tubing.
	5/02	05530	GRATINGS	Metal and glass-fiber-reinforced plastic gratings.
	5/97	05580	FORMED-METAL FABRICATIONS	Custom sheet metal fabrications; no flashing.
	5/02	05700	ORNAMENTAL METAL	Custom fabrications from nonferrous and ferrous metals.
U	8/02	05715	FABRICATED SPIRAL STAIRS	Standard units.
	2/02	05721	ORNAMENTAL RAILINGS	Ornamental metal railings assembled from either standard or custom components and shapes. Also included are glass- and plastic-supported railings, and illuminated railings.
			DIVISION 6 - WOOD AND PLASTICS	
	8/99	06100	ROUGH CARPENTRY	Framing, sheathing, subflooring, etc.
	8/99	06105	MISCELLANEOUS CARPENTRY	Furring, grounds, nailers, and construction panels.
	5/99	06200	FINISH CARPENTRY	Interior & exterior, exposed and nonstructural.
	5/98	06402	INTERIOR ARCHITECTURAL WOODWORK	Trim, cabinets, tops, paneling, and ornamental items.
	5/98	06420	PANELING	Board type, flush wood, plastic laminate, and stile and rail.
			DIVISION 7 - THERMAL AND MOISTURE PROTECTION	
	5/01	07920	JOINT SEALANTS	Elastomeric, nonelastomeric, and preformed sealants.
			DIVISION 8 - DOORS AND WINDOWS	
N	8/02	08111	STANDARD STEEL DOORS AND FRAMES	Standard units complying with ANSI A250.8.
U	8/02	08114	CUSTOM STEEL DOORS AND FRAMES	Units of nonstandard shapes and sizes.
	2/98	08125	INTERIOR ALUMINUM FRAMES	For doors, glass sidelights, borrowed lights, and fixed windows in interior partitions.
	8/99	08161	SLIDING METAL FIRE DOORS	Composite and hollow-metal types.
	5/99	08211	FLUSH WOOD DOORS	Wood-veneer and plastic-laminate-faced units.
	11/01	08212	STILE AND RAIL WOOD DOORS	Stile and rail units, stock and custom.
	5/99	08311	ACCESS DOORS AND FRAMES	Wall and ceiling units.
	8/01	08331	OVERHEAD COILING DOORS	Steel and aluminum curtains.
	8/01	08334	OVERHEAD COILING GRILLES	Open-mesh curtains.
	11/01	08343	ICU/CCU ENTRANCE DOORS	Combination swing/slide manual type.
U	8/02	08346	SOUND-CONTROL DOOR ASSEMBLIES	Swinging steel and wood doors, steel frames, and sound-control seals.
	11/00	08351	FOLDING DOORS	Accordion and panel folding doors, metal bifold doors, bifold mirror doors, and fire-rated folding doors.
	2/01	08411	ALUMINUM-FRAMED ENTRANCES AND STOREFRONTS	Standard exterior and interior systems, hardware.
	8/00	08450	ALL-GLASS ENTRANCES AND STOREFRONTS	Tempered glass without frames.
	2/98	08711	DOOR HARDWARE (SCHEDULED BY NAMING PRODUCTS)	For specifying door hardware by using a schedule that names products or indicates BHMA designations.
	2/98	08712	DOOR HARDWARE (SCHEDULED BY DESCRIBING PRODUCTS)	For specifying door hardware by using a schedule that includes nonproprietary product descriptions.
	2/02	08800	GLAZING	General applications.
	2/95	08825	DECORATIVE GLASS	Acid-etched, sandblasted, silk-screened, beveled, patterned, and laminated types.
U	8/02	08830	MIRRORS	Unframed units, wall mounted.

N = NEW   U = UPDATE

MASTERSPEC OUTLINE INTERIORS TABLE OF CONTENTS - AUGUST 2002 - Page 2 of 5

FIGURE 13.10 (continued)   Table of contents for Masterspec Outline Interiors: Construction Version.

MASTERSPEC® OUTLINE™
TABLE OF CONTENTS
© 2002 The American Institute of Architects

Issue Date	Sect. No.	SECTION TITLE	SECTION DESCRIPTION
DIVISION 9 - FINISHES			
2/02	09210	GYPSUM PLASTER	On gypsum lath and metal lath, furring, and framing.
5/99	09215	GYPSUM VENEER PLASTER	On gypsum base; includes ordinary assemblies and steel framing.
2/99	09260	GYPSUM BOARD ASSEMBLIES	Includes ordinary assemblies and steel framing.
11/97	09271	GLASS-REINFORCED GYPSUM FABRICATIONS	Ceiling coves and domes, vaulted ceilings, column covers, etc., for interior use.
8/00	09310	CERAMIC TILE	Ceramic mosaic, quarry, paver, and wall tile.
11/97	09385	DIMENSION STONE TILE	Marble, granite, limestone, and slate tile.
8/99	09401	CEMENTITIOUS TERRAZZO	Cast-in-place cementitious and rustic terrazzo and precast cementitious terrazzo.
8/99	09402	EPOXY TERRAZZO	Thin-set and precast epoxy-matrix terrazzo.
5/00	09511	ACOUSTICAL PANEL CEILINGS	Mineral-base and glass-fiber-base panels with exposed suspension systems.
5/00	09512	ACOUSTICAL TILE CEILINGS	Mineral-base tile with concealed suspension systems.
8/00	09513	ACOUSTICAL SNAP-IN METAL PAN CEILINGS	Snap-in steel, stainless-steel, and aluminum pans with concealed suspension systems.
11/00	09514	ACOUSTICAL METAL PAN CEILINGS	Lay-in, clip-in, and torsion-spring-hinged metal pans with exposed suspension systems.
8/00	09547	LINEAR METAL CEILINGS	Strip, decorative metal systems.
8/00	09580	SUSPENDED DECORATIVE GRIDS	Plenum mask ceiling systems.
2/98	09635	BRICK FLOORING	Interior applications only.
11/99	09638	STONE PAVING AND FLOORING	Exterior and interior stone traffic surfaces.
5/97	09640	WOOD FLOORING	Solid- and engineered-wood flooring.
8/97	09644	WOOD ATHLETIC-FLOORING ASSEMBLIES	Maple flooring systems.
5/00	09651	RESILIENT FLOOR TILE	Solid vinyl, rubber, and vinyl composition floor tiles.
5/00	09652	SHEET VINYL FLOOR COVERINGS	Unbacked and backed sheet vinyl products.
5/00	09653	RESILIENT WALL BASE AND ACCESSORIES	Vinyl and rubber wall base, treads, nosings, and edgings.
8/00	09654	LINOLEUM FLOOR COVERINGS	Tile and sheet products.
2/00	09661	STATIC-CONTROL RESILIENT FLOOR COVERINGS	Static-dissipative and static-conductive tile and sheet products.
2/98	09680	CARPET	Tufted and woven carpets and cushions.
2/98	09681	CARPET TILE	Modular tile for commercial applications.
2/01	09720	WALL COVERINGS	Vinyl, textile, and woven glass-fiber wall coverings, and wallpaper.
11/99	09751	INTERIOR STONE FACING	Dimension stone facings including trim and countertops.
2/97	09771	FABRIC-WRAPPED PANELS	Fabricated tackable or acoustic panels.
2/97	09772	STRETCHED-FABRIC WALL SYSTEMS	Site-upholstered ceiling and wall systems.
2/97	09841	ACOUSTICAL WALL PANELS	Spline- and back-mounted units.
11/99	09921	INTERIOR PAINTING (CONSUMER LINE PRODUCTS)	For consumer line of interior coatings.
11/99	09922	INTERIOR PAINTING (PROFESSIONAL LINE PRODUCTS)	For professional line of interior coatings.
2/97	09945	MULTICOLORED INTERIOR COATINGS	Spray-applied multicolored speckled finishes.
5/98	09960	HIGH-PERFORMANCE COATINGS	Specialty coatings for severe, moderate, and mild environments.
8/95	09980	WOOD-VENEER WALL COVERINGS	Scrim-backed flexible sheets.

N = NEW   U = UPDATE

FIGURE 13.10 *(continued)* Table of contents for Masterspec Outline Interiors: Construction Version.

MASTERSPEC® OUTLINE™
TABLE OF CONTENTS

© 2002 The American Institute of Architects

INTERIORS LIBRARY
Construction Version

Issue Date	Sect. No.	SECTION TITLE	SECTION DESCRIPTION
DIVISION 10 - SPECIALTIES			
5/01	10101	VISUAL DISPLAY SURFACES	Chalkboards, markerboards, tackboards, sliding units, conference units, and electronic markerboards.
5/01	10125	BULLETIN BOARDS AND DISPLAY CASES	Illuminated and nonilluminated types.
5/01	10155	TOILET COMPARTMENTS	Metal, plastic laminate, phenolic-core, and solid-polymer types.
5/01	10180	STONE TOILET COMPARTMENTS	Granite & marble partitions & urinal screens.
2/99	10190	CUBICLES	Curtain and IV tracks; curtains for cubicles, dressing areas, and tub and shower enclosures.
5/02	10265	IMPACT-RESISTANT WALL PROTECTION	Protection for walls, corners, and door edges.
2/00	10270	ACCESS FLOORING	Portable modular panels and support systems.
2/98	10405	BANNERS	Ornamental fabrics with applied graphics for interior and exterior use.
5/01	10410	DIRECTORIES	Illuminated and nonilluminated types with changeable message strips or changeable letters.
5/00	10431	SIGNS	Exterior and interior signs, letters, and plaques.
8/01	10505	METAL LOCKERS	Standard, quiet, corridor, athletic, open-front, and coin-operated types.
8/00	10506	WOOD LOCKERS	Wood- and plastic-laminate-faced types.
2/01	10520	FIRE-PROTECTION SPECIALTIES	Portable and wheeled fire extinguishers and fire-protection cabinets.
11/00	10550	POSTAL SPECIALTIES	Mailboxes, collection and receiving boxes, cluster box units, parcel lockers, data distribution boxes, and mail chutes.
11/00	10605	WIRE MESH PARTITIONS	Standard- and heavy-duty partitions, ceilings, storage lockers, railing insert panels, and equipment barriers.
5/98	10616	SITE-ASSEMBLED DEMOUNTABLE PARTITIONS	Demountable partition systems consisting of gypsum board or metal-faced gypsum board panels supported by concealed framing.
5/98	10620	DEMOUNTABLE UNITIZED-PANEL PARTITIONS	Demountable partition systems consisting of factory-assembled unitized panels.
2/98	10651	OPERABLE PANEL PARTITIONS	Acoustically rated, manually and electrically operated, flat-panel partitions.
2/98	10653	FIRE-RATED OPERABLE PANEL PARTITIONS	Acoustically rated, manually operated, flat-panel partitions, fire rated 1 or 1-1/2 hours.
2/98	10655	ACCORDION FOLDING PARTITIONS	Acoustically rated, manually and electrically operated, accordion folding partitions.
11/00	10671	METAL STORAGE SHELVING	Freestanding end-panel-support, post-and-shelf, and post-and-beam types.
8/99	10750	TELEPHONE SPECIALTIES	Telephone enclosures and directory storage units.
2/97	10801	TOILET AND BATH ACCESSORIES	Standard commercial and institutional units.
DIVISION 11 - EQUIPMENT			
11/97	11062	FOLDING AND PORTABLE STAGES	Portable stages, risers, acoustic shells.
11/97	11063	STAGE CURTAINS	Includes fabrics and tracks.
8/01	11132	PROJECTION SCREENS	Front and rear projection screens.
U 8/02	11400	FOODSERVICE EQUIPMENT	Commercial food service equipment.
2/02	11451	RESIDENTIAL APPLIANCES	Kitchen and laundry appliances.
8/01	11460	UNIT KITCHENS	Standard metal and plastic-laminate types.
2/01	11610	LABORATORY FUME HOODS	Walk-in hoods, hood stands, and countertop units for general laboratories.

N = NEW   U = UPDATE

MASTERSPEC OUTLINE INTERIORS TABLE OF CONTENTS - AUGUST 2002 - Page 4 of 5

FIGURE 13.10 *(continued)* Table of contents for Masterspec Outline Interiors: Construction Version.

MASTERSPEC® OUTLINE™
TABLE OF CONTENTS
© 2002 The American Institute of Architects

INTERIORS LIBRARY
Construction Version

Issue Date	Sect. No.	SECTION TITLE	SECTION DESCRIPTION
		DIVISION 12 - FURNISHINGS	
11/99	12355	INSTITUTIONAL CASEWORK	Manufactured wood- and plastic-faced units and countertops.
8/97	12356	KITCHEN CASEWORK	Manufactured cabinets and countertops.
11/00	12361	METAL LABORATORY CASEWORK	Modular type with enameled finish.
11/00	12362	WOOD LABORATORY CASEWORK	Modular type with clear finish.
11/00	12363	PLASTIC-LAMINATE LABORATORY CASEWORK	Modular type with plastic-laminate finish.
11/00	12365	METAL MEDICAL CASEWORK	Stainless- and enameled-steel units including countertops, sinks, and accessories.
8/99	12484	FLOOR MATS AND FRAMES	Recessed and surface-applied flexible floor mats and frames.
5/99	12485	FOOT GRILLES	Metal, plastic, with various tread surfaces; recessed; metal frames.
5/99	12491	HORIZONTAL LOUVER BLINDS	Manually operated and motorized venetian blinds.
5/99	12492	VERTICAL LOUVER BLINDS	Manually operated and motorized blinds.
5/99	12494	ROLLER SHADES	Manually operated and motorized roller shades.
5/99	12495	PLEATED SHADES	Manually operated and motorized Z-pleated and cellular shades.
2/96	12496	WINDOW TREATMENT HARDWARE	Conventional draw, snap pleat, and panel track.
8/98	12610	FIXED AUDIENCE SEATING	Interior applications.
8/97	12815	INTERIOR PLANTS	Plants, trees, and vines for interior spaces.
8/97	12830	INTERIOR PLANTERS	Pots and urns for interior plants.
		DIVISION 13 - SPECIAL CONSTRUCTION	
5/99	13038	SAUNAS	Modular and precut saunas; heaters; accessories.
8/01	13041	MODULAR VAULTS	Factory-formed and field-assembled modular vault panels and vault doors.
		DIVISION 14 - CONVEYING SYSTEMS	
5/99	14100	DUMBWAITERS	Preengineered, hand and power operated.
		DIVISION 15 - MECHANICAL	
3/99	15410	PLUMBING FIXTURES	Fixtures, carriers, faucets, and trim.
		DIVISION 16 - ELECTRICAL	
3/00	16122	UNDERCARPET CABLES	For building wiring.
9/00	16511	INTERIOR LIGHTING	Normal and emergency lighting.
U 6/02	16727	SOUND-MASKING EQUIPMENT	Equipment and accessories for acoustical privacy.

N = NEW   U = UPDATE

MASTERSPEC OUTLINE INTERIORS TABLE OF CONTENTS - AUGUST 2002 - Page 5 of 5

FIGURE 13.10 *(continued)*   Table of contents for Masterspec Outline Interiors: Construction Version.

Discount Schedules - Create discount by criteria, then save and apply discount schedules as negotiated. Discounting under a contract is easier. Saves time and reduces errors.

Enhanced Discounting - View item properties and discount history. Make mass changes with enhanced Edit function. Provides easier discounting and editing for sales and admin on large projects.

Undo/Redo Function - Allows unlimited back-up to the last save. Reduce time manipulating data, easily correct errors, and test ideas in CAP Worksheet.

Catalog Search - Part number search has been expanded to include quick, easy catalog search by description using any combination of letters, numbers, and symbols.

Mini-Explorer - Access catalogs and "drag & drop" product directly into a worksheet.

CAP Compare - Compare existing inventory against new configurations to determine reusable and excess product and new requirements.

Import/Export - Import and export worksheet information. Export as CAP SIF, SIF for order entry, CSV (EXCEL) or new CAP Studio XML.

Bottom-Line Pricing - Add multiple bottom-line adjustments to improve profitability and create complete proposals.

Cover Page Support - Create and store templates to print with a worksheet. Include logos, signature lines, and more to create professional, complete proposals.

CAP Options - View option numbers, descriptions, and prices while selecting finishes. Save time and manage change easily.

Contact Manager - Maintain names, addresses, and other information for project contacts.

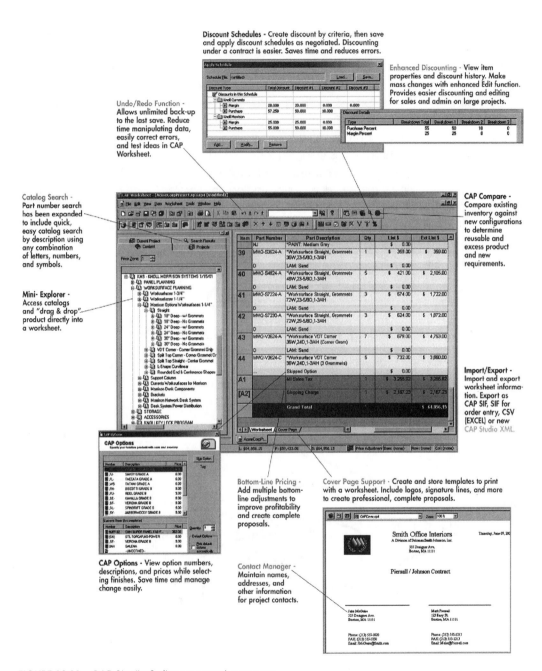

FIGURE 13.11   CAP Studio Software sample screens.

CAP also distributes CAD libraries and electronic catalogs representing over 40 furniture manufacturers, 350 catalogs, and one million products. It is the industry's most comprehensive collection of furniture catalogs and AutoCAD 2D and 3D symbols. CAP's *Offices Online* product offers a customized approach to e-procurement by connecting end-users and facility managers with their dealer. Offices Online provides online product visualization, selection, specification, and other fulfillment (Figure 13.12). CAP also uses drag-and-drop technology

Because of the increasing safety concerns and the accompanying liability factors involved in the specification of furnishings, it is essential for space planners and specifiers to maintain quality control through performance evaluation of furniture components. The precise method of specifying and ordering furniture will vary depending on a project's size and working methods of the procurement design office. The responsibilities of the client, space planner/interior designer, furniture dealer, and others are set out in the formal contract agreement between the space planner/interior designer and the client.

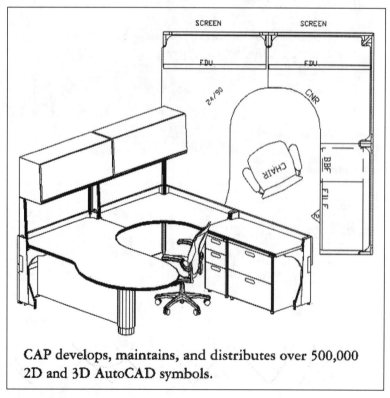

CAP develops, maintains, and distributes over 500,000 2D and 3D AutoCAD symbols.

FIGURE 13.12 CAP maintains and continuously develops 2D and 3D CAD symbols to facilitate the specification and ordering process.

Often space planners and interior designers select furniture for the client and assume the responsibility for writing purchase orders, coordinating delivery schedules and installation for the furniture. This negates the need to write furniture specifications. Selections that are approved by the client are directly listed on the purchase order and this is sent to the furniture dealer. This procedure is the most popular for residential commissions.

With regards to commercial work (and some residential projects), the space planner/interior designer may select the furniture and then turn the job (and the responsibility) of ordering, installing, and billing over to the furniture dealer or manufacturer who will supply the brands of furniture specified. The dealer or manufacturer in this case, contracts directly with the client and assumes full responsibility for on-time delivery and quality, etc.

On large commercial and government projects, price quotations are typically requested from one or more dealers bidding the same job. The specifier must ensure that the furniture specifications are written clearly and precisely to state the client's exact requirements. These specifications should be detailed and list all the individual items required. It should also stipulate bidding requirements, responsibilities, installation procedures, and methods of invoicing.

AUTOMATED SPECIFICATION WRITING SYSTEMS

Numerous firms have recently emerged that offer on-line specification-preparation services to architects, space planners and interior designers. One such firm is Building Systems Design's *SpecLink* which is an electronic specification system that has a database of over 780 master specification sections and over 120,000 data links that automatically include related requirements and exclude incompatible options as you select specification text (Figure 13.13a, b). Interspec LLC is another firm that uses a proprietary technology that connects a large database of building specifications to an electronic architectural drawing of the project. The customer can also access the specs through the internet. Moreover, the customer can make alterations as the specs are being written. Interspec also has a do-it-yourself program for designers with small projects. Using the *e-Specs* service will enable companies to increase their productivity while simultaneously reduce their costs. Also, by linking the architect's CAD drawings to the master guide specifications, the need to mail or deliver large blueprint drawings to the spec writer is eliminated. With these automated systems, the designer can input all necessary information at the earliest stages of the project, before any drawings are available, and instantly obtain an outline or preliminary specification (Figures 13.13a, 13.13b).

Another software system on the market is the *SpecsIntact System*, an automated system for preparing standardized facility construction specifications. SpecsIntact was designed by NASA to help architects, engineers, specification writers and other professionals doing business with the three government agencies using it, i.e. the National Aeronautics and Space Administration (NASA), the U.S. Naval Facilities Engineering Command (NAVFAC), and the U.S. Army Corps of Engineers (USACE).

BSD SpecLink Catalog Listing

The SpecLink database is divided into specification **sections** organized into **Divisions** corresponding to the 1995 edition of MasterFormat™. Click on the appropriate Division below to see full list of sections in that Division, along with a description of the contents of the section and the catalogs in which it is available.

Division 0 - Introductory Info, Bidding, and Contract Requirements	26 sections	Total Number of Sections: 714	
Division 1 - General Requirements	23 sections	Division 9 - Finishes	58 sections
Division 2 - Site Construction	55 sections	Division 10 - Specialties	50 sections
Division 3 - Concrete	31 sections	Division 11 - Equipment	17 sections
Division 4 - Masonry	23 sections	Division 12 - Furnishings	11 sections
Division 5 - Metals	26 sections	Division 13 - Special Construction	43 sections
Division 6 - Wood and Plastics	30 sections	Division 14 - Conveying Systems	12 sections
Division 7 - Thermal & Moisture Protection	85 sections	Division 15 - Mechanical	91 sections
Division 8 - Doors and Windows	80 sections	Division 16 - Electrical	59 sections

Catalogs:
A=Architectural
S=Structural Engineering
C=Civil Engineering

L=Landscape Architecture
ME=Mechanical/Electrical
*=the Basics

SpecLink is available only on CD-ROM because the database is over 100 MB in size and the sections are interlinked to provide coordination for project specs.

FIGURES 13.13a BSD SpecLink Summary Catalog Listing and Computer Screen printout. SpecLink is one of the many electronic specification services that have emerged in recent years.

These new systems are transforming the way architects and interior designers prepare specifications for commercial and residential buildings. They can provide greater accuracy, in less time, at a lower cost. These systems also eliminate or minimize costly construction changes due to omissions, discrepancies or improper quality controls. A firm's proprietary interactive on-line editing systems can be integrated into the specification development process over the Internet with secure password access. A completed specification manual can be delivered on-line for client downloading, printed and bound, as well as on CD-ROM. The bottom line is whether outsourcing is the most effective way to go for a particular design firm.

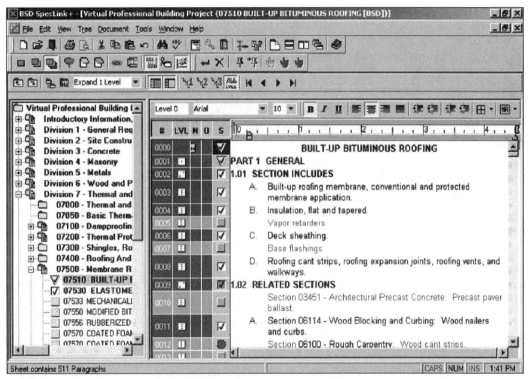

FIGURES 13.13b BSD SpecLink Summary Catalog Listing and Computer Screen printout. SpecLink is one of the many electronic specification services that have emerged in recent years.

THE PROBLEM OF LIABILITY

Space planners and architects, like other professionals, are expected to exercise reasonable care and skill in carrying out their work. Although this does not imply 100 percent perfection at all times, the level of performance should be consistent with that ordinarily provided by other qualified practitioners under similar circumstances. Law relating to professional responsibility and liability has become very active in recent years, and the zone of risk and exposure has expanded dramatically in professional practice. Indeed, under current law, whenever a designer enters into a contractual agreement and specifies furnishings or any other subsystem of a commercial or institutional space, he or she becomes responsible for the performance of that system.

Professional Liability

One of the most significant areas of exposure relates to the liability of the space planner-architect-engineer to third parties unconnected with the contract for claims of negligence or errors in design that lead to alleged injury of persons using the building. The legal bases for the majority of current liability suits include professional negligence, implied warranty or misrepresentation, implied fitness warranty, breach of contract, joint and several liability and liability without fault for design defects. Often, these legal bases overlap. Thus, a designer that fails to reject defective work by a contractor or supplier may be considered to be professionally negligent and in breach of contract.

Designers can protect themselves from possible liability suits by working within their area of expertise, using concise contracts and specifications, complying with codes and regulations, using reputable contractors, maintaining accurate records, and securing legal counsel and liability insurance.

Product Liability

Another zone of exposure is building product performance, that is, holding space planner-architect responsible for damages caused by faulty materials and components and sometimes for the cost of their replacement. This tends to place a heavy emphasis on the selection and specification of building products with long records of satisfactory performance, thus inhibiting the introduction of new materials and methods.

Product liability is mainly concerned with negligence. And while it greatly affects manufacturers, retailers, wholesalers, and distributors, designers and specifiers are increasingly becoming involved in product liability suits. Designers can minimize product liability actions by specifying products manufactured for the intended use.

CHAPTER
FOURTEEN

EPILOGUE AND
FUTURE TRENDS

*T*he tremendous strides we have witnessed over the last few decades in the evolution of technology have demanded a new office environment—one that necessitates an intelligent approach to technology management, products that support new work styles, and furniture that is characterized by total flexibility and capacity to support changing work functions.

GENERAL OVERVIEW

Integrating technology into the workspace helps make the cyber-experience appear less daunting and more friendly. Simultaneously, the built environment that we all share is becoming more interactive, more entertainment-oriented, and more colorful. Shopping malls, for example, used to consist of boxes where the retail store really was the thing to look at; and now the mall itself is much of the entertainment.

As modern civilization grows more complex, switching over from an industrial to a knowledge-based society, those responsible for the planning of environments will need to have a better understanding of the psychic makeup of people. This imposes on space planners the need to formulate a vision for the future and plan for it. The compelling necessity to be forward looking and try to anticipate how people will be living and working tomorrow without regard to present-day constraints and without regard to traditional divisions among disciplines provides a daunting challenge to space planners and designers. Looking into the future, Susan Mitchell-Ketzes, Senior Vice President, HOK Consulting, believes that, "Speed and access to connectivity and virtual workplaces will radically transform the world of work, making work across multiple time zones and irregular schedules more and more common," and that "agility will become an even greater priority as the need to respond to change becomes more acute."

Present trends strongly suggest that strategic alliances will form the cornerstone of the future for businesses, whether self-employed individuals or large corporations. However, for virtual teams to be really effective, accurate communication is essential. To achieve this, more firms are looking to centralize communications, and are moving towards the use of Web sites as project archives where colleagues and clients can send e-mail, post status reports, and view drawings and documents.

It becomes clear that all of the topics discussed in this book have been impacted to varying degrees by the rapid evolution of new technologies, particularly in communications. This has affected design methodology techniques, which continue to change and adapt to these new technologies, with computers playing an increasing if not dominant role. Cost estimating and specification writing, too, have been greatly impacted by the introduction of computers. Automation of estimating spreadsheets and the use of computer aided cost estimation systems is now commonplace, and the many tools now available allow you to estimate more effectively and efficiently. Likewise, the emergence of automated specification writing systems, providing greater accuracy, speed, and lower costs, is in keeping with the general trend of the construction industry and consulting professions.

Communication and drafting methods have likewise moved from the manual to the electronic. Presentations now consist of virtual entry and exit. The observer is placed "inside" the building before a single brick is laid. Furniture manufacturers are increasingly taking into consideration the research of anthropometrics and ergonomics, to produce more suitable furniture and an environmentally attractive workplace. To better serve their clients, they now work more closely with space planners, architects, and interior designers. This approach is exemplified by Nortel Networks, a company with an enlightened management that has positioned itself at the leading technological edge of telecommunications. The firm drew in HOK and Herman Miller to assist them to rapidly move towards a flat hierarchy, an environment that strongly encourages communication and teamwork, and furniture that is extremely agile and responsive to change. The results proved a resounding success.

Today, communication differs fundamentally from what it was a decade ago. The rising cost of real estate and changes in economic, social, and technological realities have made alternate office locations more feasible, and employees are increasingly telecommuting and maintaining home offices. Additionally, many services can now be outsourced via call centers and other new kinds of emerging companies. Commercial activities and even after-sale services are now being pursued through innovative routes as a result of e-commerce. The impact of physical distances has become almost meaningless, as transactions are completed at a stroke across the entire globe, and international teams across the spectrum now work seamlessly together.

The construction industry is also facing new challenges. Numerous technological advances continue to take place in construction materials and systems. In glazing, for example, innovations such as krypton gas glazing and holographic glazing are marketed but not often employed in commercial installations. In lighting, advances continue to be made in lamp, ballast, control, and sensor technology. One of the interesting developments involves day lighting the core of the buildings. Building cores can receive natural light via light shelves, central light courts, atriums, and overhead lighting. Nonie Niesewand, author of *Lighting*, says in his section on future lighting, "In the 21st century illumination will come in the form of light-emitting material, rather than being sculpted and molded from a material that conceals the light source." Efforts are already underway to integrate lighting and energy, and recent trends in simulation software have strengthened the relationship between HVAC design and energy use predictions.

The efficiency of heating, ventilating, and air-conditioning equipment for commercial buildings has significantly improved during the past two decades, with most of the technical advances revolving around refinements of existing technology. The perfection of heat recovery concepts and hardware continues, with profound changes taking place in system integration. Most modern buildings maintain some form of building automation system, which in turn often include energy management and control systems (EMCS).

Security issues and challenges have been highlighted by the September 11, 2001, terrorist attacks on the U.S., and promise to play a central role in future design considerations. Advanced technology is being brought to bear to resolve many of these unprecedented challenges.

The futurists' myth of the virtual office—the ability to work anytime, anywhere—captured our imagination during the early 1990s, when portable computing and wireless telephony took the workplace by storm. Yet the virtual office remains elusive. However, with security on the top of everyone's mind and businesses looking to cut back employee travel, corporate America is taking a second look at collaborative technologies such as videoconferencing and video streaming as an alternative for face-to-face communication. A Knoll/DYG research study shows that only about seven percent of the current working population spend most of their time out of the office, and 73 percent say they spend the majority of their time in an office-type environment.

The workplace is a very powerful tool for achieving business goals. Yet, there is an enormous amount of stress in today's workplace environment. Efforts are being made to explore new computing technology and hardware that will minimize or erase ergonomic stresses placed on today's users. Voice recognition capability is one of many avenues being explored, especially for general office applications, that can reduce or eliminate keyboard input. Surveys show that people are significantly more productive when their work environment has been created with a holistic approach, i.e. when architecture, furniture, and technology are integrated to create a homogeneous workplace environment.

In today's climate of an increasingly competitive global business community, companies are seeking out every available tool to help them improve employee productivity and increase profits. Productivity is a vital issue in corporate America and around the world, which is perhaps why it continues to rise year after year, as companies continuously reorganize their business strategies to improve their market position. Unlike the strategies pursued during earlier decades, when companies expanded their real estate assets and increased their corporate holdings, today they are streamlining their operations, and reengineering the way they run their business to increase efficiency and profitability.

With real estate costs often representing in excess of 25 percent of the assets of a large company, management began to closely scrutinize the investment and consider alternative methods of reducing costs and increasing space efficiency. A wealth of corporate case studies and research offers conclusive evidence of the positive impact space planning and office redesign can provide to productivity. Furthermore, it has been found that productivity can be increased by making resources, including people, information, and equipment, more accessible to employees. It is obvious that accessibility will continue to be a critical issue for years to come. Space planners can and will help companies meet this need by developing appropriate customized design solutions.

As we have seen, space planning is a complex process involving many interactive information systems from program analysis to environmental issues. The need for intuitive and comprehensive literature on space planning is intensified by the escalating cost of new construction and the assimilation of the newly emerging technology. More people today are looking for new ways to recycle existing structures, and clients are more and more requesting space planners to adapt old buildings to new uses. Space planners are being taxed to find new, innovative, and efficient solutions to existing problems.

Finally, the hallmark of a good space planner is measured by the ability to create spaces that are both functional and aesthetically pleasing. The interrelation of specialized activities places the obligation on the space planner to be conversant with the language and basic knowledge in many fields. Planning spaces within a completed building shell or making minor alterations within existing buildings make it necessary for space planners to understand basic structural systems, how they function, and the materials used to implement them. The fact that many of the larger architecture and interior design firms have established space planning departments simultaneously strengthens the union between the disciplines and creates new career opportunities. Currently space planning is a developing profession, still in its youth, and its boundaries still evolving and yet to be defined.

GLOSSARY

abacus A slab of stone, marble, or wood, placed on the top of columns in the classical orders.

accent lighting Directional lighting used to illuminate or emphasize specific objects or small areas.

accessible A building or space that can be approached, entered, and used by persons with disabilities.

acid rain Precipitation that has a pH below 5.6. Main contributors are sulfur dioxide from industrial burning of fossil fuel, and nitrogen oxides from automobile emissions, which is transformed into nitrogen dioxide.

acoustics The science or study of sound. The science that deals with the production, control, transmission, reception, and effects of sound.

achromatic (color) A neutral color such as black, white or grey.

ADA *See Americans with Disabilities Act.*

air conditioning The treatment of air within a space to control temperature, humidity, and cleanliness.

alcove A small recessed section of a room or area.

align To be or come into precise adjustment or correct relative position.

alley 1. A narrow street or passageway behind or between buildings. 2. A building for bowling.

alternating current (AC) Electric current that continually reverses its direction. It is expressed in cycles per second (hertz or Hz).

ambient lighting Lighting that provides general uniform illumination in an area. It can be provided through a direct, indirect or direct-indirect lighting system.

ambient temperature Room temperature or the temperature of the surroundings; temperature of fluid (usually air) which surrounds object on all sides.

amenity Pleasant or useful features in real estate that contribute satisfaction and pleasure rather than direct financial benefit.

Americans with Disabilities Act (ADA) Civil rights legislation enacted in 1991 prohibiting discrimination against disabled individuals; the act includes detailed requirements for the planning and design of buildings. The Act was enacted to provide fair employment opportunities, access to public and private services, and barrier-free environments for persons with disabilities.

ampere (amps or A) The unit of measurement of electric current flow.

analogous color Colors that are close or adjacent in their position in the spectrum or on the color wheel.

analogous harmony Colors which are related by containing one color in common; color harmony.

anchor tenant The main tenant in a shopping center development; a large stable tenant or tenants that are expected to attract other tenants and customers to the development.

angle of incidence The angle that a line or light ray striking a surface makes with the perpendicular at that point, the point of incidence.

angle of reflection The angle that a reflected ray makes with the perpendicular to a surface at the point of incidence.

angle of repose 1. The natural angle that a pile of a material, such as earth, sand, or gravel will assume. 2. The angle at which a body will slide down an inclined plane impelled only by gravity.

anthropometrics The study of measuring human body dimensions, like standing height, foot length and outreach of the arm, through systematic and statistical observation of large numbers of people.

antiquing Furniture finishing technique intended to give appearance of age or wear.

apartment hotel A hotel containing apartments as well as transient rooms.

apartment house A building containing three or more separate residential apartments; also called an apartment building.

apartment A suite of rooms, usually let as a dwelling; a dwelling unit.

arcade 1. An arched covered passageway. 2. An amusement center with coin-operated games.

architrave The lowest part of the entablature.

archives A collection or place containing records, documents or other material of historical interest.

atrium A central courtyard with surrounding rooms opening off it. In current usage, the term refers to an interior space usually roofed over with glass, as can be found in many modern hotels and large projects.

axis An imaginary straight line around which parts of a building or a group of buildings are arranged. A straight line of reference; in three dimensions, the three axes are referred to as x, y, and z.

axonometric projection A drafting projection in which objects on the drawing appear inclined with three sides showing and with horizontal and vertical distances drawn to scale but diagonal and curved lines distorted.

azimuth The angle between true south and the point on the horizon directly below the sun.

baffle An opaque or translucent element that serves to shield a light source from direct view at certain angles, or serves to absorb unwanted light.

ballast An electrical device used in fluorescent fixtures to obtain the necessary voltage and current to start and operate an electric discharge lamp. Electronic ballasts are replacing magnetic ballasts because they are more efficient, quieter, lighter, and can be dimmed.

balloon frame A wooden building frame composed of closely spaced members (studs) which are continuous from the sill to the top plate of the roof line; also called eastern frame; compare platform frame.

baluster Each of a series of often ornamental short posts or pillars supporting a rail or coping; also called banisters.

balustrade A row of balusters topped by a railing on a stair, porch, or balcony.

banister A light baluster supporting a stair handrail.

baroque Highly ornate, grotesque, flamboyant, and extravagant in style, especially of the architecture, art, and music of the 17th and 18th centuries.

baseboard The finish trim board covering the interior wall where the wall and the floor meet. Also called skirting.

base building A building's shell structure, including core services.

basement The part of a building that is wholly or partially below ground level; cellar.

basilica 1. An ancient Roman public hall with an apse and colonnades, used as a law court and place of assembly. 2. A similar building used as a Christian church.

bearing wall A wall which supports any vertical loads in addition to its own weight.

bidding or negotiation phase One of the standard phases of architectural service (Schematic Design Phase, Design Development Phase, Construction Documents Phase, Bidding or Negotiation Phase, and Construction Phase-Administration of the Construction Contract).

binary hue A hue that is perceptually mixed, as orange appears to be a mixture of red and yellow. All binary hues are mixtures of two of the unique hues.

BOCA Building Officials and Code Administrators International, an organization that publishes model building codes.

boiler room The space provided for a hot water or steam boiler, circulating pumps, and other mechanical and electrical equipment; engine room.

book matched Wood veneer where adjoining sheets are sliced from the same log so that the grain matches like an open book.

brick veneer A one brick thick outside facing of brickwork used to cover a wall of some other material.

British Thermal Unit (BTU) Quantity of heat required to raise temperature of one pound of water one degree Fahrenheit.

brightness Attribute of a visual sensation according to which an area appears to emit more or less light, reflecting the perceived amount of light coming from an area. "Brightness" is often restricted to apply only to lights and "lightness" is used for the corresponding dimension of the colors of surfaces. It is one of the three standard elements of color appearance along with hue and saturation.

building line An imaginary line on a plot beyond which the building may not extend.

build-out The interior construction and improvement of a space (including services and finishes) to meet the tenant's requirements (also referred to as fit-out). Build-out can be new construction or renovation.

built-up roof A seamless, roof covering traditionally made of continuous rolls or sheets of saturated or coated felt, cemented together with bitumen, and which may have a final coating of gravel or slag.

bus bar 1. A large, flat conductor, usually solid copper, used for carrying very high electrical currents. 2. An uninsulated bar or tube used as an electrical conductor at a circuit junction.

BX cable Rigid, flexible metal conduit with a wire bundle, consisting of individually insulated conductors covered by a flexible spiral-wound layer of metal or tough paper. Also refered to as metal clad (MC).

C 1. Celsius. 2. Centigrade. 3. In heat transfer, conduction of a material to the passage of heat; the reciprocal of resistance (C=1/R). 4. In seismic design, the numerical coefficient used which represents building acceleration. 5. Capacitance.

cabling The cords that connect computer components to form a single workstation or multi-user network.

CAD Computer Aided Design. Term used to define a computer function or computer system that involves predominantly design or graphics manipulation.

capital The distinguishing feature at the top of a column that identifies the order (column).

capitalization The process of converting expected future income into present value.

carbon dioxide Colorless, odorless gas. Contributor to global warming, and is formed by a combustion process. Used in manufacture of carbonates and as a propellant in aerosols.

carbon monoxide Poisonous, colorless, odorless gas formed by incomplete fossil fuel combustion. Combines with hemoglobin in blood to form carboxy-hemoglobin, which will not release oxygen to the tissue. Used in organic synthesis.

carpentry, finish The finish woodwork installation such as base, casing, doors, stairs, paneling; all woodwork installed after plastering or drywall.

carpentry, rough The preliminary framing, boxing, and sheeting of a wood frame building.

casement A window in which the sash opens with hinges and pivots on an axis along the vertical line of the frame that allows it to open up or out; casement window.

casework Assembled cabinetry or millwork.

catwalk A narrow walkway, such as used in an attic for access.

caulk 1. To seal and waterproof cracks and joints, especially around window and exterior door frames. 2. To seal small openings in wall or ceiling systems to prevent leakage of sound or to effect a finished appearance and seal between dissimilar materials.

cellular office An environment where much of the space is divided into individual offices, as opposed to an open office layout. A cellular office plan is often representative of a hierarchical organization structure.

centigrade Thermometric scale where 0 degrees represents the freezing point of water and 100 degrees the boiling point. Similar to Celsius.

change order A written and signed document between the owner and the contractor authorizing an order to change the work to be performed under a construction contract, usually given by an owner to a prime contractor or a by prime contractor to a subcontractor; a revision in the contract documents after the execution of the owner-contractor contract. A change order may be in the form of additional compensation or time, or less compensation or time in which case it is known as a deduction.

chiller A piece of equipment that produces chilled water for circulation through a building and contains a compressor, condenser and evaporator tank.

chroma Intensity of color or purity. For colors of the same hue and brightness, chroma and saturation are equivalent.

circuit The closed path over which an electric current flows. It includes the source of electric energy (Usually the electric panel box or breaker), the wiring, and the electric load.

circuit breaker An over-current protection device.

class A   Premium, most desirable office space.

clerestory   An upper row of windows in a high ceiling room, above the level of a lower adjoining roof; also called clearstory.

cloister   A covered passage on the side of a court.

codes   1. Prevailing regulations, ordinances or statutory requirements set forth by governmental agencies associated with building construction practices and owner occupancy, adopted and administered for the protection of public health, life safety, and welfare. 2. The identification marking on the back of sheets of gypsum board; denotes manufacturing plant, date, time, and other details.

coffered (ceiling)   The use of beams and cross beams to form a pattern of many sided sunken panels that are usually molded, decorated or carved.

colonnade   A set of columns occurring at regular intervals.

color rendition   The effect of a light source on the color appearance of objects, as compared with their color appearance under a reference light source.

color temperature   The color of a light source appears to be, ranging from *cool* (blue) to *warm* (orange-red).

combustion   A chemical process that involves sufficient oxidation to produce heat or light.

community property   A type of concurrent ownership by husbands and wives that allows all property acquired during marriage to be divided 50-50. This concept is the law in several states in the U.S.

complementary colors   The colors that are located on the opposite sides of the color wheel. Two color stimuli that can be additively mixed to produce an achromatic color.

console   1. An ornamental bracket supporting a shelf. 2. A cabinet or panel containing controls and switches for operating lighting, sound, television, or radio equipment.

contract documents   A term used to represent all executed agreements between the owner and contractor; any general, supplementary or other contract conditions; the drawings and specifications; all addenda issued prior to execution of the contract; and any other items specifically stipulated as being included in the contract documents.

construction documents phase   One of the standard phases of architectural service (Schematic Design Phase, Design Development Phase, Construction Documents Phase, Bidding or Negotiation Phase, and Construction Phase-Administration of the Construction Contract).

construction documents   The drawings and specifications that describe the construction requirements.

cool colors   Hues or colors in which blue-green predominates; so termed because of the association with ice, water, and sky; also called cold colors.

corbel   A projecting timber or block usually supporting a horizontal member such as a beam.

cornice   A projected molding mounted where the ceiling and wall meet, or the top of the entablature.

core   The central vertical element in a building, which usually houses the elevators, fire stairs, rest rooms, and mechanical equipment.

cost approach   One of the three classic approaches to value. It involves estimating the replacement cost new of the improvements, deducting the estimated accrued depreciation, and then adding the market value of the land.

cove lighting   A lighting source shielded from view by a ledge or horizontal recess that lights the ceiling and wall.

cost estimate   A preliminary statement of approximate cost, determined by one of the following methods. 1. Area and volume method; cost per square foot or cubic foot of the building. 2. Unit cost method; cost of one unit multiplied by the number of units in the project; for example, in a hospital, the cost of one patient unit multiplied by the number of patient units in the project. 3. In-place unit method; cost in-place of a unit, such as doors, cubic yards of concrete, and squares of roofing.

cost plus contract   A type of construction contract where the contract price is the sum of the costs of labor, materials, and subcontracts plus an established percentage fee for overhead and profit.

credenza   A furniture element, usually placed behind a desk, which consists of a surface over storage or file space.

crown molding   An interchangeable term for cornice molding.

cupola   A small dome topping a turret or roof.

current   The flow of electricity. Current is measured in amperes (amps or A).

dado (pl. dadoes)   1. Part of a column base. 2. The lower part of an interior wall when differently surfaced. 3. A groove in a piece of wood made by dadoing.

daylight factor   Under totally overcast sky conditions, the percentage of light (in foot candles) that arrives on a horizontal surface within a building compared to the amount of light (in foot candles) arriving on an unshielded horizontal surface outside.

decibel (dB)   A measure of sound volume or intensity; the smallest noticeable sound intensity difference detectable under laboratory conditions. A term that expresses two power levels used to indicate gains or losses in a system.

deciduous   Trees that lose their leaves seasonally, differing from coniferous.

deed   The formal legal document that transfers title to real property.

design-build construction   When an owner contract with a prime or main contractor to provide both design and construction services for the entire construction project. Use of the design-build project delivery system has grown from five percent of U.S. construction in 1985 to 33 percent in 1999, and is projected to surpass low-bid construction in 2005. If a design-build contract is extended further to include the selection, procurement, and installation of all furnishings, furniture, and equipment, it is called a "turnkey" contract.

diffused lighting   Lighting, provided on the worksurface or on an object, that does not appear to come from a specific direction or source.

diffuser   A translucent glass or plastic that shields the light source and spreads the light evenly in all directions.

dimmer   A device used to control the intensity of light emitted by controlling the voltage or current to it.

direct current   An electric current which flows in one direction.

direct lighting   Light cast directly on an object rather than reflected (indirect light).

directional lighting   Light provided on the worksurface or on an object, coming from a specific source.

dormer   A projection located in the slope of roof that usually contains a window.

double net lease   Lease rate, plus pro-rated share of insurance or taxes.

downlight   A small direct lighting unit that directs the light downward and can be recessed, surface mounted, or suspended.

drywall   A technique used for building interior partitions. Large panels or sheets of wallboard, gypsum board, plasterboard, or sheetrock are used in place of plaster to cover studs or other structural wall support materials.

DX split system   A cost-effective air conditioning system suitable for smaller installations, and comprised of an outdoor unit (condenser) and an indoor unit, linked together by refrigeration piping. The indoor unit can be located either above or below the ceiling, or be wall mounted or cassette.

easement   The legal right to use land that is owned by another. Such rights are created by an express writing, by implication, or by prescription and are of a fairly permanent nature.

efflorescence   A deposit of water soluble salts (in the form of white stains) on the surface of masonry or plaster caused by the dissolving of salts present in the masonry; migration of the solution to the surface and deposition of the salts when the water evaporates; the surest preventative of efflorescence is to keep water out of masonry; the process of efflorescing is also referred to as whiskering or saltpetering.

egress   The way out; exit.

elevation   A drawing showing a vertical image of an element such as a building, partition or piece of furniture, viewed to scale and usually with dimensions (unless a presentation drawing).

encumbrance   Any restriction that limits ownership interests in real property.

entablature   The complete area of the architrave, frieze and cornice area that is supported by the column in one of the classical orders.

expansion joint   A flexible joint used to prevent cracking or breaking because of expansion and contraction due to temperature fluctuations.

fan coil unit   An air conditioning system comprising of either a four or two-pipe fan coil unit and are normally installed with a fresh air supply and extract system. They are located usually above the ceilings, but can be installed at low level around the perimeter of a building.

fanlight   A transom type window usually located over a door, shaped like a fan.

fenestration   The arrangement of window and door openings in a wall or elevation.

feng shui   Running water, tropical fish and indoor rock gardens are claimed to have a soothing and rejuvenating effect on the spirit. As interest in eastern culture is increasing, more designers are using such features to relieve stress and create a calming and harmonious atmosphere.

FF&E   Furniture, fixtures, and equipment.

fiber optics   Light transmission through optical fibers for communication, including voice, video and data.

fill light   A type of accent lighting which reduces shadows or contrast.

finial   An ornament on top of a spire, pinnacle, gable, etc.

fire barrier   A continuous membrane such as a wall, ceiling, or floor assembly that is designed and constructed with a specified fire-resistant rating to limit the spread of fire and smoke. The resistant rating is based on a time factor. Only fire-rated doors may be used in these barriers.

fire rating   A system of rating materials in terms of their ability to withstand laboratory-controlled test fires for a specified period of time.

fire retardant   A chemical treatment to reduce the ignitability of the treated material; a material or treatment which effects a reduction in flammability and in spread of fire.

fire wall   A fire-rated wall that extends continuously from the foundation of a building to or through the roof with sufficient structural stability to allow collapse of one side, while leaving the other side intact, and requiring a three to four hour fire rating.

fit out   The interior construction and customization of a space (including services, space and stuff) to meet the tenants requirements; either new con-

struction or renovation (also referred to as fit-out or build-out).

fit-up   Fit out.

fixture   The hardware element that holds a lamp in position, distributes the light, and provides a connection to the power source.

flame resistance   The ability of a material not to propagate flame once the flame source is removed.

flammability   The measure of the material's ability to support combustion.

Flemish bond   A brick laying technique in which the headers and stretchers alternate every other row.

floor plate   The dimensions of an entire floor of the building.

fluorescent lamp   A type of electric discharge lamp in which a phosphor coating transforms ultraviolet energy (created by electric discharge) into visible light. Fluorescent lamps are the most common lamp used in commercial office applications. Often chosen for its ability to combine energy efficiency with good color rendering.

footcandle (fc)   A unit of measurement indicating how much illumination is reaching a surface. 1 fc = 1 lumen/ft. sq.ft.

footlambert (fl)   A unit of luminance, the brightness of a surface. 1 fl = 1 lumen/sq.ft.

furring strips   Thin strips of wood fastened to walls or ceilings for leveling and for receiving the finish surface material.

gambrel roof   A roof with two pitches, the lower slope steeper than the upper.

glare   A sensation caused by light within the visual field that is brighter than the level of light to which the eyes are adapted. Causes annoyance, discomfort, and a loss in visual performance and visibility.

gradient   The inclination of a road, piping, or the ground, expressed in percent.

gross building area   The total building area, without deductions, expressed in square feet.

gross leasable area   The total area of a building that is leasable to tenants; the gross building area less the unrentable areas.

gross multiplier A rule-of-thumb method of appraising the value of income property by multiplying the gross annual income by a multiplier; this is an unreliable method, used primarily on residential property.

headers The short side or face of the brick.

highest and best use That legal use of land that is most likely to produce the greatest long-term economic return to the owner.

hip rafter The diagonal rafter that extends from the plate to the ridge to form the hip.

hip roof A roof type with four sloped sides of equal inclination.

hue The attributes that describe and recognize a color. The name of a color. Hue differences depend mainly on variations in the wavelength of light reaching the eye.

HVAC is the acronym for heating, ventilating, and air conditioning, and includes the systems that are used for these purposes.

illuminance The level of illumination on a surface.

incandescent lamp Generates visible light by heating a filament until it radiates. Incandescent lamps come in standard voltage and low voltage versions. They produce a significant amount of heat, are less energy efficient, and have a significantly shorter life than fluorescent lamps. Incandescent lamps are used liberally in retail and entertainment applications as well as commercial lobbies, conference areas, and theatres.

income approach One of the three appraisal methods, in which the estimated gross income from the subject property is used as a basis for estimating value along with gross rent multipliers derived from the marketplace.

indirect lighting Lighting by luminaires distributing 90 to 100 percent of the emitted light upward.

infrastructure Such public facilities as roads, water lines, and sewer systems.

interior fit out The process of installing interior services, ceilings, partitions, floors, and furnishings.

International style Term used to describe architectural design that is simple, functional, and unornamented, following the theoretical teachings of Bauhaus and the leading figures of Modernism of the 1920s and 1930s.

jamb The side of a door or window frame.

joist A horizontal structural member supported by bearing walls, beams, or girders in floor or ceiling framing.

keystone The center stone in an arch.

kilowatt-hour (kWh) A unit of measuring electrical energy consumption, kilowatt/hour = watts x hours/1000. Electric energy is sold by the kilowatt-hour (kWh).

lamp A generic term for a manufactured source of light.

LAN A Local Area Network, or collection of interconnected computers, servers, and hubs within a company. Multiple LANs linked together form a WAN, or Wide Area Network.

land-use planning The development of plans for the use of land. These plans can be for the use of a particular site or the use of land in an entire community or region.

laser A light source used in conjunction with an optical fiber.

lateral file A roll-out filing compartment whose major dimension extends horizontally. The depth can vary to accept letter or legal files. The width is typically greater than the depth. This device is generally designed as a freestanding cabinet with two to five compartments.

latex paint A paint containing a synthetic resin used as a binder for emulsion (water-thinned) paints.

lease A contract by which real estate is conveyed for life, for a term of years, or at will, usually for a specified rent; also, the act of such conveyance, or the term for which it is made. A written document permitting one party—the lessee—the possession of land or a building of another party—the lessor.

  gross A lease under which the landlord agrees to pay the real estate taxes, utilities, insurance, and all other operating expenses in connection with the use of the premises.

  net A lease under which the lessee pays any one of the following: taxes, insurance, or maintenance.

  net net (double net) A lease under which the lessee (tenant) pays any two of the following: taxes, insurance, or maintenance.

net net net (triple net)   A lease under which the lessee (tenant) pays all three of the following: taxes, insurance, and maintenance. This term is generally used in commercial and industrial leased properties where the lessor (owner) provides the land and capital improvements,

sublease   A lease from a lessee to another lessee.

lessee   A tenant under a lease (the landlord).

lessor   One who leases.

lien   A claim that one person has on the property of another as security for a debt.

lintel   A short, horizontal member spanning an open space between columns or over a door, window, or other opening.

loan-to-value ratio   The percentage of a property's value that is financed with borrowed funds.

long lead   Long delay needed between an order being placed and the receipt of an item.

lumen   The unit of luminous flux. A measure of a lamp's or luminaire's light output.

luminaire   A complete lighting unit consisting of a lamp or lamps, together with the parts designed to distribute the lights, to position and protect the lamps, and to connect the lamps to the power supply.

luminance   The luminous intensity of any light-emitting surface. Often referred to as brightness. Measured in footlamberts.

marquetry   Inlaid decorative technique on furniture, doors, and floors using various colored woods or other materials.

mezzanine   Balcony or low ceiling overhang just above the main floor and below the next story. In a theater, a mezzanine is the first balcony above the stage.

millwork   A general term that includes all dressed lumber that has been molded, shaped, or pre-assembled at the mill.

modular   Units of standardized size or design, which can be arranged or fitted together in a variety of ways.

molding   The ornamental strip of woodwork or stonework either recessed or in relief, used generally for decoration.

monochromatic colors   Colors of a single hue.

Munsell color system   A widely used coloring system. Color appearances in the Munsell system is characterized using sets of three symbols, for example 2.3YR 5/7 means that the hue is 2.3YR, the value (= lightness) is 5 and the chroma is 7.

musculoskeletal disorders (MSD)   A term used to describe a variety of physical conditions including back pain, neck tension and carpal tunnel syndrome.

net floor area   Usable floor area after deducting stairs, walls, and similar features.

net leasable area   Floor space in a building that is actually under lease and able to be rented to tenants. Non-leasable areas include hallways, building foyers, areas devoted to utilities, elevators, etc.

net operating income   Gross annual income from a property less fixed expenses, operating expenses, and reserves for replacement.

net rentable   The square footage in a commercial building that is deemed rentable, according to BOMA.

niche   A recess in a wall.

noise reduction co-efficient   The rating that identifies the ability of an object to absorb rather than reflect sound.

non-territorial space   A non-ownership approach to space, usually expressed through hot-desking and hotelling.

occupancy rate   The number of units currently occupied in a facility, neighborhood or city, stated as a percentage of total capacity.

ohm   Unit of resistance such that a constant current of one ampere produces a force of one volt.

order   A typical style of classical architecture. These upright columns with the proportions and strict interrelations of its parts are found in classical buildings.

parapet   A low wall or railing, usually around the edge of a roof.

particle board   A substrate material manufactured by bonding wood particles with resins under heat and pressure.

party wall   1. A special purpose wall system used to divide compartments for different occupancies; may have requirements for fire and sound.

2. Partitions of brick or stone walls between buildings on two adjoining properties in which each of the respective owners of the adjacent buildings share the rights and benefits of the common wall. 3. A common wall between two tenancies; also called demising wall.

pediment A triangular decorative element usually located over a door, window, or fireplace. Often supported by columns.

performance specifications The written material containing the minimum acceptable standards and actions, as may be necessary to complete a project.

pigment Mineral or organic colored matter that is mixed with a material that will bind and suspend it to create paint or ink.

pilaster An upright flat pier or column-like architectural element attached to a wall surface for the purpose of strengthening the wall, although it is sometimes used for decorative effect.

plenum, plenum space The air return path of a central air handling system, either ductwork or open space over a dropped ceiling.

portico A roofed entrance porch often supported by columns.

post-and-beam construction A type of building frame in which roof and floor beams rest directly over wall posts.

Post Modernism Term that has come to describe the stylistic developments that depart from the norms of modernism. Robert Venturi, in his 1996 book *Complexity and Contradiction in Architecture*, questions the validity of the emphasis of modernists on logic, simplicity, and order, suggesting that ambiguity and contradiction may also have a valid place.

pressurized stairs These are stairs that provide protection to occupants from fire and smoke through pressurization and ventilation. Pressurization is accomplished through pressure and ventilation control. Buildings containing pressurized stairs are often required by code to be fully sprinklered.

primary colors The group of colors from which all other colors may be generated, but from which themselves cannot be made from mixing. The *subtractive* (pigment or dye) primaries are red, yellow, and blue. The *additive* (colored light) primaries are red, green and blue.

proxemics A term coined by Edward T. Hall, the father of proxemics, referring to the systematic study of the psychological impact of space and interpersonal physical distances. Proxemics deals with unconscious as well as conscious structuring of space.

raceway 1. An enclosed metal channel, usually fire-resistant, installed in a building to hold electrical wiring. 2. A chute that directs the flow of a material to a specific location in a device.

radiant heat Heat that is transmitted through an object to the other side.

radiant heating Use of radiation to generate heat such as with baseboard heating where the circulating hot water is radiated through conduction by thin metal fins at the bottom of the wall. The room is warmed by air circulating around the heating unit using convention.

refraction The process by which the direction of a ray of light changes as it passes obliquely from one medium to another. For example, light is refracted as it passes through water.

retaining wall A wall that is designed to resist the lateral pressures of retained soil; a wall that holds back a hillside or is backfilled to create a level surface.

satellite office Regional offices providing support services and meeting space to a highly mobile workforce.

saturation The vividness of a hue.

scale Size of something in relation to some known standard or recognized constant.

secondary color The color that results from mixing two primary colors.

setback line A line set by ordinance which determines how close to a property line a structure can be erected or installed.

shaft The part of the column between the capital and the base.

shell The skeletal frame of a house when only the framing, sheathing and decking have been constructed.

signage A plaque that identifies graphically and/or alphabetically, occupant or function of a workstation or area.

simultaneous contrast The phenomenon in which the perceived color of an area of a scene tends to take on a hue opposite to that of the surrounding area. Thus a grey square on a red background will take on a greenish tint.

site A plot of land prepared for or underlying a structure or development. The location of a property.

site plan Document that describes how a parcel of land is to be improved. It includes the outlines of all structures and site improvements, such as driveways, parking lots, landscaping and utility connections.

skin 1. Outside layer or covering of a structure, which may be a coating of material for protection against the weather. 2. Dry surface which appears on paint, caulk, and similar materials that are exposed to air for too long.

skirting boards See baseboards.

smoke barrier A wall, ceiling, or floor constructed to restrict the movement of smoke. It may or may not have a fire-resistant rating.

soil pipe A pipe that carries sewage containing solids.

sound transmission The ability of a solid, gas or liquid to transmit sound.

specifications A detailed, exact statement of particulars—especially statements prescribing materials and methods—and quality of work for a specific project. The most common arrangement for specifications substantially parallels the CSI and Masterspec formats.

spectrum The visible bands of color produced when light passes through a prism comprising red, orange, yellow, green, blue, indigo, and violet.

square foot cost The cost per square foot of area of land or a building or other structure; found by dividing the number of square feet of area into the total cost of the structure or land.

stack pipe A vertical main that can be used as a soil, waste, or venting pipe.

standpipe A fixed, manual extinguishing system, including wet and dry systems, with outlets to allow water to be discharged through hose and nozzles for the purpose of extinguishing a fire.

stretchers The long side or face of the brick

stucco A smooth mixture of sand and limestone often used on exterior and interior walls.

successive contrast The influence of the color of an area on the perceived color of an area viewed immediately afterward, e.g. afterimages.

systems furniture A collection of furniture elements designed to be used together to form a space efficient workstation in any of a number of different configurations.

task lighting Lighting directed to a specific work surface or area to provide illumination for visual tasks.

tenant improvements Changes, typically to office, retail or industrial property, to accommodate specific needs of a tenant. Include moving interior walls or partitions, carpeting or other floor covering, shelves, windows, toilets, etc. The cost is negotiated in the lease.

terra cotta Unglazed fired clay used for ornament, tiles, garden pots, and dishes.

terrazzo Marble or stone ships set in mortar, then finished with a polish.

territorial space One man, one desk-owned offices and workstations.

tetrad color A color scheme using four hues equally spaced on the color wheel.

tint A color made lighter by mixing with white or light gray.

tolerance The total amount by which a specific dimension is allowed to vary.

transformer A device that converts an electrical current to a lower voltage (step down) or higher voltage (step up).

transmitter The electronic unit that converts an optical signal.

triad color A color scheme using three hues equally spaced on a color wheel.

triple net lease See lease, net net net (triple net)

troffer A recessed lighting unit, usually long and installed with the opening flush with the ceiling. The term is derived from *trough* and *coffer*.

unit cost-in-place method A method of estimating the reproduction cost of a building by estimating the installed cost of each component part.

urban sprawl Unplanned and unexpected expansion of a large area of development in an urban area.

utilities Services rendered by public utility companies, for example, water, gas, electricity, and telephone.

valance A short drapery that can conceal the tops of curtains. The term also describes a decorative trim, board, or drapery hanging from an edge.

variable air volume An all-air building mechanical system that accommodates load variations by regulating the volume of air supplied through a single duct.

variance A permit that allows use to deviate slightly from a strict interpretation of the zoning ordinance to avoid placing undue hardship on an owner.

vault An arched ceiling or roof. A barrel vault is formed from the horizontal extension of an arch; a groin vault from the intersection of two arches.

vent 1. A vertical pipe connected to a waste or soil distribution system that prevents a back pressure or a vacuum that might siphon the water out of a trap. 2. Vertical pipe to provide passageway for expulsion of water vapor and vent gases from gas-burning equipment to outside air. 3. A free opening to provide air intake, expulsion, or circulation in such areas as underfloor crawl spaces and attics.

ventilation The process of supplying or removing conditioned or unconditioned air by natural or mechanical means to or from a space and sufficient to permit the removal of excess heat, fumes or vapors.

vent stack A plumbing vent pipe in a multistory building, a separate pipe used for venting, that either connects with a stack vent above the highest fixture, or extends through the roof.

virtual office A term used to describe the concept of the workplace as wherever and whenever people are working, i.e. the office is not associated to a specific place or time. A recent development in which an individual or organization utilizes an entirely remote-working or home-working workforce, communicating by telephone, fax, PC and Internet.

virtual private network (VPN) A private network built within a public network.

voltage A unit of electromotive force. The force or pressure which causes electricity to flow. Voltage is measured in volts (V).

volutes A scroll-like decoration.

waiver of lien Voluntarily relinquishing the right of a lien, usually temporarily. This waiver may be explicitly stated or implied.

wall bearing A wall that acts as a support for the roof or upper story of a house or structure.

WAN Multiple LANs linked together by physical or virtual connections.

watt Unit of measurement of electrical power. The watt is the power required to do work at the rate of one joule per second. When power is used and energy is consumed, it is measured in watt-hours or kilowatthours.

wet pipe automatic sprinkler system The most effective and efficient automatic sprinkler system, consisting of a series of water-filled pipes and sprinkler heads.

work station Space required to accommodate the performance of a task. Any of several systems of office furniture and equipment, often incorporating screens or other partitions to provide some degree of enclosure and privacy.

zoning Under the police power of government, local laws that control the use of land. Zoning regulations apply to the type of use (e.g. residential, commercial, industrial), density, height of buildings, parking requirements, etc., permitted in a specific jurisdiction.

BIBLIOGRAPHY

Adam, Robert, *Classical Architecture: A Comprehensive Handbook to the Tradition of Classical Style*, Harry N. Abrams, New York, 1991.

Adaptive Environments Center, Inc. and R.S. Means Engineering Staff, *Means ADA Compliance Price Guide*, R.S. Means Company, Inc., 1994.

Albrecht, Donald et al., *The Work of Charles and Ray Eames: A Legacy of Invention*, Harry N. Abrams, Inc., in association with the Library of Congress and the Vitra Design Museum, New York, 1997.

Abercrombie, Stanley, "Charles Eames—Legacy of Invention," *Interior Design*. Allen, Phyllis Sloan, et al, *Beginnings of Interior Environment*, 8th Edition, Prentice Hall, New Jersey, 1999.

Apgar, M., "The Alternative Workplace: Changing Where and How People Work," *Harvard Business Review*, pp.121-135, May-June, 1998.

Baker, Hollis, S., "Furniture in the Ancient World," *The Connoisseur*, London, 1966

Ballast, David K., *Interior Design Reference Manual*, Professional Publications, Inc., Belmont, California, 1998.

Birren, Faber, *Color and Human Response*, Van Nostrand Reinhold, New York, 1978.

Blakemore, Robbie G., *History of Interior Design and Furniture*, Van Nostrand Reinhold, New York, 1997.

Boethius, Axel and Ward-Perkins, J.B., *Etruscan and Roman Architecture*, Penguin Books, 1970.

Boger, Louise Ade, *The Complete Guide to Furniture Styles*, Waveland Press, Inc., Prospect Heights, Illinois, 1997.

Boss, Richard, W., *Information Technologies and Space Planning for Libraries and Information Centers*, G.K. Hall Publishers, Boston, Massachusetts, 1987.

Brand, Jay L., *Office Environments for Future Organizations*, Ideation Group, Haworth, Inc., July 2002.

Brown, G. Z., Dekay, Mark, Barbhaya, D., *Sun, Wind and Light: Architectural Design Strategies*, 2nd Edition, John Wiley and Sons, New York, 2000.

Burckhardt, Jacob, *The Architecture of the Italian Renaissance*, University of Chicago Press, Chicago, 1985.

Burgner, Lois, "Light and Color: Equipment and Application," *Architectural Lighting Magazine*.

Calloway, Stephen, Ed., *The Elements of Style, An Encyclopedia of Domestic Architectural Details*, Reed Consumer Books Ltd., London, 1994.

Caplan, Ralph, *The Design of Herman Miller*, Whitney Library of Design, 1976

Ching, Francis D.K., *Architectural Graphics*, 3rd Ed., John Wiley and Sons, Inc. New York, 1996.

Cole, Alison (in association with The National Gallery, London), *Perspective*, Dorling Kindersley, Inc., New York, 1992.

Crouch, A., and Nimran, U. "Office Design and the Behavior of Senior Managers," *Human Relations*, 42, pp.139-155, 1989.

David, William, et al, *McGraw-Hill On-Site Guide to Building Codes 2000: Commercial and Residential Interiors*, McGraw-Hill Professional, New York, 2001.

De Chiara, Joseph, Panero, Julius, *Time-Saver Standards for Interior Design and Space Planning*, McGraw-Hill, New York, 2001.

Deasy, C.M., *Designing Places for People: A Handbook for Architects, Designers, and Facility Managers*, Whitney Library of Design, New York, 1985.

Dingle, Jeffrey, "Front Line of Security," *FacilitiesNet, Building Operating Management*, Trade Press Publishing Corporation, January, 2002.

Duffy, Francis; Cave, Colin; Worthington, John, *Planning Office Space*, Nichols Publishing Company, New York, 1977.

Duffy, Francis, *The New Office: With 20 International Case Studies*, Conran Octopus, 1997.

Edwards, Sandra, *Office Systems—Designs for the Contemporary Workspace*, PBC International Inc., New York, 1986.

Egan, David M and Olgyay, Victor W., *Architectural Lighting*, 2nd Edition, McGraw-Hill Science/Engineering/Math, New York, 2001.

Foster, Norman, et al, *Construction Estimates From Take-Off to Bid*, McGraw-Hill, Inc., New York, 1995.

Freifield, Roberta; Masyr, Caryl, *Space Planning*, Book News, Inc., Portland, Oregon, 1991.

Friedmann, Arnold, John F. Pile, Forrest Wilson, *Interior Design—An Introduction to Architectural Interiors*, 3rd Ed., Elsevier, New York, 1983

Gertler, Jeffrey, "Better Than New," *Contract Magazine*, July 1999.

Giesecke, Frederick E. et al, *Technical Drawing*, Macmillan Publishing Co., Inc., New York, 1974.

Gilliatt, Mary, *Mary Gilliatt's New Guide to Decorating*, Little Brown and Company, Boston, 1988.

The Decorating Book, Pantheon Books, a division of Random House, Inc., New York, 1983.

Goldsmith, Selwyn, *Designing for the Disabled—The New Paradigm*, Architectural Press, an imprint of Butterworth-Heinemann, Oxford, 1999.

Gordon, Gary, "Light and Color," *Architectural Lighting Magazine*, May 1987.

Gunn, R. A., and Burroughs, M. S., "Work Spaces that Work: Designing High-performance Offices, *The Futurist*, pp.19-24, March-April 1996.

Guthrie, Pat, *Interior Designer's Portable Handbook*, McGraw-Hill Professional, New York, 1999.

Hall, Edward T., *The Dance of Life—The Other Dimension of Time*, Anchor Books, Doubleday, New York, 1989.

The Hidden Dimension, Doubleday and Company, Garden City, N.Y., 1966.

Hartman, Taylor, *The Color Code*, Scribner, Simon and Schuster Inc., New York, 1998

Harris, Cyril M., (Ed.), *Historic Architecture Sourcebook*, McGraw-Hill Book Company, New York, 1977.

Harwood, Buie; May, Bridget; Sherman, Curt, *Architecture and Interior Design Through the 18th Century: An Integrated History*, Prentice Hall PTR, New Jersey, 2002.

Hauf, Harold D., *Building Contracts for Design and Construction*, John Wiley and Sons, New York, 1976.

Henderson, Justin, *Workplaces and Workspaces: Office Designs That Work*, Rockport Publishers, Inc., Gloucester, Massachusetts, 1998.

Henley, Pamela E. B., *Interior Design Practicum Exam Workbook*, Professional Publications Inc., Belmont, California, 1995.

Herman Miller, *Body Support in the Office: Sitting, Seating, and Low Back Pain*, Research Paper, Herman Miller Inc., 2002.

Herrmann, Georgina, Ed., *The Furniture of Western Asia Ancient and Traditional*, Philipp Von Zabern, Mainz, 1996.

Houser, Kevin W., "How Do You Like Them Apples—Er, Oranges?," *Contract Magazine*, October 1998.

Karlen, Mark, *Space Planning Basics*, John Wiley and Sons, Inc., New York, 1993.

Kearney, Deborah, S., *The ADA in Practice*, R.S. Means Company, Inc., Kingston, MA., 1995.

Kilmer, Rosemary and Kilmer, W. Otie, *Designing Interiors*, International Thomson Publishing, 1994.

Kirkham, Pat, *Charles and Ray Eames: Designers of the Twentieth Century*, The MIT Press, Cambridge, Massachusetts, 1995.

Kirkpatrick, Beverly; James M., *AutoCAD for Interior Design and Space Planning: Using AutoCAD 2002*, Prentice Hall PTR, New Jersey, 2002.

Koomen-Harmon, S., and Kennon, K. E., *The Codes Guidebook for Interiors*, 2nd Edition, John Wiley and Sons, New York, 2001.

Kostof, Spiro, *A History of Architecture – Settings and Rituals*, Oxford University Press, New York, 1995.

Kroll, Karen, "Steps in a Green Direction," *FacilitiesNet*, Trade Press Publishing Corporation, March 2002.

Kubba, S.A.A., *Architecture and Linear Measurement during the Ubaid Period in Mesopotamia*, BAR International Series 707, Oxford, 1998.

Mesopotamian Furniture, In preparation, BAR International Series, Oxford, 2002.

Kubba, Shamil, *Mesopotamian Architecture and Town Planning*, BAR International Series 367(i), Oxford, 1987.

Laseau, Paul, *Architectural Representation Handbook*, McGraw-Hill, New York, 2000.

Leacroft, Helen and Richard, *The Buildings of Ancient Mesopotamia*, Brockhampton Press, Leicester, 1974.

Loebeison, Andrew, *How To Profit in Contract Design*, Interior Design Books, New York, 1983.

Malnar, Joy Monice and Vodyarka, Frank, *The Interior Dimension: A Theoretical Approach to Enclosed Space*, John Wiley and Sons, New York, 1991.

Manno, Paul, "Foundations of Flexibility," *Building Operating Management, FacilitiesNet*, Trade Press Publishing Corporation, August 2000.

Marmot, Alexi and Eley, Joanna, *Office Space Planning: Designs for Tomorrow's Workplace*, McGraw-Hill Professional, New York, 2000.

Measelle, R., "Arthur Andersen: Space Planning to Meet Business Goals," *Today's Facility Manger*, pp.1, 58-67, May, 1998.

McGowan, Maryrose and Kruse, Kelsey, *Specifying Interiors: A Guide to Construction and FF&E for Commercial Interiors Projects*, John Wiley and Sons, Inc., New York, 1996.

Mendler, Sandra and Odell, William, *The HOK Guidebook to Sustainable Design*, John Wiley and Sons, New York, 2000.

Meyer, Franz Sales, *Handbook of Ornament*, Dover Publications, Inc., New York, 1957.

Miller, Marjorie A., *Designing Your Law Office: A Guide to Space Planning, Renovation and Relocation*, American Bar Association Publishing, Chicago, 1989.

Mills, Sam, "Introduction to Light and Color, Part II," *Architectural Lighting Magazine*, November 1987.

Mitton, Maureen, *Interior Design Visual Presentation: A Guide to Graphics, Models, and Presentation Techniques*, John Wiley and Sons, New York, 1999.

Montague, John, *Basic Perspective Drawing—A Visual Approach*, 3rd Ed., John Wiley and Sons, Inc., New York, 1998.

Muller, Edward J. et al, *Architectural Drawing and Light Construction*, 5th Ed., Prentice Hall, New Jersey, 1999.

Nielson, Karla J. and Taylor, David A., *Interiors: An Introduction*, McGraw-Hill Higher Education, 1994.

Niesewand, Nonie, *Lighting*, Whitney Library of Design, an imprint of Watson-Guptill Publications, New York, 1999.

O'Neill, M.J., *Ergonomic Design for Organizational Effectiveness*, Lewis Publishers, Boca Raton, Florida, 1998.

Palmer, Alvin E; Lewis, Susan M., *Planning the Office Landscape*, McGraw-Hill Book Company, New York, 1977.

Pile, John F., *Interior Design*, 2nd Edition, Harry N Abrams, New York, 1995.

A History of Interior Design, John Wiley and Sons, Inc., New York, 2000.

Piotrowski, Christine M., and Rogers A., Elizabeth, *Designing Commercial Interiors*, John Wiley and Sons, Inc., New York, 1998.

Pita, Edward G., *Air Conditioning Principles and Systems*, 3rd Ed., Prentice Hall, New Jersey, 1998.

Propst, Robert, *The Office—A Facility Based on Change*, The Business Press, Elmhurst, Illinois, 1968.

Ramsey, George Charles, et al, *Architectural Graphic Standards*, 10th Ed., The American Institute of Architects, John Wiley and Sons, Inc., New York, 2000.

Rayfield, Julie K., *The Office Interior Design Guide: An Introduction for Facility and Design Professionals*, John Wiley and Sons, Inc., New York, 1994.

Redstone, Louis G., *New Dimensions in Shopping Centers and Stores*, McGraw-Hill Book Company, New York, 1973.

Reid, Esmond, *Understanding Buildings—A Multidisciplinary Approach*, The MIT Press, Cambridge, Massachusetts, 1999.

Reznikoff, S. C., *Specifications for Commercial Interiors*, Whitney Library of Design, New York, 1989.

Interior Graphic and Design Standards, Whitney Library of Design, New York, 1986.

Riley II, Charles A., *High-Access Home, Design and Decoration for Barrier-Free Living*. Rizzoli International Publications, Inc., New York, 1999.

Rosenbaum, Alvin., *The Complete House Office—Planning Your Work Space for Maximum Efficiency*, Viking Studio Books, The Penguin Group, New York, 1995.

Rosenblatt, B., *New Changes in the Office Work Environment: Toward Integrating Architecture, OD, and Information Systems Paradigms*, Ablex Publishing Corporation, Norwood, New Jersey, 1995.

Ryburg, Jon, "Emerging Work Patterns," *Best F.M. Practice Reports*, Facility Performance Group Inc, 1995-96.

Salvendy, G. (Ed.) *Handbook of Human Factors and Ergonomics*, 2nd Ed., John Wiley and Sons, New York, 1997.

Sampson, Carol A., *Estimating for Interior Designers*, Watson-Guptill Publications, 2001.

Sanders, Mark S. and McCormick, Ernest J., *Human Factors in Engineering and Design*, McGraw-Hill Book Company, New York, 1987.

Schittich, Christian, *In Detail: Interior Spaces: Space, Light, Material*, Birkhäuser Publishing Ltd. Basel, Switzerland, 2002.

Scutella, Richard M. and Heberle, Dave, *How to Plan, Contract and Build Your Own Home*, 3rd Ed., McGraw-Hill, New York, 2000,

Shoshkes, Lila, *Space Planning—Designing the Office Environment*, Architectural Record Books, New York, 1976.

Smith, Fran Kellog and Bertolone, Fred J., *Bringing Interiors to Light: The Principles and Practices of Lighting Design*, Whitney Library of Design, New York, 1986

Smith, William D. and Smith, Laura H., *McGraw-Hill On-Site Guide to Building Codes 2000: Commercial and Interiors*, McGraw-Hill Professional Publishing, New York, 2001.

Snyder, Loren, *A Closer Look at Security Audits*, FacilitiesNet, Maintenance Solutions, Trade Press Publishing Corporation, September 2002.

Speltz, Alexander, *Styles of Ornament*, Gramercy Books, Random House Value Publishing, Inc., New York, 1994

Steffy, Gary, R., *Architectural Lighting Design*, 2nd Edition, John Wiley and Sons, New York, 2001.

Steven Winter Associates, *Accessible Housing by Design*, McGraw-Hill, New York et al., 1997.

Stierlin, Henri, *Encyclopedia of World Architecture*, Van Nostrand Reinhold Company, New York, 1983.

Stokes, McNeill, *Construction Law in Contractors' Language*, McGraw-Hill Book Company, New York, 1977.

Sutherland, Martha, *Modelmaking: A Basic Guide*, W.W. Norton and Company, New York and London, 1999

Swinburne, Herbert, *Design Cost Analysis for Architects and Engineers*, McGraw-Hill Book Co., New York, 1980.

Temple, Nancy, *Home Space Planning: A Guide for Architects, Designers, and Home Owners*, McGraw-Hill, New York, 1995.

Tilley, Alvin R, (Editor), et al, *The Measure of Man and Woman: Human Factors in Design*, John Wiley and Sons, New York, 2001.

Tilton, Rita; Jackson, Howard J; Rigby, Sue Chappell, *The Electronic Office: Procedures and Administration*, 11th Ed., South-Western Publishing Co., Cincinnati, Ohio, 1996.

Trachte, Judith, A., *A Quick Start To AutoCad For Interior Design*, Prentice Hall, New Jersey, 2000.

Tuluca, Adrian (lead author). Steven Winter Associates, Inc., *Energy Efficient Design and Construction for Commercial Buildings*, McGraw-Hill, New York, 1997.

Tweedy, Donald B., *Office Space Planning and Management: A Manager's Guide to Techniques and Standards*, Quorum Books, New York, 1986.

Vanecko, Andrea et al., *FutureWork 2020*, Sponsored by ASID, Steelcase®, Armstrong World Industries, Inc., Ziff Davis Smart Business, 2001.

Wakita, Dr. Osamu A, Linde, Richard M., *The Professional Handbook of Architectural Working Drawings*, John Wiley and Sons, New York, 1984.

Wallach, Paul L., Ed., *Interior Design: A Space Planning Kit*, South-Western Publishers, 1982.

Walsh, Margo Grant, "Benchmarking the Law Office," *Contract Magazine*, May 1998,

Whiton, Sherrill, *Interior Design and Decoration*, J. B. Lippincott Company, New York, 1974.

Wilhide, Elizabeth and Copestick, Joanna, *Contemporary Decorating: New Looks for Modern Living*, SOMA Books—an imprint of Bay Books and Tapes, Inc., San Francisco, California, 1998.

Winkler, Ira, *Corporate Espionage*, Prima Publishing, 1997.

Yarwood, Doreen, *The Architecture of England*, B.T. Batsford Ltd., London, 1963.

Yates, Marypaul, *Fabrics: A Handbook for Interior Designers and Architects*, W.W. Norton and Company, New York, 2002.

Yee, Roger and Gustafson, Karen, *Corporate Design*, Interior Design Books, A Division of Whitney Communications Corporation, New York, 1983.

Zelinsky, Marilyn, *New Workplaces for New Workstyles*, McGraw-Hill, New York, 1998.

INDEX

Action Office, 57, 255-256
Ethospace system, 255, 257-258
Robert Propst, 57-58, 61
Resolve system, 256, 259-261
Human comfort, 189-196

I

Institutes and Standards Organizations, 305-308
Inventory, 73-74
furniture, 73
space, 74
Isometric drawing, *see Technical drawing*
(paraline drawing)

K

Knoll, 260, 262-264, 502
designers, 51-53, 260
Florence Knoll (Schust), 49, 51-52, 54
Hans Knoll, 51

L

Lettering, 150-152
Life cycle costing, 238
Light, 140-141, 198, 502
natural light, 198-199
artificial light, 199-207
artificial light sources, 201-205
types of lighting, 205-208
Line, 133-134
Louis XV, 36, 253
Louis XVI style, 253

M

Mesopotamia, 2-15
Middle Ages, 27-34
Byzantine design, 27, 30-31
Early Christian design, 27, 29
Romanesque design, 30, 32
Gothic design, 33-36
Models, 177, 181-185

N

National organizations, 310-311
Neoclassic period, 41-45, 253
Noise, *see Sound*
Nucraft Furniture Company, 279-281

O

Office landscape, 56-59
Quickborner Team, 56, 58-59
Orthographic drawing, *see Technical drawing*

P

Paper flow, 70, 75
Paraline Drawings, *see Technical drawing*
Pattern, 139-140
Perspective drawing, *see Technical drawing*
Phyfe, Duncan, 44, 46, 254
Pictorial drawing, *see Technical drawing*
Plumbing services, 428, 432-437
plumbing system criteria, 428, 432-434
plumbing fixture placement, 435
plumbing plans, 435-437
Post–occupancy evaluation (POE), 64, 66, 102-103
Presentation techniques, 171, 175-176
Program, the, 68, 70
Programming phase, 65
Project costs, 225
construction costs, 225-230
furniture, fixtures, and equipment (FF&E), 231
professional fees,231
insurance, bonding and permits, 232-233
contingency fund, 225, 233
Project manual, *see Specifications*
Proportion, 129-130
Proxemics, 217-219
Psychological and social settings, 216-222
Punch list, 100-101

Q

Questionnaires, 72, 76-79, 109